The American Cane Mill

The American Cane Mill

*A History of the Machines,
the Manufacturers,
Sugar Cane and Sorghum*

DON HOWARD DEAN

Foreword by Bill Outlaw

McFarland & Company, Inc., Publishers
Jefferson, North Carolina, and London

The present work is a reprint of the illustrated case bound edition of The American Cane Mill: A History of the Machines, the Manufacturers, Sugar Cane and Sorghum, *first published in 2008 by McFarland.*

Publisher's note: Don H. Dean (as he signed his letters) died on March 11, 2008, after completing all of the work on this book.

LIBRARY OF CONGRESS CATALOGUING-IN-PUBLICATION DATA

Dean, Don Howard, 1936–2008
The American cane mill : a history of the machines, the manufacturers, sugar cane and sorghum / Don Howard Dean ; foreword by Bill Outlaw.
p.   cm.
Includes bibliographical references and index.

ISBN 978-0-7864-5979-7
softcover : 50# alkaline paper ∞

1. Sugar machinery—History.
2. Sugar factories—United States—History.
3. Sugar—Manufacture and refining—United States—History.
I. Title.
TP381.D43   2010   664'.122—dc22   2008010946

British Library cataloguing data are available

©2008 The Estate of Don Howard Dean. All rights reserved

No part of this book may be reproduced or transmitted in any form or by any means, electronic or mechanical, including photocopying or recording, or by any information storage and retrieval system, without permission in writing from the publisher.

On the cover: Sugarcane ©2010 Shutterstock; *inset* Author's cane mill and syrup shed

Manufactured in the United States of America

McFarland & Company, Inc., Publishers
Box 611, Jefferson, North Carolina 28640
www.mcfarlandpub.com

Contents

Foreword by Bill Outlaw 1
Preface and Acknowledgments 3

Part I

1. The Syrup Canes 11
2. History of the Roller Cane Mill 35

Part II

3. Manufacturers of American Cane Mills 53

Bibliography 333
Index 339

This book is lovingly dedicated to members of my family, all of whom participated in this project in some way:

To Carol, my wife of forty-seven years;

To our daughter and son-in-law, Charlotte and Jerry Hartley, and grandsons Jacob and Caleb;

To our son and daughter-in-law, John and Beth Dean, and grandchildren Katherine, Georgia, and Hudson;

And to the numerous librarians across America who assisted so willingly and generously in the research.
My heartfelt thanks.

Foreword by Bill Outlaw

The American Cane Mill comprises scholarly compendia of the foundries that produced small- and moderate-sized cast-iron mills for extraction of the saccharine juice from stems of sweet sorghum and sugar cane. Readers will be delighted, however, to find that this book is much more than a collection of factual vignettes, because the author has infused each account with his passion for cane mills and his interest in the people who made and used these icons of rural America.

Sugar cane is an ancient crop that arrived in the New World with the southern Europeans; this one plant supported the economies of many tropical European dependencies and indeed anchored the cruel triangular trade. It is also adapted to the semitropical regions of the southern United States where rainfall is sufficient. Its importance and history there have been captivatingly described by Sitterson (J.C. Sitterson, *Sugar Country, 1753–1950*, University of Kentucky Press, Lexington, 1953) and others. Technical books on sugar cane likewise abound (notably, N. Deerr, *Cane Sugar,* Norman Rodger, Altrincham, Manchester 1911). These exemplars merely stand for countless monographs, bulletins, and journals, published before and since, on the myriad facets of sugar production. However, no major publication has been devoted to sugar cane syrup. Sweet sorghum, in contrast to sugar cane, was introduced in the United States in the mid-1800s. Its promoters touted its cold-hardiness, but predictions that it would become a serious contender in the sugar market were not realized. Sorghum is a leading cereal, of course, but sweet-sorghum syrup production was, like sugar cane syrup production, largely a cottage industry that has not been the focus of a major publication.

For a brief period in our history, circumstances were favorable to the production of syrup as a value-added farm product. This period was marked by an increasingly urbanized population that was accustomed to syrup traditions, sufficient transportation, and financial resources available to the producer. The period was ended by agricultural conglomerates with economies of scale, competition with other sweeteners, vertical integration, off-farm opportunities, and deficiencies in product uniformity. During its heyday, however, syrup production had an economical, culinary, and social prominence that is little appreciated now. The U.S. production of sugar cane syrup reached 41 million gallons in 1921. This value—about equal then to sweet sorghum production—indicated that the annual per capita consumption of syrups and edible molasses amounted to more than one gallon (H.S. Paine and C.F. Walton, Jr., *Sugar cane sirup manufacture*, USDA Bulletin 1370). At that time, J. S. Roddenbery, Sr., wrote that every one of the 2000 farms in Grady County, Georgia, grew sugar cane for syrup (G.B. Waldorf, W.B.

Roddenbery Company, Grady County, Georgia, unpublished 1995). By 1931 sugar cane syrup production had declined to 14 million gallons and that of sweet sorghum to 17 million gallons (E.W. Brandes, S.F. Sherwood, and B. A. Belcher, *Sugar cane for sirup production,* USDA Circular No. 284 1933). At that time sugar cane acreage in aggregate was evenly split between syrup and sugar production, but sugar production was in the realm of large plantations (and most sugar was imported), whereas syrup production remained a small-farm enterprise. Although the sugar shortage in World War II transiently stimulated sugar cane syrup production, the overall trend was a decline in production (to 2 millions gallons in 1967, http://www.hort.purdue.edu/newcrop/Crop/sugar_cane.html, accessed August 4, 2004).

By the 1950s, sugar cane syrup production was declared unprofitable (Waldorf); in the early 1970s, the Nixon administration closed the tri state USDA field station for sugar cane syrup in Cairo, Georgia (Special from J. Roddenbery to *The Cairo Messenger,* December 14, 1973); and, in 1988, the USDA published the last bulletin on sugar cane production for syrup (D.M. Broadhead and N. Zummo, *Sugar cane culture and syrup production,* USDA ARS-61). Similarly, sweet-sorghum production, centered in the U.S. Midwest and upper South, declined to 0.4 million gallons in 1975 (http://www.ca.uky.edu/nssppa/sorghumfaqs.html, accessed August 4, 2004). With the decline in syrup production, the tradition of the cane grinding and syrup making was lost. The sugar cane syrup campaign, as Wiley poetically put it (H.W. Wiley, *Manufacture of table syrups from sugar cane,* USDA Bulletin No. 70, 1902), is condensed into the narrow window after the cane has reached sufficient maturity for high-quality syrup and before freezing weather. Occurring at an otherwise idle time, cane grindings became a social focal point, bringing family and friends together with perhaps more dawdling the hours away than working. These gatherings ranged from simple visits to real occasions, with dances, candy making, and general jollification. Thus, when syrup production declined, an era passed.

Because syrup production was in the province of small farmers and plantings rarely exceeded 20 acres, these yeomen could afford, and needed only small mills; indeed, most of the mills were vertical and powered by animals, although mills powered by water or motors were available early. A few companies, such as Columbus Iron Works, Chattanooga Plow Company, and Goldens' Foundry and Machine Company, dominated production, but being simple machines in demand, cane mills were made by a surprisingly large number of foundries. As an example, over time, five companies in a twenty-mile-long swath through south Georgia produced virtually identical mills. Until now, the stories of these concerns have not been told.

The American Cane Mill was born of experience and nurtured by painstaking research. I have been privileged to watch this process. Don Dean grew up in the coastal South, where warm springs, rainfall, and the light sandy soils are ideal for syrup production. I met Don on his Heritage Farm where he and his family were hosting a cane grinding—complete with breakfast and lunch on the grounds! I studied his collection of mills and sugar cane cultivars, and in particular I watched as he "worked the crowd." It was apparent that his heritage, technical knowledge, and passion for people and syrup combined to form a unique talent. After that occasion years ago, I enjoyed a robust correspondence with Don. I have marveled at the details he pulled from dusty basements, his synthesis of stories from bits of oral history, his perseverance, and his ability to breathe fresh life into the past. Don combined this knowledge into one readable original book, and I introduce it with confidence that you will enjoy and learn from it, as I have the parts as they unfolded.

Bill Outlaw
The Peter H. Homann Professor of Biological Science
Florida State University, Tallahassee

Preface and Acknowledgments

Our landscape is enriched by the occasional sighting of an old cane mill along some winding road in rural America. Now reposing after a lifetime of labor, these mills remind us of another time that seems so far away but is actually so recent. They were the center of activity for numerous families each fall as juice was squeezed from the cane, evaporated in a kettle or evaporator pan, and converted into delicious syrup. Either sugar cane or sorghum syrup was a staple in the diet of the American people until the mid–twentieth century. A massive population shift from the countryside into the cities made a drastic cut into the demand for homemade table syrup. Soon there appeared numerous selections of exotic blends of syrup conveniently available at the local grocery, further lessening the demand for the homemade variety. As smaller families replaced the larger ones of earlier years they also diminished the labor pool upon which the farmer depended, and in so doing reduced the farmer's capabilities of producing a profitable crop. Now these grand old machines, which once were so essential to the farmers' livelihoods, sit rusting away behind weather-beaten barns, abandoned in pastures, entangled in vines, or stored unceremoniously in some decrepit shed, their history all but forgotten.

However, this is a rich part of America's history we cannot let escape. Real American people designed and manufactured these mills, real people marketed them from hardware stores along dirt streets, real people used them, and real people depended upon them for family provisions and cash income. In the following pages I attempt to document this part of our rural heritage. While there are several excellent studies on the origin and development of the three-roller mill, my chief objective is to chronicle the people of the American foundries which manufactured them. Therefore, I refer you to the bibliography, especially to the works of Deerr, Galloway, Daniels, Mazumdar and Needham, for more detailed studies of the ancient origin and modern innovations of the cane mill as we know it today.

There is a renewed interest in this part of Americana. Numerous individuals, communities and towns hold sugar cane or sorghum festivals each fall with thousands of persons attending. Those of us who sponsor festivals at our own farms find them well attended and lots of fun. More and more persons are looking for mills to buy to set up small syrup-making operations for profit, fun or fellowship, and foundries continue to get requests for mills and parts which they haven't manufactured for more than half a century. It is my sincere desire that we will capture not only the history but also a new appreciation for those grand old machines and the foundries which manufactured them.

Above: Syrup making was a necessity for food and income for many families. *Below:* Valdosta, Georgia, at a time of dirt streets, with cane mills on the sidewalks and syrup kettles leaning against posts (both photographs courtesy Lowndes County Historical Society & Museum, Valdosta, Georgia).

To research and write about the great American cane mill has been an exciting adventure—an adventure which should have begun sixty years ago, however, when memories were fresh, companies still had records, and I had my life before me to accomplish the task. When at the urging of our son, John, I began this endeavor I had absolutely no idea of the immensity of the assignment I had undertaken. I had assumed there would have been eight or ten companies manufacturing mills, ten to twelve at the most. Never would I have guessed that I would discover more than 160 companies which produced mills in some degree. The research, however, has been exciting. One discovery has often provided more leads and the joy of discovery is ongoing even after five years of research.

Above: When the author's father erected his cane mill, even though it was night when he finished, the family gathered around for a drink of delicious juice. *Below:* When P.O.J. was introduced into America it took the country by storm, and the author's father had a patch of it also.

The study of the history of sugar cane has been fascinating. My childhood sugar cane world consisted of the patch behind our farmhouse on Route One, Hartford, Alabama. Dad had P.O.J., a sweet but rather dense cane developed by the Proefstation Oost Java; some Blue Ribbon; and, last, some soft Government Improved Green cane with prickles at the base of the leaves. Little did I realize that a grass native to New Guinea had circled the globe and had, on the one hand, contributed so much to humankind in the form of sugar and syrup, and on the other been severely maligned for giving rise to the plantation system and its dependence upon slavery. Perhaps no other agricultural crop has impacted colonization, commerce, and human tragedy as has sugar. While this facet has been an interesting study, I'll not go there. Those who want to pursue this part of the history of sugar cane will again find some excellent references in the bibliography. My intent

Left: Ribbon was a favorite of the author's father, but it eventually played out. *Right:* The "Green Government Cane" with prickles on the leaves has also been called Home Green, a delicious soft cane.

is to look at those wonderful cane mills used to extract juice for the early American syrup industry, the people who designed them and the foundries which manufactured them. To accomplish this, first I will explore briefly the history of sugar cane and sorghum. Then there will follow a discussion of the history of the cane mill with its conflicting theories of origin. Next, I offer the history of numerous American foundries which manufactured cane mills, and in between, some photographs of mills in their unique and interesting settings.

Such an undertaking has had its fulfillment and regrets, with the joys of discovery and frustrations of dead ends. Had I known that I would have begun this project late in life I would have been more attentive early in life. I would have noted the kind of mill my grandfather used, which he powered with an old Buick engine, when he made syrup for the community. I would have made a mental note of where my father purchased his Goldens' Foundry and Machine Company No. 2 three-roller mill. I would have maintained a better network of persons knowledgeable about mills and syrup-making. And I would have sought manufacturers' histories before they were discarded or forgotten.

But, oh, I've met some wonderful people along the way. Of the hundreds of mills I've wanted to photograph, not a single mill owner has forbidden me to take a picture of his mill. Some have invited me in for breakfast, for lunch, to look at home videos, to show me pictures, and have invited me back to their farm, even if they were not at home, to take further pictures. Reference librarians have been more than courteous and helpful. Friends have swapped information, and e-mail contacts have shared wisdom, discoveries, insight, research, photographs, data and encouragement. There's really no way to express how much fun I've had with this research, and while I have tried to follow every lead, I just know numerous mills have escaped me. With my deepest gratitude I acknowledge the help and encouragement I've received from the following persons in the research and development of this book.

Richard and Jane Johnson, Comer, Alabama, who gave me my first sugar cane seed stock and my first syrup kettle and whose annual festival rekindled my interest in sugar cane and homemade syrup making upon my retirement.

Tommy and Beth Clayton, Hilliard, Florida, who have the largest collection of mills and kettles I've seen, who have been friends and encouragers, and whose family we love as our own.

Ken and Connie Christison, Conway, North Carolina, a syrup maker and Web page master who has stirred up a lot of interest in cane mills and encouraged my work.

Bill Outlaw, professor at Florida State University, Tallahassee, Florida, and his gracious wife, Nedra, who have shared discoveries in syrup making and cane mills so freely, and who kept nudging me on to completion of this book.

Dennis and Norma Parker, Goldens' Foundry and Machine Company, Columbus, Georgia, who have shared catalogs, files, and information. More importantly, they have been real friends.

Alison Gibson, library director, Union Township Public Library, Ripley, Ohio, for information on the Phoenix Foundry of Ripley, and for initiating further searches which resulted in numerous additional discoveries.

JoAnn Pearson, special collections librarian, Buffalo and Erie County Public Library, Buffalo, New York.

Alexander G. "Sandy" Monroe, city records manager, Richmond Public Library, Richmond, Virginia, who researches with grit and determination and hates to admit defeat.

Teresa Roane, director of library and photographic services, Richmond History Center, Richmond, Virginia.

Judy Dean, librarian, Nashville Public Library, Nashville, Tennessee.

Marilyn Wilkerson, reference librarian, Central Library, Evansville, Indiana.

Lee C. Grady, archivist, McCormick Archives, Madison, Wisconsin.

Mark Finlay, history department, Armstrong State University, Savannah, Georgia.

Sharen Lee, Live Oak Public Libraries, Savannah, Georgia.

P. Barry Stokes, reference librarian, Live Oak Public Libraries, Savannah, Georgia, upon whom I've had to call numerous times.

Wayne Everard and Irene Wainwright, archivists, New Orleans City Archives, New Orleans Public Library, New Orleans, Louisiana.

Vincent X. Ford, Georgia Historical Society, Savannah, Georgia.

Pen Bogert, reference specialist, Filson Historical Society Library, Louisville, Kentucky.

Frank Rogers, president, Excelsior Foundry Company, Belleville, Illinois.

Claire Momot, Springfield-Green County Library, Springfield, Missouri.

The Honorable Paula Tucker, mayor, Logan, Ohio.

Suzette Raney, Local History and Genealogy, Chattanooga-Hamilton County Bicentennial Library, Chattanooga, Tennessee.

Andrew Hempe, acting head archivist, Houston Metropolitan Research Center, Houston, Texas.

Casey Edward Greene, head of Special Collections, Rosenbery Library, Galveston, Texas.

Helen Mowrey, Hocking County Historical Society, Logan, Ohio.

Rita Forrester, Newburgh Free Library, Newburgh, New York.

Susan Veasey, reference librarian, Houston-Love Memorial Library, Dothan, Alabama.

Jennifer West, assistant director, Highland County District Library, Hillsboro, Ohio.

Albert "Bubba" Savage, III, president, Mobile Pulley and Gear Company, Mobile, Alabama.

Billie Murray, Brooks County Public Library, Quitman, Georgia.

Amy Plonowski, public services librarian, Brooks County Public Library, Quitman, Georgia.

Willard L. Rocker, reference librarian, Washington Memorial Library, Macon, Georgia.

T. Loeffler, reference librarian, Evansville Public Library, Evansville, Indiana.

Carol Kaplan, Nashville Room, Nashville, Tennessee.

Frankie King, Librarian II, Public Service Section, Tennessee State Library and Archives, Nashville, Tennessee.

Kassie Hassler, Librarian III, Public Service Section, Tennessee State Library and Archives, Nashville, Tennessee.

J. Gayle Camarda, reference librarian, St. Louis County Library, St. Louis, Missouri.

Ronald J. Caldwell, South Carolina Room, Charleston County Public Library, Charleston, South Carolina.

Mary E. Weisnewski, Bellevue Public Library, Bellevue, Iowa.

Sandy Day, Schiappa Library, Steubenville, Ohio.

Sarah S. Benson, local history librarian, Richland County Public Library, Columbia, South Carolina.

Suzanne Kelly, corresponding secretary, Genealogy Friends of the Library, Neosho, Missouri.

Larry A. James, historian, Neosho, Missouri.

Shanna Griffin, chamber of commerce, Neosho, Missouri.

Carol Jones, reference librarian, Fairfield Public Library, Fairfield, Iowa.

Elizabeth Harvey, local history librarian, Brooklyn Public Library, Brooklyn, New York.

Robin Copp, head, Book Division, South Carolina Library, University of South Carolina, Columbia, South Carolina.

Dr. Janet G. Hudson, historical researcher, Columbia, South Carolina.

Marcus Walker, syrup-maker in Bonaire, Georgia, for his Schofield and Taylor research.

Ann Toplovich, Tennessee Historical Society, Nashville, Tennessee.

Mary Beth Brown, graduate research assistant, University of Missouri–St. Louis Mercantile Library, St. Louis, Missouri.

Lenore J. Johnson, reference and genealogy manager, Tangipahoa Parish Library, Amite, Louisiana.

Paul Begley, reference archivist, South Carolina Department of Archives and History, Columbia, South Carolina.

Pat Gwyn, librarian, Mount Airy Public Library, Mount Airy, North Carolina.

Diane Mallstrom, reference librarian, Rare Books and Special Collections, the Public Library of Cincinnati and Hamilton County, Cincinnati, Ohio.

Sylvia V. Metzinger, manager, Rare Books and Special Collections, The Public Library of Cincinnati and Hamilton County, Cincinnati, Ohio.

Nancy Gaudette, librarian, Worcester Collection, Worcester Public Library, Worcester, Massachusetts.

Lyn Martin, special collections librarian, Willard Library, Evansville, Indiana.

Amy Reed, librarian, Willard Library, Evansville, Indiana.

Dennis Brandewie, references services, Evansville Public Library, Evansville, Indiana.

Paul O. Barker, Family Research Center, Ozarks Genealogical Society, Springfield, Missouri.

Jason D. Stratman, library assistant-reference, Missouri Historical Society, St. Louis, Missouri.

Patty Mosher, Galesburg Public Library, Galesburg, Illinois.

Mrs. Claire Bryan Hodges, granddaughter of D. T. Sutherland, Bainbridge, Georgia.

Doreen McCabe, young adult and reference librarian, Hartford Public Library, Hartford, Connecticut.

Janice Mathews, librarian, Hartford Public Library, Hartford, Connecticut.

Michelle Clark, reference librarian, Reading Public Library, Reading, Pennsylvania.

Greg Kelly, San Francisco History Center, the Public Library, San Francisco, California.

Cheryl Laugherty, Adult Reference Department, Birchard Public Library, Fremont, Ohio.

Renate Milner and Donald O. Davis, Lowndes County Historical Society and Museum, Valdosta, Georgia.

Sharon Rowe, librarian, South Georgia Regional Library, Valdosta, Georgia.

Thomas Hutchens, Huntsville-Madison County Public Library, Huntsville, Alabama.

Jerry Carroll, librarian, North Carolina Room, Forsyth County Public Library, Winston-Salem, North Carolina.

Linda Poitevint Beck, local history librarian, Augusta-Richmond County Public Library, Augusta, Georgia.

Peggy Haile McPhillips, city historian, Norfolk Public Library, Norfolk, Virginia.

Sara Nyman, librarian, Kansas City Public Library, Kansas City, Missouri.

David Stratton, Salem Historical Society, Salem, Ohio.

Jim Caccamo, head archivist, Hudson Library, Hudson, Ohio.

Joan L. Clark, head librarian, Cleveland Public Library, Main Branch, Cleveland, Ohio.

Margarete Lange, head of information services, Wheeler Basin Regional Library, Decatur, Alabama.

Renee Gimski, reference librarian, Wilmington Public Library, Wilmington, Delaware.

Jean E. Meeh Gosebrink, Special Collections librarian, St. Louis Public Library, St. Louis, Missouri.

Deborah S. Davis, archives librarian, Odum Library, Valdosta State University, Valdosta, Georgia.

Susan R. Cook, Special Services librarian, Thomas County Public Library, Thomasville, Georgia.

Kathy Mills, director, Thomasville Genealogical, History and Fine Arts Library, Inc., Thomasville, Georgia.

Jan Stokes, local history and genealogy librarian, Rockford Public Library, Rockford, Illinois.

Claudine Jenda, agriculture librarian and assistant chair, Reference and Instruction Services, Auburn University Library, Auburn, Alabama.

Andrew Wohrley, engineering librarian, Auburn University Library, Auburn, Alabama.

Boyd Addlesperger, librarian, The Sherman Room, Mansfield/Richland County Public Library, Mansfield, Ohio.

Sam Roshon, librarian, Columbus Metropolitan Library, Columbus, Ohio.

Al Zarvar, director, Lincoln Public Library, Lincoln, Ohio.

Richard C. LeRoy, librarian, Franklin Public Library, Franklin, Ohio.

Ron Davidson, Archives/Reference librarian, Sandusky Library, Sandusky, Ohio.

Lou Ann James, archivist, Belleville Public Library, Belleville, Illinois.

Wilma Atkinson, corresponding secretary, Washington County Genealogical Society, Washington, Iowa.

Jan Behrens, Director, Knoxville Public Library, Knoxville, Iowa.

Linda Rogers, senior circulation assistant, Campbell County Public Library, Newport, Kentucky.

Nancy Sherrill, genealogy librarian, Vigo County Public Library, Terre Haute, Indiana.

Marilyn M. Nobbe, librarian, Morrisson-Reeves Library, Richmond, Indiana.

Laura M. Gottlieb, reference librarian, Hedberg Public Library, Janesville, Wisconsin.

Jerry Bruce, reference librarian, Lancaster Public Library, Lancaster, Pennsylvania.

Esther Ciccioli, head reference librarian, Bridgeton Free Public Library, Bridgeton, New Jersey.

Judy Cheatham, genealogy and History Room director, Shelbyville-Shelby County Public Library, Shelbyville, Indiana.

Wendy Street, director, Pella Public Library, Pella, Iowa.

Susan Villar, night librarian, Wisconsin Historical Society, Madison, Wisconsin.

Cathy S. Hackett, reference department, Clark County Public Library, Springfield, Ohio.

Linda Neff, reference services, Goshen Public Library, Goshen, Indiana.

Linda Wilson, reference assistant, Joseph I. Simpson Public Library, Mechanicsburg, PA.

Johnny Tucker, Portland, Tennessee, for information on the United States and Cuban Allied Works Engineering Corporation, South Bradford, Pennsylvania.

Jean Kreke, telereference department, Louisville Free Public Library, Louisville, Kentucky.

Jane Pyle, Chatham County Historical Association, Inc., Pittsboro, North Carolina.

Cheryl Gleason, Freeport Public Library, Freeport, Illinois.

Jane Krebs, circulation clerk, Piedmont Regional Library, Winder, Georgia.

John Ransom, Rutherford B. Hayes Presidential Center, Spiegel Grove, Fremont, Ohio.

Andrew Storrs, research volunteer, The Monroe County Historical Society, Inc., Bloomington, Iowa.

Christopher Stokes, Washington Memorial Library, Genealogical and Historical Room, Macon, Georgia.

Allen Merry, librarian, Business, Science and Industry Department, Free Library of Philadelphia, Pennsylvania.

Linda Hatfield, reference librarian, John McIntire Library, Zanesville, Ohio.

Kathy McCoy and the Monroe County Heritage Museums, Monroe County, Alabama.

The Pioneer Museum of Alabama, Troy, Alabama.

Ms. Dollyie M. Martin, researcher, Decatur, Alabama.

Renee' G. Pruitt, Huntsville-Madison County Public Library, Huntsville, Alabama.

James Britton, reference department, Okefenokee Regional Library, Waycrosss, Georgia.

Bonnell Holmes, president, Brooks County Historical Society, Quitman, Georgia.

Jean H. Lythgoe, library assistant, Rockford Public Library, Rockford, IL.

Ellen Thomasson, public service coordinator, Missouri Historical Society, St. Louis, MO.

William A. Montgomery, Atlanta-Fulton County Library System, Atlanta, GA.

Muriel M. Jackson, archivist and genealogy librarian, Middle Georgia Archives and Genealogy, Macon, Georgia.

Laura Harrison, Brooks County Public Library, Quitman, Georgia.

PART I

1

The Syrup Canes

Table syrup can be made from either sugar cane or sweet sorghum, and each has been a staple in the American daily diet. Both are members of the *Gramineae* (grass) family, and therefore are related. Sugar cane is found in the warmer climates across the Deep South, and sorghum primarily in our sister states to the North, though some varieties grow successfully in the southern states. While there is a fair amount of certainty of the geographic centers from which they sprang, there is no documented evidence of the time of origin of either, and the history of each is at best sketchy. Even so, we'll endeavor to understand the background from which these marvelous plants came.

The History of Sugar Cane

Origins

New Guinea seems the center from which sugar cane burst forth upon the world and from which it eventually encircled the globe in tropical and subtropical areas roughly along the palm tree line. An island in the archipelago of East Indies just below the equator, New Guinea is situated about 93 miles north of Australia and, after Greenland, is the world's second largest island. While its origin of population dates back into antiquity, the Portuguese were the first Europeans to settle on the island in A.D. 1511. Its tropical climate is conducive to luxurious growth, and numerous unique plants abound in the area. From New Guinea, in the South Pacific, to Route One, Hartford, Alabama, seems such a long way. It seems so improbable that a grass of the large *Gramineae* family, which the inhabitants of New Guinea regarded as merely a vegetable, could find its way across continents and oceans to my father's garden. However, sugar cane is one of the most widely distributed agricultural crops on earth. Botanically, this grass belongs to the cohort *Glumiflorae*, natural order *Graminae*, tribe *Andropagonae* and of the genus *Saccharum*. While it has been generally accepted that there are five species of sugar cane, this has not been without dissent. Those five species traditionally held are as follows.

S. barberi **Jeswiet** is a thin, reed-type cane which had its origins in southern Asia. It was a significant cane in the early sugar industries of India and China, and a hybrid of *S. barberi* Jeswiet crossed with *S. officinarum* became the foundation of the sugar cane

The ancients who cultivated sugar cane could not have seen what a "pot of gold at the end of the rainbow" it would become (photograph by John Dean, Hartford, Alabama).

industry of the western world. *S. barberi* Jeswiet, probably native to northern India, was well adapted to the colder climate of that region. When Dr. Jeswiet revised Hackel's list of species in 1925 he named *S. barberi* after the botanist Dr. C.A. Barber, the first sugar cane expert of Imperial India, who, in 1918, had identified and described five horticultural groups of cane in India.

S. officinarum L is the original Linnean species, named for the Swedish botanist, Carl Linnaeus, who published his *Species Plantarium* in 1753. One of the cultivated species, *S. officinarum L* is rather large in size, having wide leaves and a high sugar/low fiber content. It is soft and brightly colored, and was usually grown for chewing. This cane became the major breeding stock for numerous hybrids and was called *officinarum* meaning, "of the apothecaries' shops," and its hybrids were called "noble," a representation made by the Dutch in Java about 1920 as a salute to their high sugar content, bright colors, large size, and good quality of juice. The geographical origin of this cane is no doubt the South Pacific Islands, where hundreds of varieties in an overwhelming assortment of colors are still grown. Some of the most important varieties selected and cultivated across the sugar cane belt were (1) the Othaheite, also called Bourbon cane; (2) Cheribon, or Transparent cane; and (3) Tanna, or Caledonia cane.

S. robustum **Brandes and Jeswiet,** one of the two species which can exist in the wild, is very tall, having medium to large stalks, medium leaves, and a low sugar content. This is a hardy, vigorous cane which probably originated in Indonesia and then spread into New Guinea where it cross pollinated with other canes. In a 1928 expedition to New Guinea, along with Dr. E.W. Brandes and Dr. C.E. Pemberton, Dr. Jeswiet discovered this new sugar cane and named it *robustum* because it was so vigorous. It seemed to be confined to that area of the world and was added to the species list. Only one significant commercial variety has been produced from this species, and that is 37-1933, a variety grown on irrigated estates in the Hawaiian Islands for a long time.

S. sinense **Roxb.** was identified and named by the Scottish physician and eminent botanist William Roxburgh, and is a Chinese sugar cane with its origin in southern Asia. While Roxburgh was collecting specimens for a flora of India in 1796, an officer of the East India Company stationed at Canton sent him some samples of sugar cane which he introduced into the Calcutta botanical gardens. Roxburgh noticed certain peculiarities and created a new species which he identified as *Saccharum sinense* in volume three of his *Plants of the Coast of Coromandel*, published in 1819. Dr. Jeswiet raised the cane to species status in 1925. *S. sinense* Roxb. is characterized by medium to slender yellow-green stalks, medium to narrow leaves, an intermediate sugar content and high fiber content. Developed in south China, it is a cultivated species and grows with great vigor. It was established and cultivated in India under the name Chinea, and became a viable commercial variety around 1850. Its descendant, Uba, was grown commercially in various sugar producing countries around the world. It was one of the two sugar canes important to the Chinese and Indian sugar industries, replaced the canes susceptible to mosaic disease in Puerto Rico and Louisiana, and became the principal variety in South Africa.

S. spontaneum is the second wild species, probably originating in New Guinea but found growing wild in the whole of that region. John Reinhold Forster reported finding this cane in Tahiti in 1773 when he accompanied Captain James Cook to the Windward Group of the Society Islands. It has slender stalks, narrow leaves, exceedingly low sugar content, and very high fiber content. It grows vigorously, and is immune to many sugar cane diseases, traits to be desired. Because of its vigorous growth and high immunity to disease it has been crossed with other species to produce disease-resistant hybrids. The immensity of this cane's gene pool is seen in the 300 plus varieties found in India alone.

Some sugar cane authorities insist on a sixth species, *Saccharum edule*. For a number of reasons other authorities do not consider it worthy of species status. It's an interesting cane, however, so let me mention it briefly.

Saccharum edule is a small cane having many of the vegetative characteristics of *S. robustum*, but this particular cane is characterized by its peculiar swollen, aborted and deformed inflorescence, which is used for food in New Guinea and surrounding islands. In fact, these deformed tassels are even canned and sold on the commercial market, known both as "Pit-pit" and "Fijian asparagus." It is not cultivated for its sugar content or juice. Since this cane cannot produce a normal tassel it has to be propagated vegetatively. Justus Karl Hasskarl, a Dutch botanist who became assistant curator for the Bogor Botanic Garden in Java, helped organize the garden by taxonomic families, and in 1844 wrote the second catalog of plants in the garden listing more than 2,800 species. In his catalog Hasskarl described the species now called *Saccharum edule*. Rhumphius had described a similar cane in 1747 in his *Herbarium Amboinense* and called it *Ova piscium*, because the tassel looked like fish eggs.

Now when Dad planted his cane patch in rural Geneva County, Alabama, he didn't know anything about the discussion of the number of species, nor would that have interested him. He simply wanted to know if the sugar cane was sweet, tasted good, was easy to peel and chew, and whether it came back from stubble well. So let me bring you to the "edge of the woods," but not go in too deeply. The sugar cane botanist, Jeswiet, held that there were these species: (1) *Saccharum spontaneum*, which included *S. Sinense*, Roxb. and *S. Barberi* Jeswiet, and (2) *Saccharium officinarum L*. The cane sugar historian Noel Deerr interpreted the species as, (1) *S. spontaneum*, (2) *S. robustum* Brandes and Jeswiet, (3) *S. Officinarum L*, and (4) Intergenetic hybrids between *saccharum* and sorghum. Daniels reduces his species list to three, namely, (1) *S. Officinarum L*, (2) *S. sinense* Roxb., and (3) *S. Barberi* Jeswiet. While

Left: This beautiful aqua green improved variety grows straight but is brittle. *Right:* Cayanna is an older yellow variety which might have come from Brazil.

these have been the generally accepted divisions of the species for numerous years, the discovery and discussion continues.

With today's astounding scientific technology using complicated molecular techniques, including cytoplasmic DNA and cluster analysis of nuclear DNA, amazing differences are being discovered. After looking at the phenotypic, cytological, and molecular marker analysis, Dr. J. E. Irvine, of the Texas Agricultural Experimental Station, Texas A&M University, published a paper in the journal of *Theoretical and Applied Genetics,* February, 1999, in which he questioned the traditional species. As a result of his scientific studies he concluded that *S. spontaneum* differs sufficiently to be called a separate species. Additionally, he believes the other five species should probably be placed into one species under the name *Saccharum officinarum.* He sees two authentic species, *S. spontaneum* and *S. officinarum.* We stand on the threshold of potentially new and exciting discoveries thanks to modern scientific inquiry.

Dates of origin of sugar cane are lost in the darkness of antiquity, but it is one of the oldest cultivated plants in the world. The folklore and mythology of the South Pacific attribute it to the creation of the human race. The sacred writings of ancient India refer to sugar cane somewhere in the 1500–500 B.C. period, while some estimates put the first migration of sugar cane from New Guinea as early as 8000 B.C. Ancient Hindu myths depict the antiquity and importance of sugar cane by describing the sacred mountain at the center of the world around which there are seven continents divided by seven magical seas reflecting the staple needs of humankind, namely salt, sugar, wine, ghee (clarified butter), milk, yogurt, and fresh water. "Sweet cane" is mentioned twice in the Holy Bible, but again there is no unanimity of the meaning. Some interpret the "sweet cane" (kawneh) of Isaiah 43:24 to be sugar cane, or *S. officinarum*, and that of Jeremiah 6:20 to be calamus, a ginger-grass from northwestern and central India which gave off a strong, spicy aroma when crushed. These Isaiah references date from approximately 712 B.C. Alexander the Great invaded India in 327 B.C. and encountered sugar cane. His scribes recorded that the inhabitants chewed a marvelous reed which produced a "kind of honey without the help of bees." Around 300 B.C. the Greek scholar, Theophrastus, wrote of a "sweet salt" which the people of India produced from a "reed-like" plant. Surely he was referring to sugar and sugar cane. Though no accurate records were kept and information must be gleaned from secondary sources, it is quite evident that sugar cane is of ancient origin.

Spread

To trace the spread of sugar cane across the known world we once again have to use secondary sources. There seems to have been three initial avenues of diffusion for *S. officinarum*, the noble cane from which so many economically profitable hybrids have sprung. New Guinea, the place of origin of sugar cane, also became known for six distinctive vari-

Left: A soft, delicious variety called Georgia Green doesn't come back from stubble well. *Right:* This cane, called Georgia Yellow Gal, might have come from Brazil also and was popular in Georgia's syrup industry

eties of cane. The Gogari was a dull, deep green cane which turned red on exposure to the sun. Badilla was a dark purple to black cane, and the Geru was greenish brown to copper colored. The Goru seela scelana was like the Geru but striped with red. Goru bunu bunana was yellow to yellowish green with red spots. The N.G.64, a significant hybrid of later years, was brownish to olive cane striped with claret. This survey of the spread of sugar cane from New Guinea will trace geographic lines of movement rather than time lines, which in some instances will occur simultaneously.

The first migration of *S. officinarum* from New Guinea was to the southeast about 8000 B.C. Sugar cane crossed island bridges, was taken by sailors and merchants along trade routes, and was carried by migrants looking for new homes in the Solomon Islands, New Hebrides and New Caledonia. The South Pacific, east of the Wallace Line, seems to be the place of origin for all of the standard cultivated varieties. Four, or perhaps five, significant varieties indigenous to this area made great contributions to the sugar industry. These included the yellowish-green enduring standard, and widely cultivated, Otaheite; the dark and light striped Tanna ("Tanna" means "rich earth," so Tanna canes require rich earth); a claret-colored cane with a bronze-green, almost black stripe named Cavengerie; the yellow and red striped Iscambine; and possibly the yellow violet, the purple violet and the ribbon Cheribon varieties. Several notable hybrids were developed from these and impacted the sugar industry in that area while other significant canes were developed through the years. The *To uti. S. atrorubens,* imported from Java by Bouganville in 1872, had violet stalk and pith. The *Rurutu S. rubicundum* had violet stalk and leaves, but a white pith. There was also a violet and yellow striped cane, the To oura. The *Irimotu S. fragile* was a green brittle cane and the To avae was a green and yellow striped cane. Vaihi was a white cane introduced from the Hawaiian Islands, and the *Piaverae. S. obscurum* was probably the same as the Creole cane.

A cultivated cane which came from a Florida research station has excellent growth habits but is very hard.

Then, about 6000 B.C., there was a second migration to the northwest through Southeast Asia, the Philippines, possibly to Indonesia, and to northern India, setting the stage for India's sugar industry and their great contribution to world sugar. Sugar from evaporated cane juice was first produced in India around 1000 B.C., so sugar cane had to arrive sufficiently before that date. There emerged several notable varieties in the Indian sugar industry that also influenced other sugar cane regions. There were the Bamboo Canes, called Kulloa, Kullore, or Culleroah, which were light colored white canes which grew to great heights. The Ukh and Nanal were small, thin, reed-like canes, the Creole a small yellow cane, the Restali a striped cane, and the Samsara a white cane. The Paunda seems to have been an acclimatized cane introduced into India, and the Ganna appears to have been a cross between the Ukh and Paunda types. Since India led the way in sugar production, it also led the way in sugar cane research. Two significant breeding stations emerged in later years, namely Coimbatore and Bihar Orisa, which contributed several significant varieties to the world, such as Co.281, Co.290, Co.221, B.O.3, B.O.17, and B.O.50.

Thailand became a stepping-stone for the movement of sugar cane to the west from the East Indies, and cane has been grown there since before its recorded history. The British included Burma as a part of India, so consequently its sugar cane history is submerged in that of India's. The first sugar cane was brought to the Philippines by the Spanish in 1521 and their early sugar industry depended on canes from Java, India or Hawaii. It was probably no earlier than the third century B.C. that sugar cane reached China, migrating from either southeast Asia or the easternmost parts of India, though the exact time is unknown. There is a specific mention of sugar cane in some Chinese writings as early as A.D. 286. Some of the older varieties were lu-che and chu-che, while the later years saw a variety of canes from a wealth of breeding stations, including Taiwan, India, Java, and the research station at Canal Point, Florida. It was much later, in 1788, that sugar cane was introduced into Australia, to the south, and it was only in the 1860s that it became a significant sugar producer. In the early years Australia depended upon the Indian cane, N:Co.310, but later developed their own Pindar and Q.83.

Sugar cane from India then made its way west to Persia (Iran) in A.D. 600. Because of winter temperatures in Iran a cane with early maturity is essential, therefore, canes developed in India, South Africa, Louisiana and Florida were used in Iran's later sugar industry. The major varieties used were N:Co.310 and C.P.48-103. From Iran, sugar cane migrated to Iraq about A.D. 650 and, though it has a long sugar cane history, the later years saw that industry using canes from India and Canal Point, Florida, namely, N:Co. 310 and C.P.44-101. A diffusion from India to the east takes sugar cane to Tonking in northern Indochina, in what is now Vietnam, in 250 B.C. South Vietnam is one of the world's oldest sugar cane regions outside New Guinea, and, in fact, wild cane still grows in some areas of the country. From Vietnam the migration moves to Szechwan in southwest China in A.D. 647. Another line of migration takes sugar cane from Persia (Iran) to Kashgar in western China between A.D. 700–800, and then to Shensi in north-central China. When Marco Polo, the Venetian traveler, was returning from Cathay in the latter part of the thirteenth century he observed sugar in Bangladesh, that part of Pakistan annexed into India in 1947. The area was late in developing a significant sugar market, and then depended on canes from India's Coimbatore and Bihar Orisa breeding stations. As Pakistan's sugar industry grew they were dependent upon the same varieties India used, namely Co.205, Co.213, and Co.285. Later, Co.L. 54 (Coimbatore—Lyallpur), became the dominant cane of Pakistan.

Next there was a migration to the countries around the eastern shores of the Mediterranean Sea between A.D. 700 and 800, down to Yemen, in southwest Arabia, around A.D. 900–1000, and to the island Zanzibar, off east Africa, somewhere around A.D. 1000–1100. The diffusion of sugar cane around the eastern shores of the Mediterranean had a strong advocate in the Arab Conquests. Everywhere the Arabs went in their conquests, they took sugar cane with them. So, in the first half of the seventh century A.D., we find sugar cane growing in Syria, in Palestine from Jerusalem to Lebanon, and along the Jordan River north of the Dead Sea in the Jericho area. By A.D. 640 it was growing from Cairo to Alexandria, Egypt. The later sugar industry saw Co.310 and Co.413 as the dominant canes of the area.

Between A.D. 644 and 966 cane had spread to the southern part of Cyprus, to the middle regions of Crete by A.D. 823, and to the northern coastline of Sicily by A.D. 877. Sugar cane was growing in northwest Africa by A.D. 682 and in southeast Spain by A.D. 711. It also migrated to the Greek island of Rhodes around 655 and to Malta after 820.

Much of the remainder of Africa which developed sugar industries also depended upon cane from India, with Co.310 being grown in Ethiopia, Kenya, Mozambique, Rhodesia, South Africa, Sudan, Swaziland, and Tanzania. Angola was discovered by the Portuguese in 1486. Sugar cane from São Tomé was introduced to the country soon after. Sugar cane was found on the island of Madagascar more than a thousand years ago by Arab traders. One of the major varieties was the Otaheite cane, which was one of the world's leading varieties. Cane reached Mauritius in the sixteenth century and Réunion (which was once known as Ile de Bourbon) in the second half of the seventeenth century. Their early cultivated varieties came from Barbados and Coimbatore, India, while the later industry turned to the Australian canes Ragnar and Q.75.

It took a few hundred years longer, but sugar cane finally reached the Atlantic islands off the west coast of Africa. There it was poised to capture the Americas. Madeira, an island group about 400 miles west of the Moroccan coast, became an important factor in what was to become the American sugar cane industry. There were two inhabited islands, Madeira and Porto Santo, to which Henry the Navigator arranged sugar cane to be sent from Sicily in A.D. 1425. Sugar cane became their chief crop, and sugar and wine their chief exports. There was a thriving sugar industry on these islands, with Uba, a hardy and enormously productive Japanese cane, and Creole being the two chief varieties. The Madeira Islands have a direct link with the Americas but, before we explore that, let's move on to the other Atlantic islands. South of Madeira are the Canary Islands. When sugar cane arrived on the islands is not certain, but the first sugar mill was built in 1484, with Creole cane being the cane of choice. Sugar cane, then, had to arrive before that date in order to establish a marketable crop. It was from Gomera, one of the islands in the Canaries, that Columbus secured his seed cane, which he took to Hispaniola in 1493. Still farther south, and to the west, is Sao Tome, in the Gulf of Guinea, off the west coast of Africa. The island was producing sugar by 1495, so sugar cane had to arrive earlier. Sugar cane was also carried to the Cape Verde Islands and to the Azores, but for some reason it did not develop into a thriving industry.

Now for the American connection. Columbus brought sugar cane to Hispaniola on his second voyage in December 1493, at the command of King Ferdinand and Queen Isabella, who on May 23, 1493, ordered that he carry all sorts of seeds and plants, and twenty field experts in cultivation. Columbus was no stranger to sugar cane. Acting as an agent for Italian merchants, he had sailed to Madeira in 1478 to purchase sugar. It was a lawsuit resulting from that voyage that compelled Columbus to return to Genoa in 1479 to testify, and the record of that lawsuit establishes his Genoese origins. Either in 1478 or 1479, Columbus married into an Italian-Portuguese family of some prominence. His bride was Felipa Moniz de Perestrelo and her father, Bartholomew Perestrelo, was the first governor of Porto Santo. Bartholomew was raised in the royal households of Prince John and Prince Henry (Henry the Navigator). He married and was widowed. His second wife was Isabel Moniz, who belonged to a noble family with landholdings in southern Portugal and a sugar estate on Madeira Island. Isabel Moniz gave her son-in-law, Columbus, the maps and papers which had belonged to her deceased husband, perhaps valuable information concerning sailing and world geography. Even after his wife's death Columbus still maintained his relationships on Madeira and Porto Santo islands. With such contacts it is not surprising that Columbus carried sugar cane on his second voyage to the New World. On September

25, 1493, Columbus set sail, stopped in the Canaries, at Gomera, on-boarded his cargo, and arrived in Hispaniola in December of that year. Coming to the site of his first settlement, Navidad, on the coast of Haiti, and finding it deserted, he sailed on and selected an unprotected, unhealthy shore on the north coast of Hispaniola, which he named Isabella. When he returned to the Old World his brother moved the settlement to the southern coast and began building Santo Domingo. Sugar cane had now arrived in the New World.

By 1496, sugar cane was being planted in Santo Domingo, reaching Puerto Rico about 1515, carried into Cuba by Velasque in 1511, and to Jamaica with the Spanish explorers in the first years of the sixteenth century, prior to 1527. The Salangora cane, a grayish cane which turned deep reddish purple when exposed to sunlight, became a standard in Puerto Rico. Crystallina and Otaheite were Cuba's principle canes, while Otaheite was grown primarily in Jamaica. Sugar cane was carried farther south to Brazil by the Portuguese prior to 1516 and several varieties were grown successfully. Salangore and Louzier were two important varieties, but there were also other significant ones such as Cayanna Antiga, which was probably the Otaheite

This excellent all-around cane is known locally as Government Improved Red.

cane. Others included Black Cane, probably Black Tanna; Imperial, which was a green and yellow striped cane; a butter colored cane called Manteiga; a seedling cane without hairs called Aleijada; Crystallina, or White Tanna; Rox Louizer, which was introduced into Brazil from Mauritius; Cirzenta, a cane similar to Salangore, a bright purple cane named Ferrea; a ruby red cane from Mauritius named Bois Rouge; a cane which resembled Crystallina when young and Antiga at maturity named Bronzeada; and Cayanninha, and all contributed to the Brazilian sugar industry, which ultimately grew into the largest in the world.

Sugar cane traveled into Mexico with Cortes by 1524 and reached Barbados by the late 1630s, where several varieties emerged and contributed to that industry. Bourbon, a yellowish or green cane, was popular, as were Purple Transparent Cheribon, Striped Cheribon, and White Transparent. Several seedlings also became prominent in the Barbados sugar industry, such as a yellowish green, erect cane, B.109; a yellow, very long jointed cane known as B.147; a green, erect cane named B.208; and B.306, an erect, yellow, long jointed cane. Sugar cane reached the Leeward Islands and the Virgin Islands perhaps a generation after reaching Barbados. This area became a dynamic sugar cane industry, with Cuba and Brazil leading the world in sugar production.

Sugar cane continued to spread throughout the New World, finding its way to Paraguay perhaps as early as 1580, with the Jesuits carrying it to Argentina in 1636, where the dark colored Louzier was the cane of prominence. Cane was carried to Peru by Pizarro in 1533, and reached Buenos Aires by 1545. The Jesuits, members of the Roman Catholic Society of

Jesus founded by Ignatius Loyola in 1534, devoted themselves to missionary and educational work. Wherever they established themselves they improved the agricultural conditions of the area. Jesuit orders were established in Hispaniola and Louisiana. In 1751, two ships passed through Hispaniola transporting soldiers to Louisiana. The Jesuits in Hispaniola sent sugar cane, and some slaves to tend them, to the brothers of their order in the New Colony. Though the Jesuits tried to establish this new crop, it failed, and it was as late as 1795 that sugar cane became naturalized enough to become economically profitable in Louisiana. In 1796, Etienne de Boré milled a crop of sugar cane on his plantation near New Orleans, a crop which brought a hefty return of twelve thousand dollars. Some of the colonists in Virginia and Carolina also tried to establish sugar cane in the colonies in the early 1700s, but without much success. However, sugar cane, not known to the American Indians, was now established in what was to become the United States of America. The first variety grown in America was known as Creole Cane, a small, yellow cane of probable Indian origin, which the Crusaders had introduced into southern Europe from China. This was the cane which was cultivated extensively in Sicily, southern Spain, the Canaries and Madeira and which reached the New World about 1500. When other varieties from the South Pacific were introduced into the New World, it was necessary to give this cane a name, and because of its long association with the colonies it was called Creole, or "cane of the country." Another cane, D.74, a pale green cane from Demerara, South America, was introduced into Louisiana, and because of its early maturity, grew well. Two Cheribon canes, a purple cane and a striped cane, also did well in Louisiana and became known as Home Purple and Home Ribbon.

The third migration was from Fiji, east of New Hebrides in the South Pacific, to the northeast. Sugar cane had been introduced to the area on its eastward movement through the Pacific at some unrecorded time. There Malabar, or White Tanna, was a favorite. Spreading through the various islands, Tonga, Samoa, the Cook Islands, Marquesas, Society Islands, and Easter Island, sugar cane reached the Hawaiian Islands between 500 B.C. and A.D. 1100. When Captain James Cook, the first European to discover the islands, arrived in 1778, he found five varieties of sugar cane growing there. As the Hawaiian Islands sugar industry grew it was supported by a number of significant canes. The Lahaina Cane, perhaps the same as the old standard, Otaheite, was grown in arid areas at low altitudes, while the Yellow Caledonia was grown in the rainfall areas at higher altitudes. Otaheite was introduced into the Hawaiian Islands by Captain Pardon Edwards in 1854. The Cheribon became known as Rose Bamboo and a small yellow cane was known as Yellow Bamboo. There were two Tip canes in the Islands which were grown at higher elevations. The Striped Tip was striped dark red and pinkish green which turned yellowish red and yellow at maturity, while the Yellow Tip was a light green cane which turned yellow at maturity. The Vaihi was a white cane and the Ko Kea was a greenish-white cane which predated the Otaheite. There was a green and red striped cane known as Ainakea, a yellow, very woody cane known as Oliana, and purple canes called Papaa and Palania. The Cavengerie Cane was probably introduced into the Islands from the South Pacific. Most of these were replaced by locally developed varieties. Little by little sugar cane, one of the world's greatest agricultural crops, began spreading from these centers until it encircled the globe and became established in those geographical areas with long enough growing seasons and soils conducive to its growth.

While there have been serious and intentional efforts to classify and identify canes by the countries from which they emerged, perhaps the best method is to follow the lead of Harrison and Jenman in their *Report of the British Guiana Botanical Gardens, 1890, Sugar Cane, No. 273*, and classify them by their outward appearance. This would entail consideration of five classes:

1. Yellow-Green or Green canes which are often blotched with red. This would include such canes as Bourbon, which is synonymous with Otaheite; Keni Keni; Elephant from Java; Singapore; Lakona and Lahaina.

2. White, Vinous (wine red), and Brown-tinged canes, such as Burke, Selangore, and Tamarind.

3. Grey and Pink-tinged canes which would include the true Elephant and the White Transparent, which is synonymous with Caledonian Queen, Mamuri and Rappoe.

4. Ribbon canes of several varieties and combinations, such as (a) the Red Ribbon, striped with pink, claret, or yellow; (b) Violet Ribbon, which was striped with violet and white, or violet, pink and green; (c) Green Ribbon, striped with cream and pale green, sometimes taking a pinkish tint with age. One Green and White striped cane became known as Simpson Cane. Then there was (d) the Drard, which was striped with yellow and very pale green; (e) the Large Green, which was a short green cane with faint dark green and lighter green striping; (f) the Vagabonde, a very hard cane conspicuously striped with dark claret and bright green; (g) the Grande Savanne was a pale straw-colored cane striped with almost indistinguishable bands of pale green; (h) the Batramic, a small green cane striped with chocolate; (i) the Horne, which was smaller than average with a variable color striped in very pale green, darker green, or bronze, or brown, or pale claret; (j) the Samuri, which was an average size dark purple cane striped ever so inconspicuously with lighter hues; (k) the Vulu Vulu, which had a variable color striped in shades of brown or dark claret; (l) the Vico, which was a small cane about the size of a walking stick, and was very faintly striped; (m) and the Po-a-ole, which was an average size cane very faintly striped with bright reddish claret.

5. Claret and Purple canes included several varieties. (a) The Mani was a very pale claret cane with a bronze tint; (b) Vitu-Haula was a pale claret bronze colored cane; (c) the Hillii was bronze pink; (d) one of the better known varieties, Purple Transparent, was synonymous with Java, Purple Mauritius, Queensland Creole, and Meera; (e) Bois Rouge was a small cane with a pinkish-horn tinge with dot-like blotches; (f) the Keening was a small cane colored at first in claret, then turning pink and always with dark blackish patches; (g) the Kara-Kar-awa was purple but turned claret with age; (h) the Brekeret cane was purple but turned dark claret; (i) the Nara Tara was a very dark purple cane which had a greyish powdery coating; (j) the Governor Lees was purple or claret with a slight greyish tinge toward the nodes, which turned a vinous horn shade with age; (k) the Russel was purple primrose but turned vinous grey with age; and (l) the Dama, which turned from a pale claret to a dingy metallic stone grey with age.

It is evident from the text, before and after this point, that these lists are not exhaustive but indicative of a classification procedure. Through concerted breeding improvements the number of canes in each classification would naturally continue to grow.

Improvements

The sugar cane brought into Hispaniola known as "Creole," or "cane of the country," was a rather small, soft, yellow cane, and while it became the foundation of the sugar industry of the New World, it did have its weaknesses. Around 1800 it began to fail and had to be replaced with newer varieties. Otaheiti, also known as Bourbon cane, replaced the Creole. It was an excellent producer and became widely used, but due to its susceptibility to disease it also began to fail. Cheribon, a cane from Java, then took its place. Another Java variety, Batavian Striped, or Black Java, was imported into Louisiana and was found to be more cold resistant than Creole or Otaheiti. The search for productive canes was of necessity an ongoing endeavor for the sugar industry.

Above: Note the obvious growth characteristics of these canes, which were all planted the same day. *Below:* This is CP 52-48, a highly recommended syrup variety.

Initially, any improvements made in the sugar cane culture depended solely upon the selection of choice canes from existing crops. This was done through observation of disease resistant specimens, taste of sweetness, softness, size, growth patterns, and reproductive abilities. These early improvements occurred simply through the observation and selection of better canes by the growers. When a sugar cane variety is propagated by cuttings, the subsequent plant will be a faithful reproduction or its parent. However, when sugar cane is reproduced from seed, it is never exactly the same, for every seed produces a well-defined hybrid. It was much more recent on history's time line that cross pollination became a scientific endeavor and began to produce choice hybrids. As the demand for sugar impacted the world markets, numerous research facilities were established. Some of these were privately funded by plantation owners, growers' cooperatives, or individuals, while others were funded by governments and governmental agencies. The earliest of these were established in 1886 in Java and Barbados. The first two in Java were established at Tegal and Kagok in 1886, and another, the Proefstation Oost Java, was established at Pasoeroean in 1887. These three were funded by an association of sugar growers. The Botanic Station, located at the Boys' Reformatory School at Dodds, Barbados, was a governmental funded research center located at the boys' school to take advantage of available labor there.

The Java research stations experimented with two lines of crosses, those between *S. officinarum* X *S. barberi* and *S. officinarum* X *S. spontaneum,* and produced numerous outstanding hybrids. Of all the thousands of crosses and hybrids produced in Java through the years, one was particularly outstanding. Work began on this hybrid in 1921 and resulted in a cane which was immune to most of the sugar cane diseases and had the highest output of sugar per area of any variety grown in Java at that time. The hybrid was P.O.J.2878 (for Proefstation Oost Java) and was released in 1928. In August 1922, there was only one stool of this superb cane. Yet it was so prolific that by 1927 it had multiplied enough to plant 18,000 hectares. By 1930, ninety-eight percent of Java's cane acreage was planted in P.O.J.2878. This suc-

P.O.J. 2878 has amazing growth habits and is an excellent syrup cane.

cessful hybrid has an interesting background. Cheribon was crossed with *Saccharum spontaneum* to produce Kassoer; Bandjarmasin hitam was crossed with Loethers to produce P.O.J.100; and Red Fiji was crossed with Lahaina to produce E.K.2. Kassoer and P.O.J.100 were crossed to produce P.O.J.2364 and P.O.J.100 was crossed with E.K.2 to produce E.K.28. P.O.J.2364 was then crossed with E.K.28 to produce the outstanding P.O.J.2878, a cane which gave new life to the sugar industries not only in Java but also in America, Indonesia, Haiti, Cuba, the Dominican Republic, Puerto Rico, Belize, Costa Rica, El Salvador, Colombia, Ecuador, and which influenced hybrid development in still others.

The propagation diagram of this amazing cane would look like this:

Cheribon
  +   = *Kassoer*
Saccharium Spontaneum
        +   = *P.O.J.2364*
Bandjarmasin Hitam
  +   = *P.O.J.100*   +   = *P.O.J.2878*
Loethers
        +   = *E.K.28*
Red Fiji
  +   = *E.K.2*
Lahaina

There is still some P.O.J. grown in gardens across the American Deep South but not for commercial endeavors. Java became a proverbial gold mine in its wealth of sugar cane history and development. The purple cane, Cheribon, became the standard cane of Java. It was established by Gonsalves in the mid–nineteenth century, and had three rather specific family members: (1) the light colored cane known as Rose Bamboo; (2) a dark colored cane known as Purple Bamboo; and (3) a striped variety known as Striped Bamboo. The yellow-green Port Mackay Cavangere cane with its distinctive brown blotches when exposed to the sun; a Red Ribbon cane striped with pink, reddish wine and yellow; a brown cane named Loethers; the dark red Meera; the light colored Rappoe of several varieties; Muntok, a cane introduced from Banca; Canne Morte, the Fiji cane which became parent to several significant seedlings; a purple Bourbon; the Red, White and Black Manila canes; and *To uti. S. atrorubens,* which had a violet stalk and pith, were all prominent in Java at one time. With the emergence of their experimental stations several varieties of P.O.J. came into prominence. Some of these are as follows:

P.O.J.33 was a dark violet cane which turned brown red when mature, having long joints, stood upright, and produced a strong stalk;
P.O.J.36 was a green, fairly thick, hard and strong cane;
P.O.J.100 was golden to light brown with fiery red burnt patches when exposed to the sun;
P.O.J.139 was pink when young but turned a dirty greenish pink when mature and was a very sweet cane;
P.O.J.161 was pink when young, but turned a yellowish green mixed with dirty pink when older. It was a long, sweet cane which stood strongly upright;
P.O.J.181 was a fairly thick cane, yellowish red with sunburnt patches of dark red;
P.O.J.213 was bright violet red with a long, thin, upright stalk and was also very sweet;
P.O.J.228 was violet red when young but turned dirty brown at maturity. It had a fairly thick stalk and was very sweet;
247 Bouricius was dark violet red cane having a fairly thick, long straight stalk. It ripened late and was very sweet.

The Barbados Station did extensive experimentation with a single species, *S. officinarum.* They were able to develop five distinct lines of the noble varieties. White Transparent was the progenitor of two of those lines. They achieved almost pure lines of sugar cane with high sugar content and low fiber content well suited for Barbados and the West Indies. However, there were substantial difficulties. Germination for these varieties was not as good as those from India and Java. Also, they were susceptible to many sugar cane diseases and tended to dry out and rot after being cut. The two most significant varieties were B.H.10/12 and S.C.12/4.

The Coimbatore Station was established in India, and in 1912 it became the first experimental station to intentionally use *S. spontaneum,* a wild Indian cane, in its crosses with *S. officinarum.* Hoping to capture some of the wild cane's resistance to disease and vigorous growth habits, the Coimbatore Station produced several important varieties, some giving a boost to the American sugar industry. The rich ancestry of Co.290 is another example of selective breeding. Cheribon was crossed with Chunnee to produce P.O.J.213; Kaludai Boothan was crossed with *Saccharium spontaneum* to produce Co. 291. P.O.J.213 was then crossed with Co.291 to produce Co.221, while Co.291 was crossed with White Transparent to produce D.74. Co.221 was finally crossed with D.74 to produce Co.290.

The ribbon cane grown extensively in Louisiana in the early years was imported from Java in 1817. It was a hardy cane, ripened much earlier than varieties currently used, and was soon adopted in all sections of the state. As the sugar industry grew in Louisiana growers realized more acutely the necessity of research and development. In 1885 the Louisiana Scientific and Agricultural Association founded the Sugar Experimental Station. A government research center was established in the United States at Canal Point, Florida, in the early 1900s. Some of the old dependable varieties, such as D.74 and Louisiana Purple, had begun to fail because of their susceptibility to disease. At one time D.74, a light green colored cane which originated in Demerara, South America and was introduced into Louisiana in 1873, produced a larger tonnage than the other varieties in Louisiana. It matured early, was lodging resistant, had a higher sugar content, and was preferred over purple and ribbon cane. But it, too, began to fail. Another South American cane, D.95, a purple-red cane also introduced into Louisiana in 1873, was a fairly good producer on rich land but was not accepted as extensively as the D.74. Consequently, the early years of research at the station were driven by the need to find new canes to replace the old ones. In this mission the experimental stations were looking for several desirable qualities, such as early maturity for a shorter growing season; a large yield of stalks per acre; a high percentage yield of juice per stalk; a high sugar content; light colored stalks to yield a lighter colored syrup; a high resistance to disease, both in the growing stage and in storage for future seed stock; good germinating and stooling qualities; rationing well and producing excellent stubble crops; straight stalks which resist lodging; and enough softness to make grinding easy. They produced C.P.807, C.P.28/11, and C.P.28/19, which were disease resistant, highly productive, and well adapted to the soils and climate of the area.

Sugar cane will flower and produce seed at Canal Point, one of the few places it will do so outside the tropics, so they were able to experiment with thousands of hybrids. Work continued at Canal Point, and other experimental stations were opened at Meridian, Mississippi, and Houma, Louisiana. Still other tests were conducted at Poplarville, Mississippi; Cairo, Georgia; and Brewton, Alabama. Recently the Houma station announced the development of an outstanding new variety, the L.C.P.85-384.

Some of the grand old canes of the American sugar cane culture included the Indian Co.290; Black Cheribon, or the Louisiana Purple, also called Home Purple or Red; the Japanese Cayana; Purple and Green Striped, also called Home Striped or Louisiana Striped; Green Ribbon, also called Simpson Cane; Green, or Home Green; Blue-ribbon; Georgia Yellow Gal; and P.O.J. from Java. A Japanese cane was introduced into Florida from Louisiana about 1889. It was harder to grind and extracting its juice was more difficult, though it did make an excellent syrup. One of its advantages, however, was that it grew well on soils where other canes would fail. Crystaline, from which numerous other canes originated, was one of the grand old canes, as was the Hawaiian, a large white cane which became a favorite for chewing. A cane from Brazil, Cayana-10, was introduced into the Cairo,

This blue cane of unknown origin is brittle and snaps easily in the wind.

Georgia, industry and proved to be a very promising cane. It was planted extensively and became the predominant variety of the area. It was a green cane which produced a light-colored syrup. It had many of the advantages of the Japanese canes, such as resistance to mosaic diseases. It ratooned well, and produced a prolific growth with large yields. It also had most of the disadvantages of the Japanese canes, but not in such a high degree as some other canes.

Our experimental stations have introduced other newer significant varieties, some of which are summarized here. With thousands of hybrids being produced each year it is impossible to give each one an easily remembered name, hence the code numbers. C.P.36-111 is a pale green cane, though it tends to turn purplish in color after it has been stripped and exposed to the sun. It has excellent resistance to disease and lodging. With favorable growing conditions, C.P.36-111 grows straight stalks with long internodes and produces an excellent crop through first and second year stubbles. C.P.29-116 is also a green cane with excellent resistance to disease, but it doesn't have the lodging resistance of C.P.36-111. It is an excellent syrup producer and usually produces well from the first and second year stubble. C.P.52-48 is one of the varieties recommended by the Field Station at Meridian as having excellent syrup production and it was released for commercial syrup production in southwest Georgia. It produces a good crop from first and second year stubble, and because of its considerable root system and stiff stalks it is highly resistant to lodging. It is a pale green cane and has long leaves which tend to droop, but because it shades the row well it is highly competitive with weeds. C.P.52-48 is harder than some other varieties, but because of its straight stalks it is not too difficult to harvest. C.P.67-500 is superior to C.P.36-111 in syrup yield per ton of cane, and has superior resistance to lodging. The stalks are bluish in color and have a heavy wax. C.P.67-500 has shorter, but larger in diameter, internodes than C.P.36-111 and is about the same in cane per acre.

There is a difference in cane intended for sugar extraction and cane intended for syrup production. A high sucrose content causes the syrup to tend to crystallize, so those varieties specifically bred for sugar production do not necessarily make good syrup varieties. Those recommended by the U.S. Department of Agriculture for syrup production are the C.P.36-111, C.P.52-48, and C.P.67-500. Some other notable varieties include GA.64-188; POP.63-1; POP.60-12 (for Poplarville, Mississippi); and F.31-407 (from the University of Florida.).

It's been a long way from New Guinea, both geographically and genetically, to the sugar cane belt across the southern United States. The canes out of the tropics, Creole, Otaheite, and Black Cheribon, are all but gone. Canes out of India and Indochina with such picturesque names as Chuunee, Mungo and Kansar are no longer in our vocabulary. The Japanese canes—Uba from Natal; Kavangire from Argentina; Yontanzan and Tekeha from Japan; Khera and Cayana from India; White Transparent, B.H.10/12 and S.C.12/4 from Barbados; Zwart Cheribon, Kassoer, and Preanger—from Java are in our cane's genetic background, but we speak of them no longer. Now we reap the benefits of the thousands upon ten thousands of hybrids which have been tested in experimental stations around the world. Little did those migrants, sailors, and traders who first carried sugar cane out of New Guinea know they were contributing to the spread of what was to become one of the world's greatest agricultural crops—and one of the most enjoyable! But first, the juice has to be extracted.

The History of Sorghum

Sorghum is a versatile plant with various and numerous uses, including livestock feed, human food, and industrial applications. Because of this, several types of sorghum have been identified as grain sorghum, forage sorghum, and the specialty sorghums—sweet sorghum

To make syrup or sugar, the juice must first be extracted from the cane, and for that one needs a cane mill.

and broom corn. Classified under the family *Poaceae*, like sugar cane, the various sorghums are members of the *Gramineae*, or grass, family, as well. Botanists tell us that sorghums are grouped into a subfamily, *Panicoideae*, and a tribe, *Andropogoneae*, in which *Saccharum officinarum*, or sugar cane, is also found. This makes sorghum and sugar cane close relatives, yet with distinctive differences.

Origins

The origin of sorghum—*Sorghum bicolor* (L.) Moenh—is lost in antiquity, though the oldest recorded find dates back 8,000 years to a site in southern Egypt. There seems to be some general agreement, however, that sorghum culture began in northern Africa some 5,000 or more years ago. And, like sugar cane, it spread along trade and migration routes first to other parts of Africa, then to southeast Asia and China, and finally to the New World. The earliest report of sorghum in India is from the Indus Valley at the end of the third millennium and was reported in Assyria by 700 B.C. Historical writings on sorghum in China were found in the writings of Zhang sometime in the third century. Snowden, in his monumental 1936 work on sorghum, proposed 31 species, 158 varieties, and 523 forms of sorghum. Harlan and deWet proposed a much more simplified classification in 1972, a classification which most sorghum experts have followed, which included five races and ten intermediates. Dr. Jeff Dahlberg of the National Grain Sorghum Producers, Lubbock, Texas, proposed an integrated classification in 2000 which merges the work of Harlan and deWet with that of working group descriptions by Murty and Govil of 1967. Five basic races of sorghum, namely, bicolor, guinea, caudatum, kafir and durra, make up all sorghums cultivated worldwide.

A sorghum called Chinese Amber, also known as Black Amber and Chinese Sugarcane, arrived in the United States via France in 1853, but it was with the introduction of sweet sorghum by the English sugar planter, Leonard Wray, in 1857 that the American sweet sorghum culture really began. Significant grain production began in 1874 following the introduction of two varieties from Egypt, two varieties from South Africa, in 1876, milo from Columbia, South America, in 1879, and one variety from India in the 1890s.

Sorghum is a versatile, multipurpose plant which is, along with rice, wheat, corn, barley, and millet, one of the world's major cereal grains. In Africa and Asia it is used as a food source, in the United States it is a significant feed grain and forage crop, and to some small degree it is still a source of table syrup. It is also used in numerous commercial products. The shiny seed coatings produce a wax which is used in polishes, sealing wax and electric insulators. Industrial alcohol can be made from the seed, as well as the butyl alcohol used in lacquer solvents and weed killers. Sorghum contains starch which is used in the manufacture of such products as gypsum lath, paper and cloth sizing and adhesives. This starch is also used in oil drilling slush, which lubricates the drill and seals the walls of the well. It is a substitute for tapioca and its oil is used in salad dressing. Sorghum is grown on all six continents where warm weather permits and, with over 100 million acres planted worldwide, is the fifth largest crop in the world in total acres grown. While we'll concern ourselves primarily with sweet sorghum, let it be noted that three agronomic groups of sorghum are now generally recognized. However, because of crossbreeding and development of new hybrids,

Several varieties of sweet sorghum, such as this Sugar Drip, are excellent for making syrup (courtesy Jeff and Lisa McLain, Martinsville, Indiana).

the lines of demarcation are becoming increasingly indistinct. Those groupings include the following:

Grain Sorghum, which produces a rich head of grain, is grown for the food value of the seed. Green sorghum plants contain the glucoside dhurrin, which converts to prussic acid (HCN) and is poisonous to livestock. Therefore, grain sorghums are not suitable for forage. Grain sorghum includes the following five major races.

1. Bicolor. Thought to be the most primitive sorghum; though of unclear origins, the race bicolor includes such working groups as sudangrass, bicolor, and koaling sorghums. In general, most sweet sorghums are thought to be in this race also. Koalings, which are found in China, have slender, dry stems, a sparse set of leaves, and typically are brown seeded with a bitter taste.

2. Guinea. Thought to have originated in west Africa some 3000 years ago, the race guinea contains some unique sorghums which tend to be tall and grassy-like, and have panicles which contain seeds that are quite involuted and open in the glumes. The grains are small to medium and tend to be light colored or slightly pigmented.

3. Caudatum. One of the most important sorghums agronomically, caudatum sorghums are thought to have resulted from a cross of bicolor and wild sorghum and are widely distributed in areas such as Chad, Nigeria, Sudan, Ethiopia and Uganda. Hegari, Milo, and Feterita, some of the older sorghum varieties in the United States, are classified under this race. Hegari varieties come from Sudan, tiller profusely, and bear chalky white seeds. Milo, a native to east Africa, bears large seeds and the plants tends to be more drought and heat tolerant. Feteritas also were from Sudan and are characterized by large white chalky seeds. Caudatum has become one of the most important sources of germplasm in worldwide breeding programs in producing genes for high yielding and superior seed quality sorghums.

4. Kafir. Kafir sorghums, which originated in southern Africa, are characterized as having medium height stalks and high yields and tend to have erect cylindrical and semi-compact panicles. The glumes are almost glossy at maturity.

5. Durra. Durras most likely were domesticated in Ethiopia and then spread throughout Africa and into India. They tend to have very tight, compact panicles and many are called "crooked neck" sorghums. Shallu is considered a durra which came from India where it is a late maturing sorghum with very white seed. Generally, durras are medium to tall in height, bearing lightly pigmented glumes with medium to large grain.

Forage Sorghums are cultivated specifically as a forage feed crop. In the mid 1950s there were approximately thirty distinct varieties and strains of forage sorghums grown in the United States. Today, through public and private research and experimental and breeding stations, there are more than one hundred varieties and hybrids on the market. This group includes sterile late maturing sorghums, sudangrass, sudangrass hybrids, silage sorghums and sorghum-sudangrass hybrids. Sudangrass—a thin sorghum with very small panicles, which was introduced into the United States in 1908—and its many hybrids grow rapidly in warm temperatures under favorable moisture and fertility conditions. Sudangrass is used primarily for livestock grazing or to produce hay.

Specialty Sorghums are those which are grown for a specific purpose not readily included in the groups above. Broomcorn and sweet sorghum are generally considered in the Specialty Sorghum group.

1. Broomcorn is a sorghum grown primarily for its inflorescence, or blooms. The branches of its flower cluster grow anywhere from one to three feet long and are used for

making household brooms. While Standard, Western Dwarf, and Whisk Dwarf are the most common, there are seven varieties grown in North America. The origin of broomcorn is unknown but it was probably developed in the Mediterranean region from stock from either India or Africa. There is some evidence that it has been grown in Europe for at least 300 years. Benjamin Franklin first introduced broomcorn in the United States in 1725, and in 1797, on a farm in Hadley, Massachusetts, the first commercial crop was produced.

2. Sweet Sorghum, or sorgo, was once grown primarily for making sorghum syrup. While some is still grown for that purpose, most is now grown for forage since the yield is greater than that of grain sorghum. Despite early optimism and the contention that "the time is past when this pursuit is to be regarded only as an experiment" sweet sorghum was never a contender with sugar cane for making sugar because the process was too complex and expensive. Since alcohol had to be used to make the sugar crystallize, an extensive filtration system had to be utilized and other additives used; it became easier and less expensive to use sugar cane. Now, in that sorghum syrup was once a thriving industry in America—and since that wonderful tradition continues, requiring the sweet sorghum stalks to be milled in a great American cane mill—sweet sorghum will be the object of our attention from this point.

Improvements

As with sugar cane, sorghum improvements began through the selection of choice seeds from existing crops. In 1851, Chinese Amber was sent to France from the island of Tsungming, China. From France it was imported into the United States in 1853. Fifteen varieties of sorgo were sent to several countries in Europe in 1854 by Leonard Wray. These varieties were brought from Toulouse, France, to America by Mr. Wray in 1857 and were grown under his supervision in South Carolina and Georgia. Though we no longer call them by their original names, let the record show that these fifteen varieties were: Vim-bis-chu-a-pa, E-a-na-moode, E-enga, Nee-a-za-na, Boom-vwa-na, Oom-see-a-na, Shla-goova, Shla-goone-de, Zim-moo-ma-na, E-booth-la, Boo-ee-an-a, Koom-ban-na, See-en-gla, Zim-ba-za-na, E-thlo-see. Mr. Wray got his seed into the ground on June 20 and was met with a very wet growing season that proved detrimental to his crop. Failing to make sugar, Mr. Wray abandoned his seed along with his patented process of refining sugar and returned to England, discouraged and financially strapped. However, these varieties became the progenitors of some of the varieties listed in the next section.

About 1857, E.Y. Teas of Dunreith, Indiana, selected some choice seed from his Chinese Amber crop. The result was an improved strain called Early Amber. Seth H. Kenny, from Waterville, Minnesota, selected choice seed from Early Amber a decade later and that hybrid became Minnesota Amber, which through the work of the South Dakota Agricultural Experiment Station produced Dakota Amber about 1915. Then, through the work of the Waconia Sorghum Mill in Waconia, Minnesota, Waconia Amber was produced about 1925. This became an excellent variety for sorghum syrup. Other experiments in the late 1800s and early 1900s were carried out by the Iowa Experiment Station in Ames, Iowa, and the Kansas Agricultural Experimental Station, which produced the Kansas Orange Sorghum, a leading variety for forty-five years.

What was to become an outstanding variety was begun by Mr. N. Farr, a farmer and amateur sorghum breeder from Stockton, Kansas, who crossed Sourless Sorgo with Blackhull Kafir. R.E. Getty took the seed from this first hybrid generation and planted them in the U.S. Department of Agriculture and Kansas Agriculture Experiment Station cooperative sorghum experiments at Hays, Kansas. Further experiments were done by John H. Parker until he had isolated a uniform type of sorghum with tall, strong, sweet, juicy stalks. Because of its large, tall, strong stalks it was called Atlas and after being released in 1928 it became the most popular sorghum in the mid-west.

The agricultural experiment stations played a significant role in America's development as a world leader in crop production. That in itself was an evolving process. As early as 1776, proposals were made for some type of agricultural branch in the federal government. In 1796 George Washington advocated such an agency. John Quincy Adams began the process by instructing ambassadors and naval officers serving abroad to send to the United States seeds and breeds of domestic animals which might improve our own. When Henry L. Ellsworth was commissioner of patents, in 1836, he began his own program of distributing seeds, which he secured from foreign lands, to farmers who would plant them. Three years later Congress recognized his work by appropriating $1,000 of patent office fees for gathering statistics, conducting agricultural experiments, and distributing his seeds. The experimental station was on its way. Ellsworth established the Agricultural Division in the patent office which distributed seed and gathered farm statistics. A chemist, a botanist, and an entomologist were conducting experiments by 1854, and in 1856 a five acre plot was obtained and experiments in sorghum and tea were begun. From this modest beginning the United States Department of Agriculture has grown tremendously and contributed immeasurably to the quality of life and productivity of the American farmer.

Varieties

The American sorghum syrup production began in 1853 with the importation of a single variety of Chinese origin. Over the next sixty years there were at least two hundred varieties in cultivation, though some were not well known and ceased to exist. While there are distinct differences in the various varieties of sorghum, those differences are not as obvious as those in sugar cane. The following photographs therefore will be of Sugar Drip in several stages of development rather than attempting to describe the distinctiveness of each variety. The most commonly used old lines of sorghum have been divided into five groups.

1. Amber Sorghum was developed in Indiana from the original Chinese variety, was a desirable early variety and was often referred to as Early Amber. Folger, a strain developed from it was an improved syrup variety having all the characteristics of Amber Sorghum. Red Amber and Minnesota Amber were varieties also developed from the Amber group.

2. Orange Sorghum originated in South Africa. It is larger and heavier than Amber and requires a longer growing season. A cross between Early Amber and Orange produced the Colman variety, which had a higher sugar content and was popular for syrup making.

3. Sumac Sorghum, also called Red-top Sorghum, was a short, stocky variety of Natal importation. It matured rather early, and was popular throughout the South.

4. Goose-neck Sorghum is a descendant of one of the original African varieties and is distinctive from others because the seed pod hangs down rather than standing erect. This sorghum was popular in the South, especially in Texas; because it was late maturing it could not be grown in the North.

5. Honey Sorghum, probably of African origin, was very sweet and remarkably tender in comparison to some of the larger varieties. Also called Honey Drip and Texas Seeded Ribbon, it matures very late, and therefore was best suited for the South. It is characteristic of late maturing varieties to produce a higher yield of stalks per acre than earlier varieties. Honey Sorghum makes excellent syrup, but lodges easily and is susceptible to disease.

Other old line varieties included White African, the original importation by Leonard Wray. It was highly susceptible to disease, and its high starch content made the syrup scorch easily. Williams and Iceberg were old line varieties used in syrup production, but were characterized by weak stalks. Sugar Drip, an old variety of unknown origin, made excellent syrup, but was also susceptible to disease and lodging. Some of the newer improved varieties include Sart, which was introduced in 1951. It has a strong stalk which resists lodging, and is highly resistant to diseases. It is a late maturing importation from Africa and makes a good quality syrup. Tracy was introduced in 1953, and while it has an excellent flavor because of its high starch content it scorches easily. Wiley is a 1956 introduction which has strong stalks but weak nodes. It is brittle and, because it produces a tall stalk, it breaks easily in the wind. However, it was the most disease resistant variety planted in the United States at that time. It also made more good quality syrup per acre than any other variety tested at the Meridian (Mississippi) Government Experiment Station. Brandes was introduced in 1968, and is characterized by its strong stalk and superior root system. It has a flexible stalk, and has the greatest resistance to lodging than any sweet sorghum tested at Meridian. It makes an excellent syrup but is highly susceptible to cotton insecticides and to drought. Hodo is known for its low germination. Dale, introduced in 1970, is a mid-season maturing sorghum, highly resistant, and makes an excellent quality syrup of mild sorghum flavor. The juice has enough body to give good syrup consistency without gelling. Its upright, straight medium-sized stalks grow to about nine feet. Dale makes a high yield of syrup per ton of stalks. M8I-E, introduced in 1981, is a late-maturing sorghum and has a syrup yield superior to Dale. It makes a mildly flavored, amber colored, excellent quality syrup, but is susceptible to a light frost. Theis, introduced in 1974, is late-maturing, and while it makes stalks twelve to sixteen feet tall, it has good lodging resistance. Its drought resistance is one of its major advantages, though it does make an excellent quality of amber colored syrup of mild sorghum flavor. Georgia Blue Ribbon is of uncertain origin. It lodges easily and is susceptible to many diseases. It matures in mid-season and makes a good quality syrup. Topper 76-6 was introduced in 1994. It reaches maturity in about 120 days, makes an excellent syrup, and is disease and drought resistant.

The Collier variety made its way from Natal, South Africa, to England and then to America in 1881. The Planter variety was carried from Africa to India to Australia to the U.S. in 1888. In 1891, the McLean variety came from Australia to the U.S. All of the American sorgos until the mid–thirties,

This patch of Sugar Drip is nearing maturity (courtesy Jeff and Lisa McLain, Indiana).

Top: It's harvest time in preparation for making syrup. *Bottom:* Syrup-making time for the McClain Family of Martinsville, Indiana (both photographs courtesy Jeff and Lisa McLain, Martinsville, Indiana).

with the three above exceptions, were developed from the original Chinese Amber or some of the sixteen varieties introduced into America by Leonard Wray. The early intent was to develop a sugar industry, but after forty years of trial and error sorgo was discontinued as a sugar crop. Sweet sorghum did continue to supply a thriving sorghum syrup industry, however. While the demand has fallen drastically across America, there is still some demand and still some syrup-makers more often than not doing well in their given localities. Sorghum, with its distinctive taste, makes a delicious table syrup.

But first the juice has to be extracted.

2

History of the Roller Cane Mill

Now that we've looked at the histories of sugar cane and sorghum, it is time to turn our attention to the devices used through the centuries to extract juice from these canes. On the one hand, cane juice has been used as a simple pleasurable drink. On the other, juice has been used to refine sugar, and that whole process ushered in a new economy, the plantation system, with its dependence upon slave labor. Refining even had religious ramifications. In the earlier days of the New World sugar industry, the church appointed priests to the sugar mills to make sure that the church got its share of the tithe. So, this whole business of juice ranges from the simple to the complex. But, through it all, there had to be some method of extracting juice from the stalks.

The Origin of Extraction Devices

Much of this history is lost in antiquity. In the absence of documented references we must look at other sources in art, literature, sacred writings, and oral tradition. In the bibliography there are several excellent references written by sugar historians who have looked at this issue from several vantage points. Again and again we will find that people first used what was available to them and then made improvements to suit their particular needs. In the earliest record of the history of sugar cane we find that it was cultivated as a fruit plant. People simply peeled away the hard rind and chewed the soft, sweet, fibrous core. It was a delicious, refreshing juice obtained by chewing.

Then there emerged the mortar and pestle, just like the druggist's, except on a larger scale. Chopped pieces of cane were placed in a receptacle, like a hollowed out stump or tree trunk, then a heavy pole was pulled around and around, crushing the cane. The juice would flow from an opening in the bottom. Some mortar and pestles were very primitive, and some developed into elaborate devices.

A television documentary in recent years showed a tribe in a third world country extracting cane juice by bouncing on a long, slender, flexible pole while cane was fed beneath it and a short stationary pole below. As the bouncing crushed the cane the juice would be caught in a basin under the device, or else the crushed cane would be boiled in water to extract even

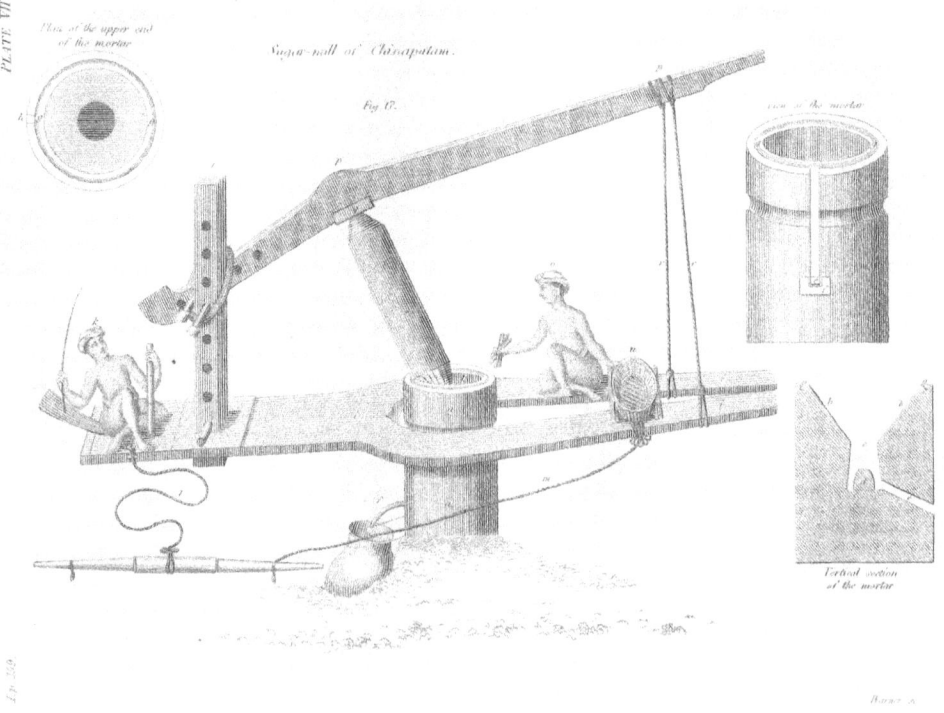

Top: The mortar and pestle mill would crush the cane but was not very efficient at juice extraction (Buchanan 1807, vol. 1, p. 159). *Bottom:* This cross section shows the principle of the mortar and pestle mill (Buchanan 1807, vol. 1, p. 159).

Top: An early version of a cane crusher was a pole mill, like this one in Panama, which crushed the cane by bouncing on it (courtesy Tommy Clayton, Hilliard, Florida). *Bottom:* The edge runner, which crushed the cane and prepared it for boiling, probably originated from the olive oil industry.

The static press, shown in the background, pressed the juice from the cane crushed in the mill in the foreground from Jan van Straet, *Nova Reperta*, vol. F81, pl. 13, circa 1600 (by permission of the Folger Shakespeare Library).

more of the sweet juice from the stalks. While this method of extraction is still used in some remote areas of the world today, such as among the Cuna Indians on Isla Rio Tigre, San Blas Islands, Panama, it is one of the oldest extraction devices known.

Other devices used through the centuries included large hammers used to pound and crush the stalks of cane. Some of these were large tilt hammers adapted for either animal or water power. The spattering caused by the hammer was messy and wasteful since there was no logical way to catch the juice. Large, heavy rollers were also used to crush sugar cane and prepare it for boiling. Stalks would be laid on wooden boards and a large roller pulled over them to crush the cane. While this method was inefficient and wasteful, it did succeed in crushing the cane. In touring Israel I had the joy of visiting Bethany. Among the interesting sites and scenes was a visit to an ancient olive press. It consisted of a large round stone, like a gristmill stone, set on edge on a raceway. When the turnpole was pulled by oxen the stone would roll around and around the raceway. Olives where placed on the raceway, and the stone would crush the oil from them.

This technology was also applied to the sugar industry, and the edge-runner became an extraction device popular throughout the Mediterranean countries and Indonesia.

Perhaps we've all seen pictures of early printing presses, with the printer turning a large static press down on a page of paper in order to print his message. Large presses not unlike these were used in the early sugar industry to squeeze juice from crushed, boiled pieces of cane. Two adaptations were leverage supplied by a long beam and pressure supplied by a screw press. Squeezing the juice in a stationary press was the principle process, however. This process was used in much of the sugar cane countries from the thirteenth century until the invention and spread of the vertical roller mill. In the above engraving of a Sicilian sugar mill from the second half of the sixteenth century one can see several steps in the sugar-making process. In the foreground workers are cutting the cane into small pieces, which are in turn carried to a waterpowered grinding mill on the left. This mill would shred the cane into pulp, and it would then be squeezed in the press seen in the center background. The juice would be evaporated in the large pots and poured into sugar molds, right center. The workman in the right front is removing cones of sugar from the molds after it had crystalized.

The Development of the Roller Mill

In all probability the greatest single advancement in the sugar industry was the development of the three-roller vertical mill. Keep in mind that this early mill had three rollers in a straight line, not triangular as were later versions. A workman on one side of the mill would feed the cane between rollers one and two, while a workman on the other side would feed it back between rollers two and three. This was a labor intensive endeavor, but it was much quicker, more efficient, and cleaner than any of the previous methods of extraction. While there are strong arguments supporting various theories, again there is no clear consensus as to the origin of the three-roller mill. At this point it is not my intent to establish its origin, nor to advance some new theory, but rather to survey current thought. Even after considering convincing arguments for various sites of origin, in the final analysis we simply do not know with any certainty. The origin of the three-roller vertical sugar cane mill is still shrouded in mystery.

This rendering shows an Indian mill with three rollers in a straight line.

For many years it was thought that the mill arose out of the Mediterranean sugar industry technology; its development was attributed to Pietro Speciale, of Sicily (1449). This was so generally accepted that it was taught as the literal truth, first by the sugar historian Edmund von Lippman, in 1890, and then in the excellent two volume work of Noel Deerr, *The History of Sugar*. However, in later years this contention has been disputed and strong arguments have been put forward for other origins. It seems the problem resulted from faulty interpretation of available sources and the inaccurate meaning of the word "trappeto," a generic term meaning cane mills in general, not specifically a three-roller. There is also the absence of common usage which would cast doubt upon Sicily as the place of origin. If the three-roller vertical mill had been developed in Sicily in 1449 there should have been evidences of its use elsewhere in the Mediterranean industry. However, there is no evidence of its use in the Mediterranean countries, Madeira and the Atlantic islands, or the Americas until the 1600s. This theory of origin is generally discounted today.

In his book, *The Sugar Cane Industry*, Dr. J.H. Galloway traces the mill to Peru and Brazil about 1610, and believes that its likely place of origin is China. There is a 1613 Portuguese sketch of a Peruvian three-roller mill in the Ajuda Palace Library, Lisbon, which is the earliest known rendering of such a mill. The three-roller mill has similarities to the Chinese two-roller mill, which was also used to gin cotton. The three-roller could well be an adaptation specifically designed to extract juice from sugar cane, a technology brought from the east through the work of the Jesuits. There is no record of the three-roller vertical mill being used in China, but the Chinese technology could well have been applied in developing this improved milling machine. Sidney W. Mintz, in his book, *Sweetness and Power*, agrees with a part of Dr. Galloway's thesis, believing that the three-roller vertical mill was invented in Peru and came to Brazil between 1608 and 1612, then spread elsewhere over the sugar industry. He bases much of his assumption on the work of Frederic Mauro (*Le Portugal et l'Atlantique au XVIIe siècle*), who reproduced the 1613 sketch of a mill with three vertical rollers and a sweep bar introduced to Brazil from Peru by a priest. This mill replaced the two-roller horizontal mill then in use and catapulted Brazil into the forefront of the sugar industry.

However, Sucheta Mazumdar disagrees with the finding that China is the place of origin for the three-roller vertical mill. In his book, *Sugar*

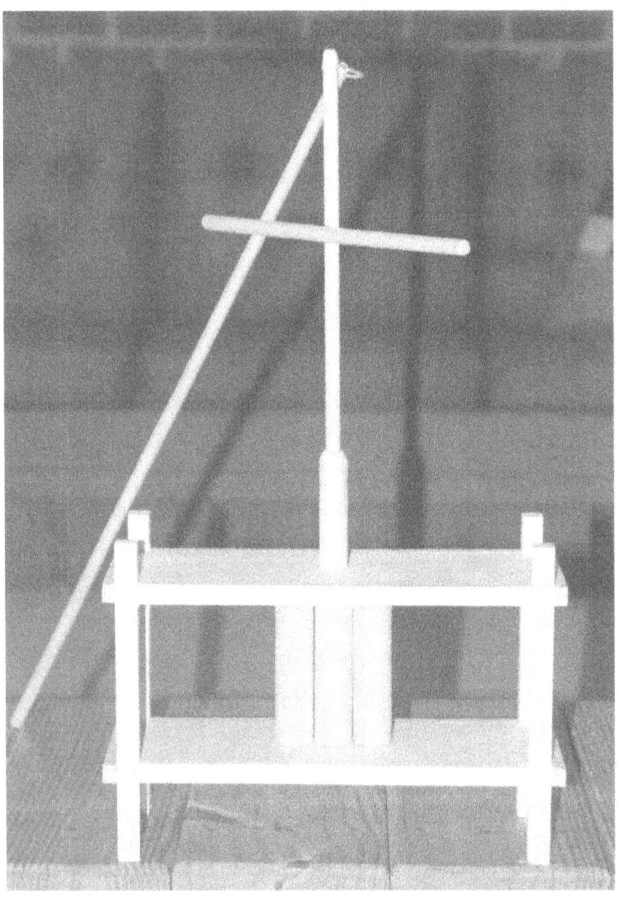

This model was based on the Peruvian mill, the earliest drawing of a three roller mill found to date (photograph by John Dean, Hartford, Alabama).

The horizontal two roller manual mill was probably inspired by the cotton gin.

and Society in China, Mazumdar reviews the mechanics of crushing cane in China's sugar industry. He describes the mortar and pestle, the edge-runner with its circumference of about ten feet, and the tilt-hammer. He asserts that two-roller vertical mills were found in the Philippines as early as 1613, about the same time they came to the Americas. But they are not mentioned in China until after the mid 1630s. He suggests that there is no evidence that the three-roller vertical mill, so common in the Americas, was ever known in China. It was used in some provinces of India, but the two-roller mill was more common. Mazumdar comes to the conclusion that the vertical cane mill was an American invention and its technology spread to China in the seventeenth century. To refute the claim that the horizontal cane mill was an adaptation of the horizontal cotton gin, Mazumdar asserts that there is no evidence of a horizontal cane mill evolving from the gin in China. However, in some cotton producing areas of the Mediterranean where two horizontal roller cotton gins existed, there is evidence of two horizontal roller cane mills as well. This led Mazumdar to conclude that the adaptation from cotton gin to cane mill took place somewhere outside Asia, and to consider the possibility that both the two-roller and three-roller mills were developed in the Americas and spread to Asia and to the world from there. Joseph Needham, in his *Science and Civilisation in China,* expresses the opinion that there was a joint origin of the sugar cane mill and cotton gin in India.

When Stuart B. Schwartz wrote in his *Sugar Plantations in the Formation of Brazilian Society* that the matter concerning the origin of the three-roller vertical cane mill was still unresolved, he apparently was exactly right. To add to this interesting discussion by world sugar historians, Christian Daniels has an enlightening dissertation in Joseph Needham's six volume work, *Science and Civilisation in China.* Daniels concludes that the vertical three-roller cane mill evolved from the primitive, manually powered horizontal two-roller cotton gin which appeared about 1100. First, there were the enlarged versions of the cotton gin which probably were developed in India about 1400. To obtain a simpler animal driven machine, the horizontal axis mill had to be converted to a vertical axis, probably developed in China in the late sixteenth century. Vertical was the typical Chinese way of arranging machinery, while the Mediterranean standard was horizontal. New World engineers took this Chinese technology and devised the three-roller vertical mill around 1600. Daniels concludes that, until other factual information proves otherwise, the most simple and logical theory is that the vertical mill originated in China. John Daniels was a sugar cane researcher in Fiji and Christian Daniels is a lecturer in Chinese history at Shujitsu Women's University in Okayama. In their article, "The Origin of the Sugarcane Roller Mill," published in *Technology and Culture*, 29, they write that though the origin of the vertical roller mill is disputed there can be no doubt that it attained maturity in Peru and Mexico. Perhaps this would be an excellent place to conclude this survey and move on to the numerous developments that produced the cane mill so characteristic of the nineteenth and early twentieth centuries.

Improvements to the Roller Mill

While there were tremendous changes going on in the sugar industry there was a time when the milling process remained basically the same. There were changes in sugar cane stock, with selection of better varieties and development of research stations. There were changes in the evaporating and refining processes with the discovery that dried bagasse could be used as fuel and the development of the "Jamaica Train," a series of evaporator pans.

Some early refinements dealt with power adaptations, such as this wind powered mill.

There were changes in methods of powering the mills, and the transition from oxen and horsepower to wind, water, and steam represented a tremendous improvement in the quality and quantity of juice which could be produced in a day. While these changes were taking place, however, the milling technology was slow to change.

For many years Brazil led the world's sugar industry. Their technology was used when the colonies were established in the Caribbean in the mid–seventeenth century. Space between the rollers was made adjustable so more pressure could be applied, yielding a higher percentage of juice. They began using smaller metal bearings which were easier to lubricate and required less power. Iron hoops were bound around the wooden rollers so more pressure could be applied without destroying them. Experiments were performed with lateral rollers larger in diameter than the center roller in order to alter rotation speed and increase friction on the cane. Cast-iron sleeves were produced to go over wooden cylinders, extending their life and increasing their efficiency. The first to do so was most probably George Sitwell of Renishaw, England, who operated a foundry, and who, in 1653, sent such a set of rollers to London. The English merchant Andrew Orgall sent a set of iron sleeves to Barbados in 1674, and a new direction was set.

One of the first improvements was a real labor-saving device. The earlier three-roller vertical cane mills had the rollers set in a straight line. A workman on one side would feed the cane through for the first squeezing, while a second workman on the other side would take the crushed cane and feed it back through for a second squeezing. In the late eighteen hundreds, about 1890, Jacques Francois Dutrone la Couture advocated the use of a "double-use," "trash-returner," or "dumb-turner," as they were frequently called. This was simply a curved plate which guided the bagasse around the first set of rollers to the second set for a second squeezing. This freed about half of the mill workers for other jobs on the plantation. Dutrone la Couture also developed rollers with shallow vertical fluting on them to allow the juice to flow away from the bagasse more freely. Heavily indented rollers appeared in 1882, having been introduced by Thompson and Black.

The trend away from rollers in a straight line to rollers with their centers at the angles of an isosceles triangle began in 1754 in a design which Smeaton made for a Mr. Grey in Jamaica. In Smeaton's design the rollers are set on a line at right angles to the lines joining the upper and lower rollers. It was John Collinge, a Lambeth axletree maker, who in 1794 designed a mill with horizontal rollers set at the angles of an isosceles triangle. This became the common design for years to come, with the first models produced and shipped to Charles Telfair of the Bel Ombre estate in Mauritius in 1818. Even with this improved design the practice of hand feeding the cane through a second set of rollers continued until 1805, when a Barbados planter, Bell, developed a curved guide plate to direct the cane for a second squeezing. Bell's device was held in place with shims. It was Watson who received a patent in 1871 for a guide plate bolted to the headstock. His design held the "dumb turner" in place but it could be replaced when worn.

Wooden timbers were used for headstock in the earlier mills. Jukes and Coulson, of London, built a mill with an iron headstock about 1825. There followed several versions of this headstock, but the modern form emerged in a mill designed by Buchanan in 1858. It had open side gaps which allowed the two lower rollers to be removed by sliding them in and out; this represented a major step forward in design. A Martinique engineer, Theophile Rousselot, advanced the technology another step by substituting cast-iron side gaps for the wrought iron tie-bars which Buchanan had used. Rousselot used two wrought iron tie-bars running from side to side to strengthen the headstock.

Several improvements came from the East. The Japanese popularized a device called a "Duck Bill" for feeding sugar cane into the rollers. They also devised a funnel shaped return feed to extract more juice from the bagasse and pioneered in adjustable rollers by using wedges to regulate the space between the rollers. The Japanese technology also simplified the gearing by making gears separate from the rollers, allowing easier replacement or repairs on the mill.

Henry Bessemer became famous for his invention of the converter process for making steel and its impact on the world steel industry. He was an outstanding industrialist whose

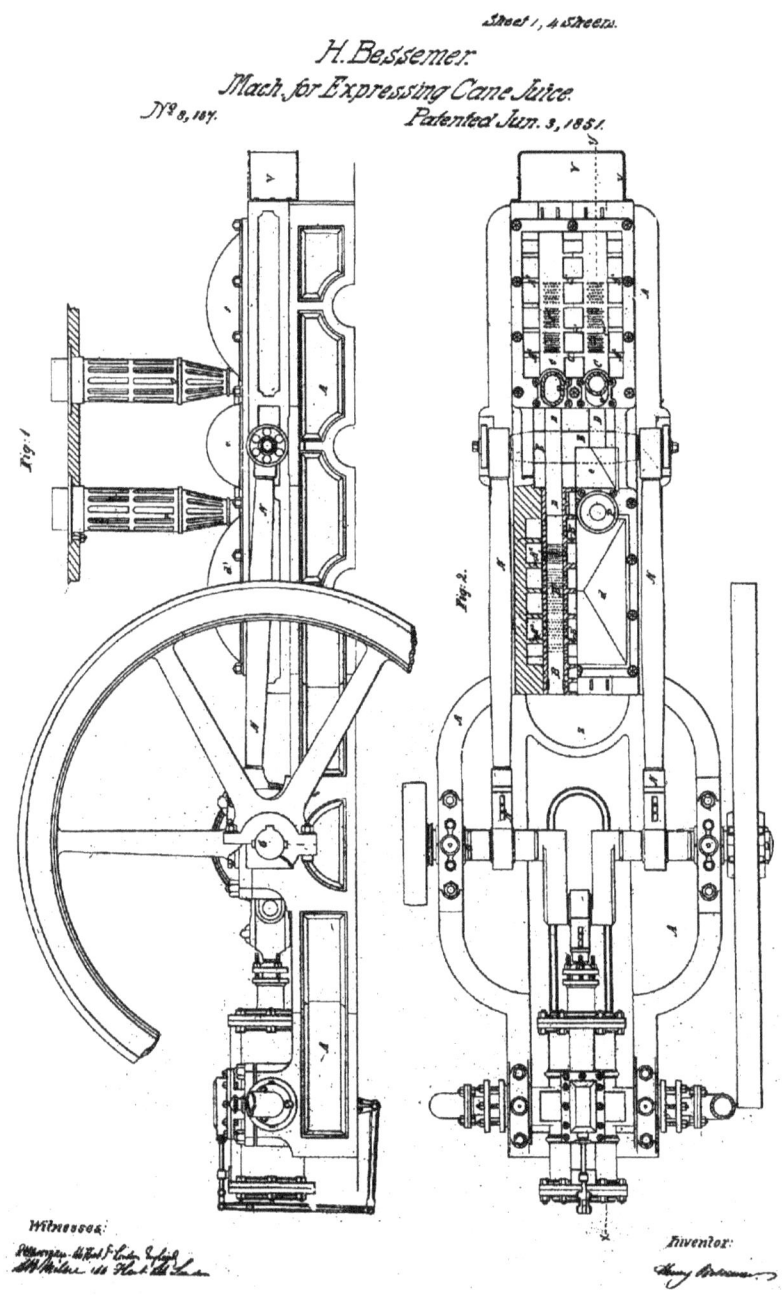

Bessemer's Plunger Mill crushed cane on the forestroke as well as on the backstroke.

inquisitive mind led him to numerous inventions in several fields, including a sugar cane press. In 1849 he became acquainted with a Jamaican sugarplanter and was struck with the wastefulness of the primitive methods of extracting juice. About this same time the Society of Arts and His Royal Highness Prince Albert announced the awarding of a gold medal to the person making the greatest improvement in methods for extracting juice from sugar cane. Bessemer, strictly an outsider and not bound by the concept of roller mills, designed and built a sugar cane press. The cane he obtained from Madeira to test his invention was the first sugar cane he had ever seen. His steam operated press consisted of two pressing tubes lined with drainage holes. A hopper held stalks of cane vertically above the pressing tubes. As the stalks slid into the pressing tube a plunger would cut off six inch sections on the forward stroke and press them on that end. On the return stroke the plunger would cut off another section of cane and press it on the other end. By using continuous pressure the bagasse could not reabsorb the extracted juice. Bessemer's press was capable of extracting six hundred gallons of juice per hour, about 20 percent more from the same amount of cane than the average roller mill. The Society of Arts was impressed with Bessemer's invention and awarded him the gold medal. However, his invention did not become the standard for extracting devices.

American Innovations

While other refinements were made to the cane mill the basic principle remained the same. Throughout the 1800s and early 1900s several innovations were developed, however. While these innovations provide us with an interesting glimpse into the emerging develop-

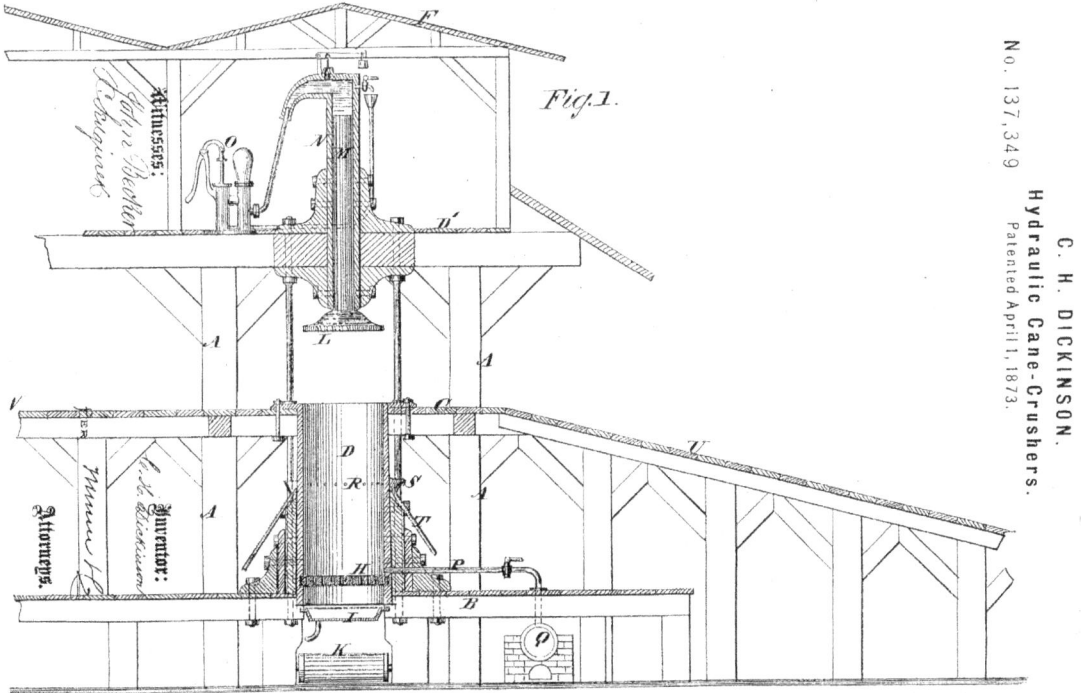

Dickinson designed a vertical hydraulic cane press.

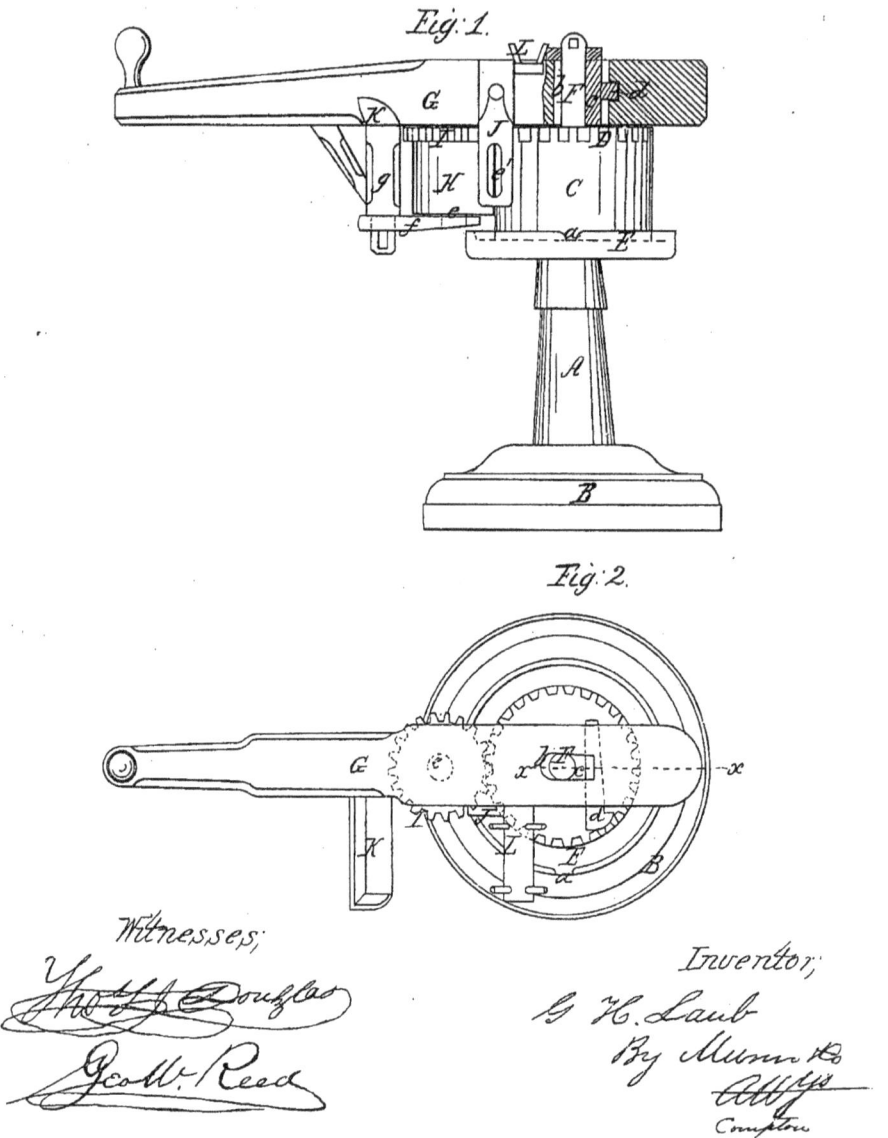

On Laub's mill the small roller rotated around the large roller.

ments of the cane mill, very few of them impacted its basic design. On April 1, 1873, C.H. Dickinson, of Rosedale, Louisiana, received Patent No. 137,349 for a vertical hydraulic cane press. While it was an excellent idea in principle, it was not generally adopted in the sugar industry.

G.H. Laub, of Macomb, Illinois, received a patent, no. 40,938, on December 15, 1863, for a mill in which the small roller rotated around the large crushing roller.

On April 10, 1860, Eugene Powell, of Conneautville, Pennsylvania, was awarded Patent No. 27,830 for a mill featuring five rollers rotating around a large central crushing roller. Each roller in his mill was set a little closer than the preceding to the main roller.

A mill with eight small rollers spaced around a large central crushing roller was awarded

Patent. No. 27,900 on April 10, 1860. The inventor, Theodore Grundmann, of Freeport, Illinois, also designed four feeding tubes in his mill, which required two workers to operate.

Thomas Hunt, of Indianapolis, Indiana, invented a mill with four beveled rollers rotating around a large beveled crushing roller, and received Patent No. 23,287, on March 15, 1858.

W.T. Dennis, of Richmond, Indiana, invented a mill for which he received Patent No. 22,711, on January 25, 1859. The uniqueness of this mill was that the rollers were covered with tin, or some other noncorrosive material, to preserve the purity of the juice from the cast-iron.

W.S. Seymour, of Ravenna, Ohio,

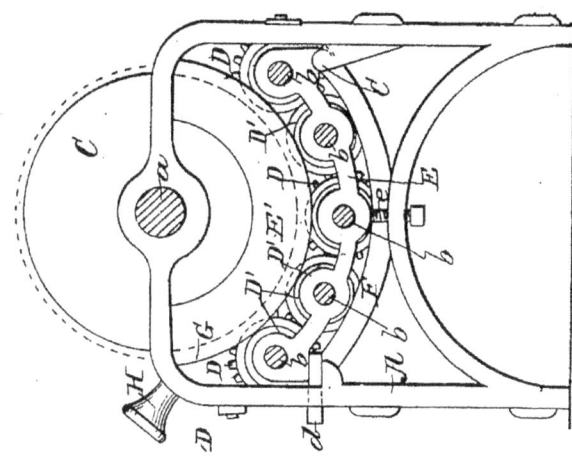

Powell's mill had five small rollers rotating around a large central crushing roller.

envisioned a mill with baked clay rollers, which he asserted would be strong, durable and clean. Baked clay rollers would not absorb juice as would wooden rollers, nor would they oxidate as would cast iron. Seymour received Patent No. 50, 281 on October 3, 1865, for his invention.

Hendrick V. Duryea, of Fulton, New York, invented a mill in which the large crushing roller was cast in two parts, assembled, and bolted together. This approach would eliminate the great weight of a single roller and would aid in assembly and disassembly of the mill. Huryea received Patent No. 19,289 on February 9, 1858, for his invention.

On May 1, 1866, Nathan B. Carr, of Madison, Wisconsin, received Patent No. 54,293 for a cane mill characterized by two protruding levers upon which an operator could place weights. These weights, which could be placed at certain intervals along the lever, would cause the upper roller to exert more pressure upon the lower rollers. The mill was designed to yield to the passing of cane through the rollers and also to be adaptable to the various sizes of cane.

Other inventions which had more lasting effects were in the nature of the headstocks, guide knives, gearing, clutches, and feed guides. Since the cane mill had already been invented, all the patents had to relate to some improvement on the mill. There were numerous patents issued for these improvements, some unique and all interesting.

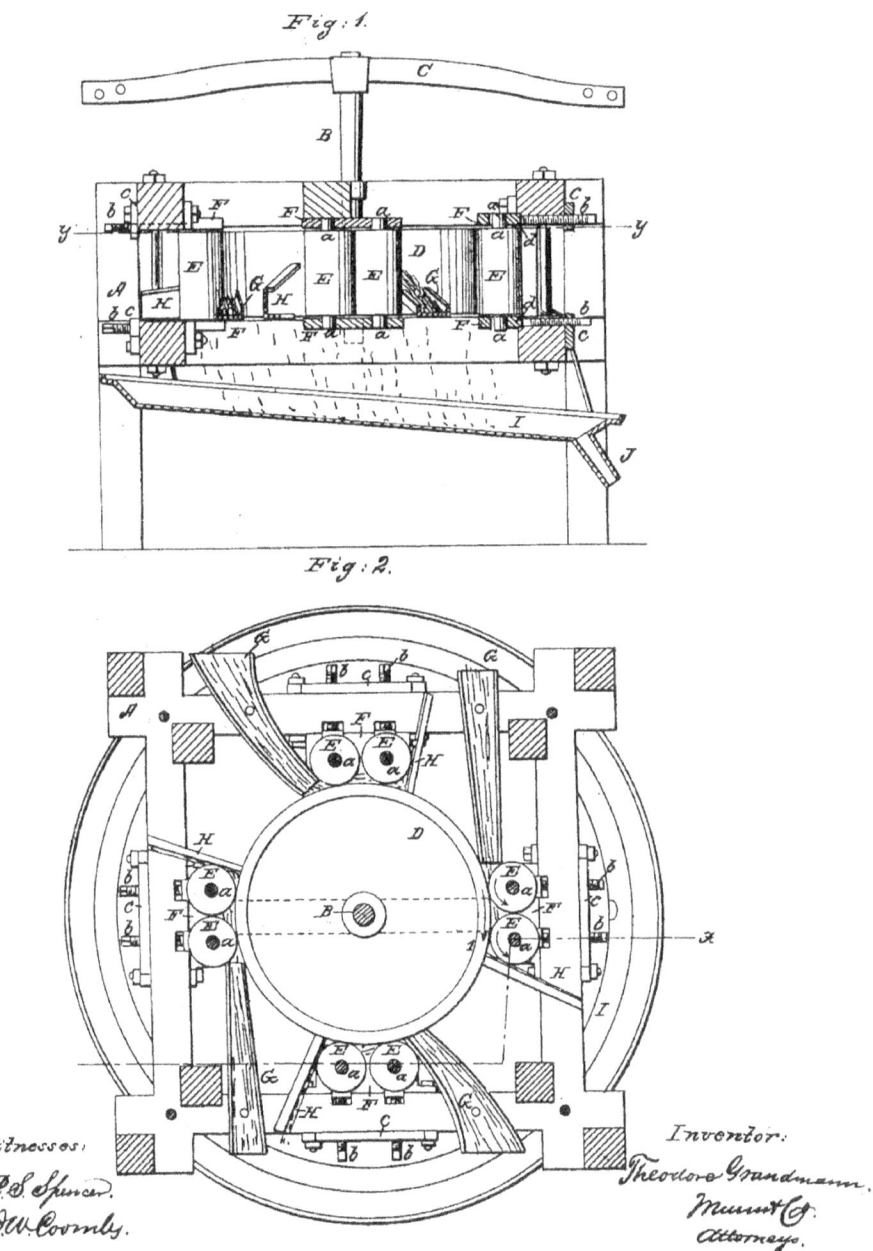

Grundmann carried the concept a little further, with eight small rollers rotating around a central roller.

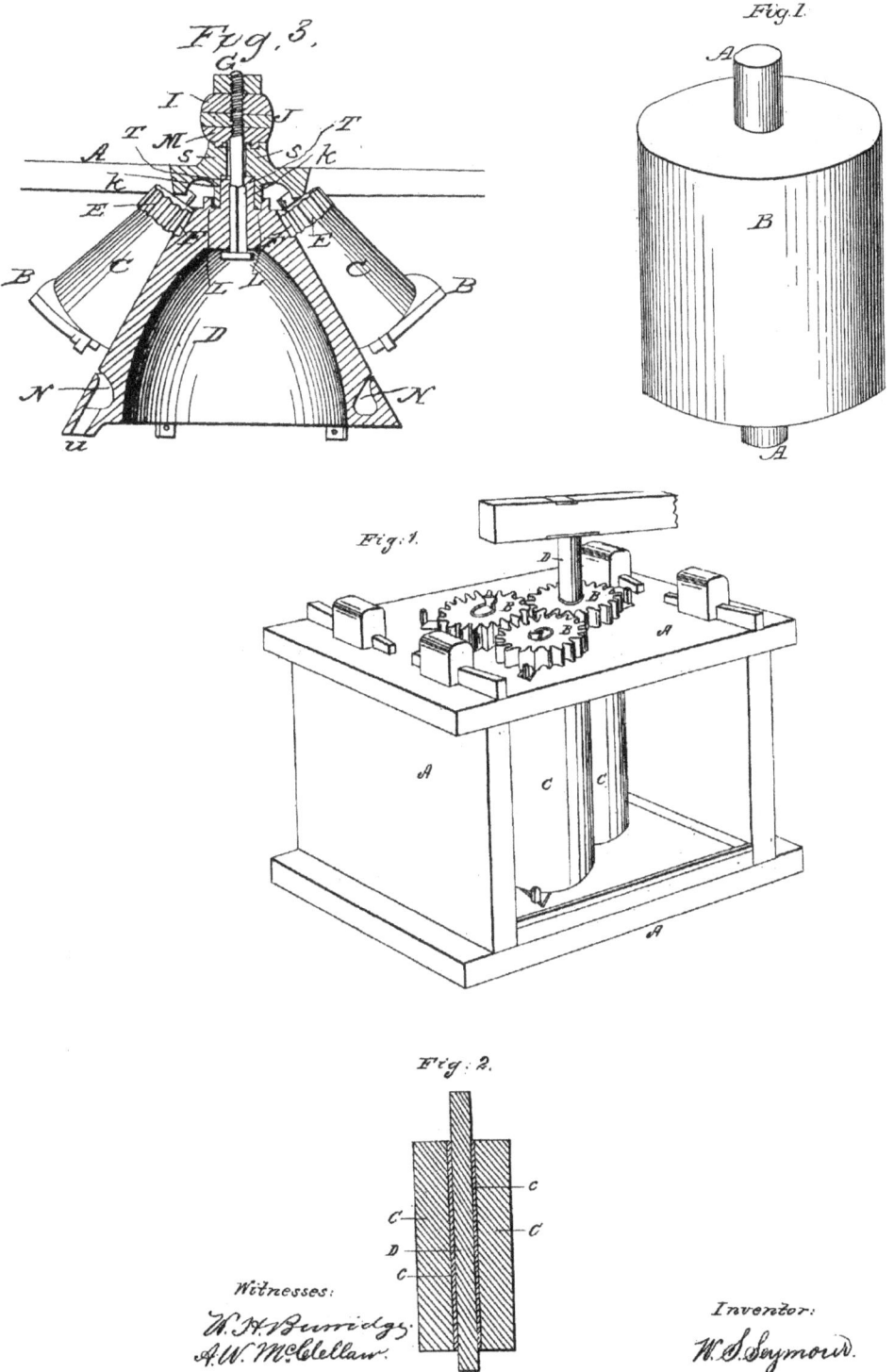

Top left: Thomas Hunt envisioned beveled rollers interacting. *Top right:* To preserve the purity of juice from contact with cast iron was the thought behind W.T. Dennis' rollers covered in a noncorrosive material. *Bottom:* Seymour conceived rollers made of baked clay for juice purity.

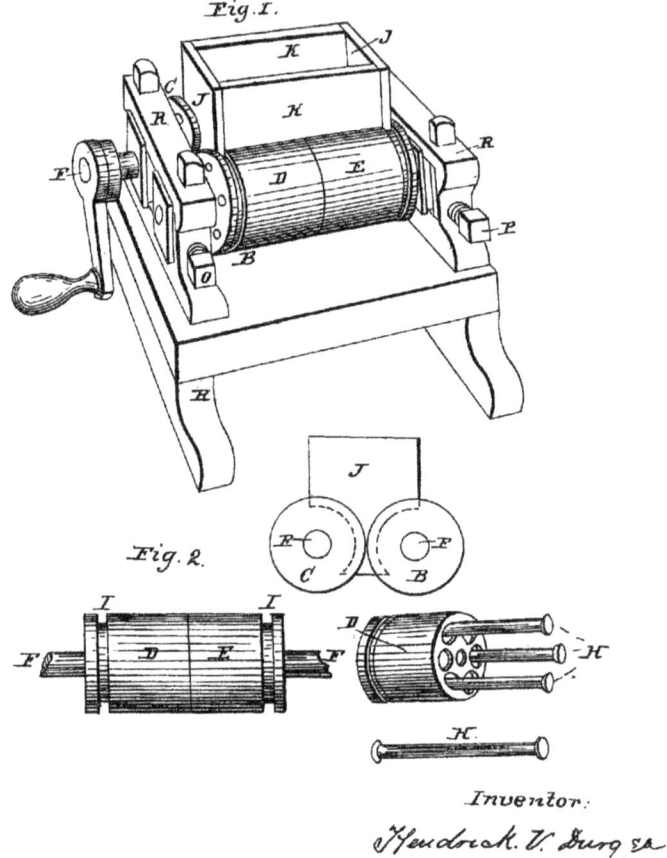

This modular mill was patented by Hendrick Duryea.

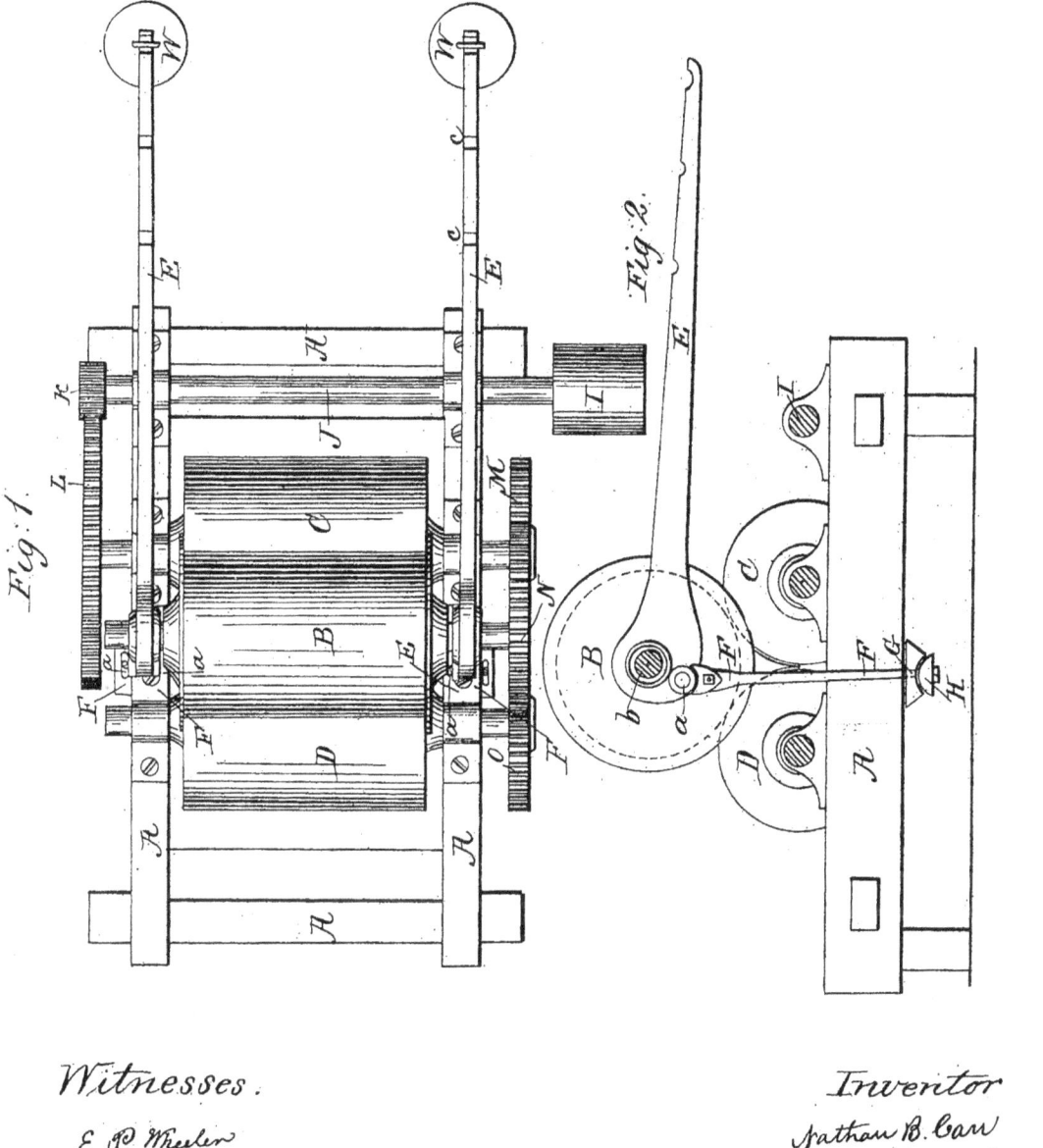

Carr invented a mill to increase pressure on rollers by adding weights.

PART II

3

Manufacturers of American Cane Mills

While the focus of our attention will be on the smaller, backyard type cane mills, let me acknowledge a newer generation of mills used in the sugar industry. These are the tremendously large three horizontal roller mills based on Rousselot's patent of 1871, wherein the rollers lie at the angles of an isosceles triangle. While there have been numerous variations on the application of this design, the mills have remained essentially the same. Headstock, king bolts, hydraulic pressure, trash turners, and bedplates are but a few variations on the basic principle.

The Puunene Mill used in the Hawaiian Islands featured a housing slanted fifteen degrees, designed to compensate for the unequal strain of the feed and discharge rollers. This led to the 1912 design of the Bolk Mill, which had a top roller completely adjustable vertically and horizontally. Hedemann completely eliminated the king bolts in his 1914 mill, and let the extra-strong housing take up the thrust. A radical design by George Squier featured a housing of only two parts, upper and lower, held together by two pins. This arrangement allowed for easy accessibility to the rollers, interchangeable bearings and a narrow trash plate. A characteristic of the De Bruin Mill was a floating (oscillating in the arc of a circle) top roller so a constant pressure could be applied to the front and rear rollers. Other giant mills for the sugar industry were made by Mirrlees Watson and Stewart of Glasgow, Scotland; George Fletcher & Co., of Derby, England; Werkspoor, of Amsterdam; Gilain; Krupp; Stork; and Hallesche. With this brief survey of the large mills, let's now return to the smaller mills used in the early American syrup and sugar industries, with a couple of exceptions when we'll look at some unique and visionary developments. For the most part, however, we'll look specifically at the foundries which made these smaller mills. In three or four instances we'll look briefly at some mail order houses which had mills made for their own brand names. The foundries which made them, though, will be our central focus.

Agricultural Implement Manufactory, Richmond, Virginia

In *Experiments with Sorghum Sugar Cane and Treatise on the Manufacture of Syrup and Sugar*, by J.W. Randolph, an 1864 publication, H.M. Smith announced the manufacture of a complete sorghum mill at his Agricultural Implement Manufactory, No. 14 Mann Street,

Richmond. This mill was built on a most improved plan with three iron rollers set in an iron frame. This mill was compact and portable, occupying "little more space than a barrel." However, when attached to a wooden sill, it was sufficiently strong for either one or two horses. Smith also announced that he would continue to manufacture mills with wooden rollers and iron gearing just as he had done in the past. By this time sorghum was being grown in central Virginia, and manufacturers were looking for ways of supplying the farmers' needs.

Alexander and Son Plow Works, Neosho, Missouri

Nestled in the Ozark Mountains in the southwest corner of Missouri, near the boundaries of Missouri, Kansas, Oklahoma, and Arkansas, lies the town of Neosho. Neosho (pronounced Nee-Oh-Show,) was founded in 1839, and is the seat of Newton County. As the town and nation grew, the business leaders of the young city recognized the need for a foundry and machine shop to meet the needs of their area. Twenty thousand dollars was raised for capital, and the Neosho Manufacturing Company was organized (see Neosho Manufacturing Company). The site selected for the company was the Alexander Planing Mill and Lumber Yard at the southeast corner of Brook and Mill Streets, and J.E. Alexander became one of the stockholders. The company was founded June 20, 1870, opened on October 2, 1870, and by January 1871 was ready to supply the area farmers with plows and agricultural implements, according to the "History of Neosho and Newton County," along with news clippings from Neosho's past.

J. E. Alexander withdrew from the firm in 1872 and with his son, J.C., began Alexander and Son Plow Works. The Alexanders began in a 7' × 9' blacksmith shop without any capital or machinery. Their first year of labor produced twenty-five plows, which they sold to local farmers. If the farmers didn't have money to buy them outright the Alexanders took meat, potatoes, and flour in part payment and in turn sold the produce to their employees in part payment for their labor. As their business grew they were able to build a 50' × 90' shop on their lot, adding a foundry and the machinery needed for the manufacture of their plows along with various castings, including the Alexander Cane Mills. These were three

Alexander and Son Plow Works and workers in Neosho, Missouri (courtesy Genealogy Friends of the Library, Neosho).

One of Alexander and Son's cane mills (courtesy John Teters, Rogers, Arkansas).

roller mills in at least four sizes. While the Alexander and Son Plow Works made a variety of items, they were especially known for their plows, one of which drew a lot of attention in its day. This was a custom plow made for the railroad contractors F.O. Baker and Son, and was super sized in every dimension. The wooden beam was ten feet long, and was 8" × 10¼" at its heaviest point. An iron reinforcement band ¾" × 4" ran full length underneath the beam, and was shaped into a clevis around the beam's end. The dimensions of the moldboard were not given, but the plow weighed 900 pounds and was designed to be pulled by sixteen horses.

The Neosho Manufacturing Company faired rather poorly those first years and was finally sold to Charles Van Riper and his son-in-law, John A. Rogers, of Joplin, Missouri. On March 8, 1907, it was consolidated with Alexander's company, which was then known as Alexander Chilled Plow Works, and the name changed to the Neosho Foundry and Plow Works. Alexander was elected president of the consolidated company and served until his death in 1918. The company produced plows, mining equipment, heavy foundry products, and stoves. The old Frame Mill, an unprofitable gristmill in Neosho, which became known later as Baurdick Mill, changed hands several times and was finally purchased by the Neosho Foundry and Plow Works for use as a pattern and woodwork shop. At the height of its productivity the foundry produced a million pounds of cast products each year and shipped them to almost every state in the Union, to Canada and to the Dominican Republic. Their production motto was "Work every day, pay every Saturday." Due to a shortage of raw materials the foundry was forced to close its doors during the early years of World War II.

John Alexander and Company, Columbia, South Carolina

Most of what we know about John Alexander and Company comes to us from the Sesqui-Centennial Commission of Columbia, South Carolina. This was one of the city's early ironworks companies in the late 1850s. In 1859, Glaze and Boatwright, who had established the Palmetto Armory in 1850, were manufacturing cotton gins. A wagon factory was operated by S.F. Moore, one of several carriage manufacturers in the city. John Alexander and Company manufactured sugar cane mills, steam engines, mill gearing, and sawmills, and made iron and brass castings to order.

Since South Carolina is on the border line for growing sugar cane, probably most of their customers were sorghum producers. In the late 1850s the promise of refining sugar from sweet sorghum was bright, and many companies rushed into the manufacture of cane mills.

Athens Foundry and Machine Works, Athens, Georgia

The predecessor companies of the Athens Foundry and Machine Works date back to their charter in 1848. The Athens Coal Gas Company became the Athens Steam Company, which began casting iron in 1851. The name was changed to the Athens Foundry and Machine Works in December of 1863. In 1862 the Athens Steam Company cast the celebrated double barrel cannon which now stands sentinel on the lawn of the city hall in Athens, Georgia. The theory John Gilleland had in mind when he designed this particular cannon was to chain two cannonballs together so when they were fired they would mow the opposing

Athens' double-barreled cannon stands sentinel at the court house.

army down like a scythe mows grain in a field. Once the cannon was cast it was taken out on Newton Bridge Road and, in April 1862 was test fired. Apparently the barrels did not fire simultaneously and one ball came out of the muzzle before the other. It was reported that this gyrating apparatus plowed up an acre of ground, destroyed a cornfield, and mowed down some saplings. The chain then broke and the balls went their separate ways. One cannonball killed a cow and the other destroyed the chimney of a nearby log cabin. A local newspaper of the day reported that the test was an "unqualified success." The foundry, however, could not interest the Confederate secretary of war in the cannon so it was placed at the city hall of Athens to signal the town if the Yankees approached. An interesting sidenote occurs in relation to the cannon. According to "Athen's Double Barrel Cannon," by Richard E. Irby, legend says that one Sunday morning while the "women and children were in church and the men napping at home" some mischievous boys fired the cannon. Well, you can imagine what happened next. That broke up the worship services, the women went screaming into the streets, and the men with their guns went "running through the town in their underwear" looking for the Yankees.

The product line of these early companies included coal grates, andirons, municipal grates, construction components, and houseware items. The Athens Foundry and Machine Works advertised portable and stationary steam engines, sawmills, cotton presses, mining and mill machinery, water wheels, plow stocks, cotton planters, miscellaneous items and cane mills. The company moved to Elberton, Georgia, in 1972 as the Athens Boiler and Machine Works, and ceased operations in 1994.

B.F. Avery and Sons, Louisville, Kentucky

The Avery and Sons Company of Louisville, Kentucky, manufacturers of agricultural implements, was founded by B.F. Avery in Clarksville, Virginia, in 1825. Making a move which would lead to vast expansion, the company relocated to Louisville in 1845. Ultimately they opened branches in Memphis, Tennessee; Dallas, Texas; Atlanta, Georgia; New Orleans, Louisiana; Oklahoma City, Oklahoma; Shreveport, Louisiana; New York City; and Mexico City. Avery and Sons built a new plant in 1910 which covered forty-eight acres of land and had 800,000 square feet of floor space. The company manufactured two sizes of farm tractors with attachments and a full line of horse-drawn farm implements. While their business interests reached from New York City to Mexico City, most were concentrated in the Southern and southeastern states.

One of the things for which they were noted was their patented Moon Coulter, wonderfully designed for plowing in vines, weeds, stalks, crab-grass and trash. Avery manufactured a patented all steel, indestructible singletree with self-locking end hooks for horse-drawn implements. Avery and Sons' product list of agricultural implements was much longer, however, and included walking plows, sulky plows, gang plows, disc plows, riding, combined and walking cultivators, disc cultivators, cotton planters, cotton and corn planters, corn drills, disc harrows, spike-tooth harrows, riding listers, potato diggers, stalk cutters, land rollers, garden plows and cultivators, plow stocks, cotton scrapers and one-horse guano distributors. And, according to Thomas' Registry of American manufacturers, *The Buyers' Guide 1905,* they additionally manufactured sugar cane mills.

Avery and Sons was taken over by the giant Minneapolis-Moline Company in 1951 and after more than a hundred years their name disappeared from the Louisville City directory. However, Avery and Sons was another great American company which made significant contributions to the success of the American farmer.

A. Baldwin and Company Ltd., New Orleans, Louisiana

The "King of the South" cane mill was marketed by A. Baldwin and Company of New Orleans, importers and dealers in hardware. The origin of the company dates back to the infancy of the city. In 1822, three men, all natives of Philadelphia, founded a hardware business in the teeming young city. Rogers, Sill and Slocomb established their business in a most advantageous location at 11 Chartres and 10 Exchange Place. (At that time Chartres was the only street in New Orleans paved its entire length.) Their company bought directly from the manufacturers and were thus able to wholesale their merchandise at competitive prices. They carried a wide stock of hardware with a line unsurpassed in the United States. At one time their huge catalog carried items from nails to locomotives, with axes, cutlery, guns and cane mills their specialties. By 1885 their business territory covered a geographic area from the Missouri River to the Amazon, and from the Rio Grande to the Florida Keys, according to *The Industries of New Orleans*. With a developing sugar industry emerging in New Orleans the company was poised for significant growth. Numerous trials, along with the ebb and flow of life, necessitated several changes in the composition of the company. Mr. Sill fell ill with yellow fever and the company was changed to Rogers, Slocomb and Company. Yellow fever and cholera epidemics killed 10,000 people in New Orleans and the Civil War brought a temporary dissolution of the company. Upon resumption of business, the Panic of 1873, with its soaring unemployment and thousands of failing businesses, were all weathered successfully by the company. When Rogers died, the company became C.H. Slocomb and Company. Albert Baldwin, a native of Massachusetts, joined the firm in 1867 with the founder's son, Cuthbert Slocomb, and the name was changed to Slocomb, Baldwin and Company. The firm was moved to old No. 74 Canal Street. Albert Baldwin was a prominent citizen of New Orleans and served as president of the New Orleans National Bank and of the Gullett Gin Manufacturing Company. Cuthbert Slocomb died in 1874 and Cartwright Eustis joined the firm. At this point the company name was changed to A. Baldwin and Company, the name by which it would be known for many years. In the passing of time and through several personnel changes, L.M. Stratton, Sr., was elected chairman of the board in 1932. In July 1943, the firm's name was changed to Stratton Baldwin Company, Incorporated. While they sold cane mills with their own imprint, it is believed that the Squier Company of Buffalo, New York, made them for Baldwin.

Belknap Hardware Company, Louisville, Kentucky

The Belknap Hardware Company was founded in 1840 in Louisville, Kentucky, and for over a century was one of the nation's largest hardware suppliers. Carriage supplies, blacksmith supplies, and horseshoes were the first items sold by the company, but before its demise its catalog was over 3,500 pages thick and carried thousands of various items. Mr. W.B. Belknap began the company in 1840 in a small three-story building on Washington Street in Louisville. The firm continued to grow and was incorporated in 1880. From that humble beginning the company grew to fifteen buildings housing forty acres of floor space that covered several city blocks, as chronicled by "The City of Louisville and Its Resources," published by the Louisville Post Company, 1892. The company enjoyed the reputation of fair dealing, quality merchandise, and vision. In the early years it carried the older lines of hardware items but was innovative enough to carry the newer, finer grades of builders' hardware, household utensils, fine tools, sporting goods and cutlery as they were being developed.

Belknap Hardware, Louisville, Kentucky, in 1840.

The Belknap Hardware Company became quite a complex. Each of the buildings was built and equipped for a special purpose in the grand scheme. In the early 1890s, builders' hardware, tools, bolts, nuts, washers, and chains were stocked on the first floor on Main Street. The second floor contained shelf hardware, carriage hardware, wagon supplies and saddlery. Forges, bellows, blacksmiths' tools, brass and copper kettles, handles and other woodwork was stocked on the third floor. The fourth floor carried agricultural implements, such as scoops, spades, posthole diggers, hoes, scythes and cradles. Later, spiral chutes connected the upper floors to shipping floors and packing rooms. Automatic conveyors, underground tunnels, overhead bridges, large, fast freight elevators and a complete pneumatic tube system connecting all departments were added, which enabled Belknap to receive freight and fill orders quickly. The warehouses were situated with railroad sidings so that workers were able to unload and reload sixty-eight cars daily. There were forty-five railroad, truck, and boat line terminals within less than a mile and a half of their plant. The Ohio River's shipping facilities were just one block from the Belknap complex and the approach to the George Rogers Clark Memorial Bridge linking Kentucky and Indiana ran by their west door.

From 1840 to 1860 the hardware giant was known simply as W.B. Belknap. From 1860 to 1880 it was known as W. B. Belknap and Company. From 1880 to 1907 it was W.B. Belknap and Company, Incorporated, and finally, in 1907, it became Belknap Hardware

Belknap's "New Blue Grass 1896 Model" cane mill.

and Manufacturing Company, Incorporated. Belknap ceased operations in 1986, but not before it made "Blue Grass" and "John Primble" household words across the homes, farms, ranches, villages and cities of America. Everything the company sold was purchased in large quantities from manufacturers, enabling them to sell at a reasonable price to retailers.

Belknap sold several models of cane mills under their own brand name. Most often seen is the "New Blue Grass 1896 Model." These mills were consistent with those manufactured by Brennan and Company of Louisville.

C.S. Bell Company, Hillsboro, Ohio

With a name like "The Bell Foundry," it would seem logical that the foundry made bells. While this is how the foundry ultimately distinguished itself, it was in fact named for its founder, C.S. Bell. Charles Singleton Bell was born February 2, 1828, in Cumberland, Maryland. At fifteen years of age he became an apprentice to the founder's trade in Pittsburgh, then sharpened his skills through work in Cincinnati, Springfield and Dayton. Having mastered the art of casting metals, he moved to Hillsboro, Ohio, where as a stranger with very little capital he opened a small foundry and began producing cook stoves of exceptional quality. As his reputation for quality and integrity grew his business prospered and the Bell Foundry soon needed larger facilities. In January 1858, Bell purchased the Speedwell Foundry on W. Beech Street and there, with one young helper and a weekly expense of seven dollars, he made stoves, plow points and other castings. When additional space was needed, a second foundry and showroom were built at the corner of Main and West streets. James K. Marly became Bell's partner and was placed over the showroom, while Bell operated the foundry. They continued to produce an expanding list of quality products.

When sweet sorghum was introduced into the United States many Northern growers, who could not grow sugar cane, began a sorghum syrup industry. To meet the needs of these Northern growers, Bell designed an efficient, simple to operate, strong, inexpensive, and sufficiently durable cane mill to grind sorghum or Southern sugar cane. In later years his mills were sold through the Montgomery Ward Company chain of stores. The foundry also produced evaporators, sugar mills, steam generators, plows, agricultural machinery, and improved beehives. Bell bought out Marlay's interest in the foundry in 1869 and continued to add various items to the product list.

Bell had a natural aptitude for metallurgy and constantly experimented with different formulas of iron, steel, and other metals in search of an alloy cheaper and more durable than iron. One day he accidentally dropped a piece of metal that struck another piece and rang like a bell. This began the foundry's illustrious career in bell making. The first year after discovering the right formula for making bells, which was kept secret, the company sold 100 bells for farms, taverns, factories, schoolhouses and churches. In 1875 the foundry sold 5,000 bells and 700 cane mills and in 1889 some 20,000 bells were shipped worldwide. During this time the company made "Mogul" stoves, caboose stoves, grinders, coffee pulpers, burr and hammer type food and feed grinding mills, cane mills, evaporators and agricultural equipment.

A son, Charles E. Bell, was taken into partnership in 1882 and the C.S. Bell Company was formed. Charles E. traveled the world opening new markets and orders poured in to the Hillsboro foundry. South Africa, Brazil and Central America needed cane mills and evaporators. China needed rice mills. Mexico needed gristmills and feed grinders. Bell's products were shipped to the four corners of the globe. By 1892, a new plant on a seven acre tract had been built on the edge of town and the foundry produced 2,000 tons of bells, 400 tons of cane mills, and 400 tons of other manufactured goods.

C.S. Bell died in 1905, and his son, Charles, continued the foundry as the Charles E. Bell Company. Charles S. Bell had been one of Hillsboro's most public-spirited citizens. In addition to the foundry, Bell built other facilities and was a stockholder in grocery, bank, hardware and railroad companies. In 1895 he built Bell's Opera House for the community at a personal cost of $40,000. He served for twenty-one years as a member of the school board, served numerous years on the city council, and, while he was not affiliated with any church, he was known as an energetic, honest, and trustworthy worker and adviser. Testimonials at his death bore witness to a generous and sympathetic man who contributed greatly to Hillsboro's economic, cultural, and educational life. With the sale of bells declining, the company concentrated on labor-saving machinery for the farm. Charles E. passed away in 1929. Although the company was run by family members, it lacked the focus of a dynamic leader to take it into the future. Finally, Virginia Bell, the daughter of Charles E., gave up an acting career in New York, returned to Hillsboro and brought order to the floundering company.

With the onslaught of World War II there was a shortage of brass and copper used for making bells for military ships. The Bureau of Ships began looking for a metal bell to substitute for their regulation bells. Virginia Bell loaded one of their bells in her car, drove to Washington, conferred with the authorities and returned with a contract. Subsequently, the foundry made all ship's bells for the United States, Great Britain and their allies during the war. They cast more than 26,000 bells for the Navy, for civilian defense, for the Maritime Commission and Lend-Lease, from six-inch baby bells to thirty-six-inch, four hundred pound battleship watch bells. In 1969 the business was sold and the C.S. Bell Company is no longer in existence. An interesting account of the company may be found at www.hillsboro-ohio.com/c_s_bell_company.htm.

During their illustrious years of production the company made the "Climax" cane mill, a three vertical roller cane mill in five sizes. An early catalog extolled the strength and efficiency of their mills with these features: four corner bolts for added strength; cog gearing cast separately from the rollers, using clutches to minimize breakage; brass boxes for all journals; serrated faces on all rollers; a feed guide; encased gearing for safety and gear protection. The main roller was flanged top and bottom to prevent jamming and the mills were made of iron 50 percent stronger than ordinary foundry iron.

The Climax Mill

Bell's brochure is one of the few to give the dimensions for a turn-pole. It states, "The circle where the horse walks should be level, the sweep 12 to 13 feet from the center of the mill and extend beyond to partially balance."

Chart for Bell's Climax Mill

Model No.	Horsepower	Main Roller- D × H	Small Rollers- D × H	Juice Per Hour	Weight	Price
No. 0	One Horse	10¼" × 5½"	5⅞" × 5½"	40 gals.	440 lbs.	$30.00
No. 1	One Horse	11½" × 6¼"	6⅝" × 6¼"	60 gals.	540 lbs.	$40.00
No. 2	Two Horse	13⅛" × 7½"	7⅛" × 7½"	80 gals.	755 lbs.	$60.00
No. 3	Two Horse	14¾" × 9¾"	8" × 9¾"	100 gals.	1,000 lbs.	$80.00
No. 4	Two Horse-hvy	16" × 12¼"	9⅝" × 12¼"	120 gals.	1,375 lbs.	$100.00

The Climax Mill by C.S. Bell (courtesy Highland County District Library, Hillsboro, Ohio).

Bell's horizontal mill, one of many models made by the company (courtesy Tommy Clayton, Hilliard, Florida).

In addition to the Climax mill, Bell also manufactured the America, Atlas, Bounty, Champion, Domestic, Eclipse, Economist, Farmer's Choice, Globe, Globe Special, Gold Medal, Lone Star, Monarch, New South, Paragon, Pioneer, Star, Delta, Jumbo 88, Monitor, Poderoso, Progreso, Trojan, Tropic and Western Cane Mills. Bells did ultimately become the focus of the C.S. Bell Foundry. However, during its long and renowned existence it made extensive equipment for the domestic and foreign sugar cane and sorghum industries.

Bellevue Foundry and Machine Shop, Bellevue, Iowa

The Bellevue Foundry and Machine Shop was founded in 1860 by William Wilson, one of Bellevue's old settlers. *The History of Jackson County, Iowa* reports that Wilson had an unfortunate mishap and was killed by a threshing machine on August 20, 1877. One of his sons, W.W., had just turned twenty years old the month his father was killed. He and a brother, John G., became proprietors of the ironworks and had the reputation of being young men with practical knowledge and a great degree of skill in their trade. The shop from which they operated their foundry and machine shop was a 30' × 90' stone building erected in 1865 that is still being used today as part of an automotive garage. The two primary products which the Bellevue Foundry and Machine Shop manufactured were steam engines and sorghum equipment. This was the era in which much sorghum research was going on in the Midwest and foundries did their best to supply local farmers with the much needed equipment.

George W. Bevitt, Madison, Wisconsin

Though no information has yet been located as to George W. Bevitt's business affiliation, he did demonstrate his Adjustable Sugar Mill at the 1866 Wisconsin Sorghum State Convention. Bevitt designed a mill with adjustable lower rollers and a unique scraper arranged between them, for which he received Patent No. 52,127 on January 23, 1866. His design mounted the lower rollers in bearings made adjustable by means of a spring. This would allow some yielding when the mill was overloaded by too much cane. A grower as well, Bevitt expressed to the 1866 Wisconsin State Sorghum Convention, as reported in the *Appleton Motor*, February 15, 1866, that he believed that the pith of sorghum would one day be used in the manufacture of paper.

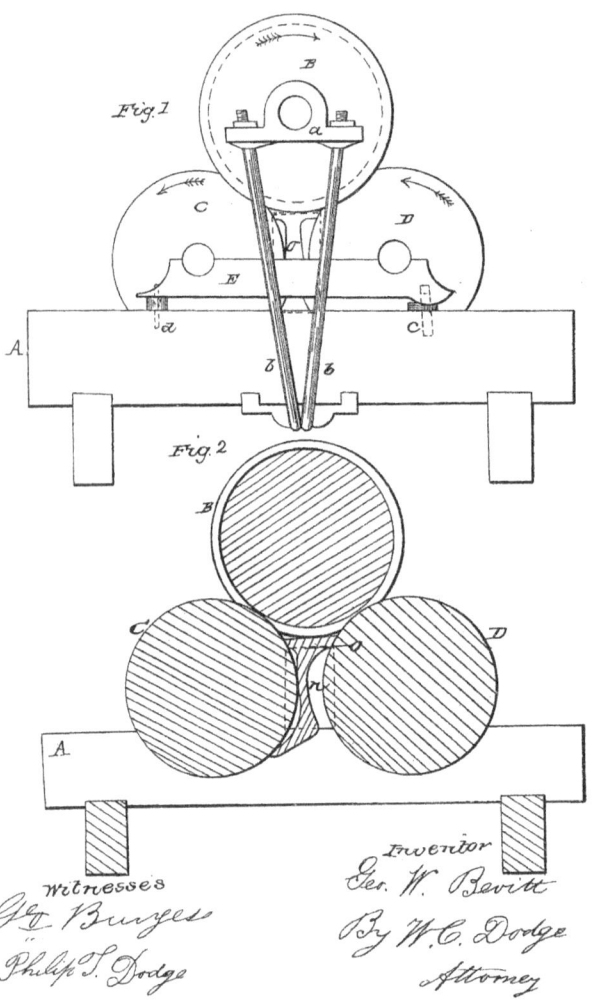

Bevitt's spring mounted rollers allowed some give under pressure.

Blandy's Steam Engine Works, Zanesville, Ohio

When John McIntire laid out the settlement called Wellbourne in the 1790s at the confluence of the Licking and Muskingum rivers he could not have known what significance lay in store for the little community. Colonel Ebenezer Zane had been commissioned by the United States Congress to blaze a trace into the old Northwest Territory and his son-in-law laid out the first settlement. The two also established three ferry crossings. The little settlement was renamed Zanesville in honor of Colonel Zane in 1801, and from 1810 to 1812 it served as the temporary capital of Ohio. A Y-shaped bridge was built in 1814 in the center of town to cross the junction of the Licking and Muskingum rivers. The rich natural resources of the area made it an ideal location for manufacturing of various kinds, including iron works.

Perhaps Blandy's Steam Engine Works of Zanesville, Ohio, owned and operated by Henry and F.J.L. Blandy, was best noted for its portable steam engine sawmills. In the 1860 United States Fair, held at Cincinnati, Ohio, the Blandy's mill was awarded First Premium as the smoothest working, easiest handling and fastest cutting mill exhibited. Using two mill hands, the Blandy's mill cut 675½ feet of lumber from two logs in eight minutes and fifteen seconds. Their mill also won First Premiums at the Ohio State Fairs in 1857, 1858, and 1859. Their mills were warranted to cut from 5,000 to 10,000 feet of lumber per day with careful management. However, sawmills were not the only machinery made by the company. An 1863 advertisement emphasized four major items, namely canal boat steam engines and propellers, Blandy's portable steam engines, Blandy's portable steam engine sawmills, and Blandy's improved sugar mills and sorgho apparatus. In 1858, F.J.L. Blandy received a patent for a steam engine of revolutionary design, which was manufactured in 4 to 50 horsepower models, and it became quite popular in its day.

Business was good in that era and Blandy's Steam Engine Works advertised for 100 machinists, 50 boilermakers, and a few good smiths. Highest wages in cash and steady jobs in a large, first class plant were promised. As an inducement for mechanics to move to Zanesville, the advertisement touted inexpensive rental, living expenses, fuel and property in the community with good, free schools and everything needed to make permanent residence pleasant for married or single mechanics. A branch, Blandy's Newark Machine Works, was opened in Newark, Ohio. No specifics other than the reference "Blandy's Improved Sugar Mills and Sorgho Apparatus" has been located by this writer. An ad in the *Zanesville Daily Courier* on October 9, 1865, did show a three roller mill with gears exposed on top, offered at "greatly reduced prices."

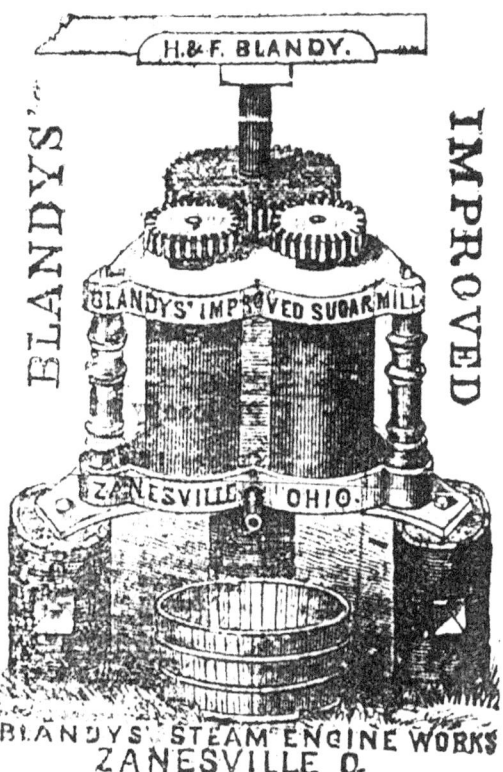

A rendering of Blandy's cane mill is an interesting one from an edition of the 1865 *Zanesville Courier* (courtesy Muskingum County Library System, Zanesville, Ohio).

The Blymyer Iron Works Company, Cincinnati, Ohio

The Blymyer Iron Works Company, 664-694 W. Eighth Street, Cincinnati, Ohio had its origin in Mansfield, Ohio, and specialized in farm machinery and bells. Their price list of July 1, 1874, included in their agricultural line cane mills, evaporators, furnace irons, shaker threshers, corn and cob crushers, feed cutters, corn shellers, crosscut sawing machines, agricultural boilers, garden cultivators, sulky revolving rakes, kitchen mills, cast-iron cider mills and tobacco screws. In addition, Blymyer produced bells for churches and schools, fire alarm bells, and a new series of farm bells.

Blymyer's line of cane mills dates back to at least 1859, though some models were already in use for over a decade by that time. The 1892 Catalogue of Sorghum and Sugar Cane Mills and Evaporators is designated as their thirty-third annual edition. It contains not only their various models of mills, but their philosophy of design, construction, and workmanship as well. Apparently their philosophy of design and craftsmanship paid off in that they were awarded the Grand Medal by the Centennial Exhibition in Philadelphia in 1876. They claimed, "Our sugar cane machinery has been given more awards, national and state, than all others combined. It has been successful at all competitive trials." They stated, "Our

SIX ROLLER NILES CANE MILL
THIS TYPE USED AT U. S. EXPERIMENT STATION, WAYCROSS, GA.

SYRUP AND SUGAR MACHINERY

"SANTA CLARA" STEAM DEFECATOR AND EVAPORATOR

CANE MILLS
ANIMAL, STEAM OR WATER POWER

EVAPORATORS
DIRECT FIRE AND STEAM

VACUUM PANS
CENTRIFUGALS
ENGINES
BOILERS
PUMPS, ETC.

Our machinery is of the most modern design and embodies every practical improvement which our fifty years of experience has suggested.

Estimates cheerfully furnished. Address,

THE BLYMYER IRON WORKS COMPANY

CINCINNATI, OHIO

EUREKA CANE MILL

This is an ad from a convention program.

machinery is not gotten up to compete in price with inferior, cheaply constructed machinery, but is strictly first class in every respect, equal to the best, and in some features superior to any."

Their 1892 company catalogue contains a statement about the importance of getting the largest possible percentage of juice from the cane and the loss of profit in losing juice in the bagasse by using an inferior mill. It's the old premise that "cheap is not always cheap." Then they have this interesting statement:

> The office of a cane mill being to press out the juice, it is all important that it press out the largest possible percentage thereof. Only a heavy mill of the best construction will do this.
>
> Mills with cast shafts, or unturned rolls, or with rolls in wooden frames, and two-roll mills, are all mere *makeshifts*, and will leave a large percentage of juice in the bagasse. *Flexible mills*, or those with rolls arranged to *yield under pressure*, by means of *rubber cushions* or otherwise, are also *wasteful of juice*. The *loss of juice* by the best flexible mill over a good rigid mill is not less than *ten per cent*, and in general, the loss is from *twenty to thirty per cent*. Any one can figure out how long it will take such a mill to waste more than its price.
>
> Mills with *flexible, or yielding*, rolls are all right *for the makers* (for this arrangement enables a weak mill to do its work without breaking), but they are *hard on the purchasers*. Such mills are not used in Louisiana or Cuba by intelligent planters, who know how a good mill should be made. In Louisiana, where the best improved mills are used, none of the leading planters could be induced to buy a flexible mill. In fact, so far as we know, there is not now in use in that state a single large mill with flexible rolls. It is the *cane* that should yield, not the mill. A good cane mill is made so powerful that the rolls can be held face to face, and when the cane is forced through, the bagasse comes out dry, no difference whether the feed of cane is light or heavy.
>
> The assertion, by makers of flexible mills, that the yielding of the rolls under pressure (thus adapting the pressure to the feed) secures an even pressure and a greater yield of juice is so *plainly unwarranted* that it is hard to understand how it could impose on any intelligent person. Nor are these flexible mills, with their great waste of juice, even secure against breakage, for they are so poorly constructed, and made so light, that breakages are numerous.
>
> The *Victor* and *Great Western* Animal-Power Mills, and the *Victor* and *Niles* Mills for steam or water power, are universally recognized in all sugar-producing countries as the *Standard* Sugar Mills, *superior in important respects* to all others. These mills are made of the best material and construction, and sufficiently strong to press out the *largest possible* percentage of juice. We are the *sole makers* of these mills.

Here are the various cane mills, and their descriptions, produced by the Blymyer Iron Works Company according to their 1892 and 1904 Catalogues.

The Victor Cane Mill

For Animal Power. Some of the advantages of the Victor Cane Mill claimed by Blymyer were:

1. It has Great Strength. It was secured by the amount of metal used (15 to 40 per cent heavier than other mills of the same horsepower), by its quality, and by the exact adjustments of its parts.
2. It Presses the Cane Dry. Only a strong mill can do this.
3. It Cannot Choke. By using lapped gearing the guide knife is dispensed with and therefore it cannot choke.
4. It Works Easy. Its design frees it from most friction common to other mills.
5. Oiling and Wear. There is protection against wear in the perfect arrangement for oiling the journals.

6. It Feeds Easy. The feed box is the best made and the fluted feed roll is of great advantage.

7. It Does Clean Work. Flanges keep the cane from working over or under; the rolls' wipers clean the faces of the rolls; and the channel in the bottom plate receives the juice as it comes from the rolls.

8. Its Work is Even and Regular. Screws hold the rolls to their exact positions, no matter how hard the pressure may be.

Patents for this mill include three rolls so arranged to dispense with "return plate," diagonal braces, oil tight boxes, movable sweep cap, cleaning scrapers, juice channel in bottom plate, juice plate, and fastening the gearing to vertical rolls with clutches.

Chart for Victor Mill

Model No.	Horsepower	Main Roller- D × H	Small Rollers- D × H	Juice Per Hour	Weight	Price 1892
No 0	One Horse	9¾" × 5½"	6" × 5⅛"	40 gals.	400 lbs.	$40.00
No. 1 Jr.	One Horse	10" × 5¾"	7¼" × 5¾"	50 gals.	600 lbs.	$55.00
No. 1	One Horse	12" × 6"	8" × 6"	60 gals.	775 lbs	$70.00
No. 2	Two Horse	12" × 8"	8" × 8"	80 gals.	875 lbs	$80.00
No. 3	Two Horse hvy	14" × 10"	8" × 10"	100 gals.	1,250 lbs.	$110.00
No. 4	L. Two Horse	12" × 12"	8" × 12"	120 gals.	1,350 lbs.	$125.00
No. 6	Four Horse	20" × 12¼"	8" × 12¼"	170 gals.	1,850 lbs.	$160.00

A distinguishing characteristic of the Victor No. 6 vertical mill was that the gears were separate from the rolls. The main roller was 20" D × 12¼" H and the small rollers were 8" D × 12¼" H. The mill weighed a whopping 1,850 pounds. To work this mill at full capacity required four large horses or six small ones. Blymyer claimed the No. 6 vertical mill would

The Victor Mill was a standard in its day.

The Victor Mill.
SWEEP BELOW.

The Mill, with sweep below, presents these advantages: 1. The Mill is more steady. 2. Horses and cane do not interfere with each other. 3. Bagasse is more easily removed. 4. Juice can flow down to the Evaporator.

Prices: No. 1, $75.00; No. 2, $85.00; No. 3, $120.00; No. 4, $135.00; No. 6, $175.00.

This model of Blymyer's mill featured a sweep below.

do as much work as any eight-horse horizontal horsepower mill made. At full capacity the No. 6 would produce 170 gallons of juice per hour and could grind 35 to 40 acres of cane per season. The 1892 price was $160.00.

The Victor Mill with Sweep Below

Blymyer offered its Victor Mill with a unique sweep below. The advantages of such an arrangement were touted as "(1) The Mill is more steady, (2) Horses and cane do not interfere with each other, (3) Bagasse is more easily removed, and (4) Juice can flow down to the Evaporator."

1892 Prices for the Victor Mill with Sweep Below

No. 1, $75.00   No. 2, $85.00   No. 3, 1120.00   No. 4, $135.00   No. 6, $175.00

Great Western Cane Mill

For Animal Power. In the Great Western Vertical Cane Mill the cog wheels, which were separate from the rolls, each had two clutches which fastened into corresponding clutches on the rolls. This made a simple, strong fastening gear, did away with keys, and enabled the mill to be readily and quickly taken apart. Oil chambers which held nearly half a pint of oil, brass bearings, and carefully turned wrought iron shafts made the Great Western a quality cane mill.

Cogs were enclosed in this Great Western mill.

Chart for the Great Western Mill

Model No.	Horsepower	Main Roller- D × H	Small Rollers- D × H	Juice Per Hour	Weight	Price 1892
No. 0	1 Horse L.	9¼" × 5"	6¼" × 5"	40 gals.	370 lbs.	$35.00
No. 1	1 Horse	10" × 5⅜"	7" × 5⅜"	50 gals.	470 lbs.	$45.00
No. 2	1 Horse H.	123" × 6½"	7" × 6½"	60 gals.	570 lbs.	$55.00
No. 3	2 Horse	14" × 7⅜"	8" × 7⅜"	80 gals.	875 lbs.	$80.00
No. 4	2 Horse H.	16" × 9"	8" × 9"	100 gals.	975 lbs.	$90.00

Great Western Horizontal Mill

Blymyer made only two sizes of the Great Western horizontal mills. The extra gearing required in horizontal mills for horsepower increase the weight and cost of a mill and requires more power than vertical mills to do the same work.

Chart for the Great Western Horizontal Mill

Model No.	Horsepower	Main Roller- D × L	Small Rollers- D × L	Weight	Price 1892
No. 1	Two to Four HP	12" × 15"	9" × 15"	2,200 lbs.	$200.00
No. 2	Four to Six HP	12½" × 20"	9½" × 20"	2,800 lbs.	$250.00

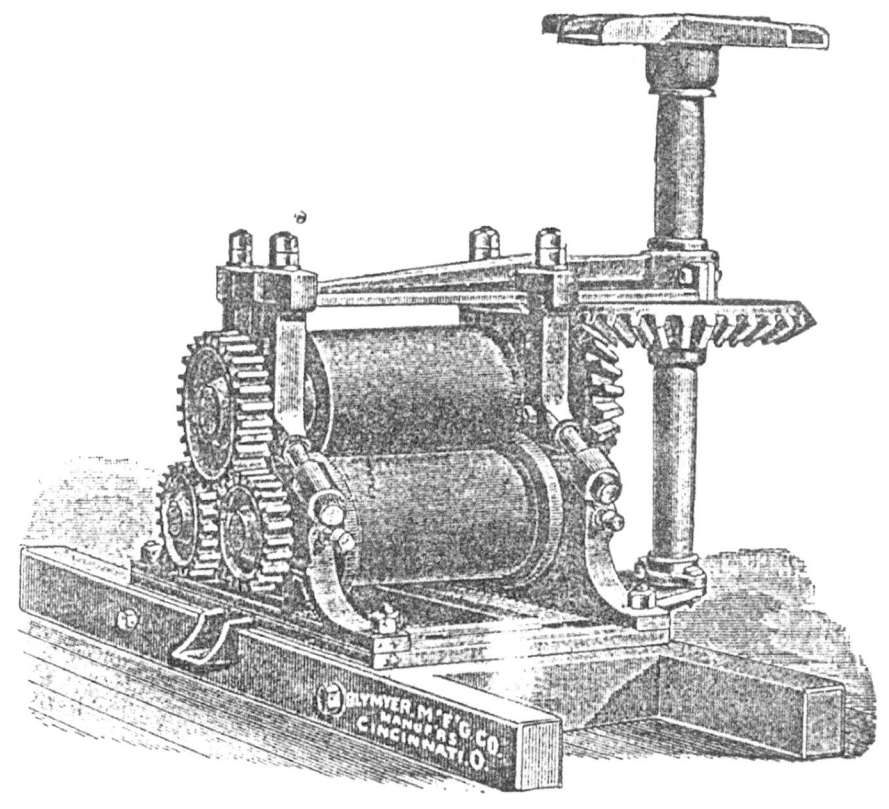

This Great Western horizontal mill had a shaft for animal power.

This horizontal Victor could use steam or water power.

Horizontal Victor Cane Mill

FOR STEAM OR WATER POWER. The horizontal Victor Mill has the same plan as the vertical in dispensing with the guide knife between the rolls. The horizontal mill featured three rollers made extra heavy and strong. A bagasse carrier came with this mill as did a feed box. Upon request, Blymyer would change the pulley to the opposite side of the mill. Four models of this mill were available in 1892.

Chart for the Victor Horizontal Mill

Model No.	Horsepower	Juice Per Hour	Cane in 12 Hours	Cane in a Season	Weight	Price 1892
No. 0	Four HP	140 gals.	8–10 tons	40–50 acres	2,350 lbs.	$250.00
No. 1	Six HP	180 gals.	12–15 tons	50–60 acres	3,350 lbs.	$325.00
No. 2	Eight HP	230 gals.	15–20 tons	60–70 acres	3,700 lbs.	$400.00
No. 3	Ten HP	280 gals.	20–25 tons	70–90 acres	4,000 lbs.	$475.00

Niles Cane Mill

THREE ROLLS, DOUBLE GEARED. This was the "Big Man" of the Blymyer line, designed and constructed for the sugar industry, the leading mill of its class since the 1840s. Blymyer suggested that probably three-fourths of all the plantations in Louisiana were using the

The Niles Mill was the "Big Man" of the Blymyer line.

Niles Mill by the late 1800s. They were first introduced in 1836 by the Niles brothers and quickly became the standard for sugar mills. Twenty sizes were offered in the Niles models in Blymyer's 1892 catalog.

Chart for the Niles Mill

Size Number	L × D of Rolls	Weight	Size Number	L × D of Rolls	Weight
No. 3	16" × 16"	7,500 lbs.	13	54" × 26"	54,000 lbs.
No. 4	20" × 16"	9,000 lbs.	14	54" × 28"	58,000 lbs.
No. 5	24" × 16"	11,000 lbs.	15	60" × 28"	65,000 lbs.
No. 6	24" × 20"	20,500 lbs.	16	54" × 30"	...
No. 7	30" × 20"	23,000 lbs.	17	60" × 30"	...
No. 8	36" × 20"	31,000 lbs.	18	66" × 30"	...
No. 9	36" × 24"	36,000 lbs.	19	60" × 34"	...
No. 10	42" × 24"	39,000 lbs.	20	60" × 34"	...
No. 11	48" × 24"	42,000 lbs.	21	66" × 34"	...
No. 12	48" × 26"	48,000 lbs.	22	72" × 34"	...

Blymyer's 1904 catalog carried this model in thirteen sizes, from the No. 3, which had 16" D × 16" L rollers, could grind 2,970 gallons of juice in a day, weighed 12,500 pounds, and cost $900, to the No. 15, which had 30" D × 60" L rollers, could grind 24,300 gallons in a day, weighed 145,000 pounds and a cost figured on gearing application. The most expensive model listed was the No. 9, which cost $3,500 in 1904.

The Blymyer Iron Works Company purchased the American Seeding Machine Company,

THE "OPAL" HORIZONTAL CANE MILL,
FOR HAND AND POWER.

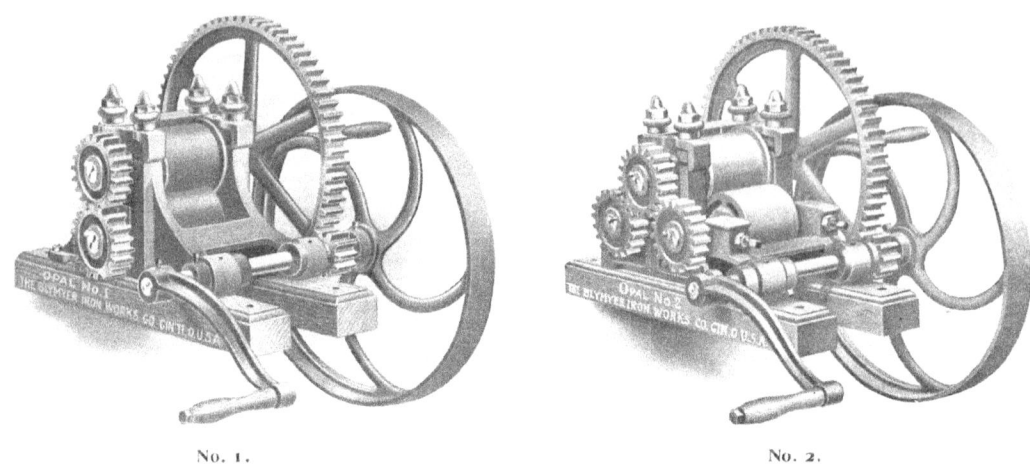

No. 1.   No. 2.

The Opal was a small hand-powered mill.

successors of Brennan and Company, Southwestern Agricultural Works of Louisville, Kentucky, on January 25, 1904. This acquisition gave Blymyer a significantly expanded inventory of mills offered to the public. In addition to the above, the following mills were offered in their 1904 catalog.

The Opal Horizontal Mill for Hand Power

The No. 1 Opal was a two roller mill equipped with single gearing for hand power only. The No. 2 was a three roller mill equipped with single gearing but could be equipped with a pulley so it could be driven by belt. The No. 3 Opal was like the No. 2, except it had double gearing and rather than having a fly wheel with a crank it had a pulley making it a power mill exclusively.

Chart for the Opal Horizontal Mill

Model No.	Power	Rollers D × L	Juice-12 hrs	Tons-12 hrs	Weight	Price 1904
No. 1	1 Man	4" × 4"	100 gals.	⅔	225 lbs.	$25.00
No. 2	2 Men	5" × 5"	175 gals.	1¼	350 lbs.	$40.00
No. 3	½ Horse	5" × 5"	175 gals.	1¼	400 lbs.	$50.00

The Topaz Mill

FOR ANIMAL POWER. The Topaz Mill was designed as an efficient, inexpensive mill for farmers with small operations. However, many features were designed into the mill, making it an excellent operating mill.

Chart for the Topaz Mill

Model No.	Horsepower	Rollers D × L	Juice-12 hrs	Tons-12 hrs	Weight	Price 1904
No. 1	1	6" × 6"	200 gals.	2	250 lbs.	$25.00
No. 2	1	8" × 8"	300 gals.	3	450 lbs.	$35.00
No. 3	2	8" × 10"	400 gals.	4	500 lbs.	$40.00

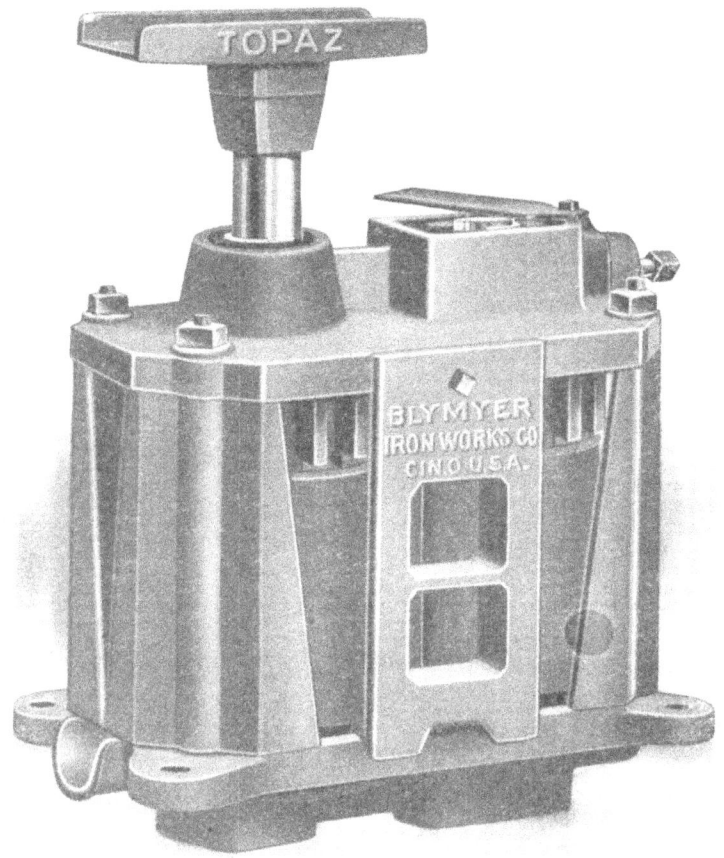

This Topaz mill was an inexpensive mill for small operations.

The Gem Mill

FOR ANIMAL POWER. This little Gem was an all iron two vertical roller mill which came in one size only. This was one of the patents secured from Brennan and Company.

Chart for the Little Gem Mill

Model No.	Horsepower	Rollers D × L	Juice-12 hrs	Tons-12 hrs	Weight	Price 1904
1	1	7⅝" × 8"	250 gals.	2½	275 lbs.	$25.00

The Improved Kentucky Mill

FOR ANIMAL POWER. This is another of the vertical mills which Brennan and Company of Louisville, Kentucky, manufactured before Blymyer purchased the company. Note the covered oil channels on the bottom plate which allowed oiling the mill without removing any part. Gears were cast separate from the rollers and were held with strong clutches. The shaft of the main roller was cast heavy and strong, and is just long enough to enable the mill to be set near the ground without the danger of bending or twisting the shaft. The divided feed guide keeps the cane from lapping and crowding in one place. This mill came in five models.

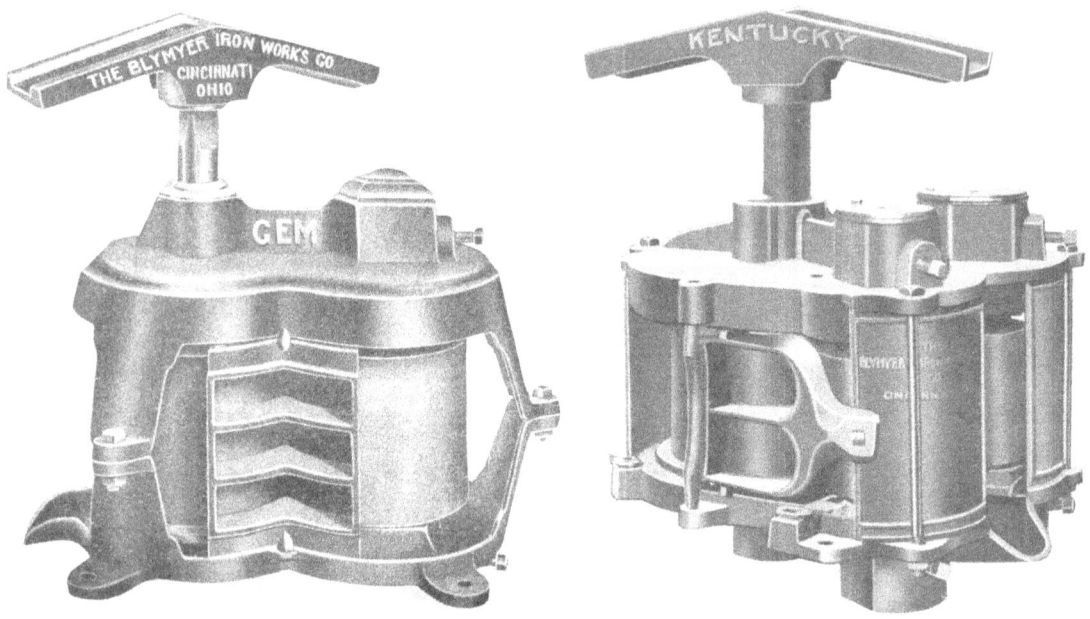

Left: Blymyer's Gem was a small two roller mill. *Right:* The Improved Kentucky was originally one of Brennan's mills.

Chart for the Improved Kentucky Mill

Model No.	Horsepower	Main Roller- D × H	Small Rollers- D × H	Juice- 12 Hours	Weight	1904 Price
No. 0	1 Horse	10⅛" × 5½"	6⅛" × 5½"	400 gals.	400 lbs.	$30.00
No. 1	1 Horse	11⅜" × 6¼"	6¼" × 6¼"	600 gals.	500 lbs.	$40.00
No. 2	2 Horse	13½" × 7½"	7⅛" × 7½"	800 gals.	725 lbs.	$60.00
No. 3	2 Horse	14¾" × 9¾"	8" × 9¾"	1,000 gals.	925 lbs.	$80.00
No. 4	2 Horse	16" × 12"	9¾" × 12"	1,200 gals.	1,300 lbs.	$100.00

The New Live Oak Mill

FOR ANIMAL POWER. The New Live Oak Vertical Mill, with its distinctive sweep cap which eliminated boring holes in the turn pole, came in five sizes and carried quality features similar to the mill above.

Chart for the New Live Oak Mill

Model No.	Horsepower	Main Roller- D × H	Small Rollers- D × H	Juice- 12 Hours	Weight	1904 Price
No. 0	1 Horse	10⅛" × 5¼"	6⅛" × 5¼"	400 gals.	400 lbs.	$30.00
No. 1	1 Horse	11⅜" × 6¼"	6¾" × 6¼"	600 gals.	500 lbs.	$40.00
No. 2	1 Horse	13½" × 7½"	7⅛" × 7½"	800 gals.	725 lbs.	$60.00
No. 3	2 Horse	14¾" × 9¾"	8" × 9¾"	1,000 gals.	925 lbs.	$80.00
No. 4	2 Horse	16" × 12"	9¾" × 12"	1,200 gals.	1,300 lbs.	$100.00

The Kentucky Horizontal Mill "A"

FOR ANIMAL POWER. This is another mill which originated with Brennan and Company and with refinements was manufactured by the Blymyer Iron Works Company. The

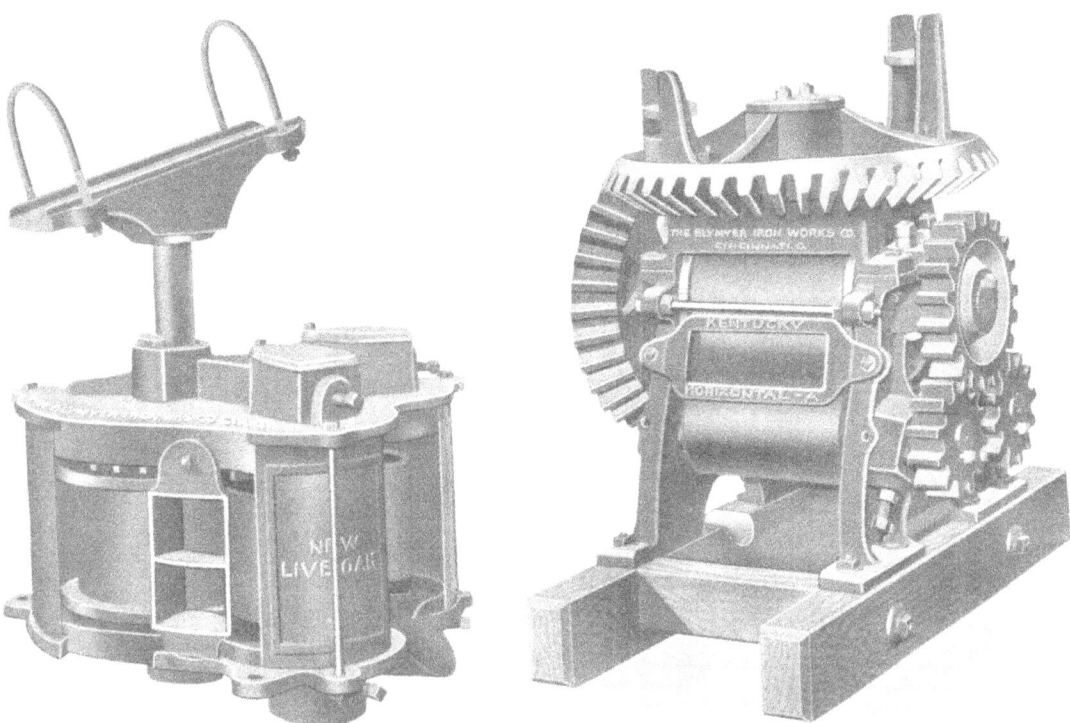

Left: The Live Oak had a distinctive sweep cap. *Right:* Blymyer's Model A was geared for animal power. *Below:* The Model B could grind 150 to 200 gallons of juice per hour.

Kentucky Horizontal size "A" mill was a two horsepower mill having an 11" D × 12" L main roller and two 6⅞" D × 11⅞" L small rollers. This mill could grind 100 to 150 gallons of juice per hour, weighed 1,150 pounds, and cost $125.00

The Kentucky Giant Cane Mill "B"

FOR STEAM POWER. This mill was also formerly made by Brennan and Company of Louisville, and was a heavier mill than the Kentucky Horizontal horsepower mill above. It had scrapers on all rollers and the journals ran in brass lined boxes. This was for the planter growing a larger than average crop of cane. The "B" mill was a four to six horsepower mill having a 12½" D × 14" L large roller and two 8½" D × 14" L small rollers. This mill was

This Kentucky Giant is in service in Tennessee today (courtesy Johnny Tucker, Portland, Tennessee).

capable of grinding 150 to 200 gallons of juice per hour, weighed 1,800 pounds, and listed for $200.00 in Blymyer's 1904 catalog.

The Aurora Horizontal Mill

FOR ANIMAL POWER. One feature which distinguished this Aurora Horizontal Mill from other similar mills is the arched support extending over the main roller from one housing to the other. In the center of this arch a brass cup-shaped journal box is placed in which the sweep shaft turns.

Chart for the Aurora Horizontal Mill

Model No.	Horsepower	Main Roller- D × H	Small Rollers- D × H	Juice- 12 Hours	Weight	1904 Price
No. 1	1 Horse	8" × 9"	6" × 9"	675 gals.	1,250 lbs.	$100.00
No. 2	2 Horse	10" × 10"	8" × 10"	1,000 gals.	1,750 lbs.	$130.00
No. 3	2 Horse	10" × 12½"	8" × 12½"	1,350 gals.	1,900 lbs.	$160.00
No. 4	4 Horse	12" × 16"	10" × 16"	2,100 gals.	4,100 lbs.	$300.00
No. 5	8 Horse	12" × 20"	10" × 20"	2,700 gals.	5,300 lbs.	$450.00

The Ohio Horizontal Mill

FOR ANIMAL POWER. The Ohio horizontal mill was constructed on the French pattern. Notice the heavy horizontal and vertical bolts holding the frame together. Notice also the space between the bottom rollers and the bed plate. The mill was open so all parts were accessible for inspection, cleaning and oiling.

Left: A distinctive arched support over the main roller characterized the Aurora mill. *Right:* The Ohio, constructed on the French pattern, was geared for animal power.

Chart for the Ohio Mill

Model No.	Horsepower	Main Roller- D × H	Small Rollers- D × H	Juice- 12 Hours	Weight	1904 Price
No. 1	1 Horse	8" × 9"	6" × 9"	675 gals.	1,500 lbs.	$130.00
No. 2	2 Horse	10" × 10"	8" × 10"	1,000 gals.	2,050 lbs.	$175.00
No. 3	2 Horse	10" × 12½"	8" × 12½"	1,350 gals.	2,150 lbs.	$200.00
No. 4	4 Horse	12" × 16"	10" × 16"	2,100 gals.	4,700 lbs.	$350.00
No. 5	6 Horse	12" × 20"	10" × 20"	2,700 gals.	5,000 lbs.	$450.00

The Garland Mill

FOR STEAM AND WATERPOWER. The grinding part of the Garland Horizontal Mill is identical to the Aurora Mill. The housing is constructed for steam and water power rather than animal power, and the gearing is of a heavier pattern. The main gear is dished, and the secondary gear and all pinions are half-shrouded. The Garland was offered in five sizes.

Chart for the Garland Mill

Model No.	Horsepower	Main Roller- D × H	Small Rollers- D × H	Juice- 12 Hours	Weight	1904 Price
No. 1	1 Horse	8" × 9"	6" × 9"	675 gals.	1,700 lbs.	$125.00
No. 2	2 Horse	10" × 10"	8" × 10"	1,000 gals.	2,150 lbs.	$155.00
No. 3	2 Horse	10" × 12"	8" × 12"	1,350 gals.	2,300 lbs.	$185.00
No. 4	4 Horse	12" × 16"	10" × 16"	2,100 gals.	4,150 lbs.	$340.00
No. 5	8 Horse	12" × 20"	10" × 20"	2,700 gals.	5,000 lbs.	$475.00

The Colon Horizontal Mill

FOR STEAM AND WATERPOWER. The Colon Horizontal Mill was essentially the Ohio Mill geared for steam and water power rather than animal power. It embodied all the latest

Blymyer's Garland was identical to the Aurora except that it was geared for steam power or water power.

research, technology and improvements fifty years of manufacturing could offer. The Colon was designed so the smaller planter could have a simple, powerful, and rigid mill at his disposal.

Chart for the Colon Horizontal Mill

Model No.	Horsepower	Main Roller- D × H	Small Rollers- D × H	Juice- 12 Hours	Weight	1904 Price
No. 1	1 Horse	8" × 9"	6" × 9"	675 gals.	2,000 lbs.	$160.00
No. 2	2 Horse	10" × 10"	8" × 10"	1,000 gals.	2,300 lbs.	$200.00
No. 3	2 Horse	10" × 12½"	8" × 12½"	1,350 gals.	2,650 lbs.	$220.00
No. 4	4 Horse	12" × 16"	10" × 16"	2,100 gals.	5,000 lbs.	$390.00
No. 5	6 Horse	12" × 20"	10" × 20"	2,700 gals.	5,200 lbs.	$500.00

The Eureka Mill

FOR STEAM AND WATERPOWER. Select materials, the best of workmanship, great strength, durability, simplicity, and the correct proportions of every part made Blymyer consider the Eureka Horizontal Mill to be an ideal mill. The housing is of the French pattern as you will note by the vertical and horizontal bolts holding it together. This mill was offered in six sizes.

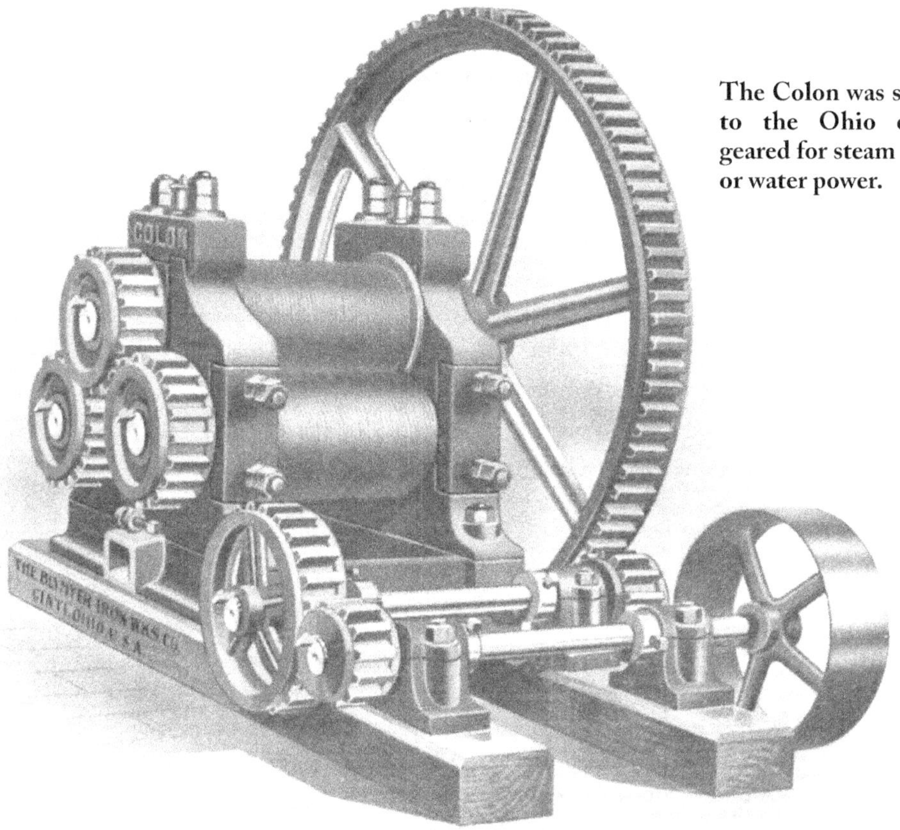

The Colon was similar to the Ohio except geared for steam power or water power.

Blymyer considered the Eureka to be the ideal mill.

Chart for the Eureka Mill

Model No.	Horsepower	Main Roller- D × H	Small Rollers- D × H	Juice- 12 Hours	Weight	1904 Price
No. 1	4 Horse	12" × 15"	9" × 15"	2,400 gals.	4,400 lbs.	$350.00
No. 1 A	4 Horse	12" × 15"	12" × 15"	2,500 gals.	4,600 lbs.	$400.00
No. 2	6 Horse	12" × 18"	9" × 18"	2,700 gals.	5,100 lbs.	$450.00
No. 2 A	6 Horse	12" × 18"	12" × 18"	2,800 gals.	5,400 lbs.	$500.00
No. 3	10 Horse	15" × 22"	15" × 22"	4,050 gals.	9,300 lbs.	$700.00
No. 4	12 Horse	15" × 24"	15" × 24"	4,800 gals.	9,600 lbs.	$875.00

The Blymyer Iron Works Co. carried evaporator pans, cast iron and copper kettles, furnace doors and grates, automatic steam evaporators, and assorted equipment for the sugar and syrup industries.

Blymyer, Day and Company, Mansfield, Ohio

In 1857–58, Mr. Benjamin Blymyer owned and operated a stove and tin store in Mansfield, Ohio. At some subsequent date, Blymyer and Day became associated in business and opened a foundry in Mansfield manufacturing blacksmith drills, screw cutters for hand use, drag and circular saws, cutting boxes, corn shellers, cider mills, sulky revolving rakes, Crawford's patent garden cultivator, the Victor cane mill, amalgam bells for churches, schools and farms, the New Principle refrigerator; they also offered pure Sorgho and Imphee seed. In the later years they manufactured Cook's evaporators and cane mill equipment. About 1874, the Blymyer, Day and Company property on East Diamond Street was purchased by the Mansfield Machine Works, according to the *History of Richland County*. This company manufactured steam engines, circular and Mulay sawmills, plows, turbine waterwheels, reapers, mowers and general foundry castings.

Brennan and Company, Louisville, Kentucky

The Southwestern Agricultural Works was established in 1855, and operated at 312 to 324 Green Street, between Eighth and Ninth, in Louisville, Kentucky, with Abraham G. Munn and Thomas Brennan as chief proprietors. The company was a manufacturer and wholesale dealer in Evans' Patent corn drills; Excelsior cider mills in two sizes; iron road scrapers in three sizes; twelve kinds of hand and power corn shellers; nine varieties of hay, straw, and fodder cutters; iron field rollers; two varieties each of hay and cotton presses; overshot and undershot threshers; four- and eight-horse separators; three varieties of wheat fans; Lynam's patent Kentucky grain drill; Kentucky grain drills and fertilizer spreaders; Kentucky rice drills; one- and two-horse railroad powers; two-, four- and eight-horse lever powers; four-, eight- and ten-horse mounted powers; Varian's wheel harrows; McGinness' steel tooth harrows; circular saw benches; shingle machines; lath benches; saw mandrels; Meiner's patent head blocks; Mulay and circular sawmills.

On June 19, 1877, Abraham G. Munn, Charles T. Clark, and Thomas Brennan were awarded a patent for a cane mill geared for reverse motion, and for a feed guide adapted to operate from either side. The top and bottom plates were so constructed that the feed guide could simply be taken from one side, flipped, and bolted to the other side. This allowed the mill to rotate in either direction. The main roller was constructed with open V shaped lugs with perfectly vertical sides which meshed snugly with matching gears on the small rollers.

Note the prices on this Brennan invoice.

In such a way, the three rollers were held together to prevent any gear from rising up, thus permitting the mill to be operated in either direction.

The company originally operated as Munn and Company. Brennan and Company later became successors to the business and manufactured the Blue Grass mills for the large Belknap Hardware Company. The mechanical genius Thomas Brennan was born in Clogremon, Queens County, Ireland, in 1838 and immigrated to the United States with his grandmother when he was three years old. He got his early training as a machinist in shops in St. Louis, Cincinnati, and Louisville and exhibited an early aptitude for metalwork. Brennan was awarded twenty-seven first prizes for his inventions, including two at the 1893 Chicago World's Fair. He had numerous business interests, including being co-owner and vice president of Brennan & Co., Southwestern Agricultural Works, in Louisville, Kentucky, and along with his brother operated T.M. Brennan and Company in Nashville, Tennessee.

Brennan was a man of strictest integrity, of indomitable will and purpose, yet there lay within him the deepest and warmest sympathies. Not only was he an industrious man, but his entire family were achievers, according to the Brennan House of Louisville. His wife, Anna, the daughter of an Episcopal minister, was well educated, and was an accomplished linguist. She bore nine children, eight of whom lived into adulthood. Two daughters became gifted performing musicians. One son was inspector of customs for the Port of Louisville, another was treasurer of the New York Yankees baseball organization, two sons became doctors, another became an attorney and still another worked with his father at Brennan and Company.

The Nashville foundry, T.M. Brennan and Company, was a manufacturer of steam engines, boilers, sawmills, mill gearing, and ornamental castings. Brennan had already been in business for a number of years at the eruption of the War Between the States, but then turned his attention to the war efforts. His foundry, known locally as the Claiborne Machine Works, on Front Street near Broad, entered into a contract with the state of Tennessee on May 16, 1861 to produce two batteries of iron cannons. This consisted of four 6-pounder and two 12-pounders. Five days later another contract was granted for an additional battery of four 6-pounder and two 12-pounder howitzers. Still another contract was granted on May

25, 1861, for equipment for the guns, such as carriages, caissons, and limbers. The work was apparently completed by August 31 and the state paid the firm $17,639.99. By November Brennan's company was making monthly deliveries of cannons to the Confederate States government. When Nashville fell before the advancing Union troops in February 1862, fourteen Brennan cannons were hurriedly moved to Atlanta, while probably at least a dozen unfinished

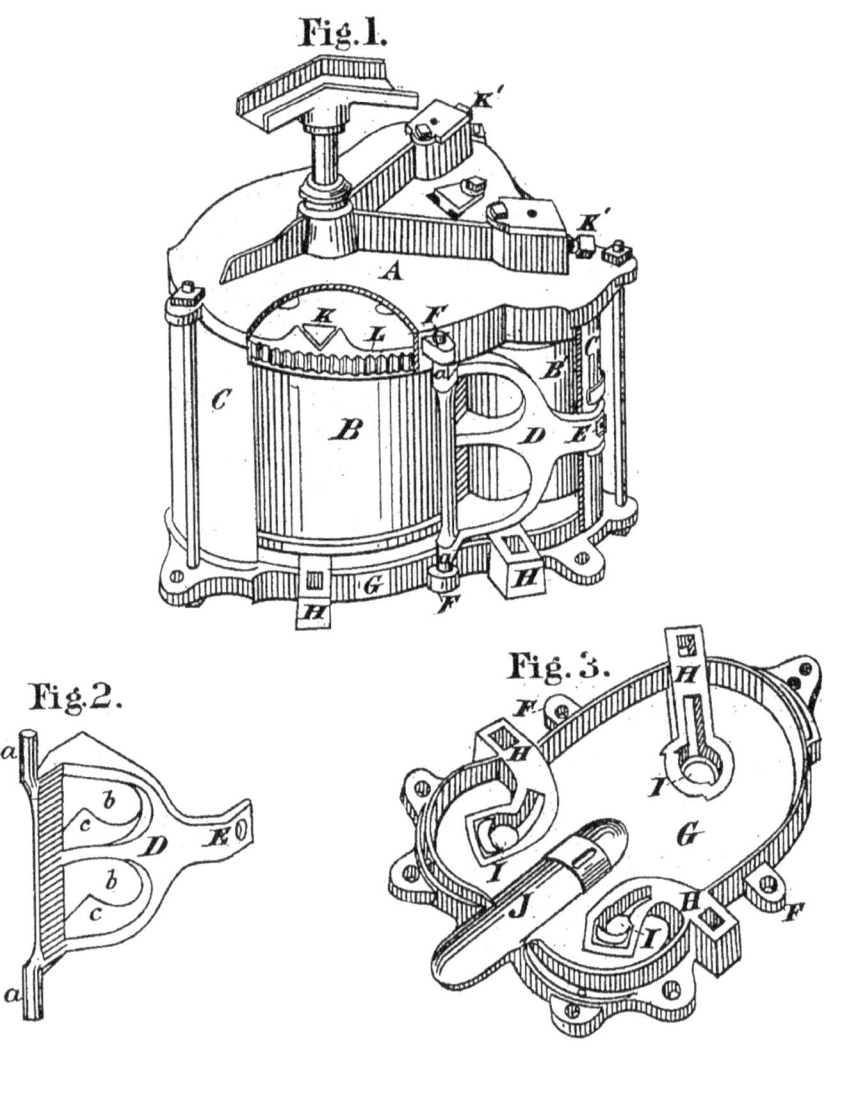

Brennan's mill patent showed its distinctive feed guide.

ones were left at the foundry. On Sunday, March 30, Thomas Brennan and his brother, Joseph, were arrested and tried for treason for their part in arms production for the Confederate army. On July 1, 1863, the machinery from the Brennan foundry was offered at auction by the federal authorities. Somehow Brennan survived the ordeal and his company appeared in the city directory as late as 1874, at which time he was also engaged in business in Louisville, Kentucky. He retired in 1897.

Brennan and Company manufactured the "Kentucky" Sorghum and Sugar Cane Mills, which were three vertical roller mills in five sizes like this model manufactured for Belknap.

Chart for the Brennan Mill

Model No.	Horsepower	Main Roller- D × H	Small Rollers- D × H	Juice- Per Hour	Weight	1879 Price
No. 0	Small 1 horse	10⅜" × 5⅜"	4⅜" × 5⅜"	40 gals.	370 lbs.	$50.00
No. 1	Light 1 horse	11⅜" × 6³⁄₁₆"	6¼" × 6³⁄₁₆"	60 gals.	500 lbs.	$55.00
No. 2	Reg. 1 horse	13⅜" × 7½"	7⅜" × 7½"	90 gals.	720 lbs.	$70.00
No. 3	2 Horse	14¹³⁄₁₆" × 9¼"	8" × 9¼"	100 gals.	900 lbs.	$85.00
No. 4	Hvy. 2 horse	16" × 12"	9" × 12"	120 gals.	1,200 lbs.	$120.00

The distinctive Brennan mill (courtesy of Bill Outlaw, Tallahassee, Florida).

Brennan additionally manufactured horizontal mills which they called the "Amber" Cane Mill. This mill, geared for horsepower, came in three sizes.

Chart for the Brennan Horizontal Mill

Model No.	Horsepower	Main Roller- D × H	Small Rollers- D × H	Juice- Per Hour	Weight	1879 Price
No. 1	1 Horse	9" × 6¾"	6" × 6¾"	60 gals.	500 lbs.	$50.00
No. 2	1 or 2 Horse	9" × 9¾"	6" × 9¾"	75 gals.	575 lbs.	$75.00
No. 3	2 Horse	9" × 13"	6" × 13"	100 gals.	700 lbs.	$100.00

On January 25, 1904, the following announcement appeared in the Blymyer Iron Works Company Catalog.

To Whom It May Concern:

We have sold to the BLYMYER IRON WORKS CO., of Cincinnati, Ohio, the Cane Mill and Evaporator business of which we were the successors of Brennan & Co., Southwestern Agricultural Works, of Louisville, Ky., the sale including the good-will, patterns, patents, etc., of all the cane machinery business heretofore controlled by that Company. As The Blymyer Iron Works Co., is under able management, favorably known to the general trade, and being thoroughly conversant with all the details of this business, we bespeak for them the same liberal patronage which has heretofore been extended to us.

AMERICAN SEEDING CO.
Successors to
Brennan & Co., Southwestern Agricultural Works,
Louisville, Ky.
Springfield, Ohio, January 25, 1904

Buerkens Manufacturing Company, Pella, Iowa

The Buerkens Manufacturing Company had its humble beginning in 1865 in an unassuming blacksmith shop on Main Street, Pella, Iowa. Here the first Buerkens wagons were built, and in the succeeding years the company grew into a sprawling complex doing volumes of business throughout the Midwest. J.B. Sexton, of Burlington, Iowa, had invented a wagon brake, and upon moving to Pella entered into a partnership with Barney Buerkens. His brake came to be used on wagons all over the country. At the height of its productivity the Buerkens Manufacturing Company manufactured 1,500 wagons annually carrying the motto, "Once Tried Always Used." The Buerkens company was known for the sterling quality of its products. Mr. Buerkens often remarked that when he started he had his tools, seventy dollars and a good wife.

Farm wagons were not the only items manufactured by Buerkens, however. Delivery wagons, buggies and bobsleds were produced by this Iowa firm. While no specifics have been found, an ad in *A History of Pella, Iowa, 1847–1987* revealed that they also manufactured cane mills. Experiments in producing sugar were being carried on in Iowa during this time and more desirable strains of sorghum were being produced. This was a productive time for foundries to supply sorghum growers with the needed mills. In 1957 a fire ravaged the ninety-two year old landmark, burning it to the ground and leaving only the bare brick walls of the original structure.

The small print beneath the wagon on this ad advertises cane mills (courtesy Pella Historical Society, Pella, Iowa).

Burdon, Hubbard and Company, Brooklyn, New York

Burdon, Hubbard and Company, 102 Front Street, Brooklyn, New York, had its beginning in a foundry and machine shop established by William Burdon, who, as early as 1836, was manufacturing steam engines of various sizes. For more than two decades Mr. Burdon sustained an excellent reputation as an engine builder, and much of what we know about the company comes from *Scientific American* from the early 1860s. He manufactured and kept on hand steam engines from 3 to 40 horsepower, and engines from 40 to 200 horsepower were made to order. He utilized the latest styles, patterns, and modern improvements and manufactured high pressure engines and engines with condensers, both stationary and portable engines attached with wheels. At some time around 1860, Hubbard joined the firm and the establishment became known as Burdon, Hubbard and Company, machinists and manufacturers. In addition to steam engines the company manufactured steam pumps, saw and gristmills, marble mills, rice mills, quartz mills for gold quartz, waterwheels, shafting and pulleys, hydraulic presses, pumps and gearing for working mines. They maintained an extensive complex where they also manufactured sugar machinery, including cane mills, sugar kettles and vacuum pans. Mr. Burdon was a congenial man who advertised "advice given gratis" and promised that plans could be drawn on short notice. Apparently, either through death, retirement, or sale, Mr. Burdon withdrew from the company in the late 1860s and by 1869 it became Hubbard and Whittaker, still doing business as Burdon Iron Works at 102 Front Street, New York City, and still manufacturing cane mills.

Burlington Foundry and Machine Works, Burlington, Iowa

The Burlington Foundry and Machine Works, Burlington, Iowa, were successors to the C. Hendrie and Company. An early advertisement, prior to 1865, listed Charles Hendrie as president and William C. Hendrie as secretary and treasurer. Their iron foundry and machine works manufactured steam engines, boilers, steam pumps, mining machinery of every description, plain and ornamental fencing, Low's Patent shingle mill, Scarlett Eagle corn and cob mills, amalgam farm bells, jack screws, steam and gas pipe and fittings, sugar mills and evaporators, according to the *Iowa State Gazetteer* published in 1865. The Burlington Foundry and Machine Works also made iron and brass castings to order. Again we see by their production of cane mills that the farmers of Iowa were interested in sugar and syrup production from sweet sorghum.

Central City Iron Works, Selma, Alabama

In September 1856, Edward G. Gregory and R. Coe established the Central City Iron Works and Machine Shops in Selma, Alabama. Their venture was an astounding success, and soon they were having more orders for foundry work than they could fill, according to *Selma: Her Institutions and Her Men*, by John Hardy. To meet the demands upon their company, Central City Iron Works employed Joseph Pollock, by reputation one of the best foundrymen in the South. The forward-looking company also installed the latest equipment available, such as the National Bolt Cutter and the Sturdevant Blower. With the expertise of their laborers and the well equipped shops, Central City Iron Works made steam engines of all kinds to order, and manufactured sawmills, cotton presses, and castings in iron and brass. They were the manufacturers of the famous Alabama Cotton Press, and in their well equipped machine shop they did repairs of all kinds. Central City Iron Works produced sugar cane mills, but to date no sample of their work has been found by this writer.

O.L. Chase Mercantile Company, Kansas City, Missouri

While there are cane mills found bearing the name of O.L. Chase, the company was a mail order house located at 1408 West Eleventh Street, Kansas City, Missouri. A 1900 city directory carried an advertisement for the company and their furniture catalogue. The catalogue contained prices of furniture, baby carriages, organs, pianos, bicycles, and ball bearing sewing machines. One cane mill bearing the O.L. Chase name is consistent with Goldens' flat top models, manufactured by that Columbus, Georgia, firm.

Chattanooga Plow Company, Chattanooga, Tennessee

Newell Sanders was the founding father and guiding influence of the Chattanooga Plow Company, Chattanooga, Tennessee. The Newell Sanders papers in the Chattanooga Public Library helps us understand what a sterling and keen businessman he was. Born July 12, 1850, in Owen County, Bloomington, Indiana, Sanders attended rural schools of the area then graduated from Indiana University in 1873. From 1873 to 1877 he owned and operated a bookstore in Bloomington. Looking for a milder climate for his young family, he visited Chattanooga, where he met and came under the influence of Gen. John T. Wilder. Gen. Wilder envisioned a plow manufacturer in Chattanooga who could entice the Southern farmers to improve their lot by discarding their primitive plows in favor of newer, more productive implements. Sanders began to see the possibilities of such an endeavor and shared his vision with his family in Indiana. His impassioned vision persuaded his stepfather, Mr. Buchanan, to sell the family farm and invest in the venture. Buchanan raised about $6,000, which he loaned to Newell, and in December 1877, Newell moved his wife and two young children, his mother and stepfather and their two children, to Chattanooga, where the Newell Sanders and Company was founded. Sanders was able to start manufacturing his plows in 1878. When chartered in 1883, the company was operating out of a 20' × 40' frame building which had been a stable on the back side of a tract of land in the city. With fewer than ten employees the newly formed company began manufacturing plows. In those early days one to three plows comprised a good order, and the company sold about fifty plows a month. In 1884 the growing company moved to the corner of Carter and Montgomery avenues and employment rose to over three hundred workers. Using up-to-date facilities in which they produced high quality goods closely identifying with the agricultural development of the South, the Chattanooga Plow Company became the nation's second largest manufacturer of chilled plows, the first in manufacturing disc plows, and the first in production of cane mills. Their first plows were sold to Hill & Ledbetter of Resaca, Georgia. Castings for those first plows were purchased from a foundry in Chattanooga run by G.W. Wheland, who would later become a stockholder.

Friction among the stockholders in 1901 led to Newell Sanders' retirement as president of the company. He then developed the Newell Sanders Plow Company, specializing in disc plows, which he made famous. This company was not included in the later International Harvester Corporation's purchase since he made plows almost exclusively for use with tractors. A subsequent conflict among the stockholders led to Sanders being reinstated as president of the company in 1913.

In 1903 the company purchased a large tract of land adjacent to their site where they built a large brick fire-proof pattern house. Their business was thriving, and they needed expanded facilities to meet the growing demands for their products. Chattanooga Plow was shipping car loads of plows to Mexico, South America, and various countries of Europe and Asia, as well as doing an enormous trade in the United States. With this additional space, the company would occupy more space than nearly all industry in or around the city and would become the largest plow manufacturer in the world.

In 1919 the International Harvester Company purchased all 500 outstanding shares of the Chattanooga Plow Company. They had been late getting into the plow business, since threshers had constituted their major line. On May 1, 1919, they purchased the plant and business of the Parlin and Orendorff Company of Canton, Illinois, the oldest plow manufacturer in the country. This gave the International Harvester Company a full and long-established line of implements, but it did not give them chilled plows. The Chattanooga Plow Company had become one of the three largest manufacturers of plows and agricultural

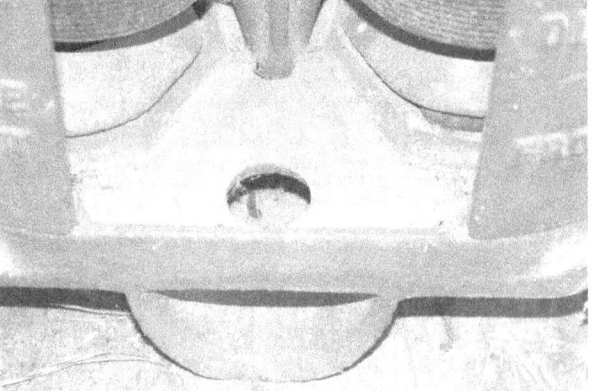

Left: The "Old Red Mill" was Chattanooga Plow's standard mill (photograph by John Dean, Hartford, Alabama). *Top right:* Notice the juice spout drops below the bottom place on this mill found at the Pioneer Museum of Alabama in Troy, Alabama. *Bottom right:* The juice spout is below the hole in the bottom plate.

implements in the United States. Their philosophy, "We belong to no trust but we make goods the farmers' trust," and their motto, "Chattanooga Plows are Crop Makers," served them well. By 1902 they were producing the No. 32 one-horse sandy land plow; a reversible hillside two-horse plow with either wood or steel beam; subsoil plows with either wood or steel beams; double moldboard chilled plows; the No. 17 potato digger; the Chattanooga-Hancock single, double and triple disc plows ("Principle right, Construction right, Results right"); double shovel plows; cane mills and evaporators. They advertised their chilled plow as "The plow that sheds where others fail," and proclaimed that "nothing sticks to it—except farmers." They continued to add to their list of implements until they were purchased by McCormick-Deering in 1919, and that began a new chapter for the company. The earliest reference to the manufacture of cane mills in existing material is 1887. From 1887 to 1905 Chattanooga Plow produced the second and third series of three vertical roller mills, the Nos. 11, 12, 13, and 14, known as The Old Red Mill. In 1905 they began the fourth series of the same mills. The second and third series of mills had a juice spout, as seen below on the left. The fourth series, begun in 1905, had a hole in the bottom plate through which the juice ran into a spout below, as seen in the mill on the right below.

Chart for Chattanooga Plow Three Roller Mills

Model No.	Horsepower	Main Roller- D × H	Small Rollers- D × H	Juice- Per Hour	Weight	1905 Price
No. 11	1 Horse	10" × 5"	5" × 5"	30–40 gals.	380 lbs.	$30.00
No. 12	1 Large Horse	12" × 6"	6" × 6"	40–50 gals.	560 lbs.	$40.00
No. 13	2 Horse	14" × 7"	7" × 7"	50–75 gals.	800 lbs.	$60.00
No. 14	2 Large Horse	16" × 8"	8" × 8"	75–100 gals.	1,024 lbs.	$80.00

In 1897 Chattanooga Plow produced an export series of three-roller mills, the Nos. 22, 23, 24, 25, 122, 123, and 124. These were mills built on the same pattern, but were heavy, powerful mills capable of grinding the heaviest tropical sugar cane at a high rate of extraction.

Chart for Chattanooga Plow's Export Models

Model No	Horsepower	Main Roller- D × H	Small Rollers- D × H	Juice- Per Hour	Weight
No. 22	1 Horse Heavy	12" × 6"	6" × 6"	45–60 gals.	690 lbs.
No. 23	2 Horse	14" × 7"	7" × 7"	60–75 gals.	959 lbs.
No. 24	2 Horse Heavy	16" × 8"	8" × 8"	75–100 gals.	1,470 lbs.

While later repair and parts catalogs carried parts for the No. 25, manufactured 1897 to 1915, no specifics for that model are available. The Nos. 122, 123, and 124 were like the Nos. 222, 23, and 24, but having fluted rollers. A two-roller, steel frame mill, the No. 16, was manufactured from 1905 to 1920. In 1908 they added another two-roller mill, the No. 7, to their production line. This was a one-horse mill having 7" D × 7" H rollers, weighing 499 pounds, and capable of grinding 25 to 40 gallons of juice per hour.

No. 7 Two-Roll Vertical

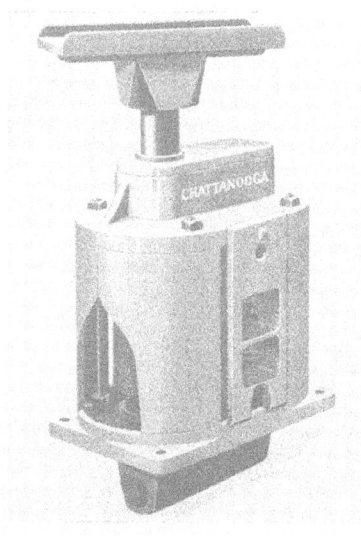

The No. 7 had two vertical rollers.

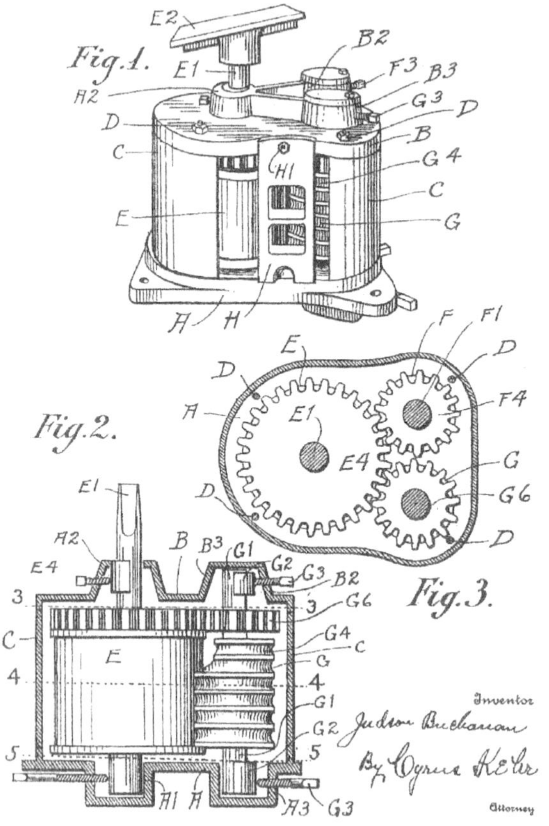

Top left: A Chattanooga Plow mill patent by Buchanan. *Top right:* Some of the Chattanooga company's mills had fluted rollers. *Below:* The No. 44 and No. 144 were geared for steam power or water power.

From 1913 to 1920 a two-horse, three-roller mill, No. 34, was manufactured. Application for a patent for a three-roller mill with a fluted roller was filed October 31, 1916, the patent awarded July 8, 1919, and production began in 1925, after the company was sold. These were the Nos. 111, 112, 113, and 114 fluted.

Chattanooga Plow manufactured horizontal power belt mills as well. In 1897 they produced Nos. 44 and 144 three-roller horizontal mills. These mills had 9" D × 9" L main rollers and 6" D × 9" L small rollers, could grind 175 to 200 gallons of juice per hour, and weighed 1,288 pounds. The No. 144 model had a fluted feed roller.

From 1897 to 1918 they produced a series of horizontal mills geared for steam power.

Chart for Horizontal Mills geared for Steam Power

Model No.	Horsepower	Main Roller- D × H	Small Rollers- D × H	Juice- Per Hour	Weight	Price
No. 44	4 Horse	9" × 9"	6" × 9"	100–150 gals.	1,025 lbs	$150.00
No. 46	6 Horse	12" × 12"	8" × 12"	150–200 gals.	1,825 lbs.	$175.00
No. 72	6 Horse	12" × 12"	8" × 12"	150–200 gals.	2,100 lbs.	$200.00
No. 60	15 Horse	12" × 24"	12" × 24"	300–400 gals.	8,000 lbs.	$1,000.00

In 1903 they added the numbers 45 and 145 to their production line. The 45 and 145 had 9" × 9" main rollers and 6" × 9" small rollers. The 71 and 171 had 9" × 12" main rollers and 6" × 12" small rollers. The 145-A and 171 had fluted feed rollers. The 45-A could grind 175 to 200 gallons of juice per hour and the 71 could grind 200 to 225 gallons per hour. From 1908 to 1921 they manufactured the No. 70 mill. The large roller was 9" D × 7" W and the two small rollers were 6" D × 7" W. The mill weighed 1,000 pounds and could grind 900 to 1,200 gallons of juice per day. Two horizontal three-roller mills were added in 1913. Model No. 92 required 8 horsepower if powered by steam or 12 horsepower powered by gasoline engine. This mill had a 12" D × 12" L main roller and two 8" D × 12" L small rollers, weighed 2,750 pounds, and could grind 2,000 to 2,500 gallons of juice per day.

Several additional mills were produced by Chattanooga Plow in 1915. From 1915 to 1928 they produced the No. 71. This mill required 4.53 horsepower, had a 9" D × 12" L main roller and two 6" D × 12" L small rollers. Weighing 1,388 pounds, this model could grind 175 to 200 gallons of juice per hour.

From 1915 to 1921 they manufactured the No. 109. From 1915 to 1922 the No. 112 was produced. The company

The No. 72 was one of Chattanooga's larger power mills.

manufactured a four horsepower horizontal mill, the No. 44, and a six horsepower horizontal mill, No. 46.

Chattanooga Plow produced a sugar house pattern, the No. 60, with 12" D × 24" L horizontal rollers, adapted for steam power. This mill, without attachments, weighed 6,000 pounds. Though they did not recommend the use of roller cane mills designed to be set in wooden frames, they did manufacture and offer for sale two of them.

Top: The 45A would be classified as a midsize power mill. *Bottom:* The No. 70 had a main roller, 9 inches in diameter by 7 inches wide (photograph by John Dean, Hartford, Alabama).

Several other mills were produced during the 1920s, but that was after McCormick-Deering purchased Chattanooga Plow. Please see the chapter on McCormick-Deering for additional history of this proud and productive company.

Power adaptations were available from Chattanooga Plow. There were the belt-power attachments for mills numbers 22, 122, 23 and 123.

Mills equipped with clutch couplings for water power were available in the later years. Chattanooga Plow manufactured some mills, like this one shown below, which are now

Top: The No 92 was one of Chattanooga's larger power mills. *Bottom:* The No. 92 weighed more than 2,700 pounds.

Above: Model 109 was only produced six years. *Below:* The No. 46 was a six horsepower mill.

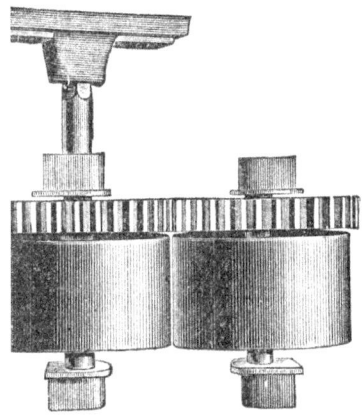

Top: The sugar house pattern was No. 60. *Bottom:* Chattanooga Plow offered rollers without frames.

difficult to identify. This mill is mounted on four pieces of railroad irons. The only visible identification is the name of the company and 567 Patent Pending stamped on the feed guide.

Other syrup-making accessories were produced by Chattanooga Plow, such as water power connections, bagasse carriers, feed tables, juice pumps, evaporators, kettles, brick and stone furnaces.

The Chattanooga Plow Works plant and equipment of the International Harvester Company were sold to the Harriman Manufacturing Company of Harriman, Tennessee, in 1944. Harriman, a company which had been incorporated on March 13, 1913, had purchased the patterns and the right to use the trade name of the famous Chattanooga Plow in 1941 and had begun manufacturing at their Harriman plant. The International Harvester Company was building new and larger facilities in Memphis, where they were transferring their operations to, but retained a portion of the Chattanooga property for a retail store and service

Above: Power adaptations were also available from the company. *Below:* The No. 192 was designed for water power.

Rollers attached to rails makes this an unusual mill.

department. Once the Chattanooga property was vacated, Harriman moved their operations to those facilities, where they manufactured chilled plows.

Newell Sanders, the founder of Chattanooga Plow, served his community as Alderman of Chattanooga from 1882 to 1886, and, upon the death of Senator R.L. Taylor, was appointed to fill the vacancy in the U.S. Senate. He served his state in this capacity from April 11, 1912, to January 24, 1913, and declined to seek reelection. Retiring from public life in 1927 Sanders lived out his life in his home on Lookout Mountain overlooking the city he loved and in which he had labored.

Christiana Machine Company, Christiana, Pennsylvania

In 1833, Mr. William Noble built a foundry to cast necessary parts for his mills, factories and farm machinery, as well as for building and repairing railroad cars on the newly expanded line. He withdrew from the foundry business and leased the works to Col. James Boon and William Dripps, who continued the work until the spring of 1838. At that time, Dripps secured a site, erected a foundry at Midway and did such an extensive business that he took much of the trade away from the Noble foundry. Due to loss of business, lack of skilled workers, and the general dilapidation of the equipment, all operations ceased at the Noble foundry by the middle of 1844. In the summer of 1846, S.L. Denney purchased Noble's foundry and twelve acres of land. He revived the foundry, installed a machine shop, and established the Christiana Machine Shop, according to the *History of Lancaster County*, by Ellis and Evans. Other businesses were established in the community in 1847, and at that time the town was named Christiana, in honor of William Noble's first wife, Christiana.

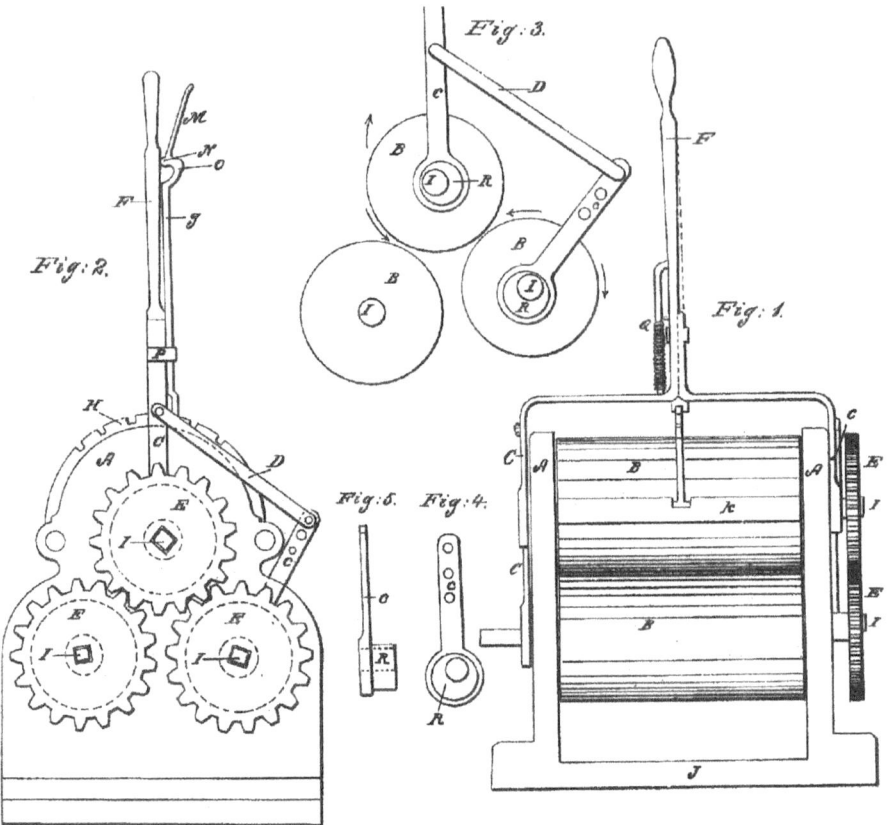

Isaac Broomell purchased the property, tools and fixtures in April 1863. On September 28, 1858, S.L. Denney had received Patent No. 21,601 for improvements in a cane mill. He sold the rights to Isaac Broomell, who began manufacturing them. The mills sold quickly until the end of the war when the demand suddenly ceased. A large number of the mills had to be remelted and converted to other uses. In the spring of 1864, E.G. Broomell joined his father in the firm and the name was changed to I. Broomell and Son. Other sons were subsequently admitted to the firm and the company name was changed to I. Broomell and Sons.

The cane mill designed by S.L. Denney and manufactured by Isaac Broomell was designed to simplify regulating space

Top: Denney's patent provided for pressure to be regulated with a lever. *Right:* A rendering of how Denney's mill looked.

between the rollers and was aimed at persons not accustomed to adjusting machinery. Denney's design accomplished this by mounting, supporting and adjusting the rollers in eccentric bearings. The space between the rollers was regulated by an upright lever which carried a stop, the lower end of which entered and fit snugly into the notches in the toothed selector. The top roller and the front bottom roller were so made that when the space between them was decreased the space between the top roller and the back bottom roller was decreased in an exact ratio. One could simply manipulate the lever to secure the desired spacing between the rollers. A wonderful rendering of the mill is found in *Scientific American*, June 11, 1864. Denny's mill was manufactured in various sizes, both in vertical and horizontal models. Power adapters for steam, water or animal power were also available.

Clark Sorgo Machine Company, Cincinnati, Ohio

Much of what we know about the Clark Sorgo Machine Company is from *The Sorgo Journal and Farm Machinist* of 1863, and from their company catalog. The Clark Sorgo Machine Company, successor to the W. H. Clark Company, was incorporated in March 1863 with a capital stock of $50,000 for the purpose of establishing in Cincinnati a complete and permanent factory for the production of sugar cane mills and other farm machinery. Special efforts were made by the fledgling company to secure and maintain high standards in management and production to the end that every article produced was the best of its kind. To this end extra precaution was taken to employ competent managers and skilled workmen. The introduction of sweet sorghum into America in the early 1850s, and its subsequent widespread cultivation, gave rise to a demand for cane mills and other related equipment. Clark's special aim was to improve the sugar cane mill to the utmost. Their company held no less than eleven original patents which covered about all the advances attainable in a cane mill. In every state where sorghum is grown, when these mill have entered competition at state fairs, they have received the award of first premium. Their mechanical department was under the management of William H. Clark, who had been associated with the manufacture of cane mills "since the first mill for crushing Northern Cane was made in the country."

Clark offered their sorgo cane mills in several sizes and patterns, including the Hedges patented vertical mill to which they applied their own improvements. Hedges' Clark mills of 1860, 1861, and 1862 were designated as Old Style, and the newer models labeled as the Victor Mill. Nineteen different sizes and patterns were offered by the company.

Clark Old Style Mill

The Old Style Mill was of Hedges patent of 1859 with Clark's improvements of 1860–1862. This engraving represents the series consisting of numbers 3, 4 and 5 of the Old Style Mills. Since they made so many other styles, they discontinued the numbers 1 and 2. The No. 3 light, was a two horse mill capable of grinding 80 gallons of juice per hour. The No. 4 heavy, was considered a two horse mill capable of grinding 100 gallons of juice per hour. The No. 5 "Invincible" was either a two or four horse mill and could grind 120 gallons of juice per hour.

There were several advanced features about this mill which the company lauded. The feed box was a narrow vertical opening to insure parallel entrance of cane between the rollers, and thus prevented overlapping. The fluted rollers grabbed the cane upon entry into the mills, and the fluted rollers also crushed the cane at short intervals insuring a more ready flow of juice. A hand hole was built into the top plate so that, in case there was an accumulation

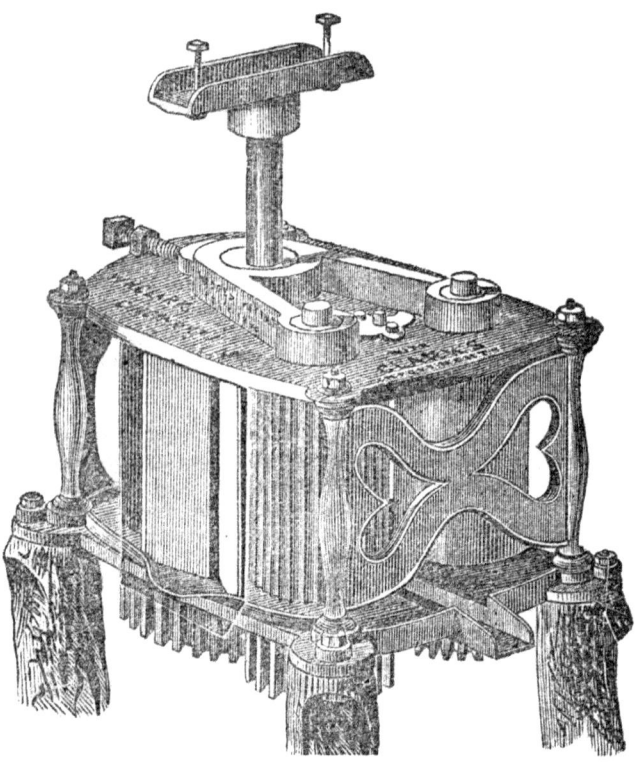

Above: Clark's "Old Style" mill. *Below:* Clark's Victor mill was a favorite (courtesy of Bob McGuire, Lenexa, Kansas, and Bill McGuire, Oregon, Missouri).

of cane between the rollers, the cane could be easily removed without removing the top plate. The company noted that to remove the top plate involved "necessarily a loss of time, and sometimes the loss of temper." The mill also had an adjustable scraper held in place by means of a spring, thus held against the feed roller cleaning it and insuring the clear passage of bagasse. Oil tubes passed down along the shafts, through the center of the rollers, carrying oil from the upper to the lower journals. Annular ledges were build around the lower journals to keep juice from coming into contact with the oil. A bridge plate enabled the juice channel to go into the triangular space between the rollers where it received the juice as it fell from the rollers without spreading all over the bottom plate and picking up impurities which collected there.

Victor Vertical Mill

The Victor Mill was also called the New Style vertical mill. It was offered in six sizes. The No. 0 was a light one horse mill capable of grinding 40 gallons of juice per hour. The No 1 was a small, one horse mill which could grind 60 gallons per hour. The No. 2 was a large, one horse mill capable of grinding 80 gallons of juice per hour. The No. 3 was a small, two horse mill which could grind 100 gallons per hour. The No. 4 was a regular, two horse mill capable of grinding 120 of juice per hour, and the No. 5 was a large, two horse or four small horse mill capable of grinding 170 gallons of juice per hour. The gearing on the No. 5 was above the top plate.

In common with the Old Style, the Victor had the slotted feed box, fluted feed roller, oil tubes with annular ledges, and in addition the lapped gearing of the master roller was made double the width of that on the small rollers. This caused the gearing of the small rollers to overlap, bringing the faces of the small rollers in direct contact, and dispensed entirely with the guide or scraper between the rollers.

The Victor Mill had flanges on the master roller to keep the cane from traveling off the rollers. Diagonal braces of wrought iron, projecting outward gave the mills much more strength than those with upright supports. Oil tight boxes insured perfect oiling of the lower journals. A removable sweep cap by means of a square eye in it allowed the operator to remove it at will. An adjustable false plate was supported under the feed roller and extended over the edge of the bottom plate insured the bagasse didn't drag through the juice reabsorbing it. Cleaning scrapers were attached to the stay braces on the discharge side of the mill, held in place by springs against the face of the rollers, insuring the working portion of the mill was always kept clean.

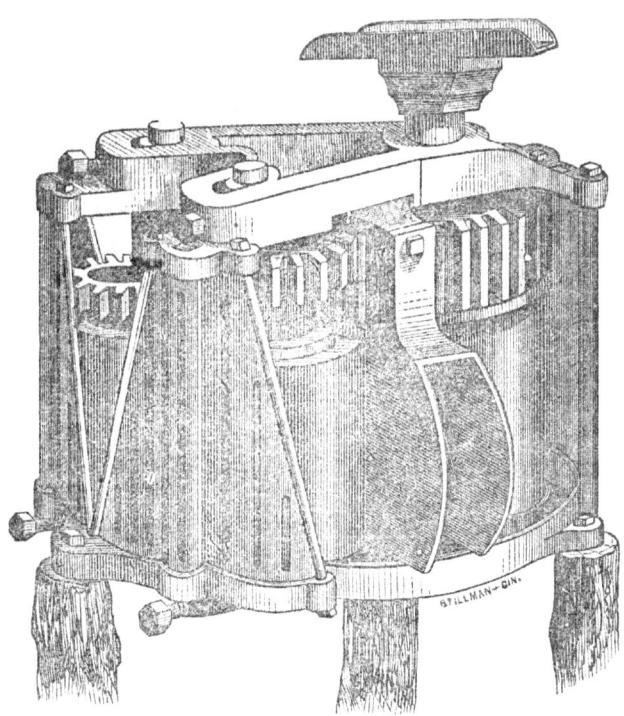

Above: **This is Clark's "New Style" vertical roller mill.**
Below: **Clark made the Victor mill with a sweep below.**

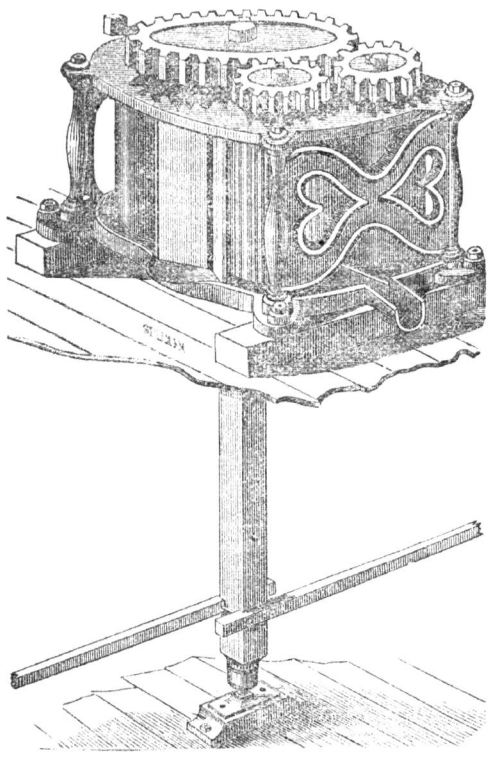

Vertical Mill with Sweep Below

The Old Style mills with sweep below were offered in styles Nos. 3–5, and the Victor New Style mills were offered in Nos. 0–5. The advantages of the sweep below were that the mill was more steady, the horses and the cane did not interfere with each other, the bagasse was more easily removed and the juice could flow downward to the evaporator.

New Back-Geared Horizontal Mill

This mill was designed for working with heavy and detached power, horse, steam, or water. This model was offered in four sizes. The No. 1 was a four horse mill capable of grinding 30 gallons of juice per hour per horse. The No. 2 was a six to eight horse mill, and could grind

30 gallons of juice per hour per horse. The No. 3 was a ten horsepower steam powered mill capable of grinding 450 gallons per hour. Clark also manufactured a Plantation Mill capable of grinding 300 gallons of juice per hour.

In addition, the Cincinnati company manufactured plain iron pans; steam coil evaporators; bells for churches, fire engines, schools and farms; corn crushers; hand and power cider mills; road scrapers; cider, wine, lard and tobacco screws; kitchen mills; small power grinding mills; agricultural boilers; furnace irons; circular crosscut saws; skimmers and other syrup related items. Clark sold cane seed as well and was a general agent for the purchase and sale of Northern Cane Syrup, as advertised in *The Sorgo Journal and Farm Machinist*, a publication of the company.

In December 1866, this announcement was made in the Cincinnati newspaper relative to the Clark Sorgo Machine Company:

Notice.

Office of SORGO MACHINE CO.,

Cincinnati, Dec. 15, 1866.

Notice is hereby given that the CLARK SORGO MACHINE COMPANY has re-organized, with a capital of $300,000, under the corporate name of BLYMYER, NORTON & CO.

All the members of the original company remain in the new organization. The same line of business will be continued, together with the manufacture of Agricultural Implements and other Machinery, and with enlarged facilities. All unsettled business with the former company will be adjusted by their Successors, *Blymyer, Norton & Co.*

CLARK SORGO MACHINE CO.
BLYMYER, NORTON & CO.

Notice.

Office of BLYMYER, BATES & CO.

Mansfield, O., Dec. 15, 1866.

Notice is hereby given that the firm of BLYMYER, BATES & DAY, has organized, with a Capital of $300,000, under the corporate name of BLYMYER, DAY & CO.

All the members of the original firm remain in the new organization. The same line of business will be continued, together with the manufacture of Agricultural Implements and other machinery, and with enlarged facilities.

All unsettled business with the firm of BLYMYER, BATES & DAY, will be adjusted by their successors, *Blymyer, Day & Co.*

BLYMYER BATES & DAY,
BLYMYER, DAY & CO.

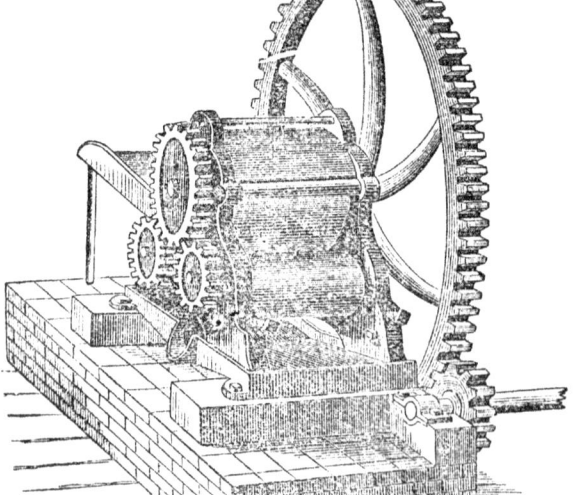

Clark's new version of a back-geared mill.

Clinton Foundry, New York, New York

Reaney and McKinley were owners and operators of the Clinton Foundry, 502 and 504 Water Street, New York, New York. The foundry did loam and dry sand casting to order, and kept a large, valuable set of pulley and machinery patterns on hand. They maintained a large general assortment of pulleys in stock. Reaney and McKinley manufactured printing and steam cylinders, sugar pans, kettles, vats, and curbs. They manufactured cane mill rollers but, though *Scientific American* made numerous references to the work of the foundry, none of the resources searched described their models.

Hiram Close, M.L. Parry and James A. Cushman, Galveston, Texas

Hiram A. Close, M.L. Parry, and James A. Cushman manufactured steam engines, boilers, sugar mills, kettles, iron and brass fittings in Galveston, though it is unclear what kind of business these gentlemen had. Mr. Close was the founder of the first iron foundry and machine shop in the city of Galveston, a business he established in 1844. As the sugar region of south Texas grew there was a demand for cane mill and sugar mill equipment. The first year in business was a disaster, and Mr. Close could not even pay his laborers. With interest on his capital invested continuing to grow, and his machinery wearing out, his future looked dismal. However, in his third year of operation he produced a net return of approximately $3,000. By 1860, his capital investment was $80,000 and he employed over sixty hands. Hiram A. Close passed away on March 9, 1876, at eighty years of age.

In *History of the Island and the City of Galveston*, by Charles W. Hayes, the author reports that Morgan L. Parry established an iron foundry in Galveston in 1850, and its value increased to $40,000 by 1861. When the Federals occupied the city in October 1862, the foundry closed. It could have well been producing cannons for the Confederate army, but it never opened again.

Other than these references this writer cannot offer any further history of the companies nor explain the relationship between these men other than they have been named together as manufacturing cane mills in Galveston.

Coldwell-Wilcox Company, Newburgh, New York

The Coldwell-Wilcox Company was founded in Newburgh in 1884 with a shop at 118 Washington Street. Early city directory entries listed them as machinists, builders of iron fences, crestings and lawn mowers. The product list included rock and ore crushing machinery and sugar cane mills.

H. Dudley Coleman Machinery Company, New Orleans, Louisiana

H. Dudley Coleman enlisted in the Confederate army and, at the end of the Civil War, returned to New Orleans as a nineteen-year-old lad with a life's savings of fifty cents Confederate currency. He soon found a job as a clerk making five dollars weekly, but then moved on to work with a machinery and agricultural implement dealer for fifty dollars per month. His father, Willis P. Coleman, established a business in 1850 manufacturing corn mills of

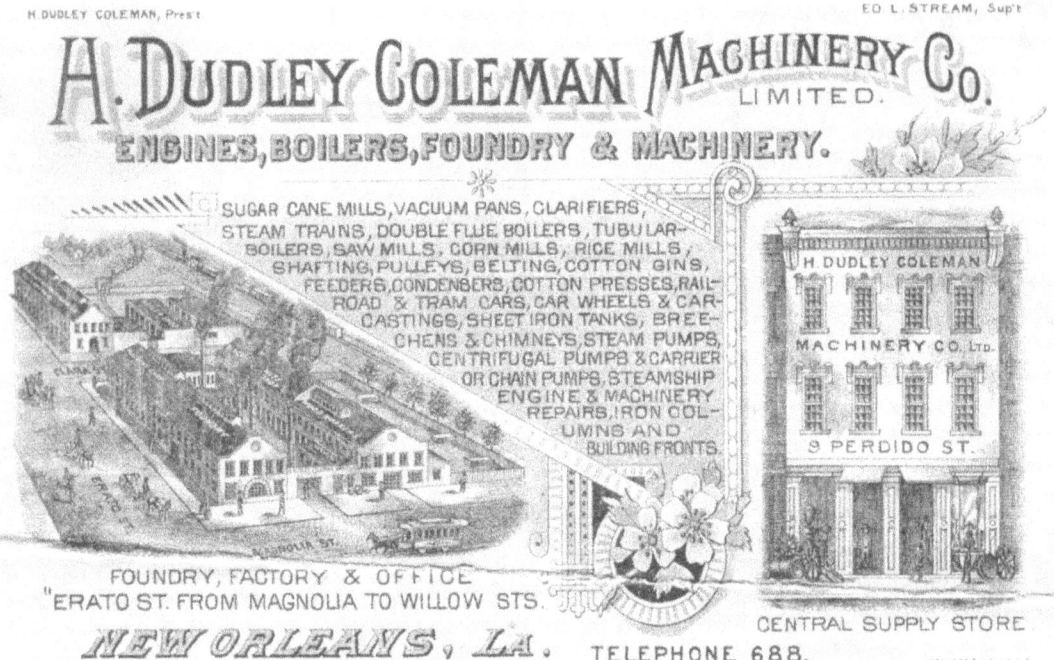

Coleman's business card states that he made cane mills among other items (courtesy Louisiana Division, New Orleans Public Library).

his own invention. When the elder Coleman passed away in 1868 H. Dudley and his brother, Will H. Coleman, succeeded him in business, establishing the H. Dudley Coleman and Brother Company. In the spring of 1879 the brothers purchased the Bennett and Lurges Foundry, occupying nearly all of a square bounded by Magnolia, Erato, Clio and Clara streets, with the intention of manufacturing their famous mills, presses, sawmills, steam engines, and plantation equipment. The brothers manufactured the large steam engine which powered their machinery. In 1884 Will resigned from the partnership and H. Dudley became the sole owner, quite a step for a young man who entered the working world with fifty cents in his pocket. Now the H. Dudley Coleman Machinery Company was poised for excellent growth. In *Pen Illustrations of New Orleans, 1881–1882* (Jno. E. Land, 1892), we find an excellent overview of the company. With one hundred fifty employees manufacturing four hundred mills annually, the company shipped their products throughout the South, West, and Northeast, and had a branch house in St. Louis which carried their goods. Coleman's company was a representative and agent for numerous prestigious manufacturers of agricultural machinery, including Brennan and Company of Louisville, Kentucky.

Coleman's product list was much more extensive than just cane mills. He produced Coleman's corn mills; Coleman's Pony sawmills; standard sawmills; simple screw cotton presses; Simmon's Patent Friction Power Presses for baling cotton, hay, hides, grass or moss; cotton seed carriers; shafting; pulleys; castings; gearing; grate bars; boiler fronts; boiler irons; and "Maid of the South" gristmill. When, in 1891, Coleman was asked what constituted the business of the foundry, he replied that steam boilers and sheet iron work was the largest segment of their business and next was power transmission machinery such as shafting, pulleys and hangers. Miscellaneous work was next followed by corn mills and repair work. The fifth largest segment of their work included sugar cane mills, draining pumps, elevators, rice mill pounders and machinery, sawmill engines and repairs, railroad work, castings and repairs on second hand machinery. The H. Dudley Coleman Company, New Orleans, Louisiana, was one of several companies in New Orleans which manufactured sugar cane mills.

Columbus Iron Works, Columbus, Georgia

Adaptability was the key to success and an ongoing characteristic of the Columbus Iron Works from its beginning in 1853. The driving force in those early days was William Riley Brown, founder of the company. Brown was born in Monticello, Georgia, on April 27, 1822, and moved to Columbus in 1839. By 1848, while just a young man, he had unofficially established Columbus Iron Works as a working combination of Brown's Foundry, Goldens' Machine Shop, Love's Variety Shop, Churchill's Rolling Mill, Fell's Cannon Factory, and Stanford Boiler Manufactory. Brown's collegial spirit, adaptability and drive continued to influence the company over the next forty years.

The official beginning of Columbus Iron Works occurred in 1853 when W. Riley Brown met with Harvey Hall, Isaac J. Moses, and William A. Beach and formally organized the company. Incorporated in 1856, the company positioned itself to meet the needs of a growing industrial city. Located on the banks of the Chattahoochee River near the steamboat landing, Columbus Iron Works was in the heart of a flourishing community. By 1860 the company was offering a wide variety of cast iron products, including cauldrons, kettles, ovens, gears, steam engines from six to forty horsepower, brass castings, cane mills, gristmills, sawmills and cast iron columns.

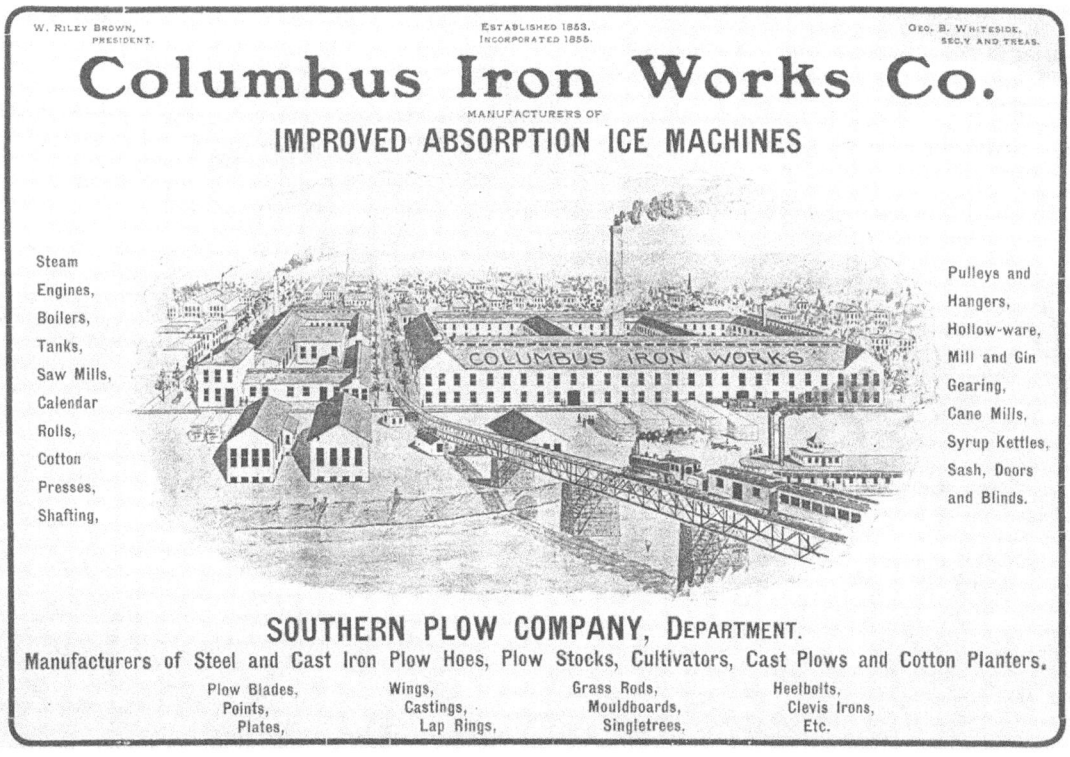

This early ad shows Columbus Iron Works' massive plant.

At the onslaught of the Civil War, Columbus Iron Works had to prove its adaptability once again. Turning its resources to the war effort, the company first made small cannons for local military units. They made the "Ladies' Defender," a small cannon cast in brass collected by the women of Columbus. The company also made the "Red Jacket," the cannon used by the Columbus Guards to salute Jefferson Davis at his inauguration in Montgomery, Alabama, the capital of the Confederacy. They entered into a contract with the Confederate Ordnance Department in 1862 to manufacture brass twelve-pounder cannons, mold and machine mortars, and a wrought-iron rifled cannon. In June 1862, the Ordnance Department established the Columbus Iron Works as the Columbus Arsenal and they manufactured all the large cannons made in the city of Columbus.

Also in June 1862, the Confederate navy leased the ironworks and its adaptability came into play again, as a large part of the plant was converted to the manufacture of steam engines and boilers for the navy's ships. Columbus engines powered at least fourteen vessels for the Confederate navy, including the iron-clad *Muscogee* and the gunboat *Chattahoochee*. James H. Warner headed the conversion of the facilities to military production. Warner was a chief engineer of Gosport, Virginia, and was one of the highest ranking chief engineers in the Confederate navy at the outset of the war. Columbus Iron Works made the transition to supplying the war cause by operating twenty-four hours a day with over 400 employees producing boilers and engines, cannons, and constructing gunboats.

During the night of April 16, 1865, a week after Gen. Robert E. Lee's surrender, Gen. James Wilson's cavalry captured Columbus. Then, on April 17, the Union Troops methodically burned all the cotton within the city of Columbus, along with all war-related industries, including the Columbus Iron Works. Once again the company's adaptability was called upon. Rather than declaring bankruptcy the stockholders doubled the company's capital and rebuilt a larger facility. Columbus Iron Works resumed operation in August 1866 with W. Riley Brown as president and George J. Golden, whose sons would later build Goldens' Foundry, as superintendent. The reinvigorated company's gears, pulleys and shafts helped rebuild the devastated industry of Columbus. Following the war there was a great demand for agricultural implements. This led to the creation of a subsidiary, and in 1877 the Southern Plow Company was formed. During the difficult period of Reconstruction in the South, and the tremendous depression of the economy, Columbus Iron Works paid its employees with its own issue of money.

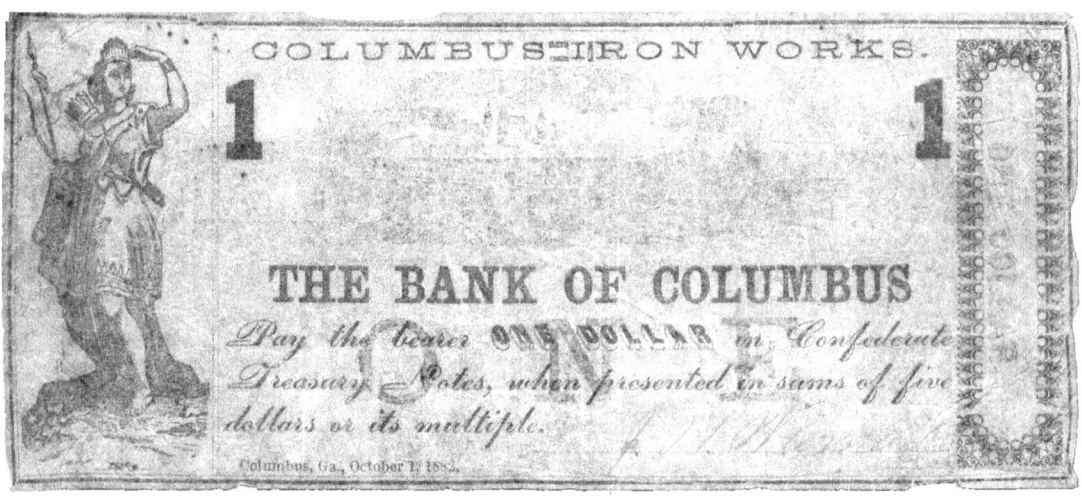

This company dollar bill was issued after the Civil War.

The demands of the war had challenged the capacity of the company, and each new demand developed new technologies. This adaptability enabled the company to successfully market its most distinctive product—the commercial ice machine. In 1870 they began designing a unit, and in June 1872 the Columbus Ice Manufacturing Company was put into operation by Columbus Iron Works. A partnership with H.D. Stratton was established in 1883, and they began producing the Stratton's Improved Absorption Ice Machine, one of the earliest units to be mass-produced in America. Columbus Iron Works led the field in these refrigeration systems for the next thirty years. Nancy Telfair states in *A History of Columbus* that at the height of the company's productivity it was "the largest foundry south of Richmond."

Some mills were issued with the Teague nameplate (photograph by John Dean, Hartford, Alabama).

On April 11, 1902, Columbus Iron Works burned, and only the 1890 foundry of the two-block complex remained standing. Being adaptable once again, a large plant was built from 1902 to 1907 and it remained basically unchanged for the next sixty-five years. The ironworks layout was complex, but productive. There was a large southern bay which held the foundry. The east-west bay contained the machine shop where ice machines, steam engines, cane mills, and stoves, along with its other products, were machined and assembled for market. This machine shop expanded its work by maintaining steam locomotives servicing Columbus. North of the machine shop was a planning area and powerhouse where a steam engine supplied the company's electricity from 1907 to 1930. The corporate offices were located north of the railroad trestle.

For all these years William Riley Brown had been the inspiration and driving force of the company, and upon his death in 1902 the Teague hardware family of Montgomery took over controlling interest. Columbus Iron Works continued to produce a wide variety of hardware items, which fit nicely into the Teague's Montgomery business. However, the refrigeration division began to fall upon hard times. The industry was moving toward smaller units, and here Columbus Iron Works failed to adapt and change with the times. They discontinued production in the 1920s.

In 1925 the controlling interest of the company was purchased by long-time stockholder and prominent businessman W.C. Bradley, and under his leadership the company offered the same variety of products, but gradually concentrated on fewer, more profitable items. These were turbulent times for the foundry. The Great Depression and the expansion of rural electrification hurt some sales, especially the coal and wood burning stoves and heaters. Looking for new markets, the company began experimenting with barbeque grills in the 1940s and sold the first covered barbeque grill under the name Char-Broil in 1953. The W.C. Bradley Company absorbed the Columbus Iron Works in 1965 and in 1974 moved to new facilities north of the city. After 121 years of operation in downtown Columbus the foundry was closed. The Columbus Foundries, a separate manufacturer, purchased the automated foundry and continued to sell cast-iron products across the nation.

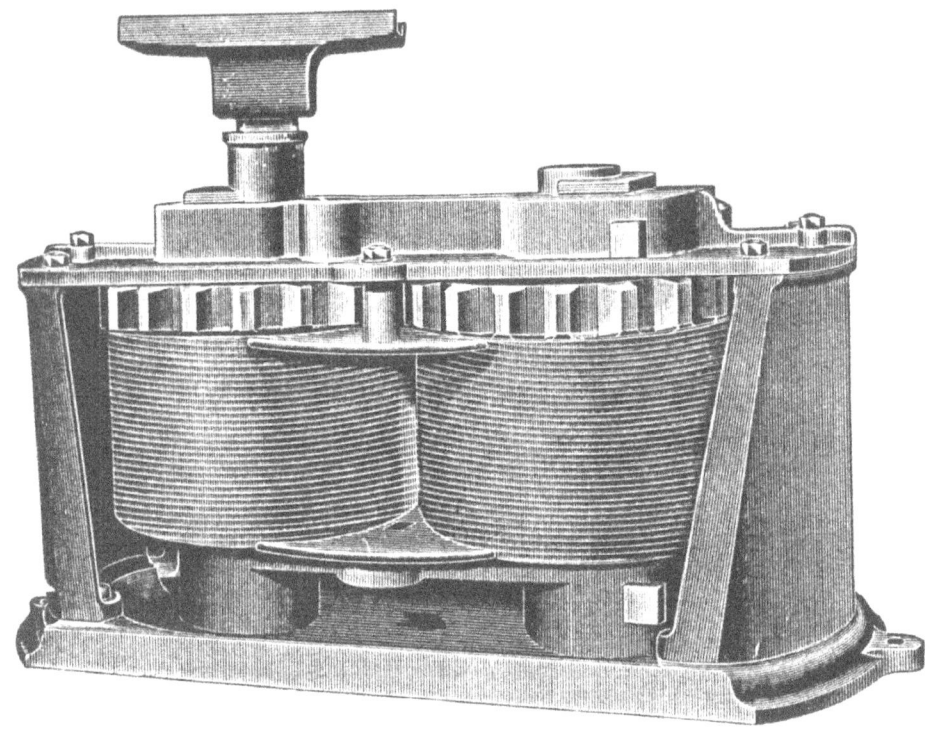

Above: The company engraving of its two roller mill. *Below:* This is a Columbus Iron Works two roller mill.

Yet, the Columbus Iron Works lives on. In 1975 the W.C. Bradley Company sold the southern half of the old ironworks to the city of Columbus well below market value and the Columbus Iron Works Convention and Trade Center was established at a cost of $8,000,000. It is now a beautiful National Historic Landmark Site. During the first seventeen hours after its opening on September 15, 1979, over 66,000 persons passed through to admire the proud structure. It is a convention and trade center of which the people of Columbus can be justly proud.

Two-Roller Cane Mills

Columbus Iron Works made two roller mills in four sizes. This mill featured very large bearings made of babbitt metal.

Chart for Colombus Iron Works Two Roller Mills

Model No.	Horsepower	Roller Size- D × H	Juice Per Hour	Weight
No. 12	1 Horse	12" × 8¼"	50 gals.	900 lbs.
No. 14	1 Horse Heavy	14" × 9¼"	60 gals.	1,090 lbs.
No. 16	2 Horse	16" × 9½"	80 gals.	1,280 lbs.
No. 18	2 Horse Heavy	18" × 12"	100 gals.	1,620 lbs.

Standard Three-Roller Cane Mills

Columbus Iron Works manufactured a series of standard three-roller cane mills which they claimed were largely used in almost every section of the globe where cane is grown.

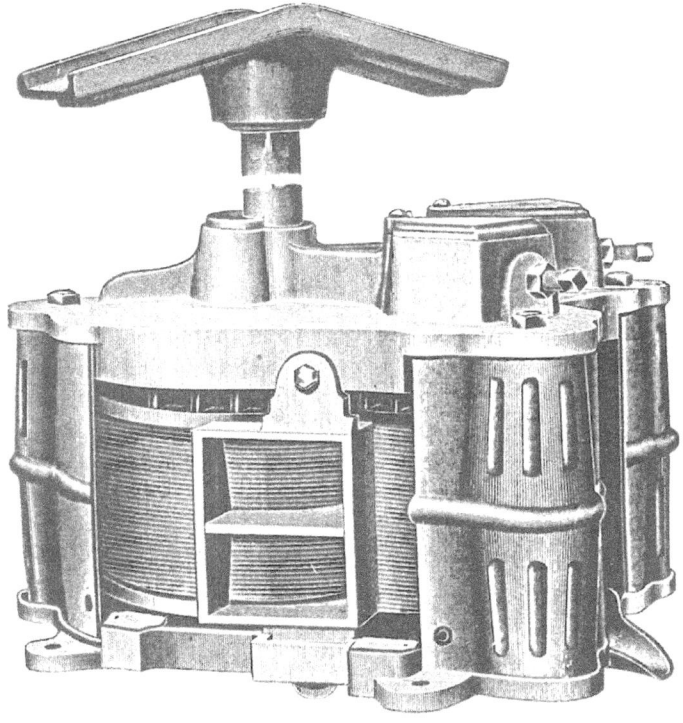

An engraving of Columbus' Standard Three Roller mill.

This is one of Columbus' Standard Three Roller mills.

The rollers on this mill were perfectly balanced, the shafts made of extra quality steel, turned true, and set in boxes fitted with removable brass bearings. The gears were accurately bored to insure proper meshing. This mill came with either a double-drop, single-drop, or straight turn cap.

Chart for Columbus Iron Works Three Roller Mills

Model No	Horsepower	Main Roller- D × H	Small Rollers- D × H	Juice- Per Hour	Weight
No. 0	1 Horse	10⅛" × 5½"	6⅛" × 5½"	40 gals.	410 lbs.
No. 1	1 Regular Horse	11⅜" × 6³⁄₁₆"	6¾" × 6³⁄₁₆"	60 gals.	550 lbs.
No. 2	2 Horse	13⅛" × 7½"	7⅛" × 7½"	80 gals.	740 lbs.
No. 3	2 Regular Horse	15³⁄₁₆" × 9¾"	8" × 9¾"	100 gals.	1,125 lbs.

Their horizontal power mills were huge workhorses.

Before Southern Plow took over the farm implement business, Columbus Iron produced horizontal mills as well.

Horizontal Three-Roller Belt Power Cane Mill

These horizontal mills were double-geared, and the gears were made from machine-cut patterns to insure even contact and uniformity of speed with a gear ratio of 16 to 1. The roller gears were situated outside the frame so no oil could get into the juice. The large rollers had strong flanges, all gears had complete guards, and the mills came with adjustable steel scrapers to keep the rollers clean. The overall design, quality of workmanship, and strength of materials made this an outstanding mill.

Chart for Columbus Iron Works Horizontal Mills

Model No.	Horsepower	Main Roller- D × L	Small Rollers- D × L	Pulley Size	Juice Per Hour	Weight
No. 18	5 Horse	9" × 14"	6" × 14"	20" × 8"	175–200 gals.	1,980 lbs.
No. 20	6 Horse	12" × 12"	8" × 12"	24" × 8"	200–250 gals.	2,590 lbs.

Heavy rollers to be set in wooden frames were also manufactured by the company, and were offered in four sizes.

Chart for Columbus Iron Works Rollers for Wooden Frames

Size	Weight with Boxes	Weight without Boxes
2 Rollers, 12" in Diameter	450 lbs.	400 lbs.
2 Rollers, 14" in Diameter	575 lbs.	525 lbs.
2 Rollers, 16" in Diameter	750 lbs.	650 lbs.
2 Rollers, 18" in Diameter	975 lbs.	900 lbs.

As previously mentioned the Columbus Iron Works made a significant contribution to the industrial and economic life of the city of Columbus. Its legacy lives on through a magnificent convention and trade center in the heart of the city it helped build and rebuild.

Congaree Iron Works, Columbia, South Carolina

The Congaree Iron Works, Columbia, South Carolina, had its origin in a foundry and machine shop established in 1847 by a Mr. Alexander and a Mr. McDougal, according to the *City of Columbia and Richland County's Business Directory, 1893*. At some point between its founding and 1854, a Mr. G. Sinclair also became associated with the business. John Alexander purchased the ironworks in 1854 and led it through some difficult times over the next forty turbulent years. John Alexander was born in Scotland in 1829 and moved to Columbia with his family in 1830. For most of his adult life he was a prominent civic, industrial, and political figure in Columbia. While serving in the Confederate army he participated in firing on Fort Sumter in April 1861, an act which began the Civil War, and he eventually left the military as a major. The Congaree Iron Works also participated in the war by producing a large number of shot, shells, and cannons for the Confederacy. Major Alexander served his community of Columbia as mayor from 1870 to 1876, serving as a Republican during this Reconstruction period. The ironworks apparently closed in 1893, and Alexander died in June 1898.

Through the years the Congaree Iron Works manufactured a variety of products, including steam engines, gristmills, iron and brass castings, cane mills and syrup kettles. They secured the rights to manufacture the Mulay Saw Mills, invented by A. Winter of Fair Play, South Carolina, and patented in 1857. They produced storefronts and pillars, ornamental castings for dwellings, gardens and cemeteries. The ironworks also produced the first twelve inch pipes used by the city waterworks and manufactured bells for churches and schools. They ran a full service ironworks industry, their products were "Equal to any in the North or South," and they enjoyed a good reputation for quality work throughout the state. With sweet sorghum spreading across the nation in the 1860s and 1870s many foundries produced cane mills to meet the growing demands of syrup and sugar producers.

Continental Works, Brooklyn, New York

Much of what we know about this "model foundry" comes to us from *The Manufacturer and Builder* 2, No. 4 (April 1870). T.F. Rowland was the proprietor of the Continental Works located at Greenpoint, Brooklyn, New York. Rowland manufactured portable and stationary steam engines of various sizes, keeping a selection on hand, and was ready to make custom engines to order. He also manufactured sawmills "adapted to the requirements of the Southern market." Through his Continental Works he produced rice mills and gristmills, and in 1866 was manufacturing sugar mills as the sugar refining industry began spreading across New York.

D.M. Cook, Mansfield, Ohio

While this is primarily a book about manufacturers of cane mills I feel a deep sense of need to digress from that purpose long enough to include Mr. D.M. Cook of Mansfield, Ohio, in this work. Though he did patent an evaporator on June 22, 1858, which was featured in *Scientific American* on January 8, 1859, and a cane mill in 1863, he was not engaged in their actual manufacture. Cook was an inventive genius and visionary, so misunderstood by his contemporaries that his neighbors gave him the uncomplimentary nickname of "Crazy Cook." By including him in this work it is my purpose to honor him as one who could see the unseen, dream the undreamable, and reach for the unreachable. He was a man ahead of his times and it is unfortunate that time and finances kept him from accomplishing all the things his creative mind envisioned.

While I've found no samples of cane mills of his design, the records say that the Blymyer-Day Company of Mansfield, Ohio, manufactured Cook's evaporator and cane mill equipment. The idea for the evaporator came to him while he was working in the maple syrup industry and it became a standard. He conceived the idea of an evaporator with channels through which the juice ran on its way to becoming syrup. The evaporator was patented and produced first by Blymyer and Day of Mansfield and later by the huge Blymyer Company of Cincinnati. With the proceeds from the evaporator Cook was able to purchase forty acres of his father's farm. There he built two houses, one for a residence and another for servants' quarters. He also erected a laboratory, a part of which doubled as a stable.

The *Mansfield News* of October 13, 1929, gave a biographical sketch of his life, and stated that Cook envisioned a machine that would one day fly like a bird. Creating his "Aerial Car" became an obsession. He built a cylinder eight feet in diameter and twelve feet high, in which he placed a door and some tiny windows, much more like a passenger plane than the one of Kitty Hawk fame. He then set about developing an electric motor that would generate its own electricity from the air. He was so obsessed with air travel that he even named his daughter Aeria. His labors did not go unnoticed. The *Mansfield Herald* published an article about Mr. Cook's air car which was subsequently published in the *Scientific American* with this commentary: "We are ignorant of the details on which his air-ship is to be built, but we understand that, while a balloon is to be used for elevation, steam is to be the motive power. The inventor is quite sanguine that he has discovered the proper machinery whereby the air may be navigated at will." Unfortunately, he was never able to create the motor, and his wingless air car never got off the ground.

He also experimented with electricity. When Edison invented the glow light in 1879, Cook laid aside his aerial car and began working on electric lights. He told his neighbor, Joseph Palmer, to hold a newspaper against the window on a certain night and he would throw a light on it bright enough for the paper to be read. Cook ran a wire from his laboratory to his house, then directed the light toward his neighbor's house one thousand feet away. The light

Cook's evaporator was a standard in the industry.

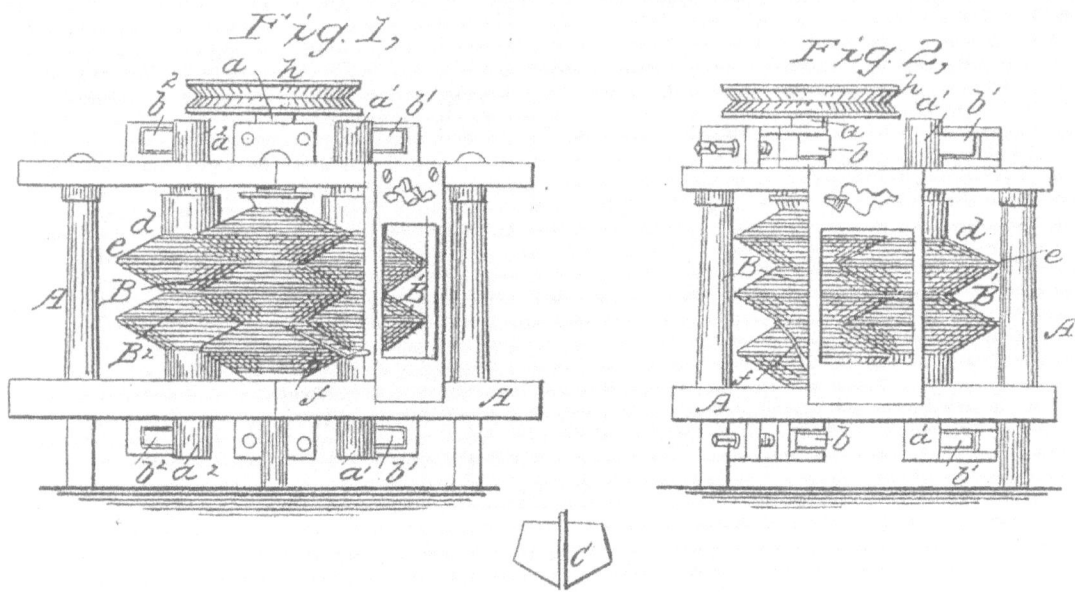

Cook's patented mill was a shredder and press.

was so bright that Palmer could indeed read his paper. However, because of financial difficulties Cook was unable to market his invention.

D.M. Cook foresaw things we take for granted today. He once saw his neighbor, Palmer, plowing with his horses and told him, "Some day that is going to be easier for you. I hope to have a riding plow propelled by a motor. All you will need to do will be to direct the lever which will control the operation." He predicted the electric cars and buggies running everywhere. Unfortunately, Cook exhausted all his resources on his inventive efforts and died poor, obscure, and disappointed. Yet, thousands have benefited from his invention of the portable evaporator.

He was awarded Patent No. 39,467 on August 11, 1863, for a cane mill of unique design. Cook's mill consisted of rollers with their crushing surfaces constructed in circular wedge, or "V" form. The wedges of the small rollers fit snugly into the wedge-shaped spaces of the main roller.

The purpose of this configuration was to splinter the rind of the cane and expose the pith inside. Once the cane was split open the rollers could press out the juice with less pressure. With less pressure the rollers would not press out the bitter albuminous and coloring matter of the rind.

D.M. Cook, of Mansfield, Ohio, was the inventor of Cook's Patented Evaporator, and a misunderstood creative genius whose "Aerial Car" never quite got off the ground but whose evaporator became a standard in the industry. I thought the reader would want to know.

Cook Cane Mill and Evaporator Company, St. Louis, Missouri

The Cook Cane Mill and Evaporator Company, 122 N. First Street, St. Louis, Missouri, was established in 1890 and specialized in cane mills, evaporators and furnaces. An interesting letter from the president of the company, J.L. Cook, dated July 15, 1935, seems to indicate that a significant part of the company's business was directed toward "sorghum-syrup-making customers." Cook gave his salesmen a peptalk, then gave them some hints for interesting customers in purchasing new sorghum equipment. He closed his letter by stating, "It's a sweet business."

Their product catalog is not only a listing of their products, but also a helpful piece of information. Catalog No. 46, copyrighted in 1919, has the usual general information concerning guarantees, capacities of various mills, repair parts and deliveries, but also has a page of directions for "building arches" (for the furnace) and using their stationary evaporator pans. Then, there's a helpful page on using their evaporator pans with their portable furnaces. With these directions even a novice would be able to set up a syrup-making system, with either their stationary or portable evaporators.

Cook Cane Mill and Evaporator Company did offer a significant variety of cane mills, both in animal and power models.

The New Improved Cook Cane Mill

FOR SORGHUM OR RIBBON CANE. The New Improved Cook Vertical Mill had several new advantages. The front plate was made in one solid piece, strengthening the mill. It had steel shafts, brass bearings, and cog wheels cast separate from the rolls so they could be easily and cheaply replaced. The gears were not keyed, but held in place by clutches cast on the gears to correspond with those cast on the rollers. The gearing was encased and the rollers were flanged top and bottom to prevent clogging.

Chart for the New Improved Cook Mills

Model No.	Horsepower	Main Roller- D × H	Small Rollers- D × H	Juice Per Hour	Weight	1919 Price
No. 0	1 Light	8½" × 5¾"	5½" × 5¾"	35–40 gals.	435 lbs.	$46.00
No. 1	1 Regular	10" × 6½"	6" × 6½"	45–60 gals.	550 lbs.	$58.00
No. 2	1 Heavy	11" × 6¾"	6¼" × 6¾"	60–75 gals.	635 lbs.	$69.00
No. 3	2 Light	13 ⅝" × 7½"	7½" × 7½"	75–90 gals.	900 lbs.	$90.00
No. 4	2 Regular	13 ⅝" × 8½"	7½" × 8½"	90–100 gals.	950 lbs.	$95.00
No. 5	2 Heavy	13¾" × 9"	7½" × 9"	100–120 gals.	1,035 lbs.	$112.50

Southern Queen Cane Mill

The Southern Queen Vertical Mill was a four-bolt mill, making the mill extra strong and rugged. Gear wheels fit into corresponding clutches on each roller, and many of the same features of the New Improved Cook were also found on the Southern Queen. The sweep cap of the Southern Queen was so constructed that the owner would not have to bore holes in the sweep pole.

Chart for the Southern Queen Mills

Model No.	Horsepower	Main Roller- D × H	Small Rollers- D × H	Juice Per Hour	Weight	1919 Price
No. 9	1 Light	8¼" × 5 ⅝"	5½" × 5½"	40–50 gals.	450 lbs.	$48.00
No. 10	1 Regular	9½" × 6⅜"	6" × 6⅜"	40–60 gals.	757 lbs.	$60.00
No. 11	1 Heavy	11½" × 6¾"	6⅝" × 6¾"	60–75 gals.	650 lbs.	$72.50
No. 12	2 Regular	13" × 7⅜"	7⅛" × 7⅜"	75–90 gals.	925 lbs.	$95.00
No. 13	2 Heavy	14" × 9¼"	8¾" × 9¼"	90–100 gals.	1,050 lbs.	$116.00

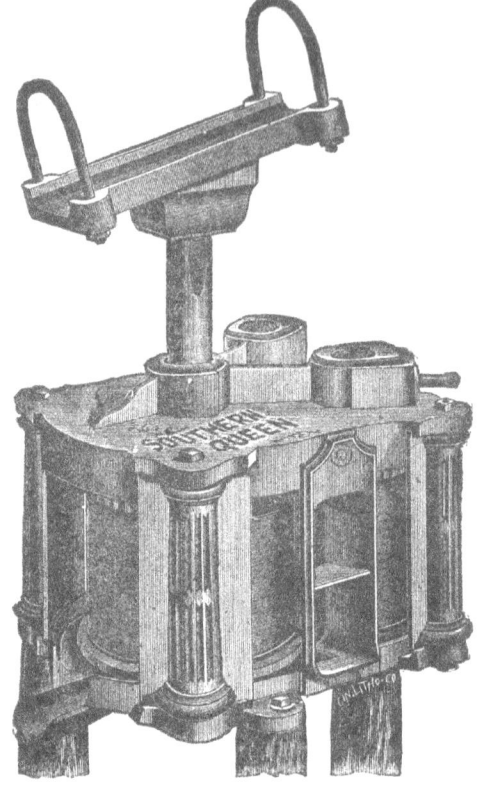

Left: Cook's "New Improved" mill had a one piece front plate. *Right:* The Southern Queen had a distinctive sweep cap. *Below:* Cook Superior Horizontal cane mill was geared for animal power.

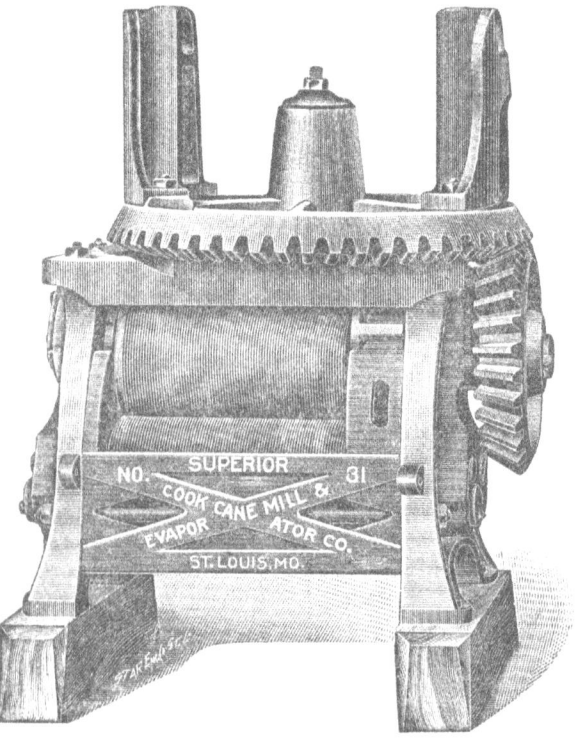

Cook Superior Horizontal Cane Mill

FOR ANIMAL POWER. Cook claimed that this was the strongest and best horizontal sweep power mill made. It had all the dependable features of mills of this type and many advantages not found on any other makes. With their improvements they put it at the "head of the cane mill line." The driving wheel was twice as large as the pinion, which gave two revolutions of the rolls to one of the team. This gave this mill a capacity equal to vertical mills with rolls twice the size. The Cook Superior had steel shafts, lathe-turned rolls, bronze-lined boxes and elastic bearings.

Chart for Cook's Superior Cane Mills

Model No.	Horsepower	Main Roller- D × H	Small Rollers- D × H	Cane Per Hour	Weight	1919 Price
No. 30	1 or 2 Horse	10" × 10"	7" × 10"	¾ ton	1,150 lbs.	$138.00
No. 31	2 or 4 Horse	10" × 16"	7" × 16"	1 ton	1,375 lbs.	$175.00

The Cook No. 39 Superior Horizontal Cane Mill

The Model No. 39 was an answer to numerous requests for a small power mill which could be operated by a small gasoline engine. In 1919 Cook designed the No. 39 Superior Mill, modeled after the Nos. 44 and 45 mills, featuring adjustable small rollers and bronze bearings.

Chart for Cook's No. 39 Superior Cane Mill

Model No.	Horsepower	Main Roller- D × H	Small Rollers- D × H	Cane Per Hour	Weight	1919 Price
No. 39	1–4 Horse	8" × 8"	5½" × 8"	¾ ton	650 lbs.	$110.00

Cook's Superior Horizontal Power Cane Mill

These horizontal mills were made to be operated with a variety of applications, gasoline, steam, water, or electric power. All shafts were cold rolled steel, the rollers were flanged and lathe turned, all boxes had bronze bearings, and the small rollers were adjustable.

Chart for Cook's Superior Horizontal Power Cane Mill

Model No.	Horsepower	Main Roller- D × H	Small Rollers- D × H	Juice Per Hour	Weight	1919 Price
No. 40	4 Horse	10" × 10"	7" × 10"	150–200 gals.	1,200 lbs.	$165.00
No. 41	6 Horse	10" × 16"	7" × 16"	200–250 gals.	1,350 lbs.	$187.50

The No. 39 was a small power mill.

This mill was made to operate with a variety of power applications.

Cook's Superior Horizontal Power Cane Mill

WITH DOUBLE BACK GEAR. This horizontal model featured double back gears, making it a more powerful machine. This model was recommended for those using a gasoline or kerosene engine for power.

Chart for Cook's Superior Horizontal Power Mill with Double Back Gearing

Model No.	Horsepower	Main Roller- D × H	Small Rollers- D × H	Juice Per Hour	Weight	1919 Price
No. 42	4 Horse	10" × 10"	7" × 10"	200–250 gals.	1,250 lbs.	$190.00
No. 43	6 Horse	10" × 16"	7" × 16"	250–300 gals.	1,450 lbs.	$240.00

Cook's "New Superior" Horizontal Cane Mill

The "New Superior" Mill was the same as the Numbers 42 and 43 with a modification which gave the rollers 2½"" more width. The gears were keyed to the rollers outside of the side plates instead of being cast onto them giving the mill 2½" more squeezing surface. This mill was designed for any type ordinary farm engine, and featured a 24" × 6" pulley.

Chart for Cook's "New Superior" Cane Mill

Model No.	Horsepower	Main Roller- D × H	Small Rollers- D × H	Cane Per Hour	Weight	1919 Price
No. 42A	4 Horse	10" × 12½"	7" × 12½"	2 ton	1,350 lbs.	$225.00
No. 43A	6 Horse	10" × 18½"	7" × 18½"	2½ tons	1,500 lbs.	$255.00

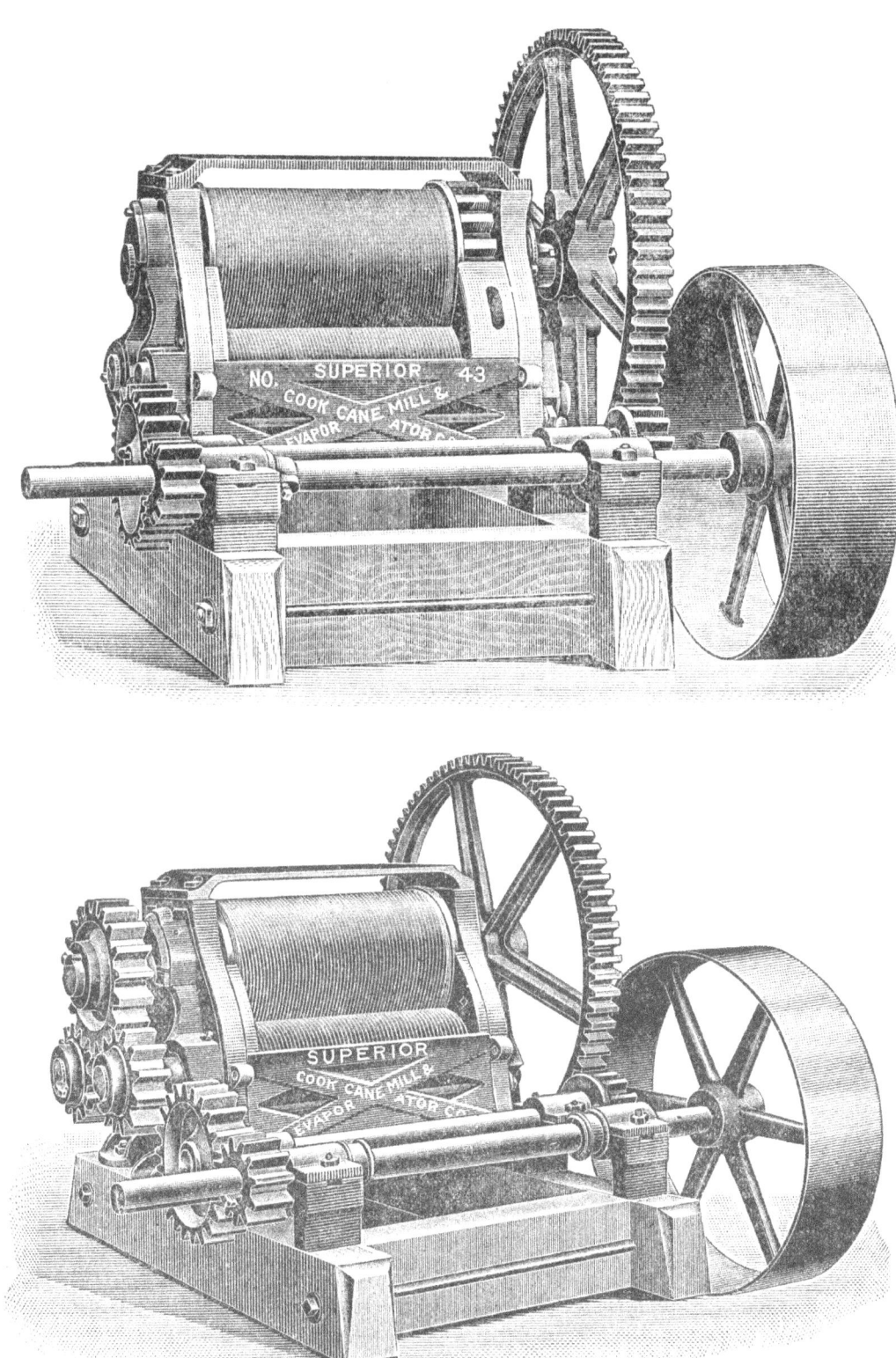

Top: **Double back gearing made this a powerful mill.** *Bottom:* **The rollers on the "New Superior" were 2½ inches wider than the mill above.**

This mill was made for those needing a heavy and powerful mill.

Cook's Superior Heavy Cane Mill

HEAVY AND POWERFUL. The Nos. 44 and 45 Superior Horizontal Cane Mills were designed stronger and heavier for those needing a big mill powered by gasoline, steam, water, or electric power.

Chart for Cook's Superior Heavy Cane Mill

Model No.	Horsepower	Main Roller- D × H	Small Rollers- D × H	Cane Per Hour	Weight	1919 Price
No. 44	10–12 Horse	16" × 12"	10" × 12"	2 tons	2,800 lbs.	$430.00
No. 45	12–15 Horse	16" × 18"	10" × 18"	3 tons	3,200 lbs.	$490.00

The Cook No. 50 Superior Horizontal Cane Mill

The No. 50 horizontal mill was an extra heavy mill designed similar to the large mills used in the sugar industry. The rollers were cast from a special iron that gave it a hard surface. The heavy steel shafts were secured to the rollers by three heavy steel keys assuring no slippage. This model featured a new invention which was attached over the main roller to prevent the bagasse from clogging the machine.

The No. 50 was an extra heavy mill.

Chart for Cook's No. 50 Superior Horizontal Cane Mill

Model No.	Horsepower	Main Roller- D × H	Small Rollers- D × H	Cane Per Hour	Weight	1919 Price
No. 50	12 to 18 Horse	16" × 15"	10" × 15"	4 tons per hr.	4,500 lbs.	$690.00

All of Cook's power mills also offered feed tables and bagasse carriers. They also sold hydrometers, skimmers, and thermometers. While Cook Cane Mill And Evaporator Company did not produce syrup kettles, at least later in its existence, it did manufacture a "Triple X" evaporator made of cop-r-roy. This was a refined steel alloyed with pure copper, producing strength, long wear, and resistance to decay and corrosion.

J.B. and J.M. Cornell Company, New York, New York

The J.B. and J.M. Cornell Company, Twenty-sixth Street and Eleventh Avenue, New York City, was primarily a manufacturer of iron items for building purposes and grew to become the most extensive and largest in the United States. While columns, lintels, girders, beams and channels were their specialty, they also manufactured sugar cane machinery. J.B. Cornell was a creative individual receiving United States patents for several items, includ-

The Cornell Company made large sugarhouse equipment.

ing continuous sheet metal lapping surface in 1856, a system of protection of iron columns in case of fire in 1860, improvements in metallic rolling shutters in 1860, and a fireproof skylight in 1869. In 1881, J.B. and J.M. joined with others in purchasing four lots on the northeast corner of Madison Avenue and Sixteenth Street and helped subscribe $110,000 for a large and substantial house of worship for the Methodist Episcopal Church. No details on their cane mills have been found other than the fact that they manufactured them.

Crockett's Iron Works, Macon, Georgia

Mr. E. Crockett, the sole proprietor of Crockett's Iron Works, opened his shop for business on Fourth Street, Macon, Georgia, on January 1, 1869. Though not endowed with immense capital, Crockett was blessed with vast energy and a practical knowledge of machinery. His ironworks consisted of a foundry, machine shop and blacksmith shop. He made gin gears and horsepowers, and advertised his horsepower as an "Old reliable movement that never fails." They were so substantially and practically made that one once took the premium at the Georgia State Fair. In the mill category he also produced flour mills, sawmills, gristmills and cane mills. For the farmers he made threshing machines and fans, stationary and portable steam engines, and shallow and deep well pumps. Crockett manufactured steam gauges, iron railings, settees, chairs, valves, steam, gas and water fittings, iron storefronts, cotton presses and brick machines.

Crockett's business philosophy was quite simple. He set out to make what people wanted, to make it as cheaply as possible, and to make it as well as it could be made anywhere in the United States. He was known as a fair man, was noted for promptness in filling orders, and always guaranteed the quality of his workmanship.

J.H. Day and Company, Cincinnati, Ohio

J.H. Day and Company, 1144 Harrison Avenue, Cincinnati, Ohio, manufactured ball pebble machines, bur stone machines, drug grinders, paint and spice grinding machines. The Day Company merged with Blymyer to form the Blymyer-Day Company, manufacturers of rice hullers, coffee hullers, portable mills and pulpers, tortilla mills, corn mills, cob grinders, sugar cane/sorghum mills and evaporators. The Blymyer Company became a giant in the cane mill industry.

Robert Deely and Company, New York, New York

The Robert Deely and Company, 507 W. 23rd Road, New York City, manufactured sugar cane machinery; however, no specifics of their mills or further information has been found.

John Deere and Company, Moline, Illinois

Plowing is basic to productive, profitable farming, and the quest for a plow to successfully break the prairie sod led to the formation of the John Deere Company. Earlier American plows had wooden moldboards and small iron points which were not too effective and wore out quickly. In 1797 John Newbold developed a cast-iron plow which had share, moldboard and landslide all cast in one piece. This was a great improvement, but when one piece broke or wore out the whole plow had to be discarded. This led to R.B. Chenaworth's 1813 invention of a cast-iron plow cast in separate pieces so broken or damaged parts could be replaced. The need for an effective plow was so urgent that Thomas Jefferson pondered the problem, applied scientific principles, and wrote a treatise in 1789 describing the necessary design of a moldboard. Daniel Webster made recommendations and produced a cumbersome plow in 1836. However, soil stuck to all of these plows so quickly that frequent and time-consuming scraping was necessary.

John Deere, a young blacksmith who had recently moved from Vermont to Illinois, developed a theory which revolutionized the American plow. Deere was born in Rutland, Vermont, on February 7, 1804, and grew up in Middlebury. He served a four-year apprenticeship learning the blacksmith's trade, then began his career as a journeyman blacksmith in 1825 and soon became well known for his creativity and craftsmanship. Numerous people from New England were moving west in search of a better life, and tales of golden opportunities made their way back to Vermont. Deere joined the pioneers migrating west, and found his way to Grand Detour, Illinois. There was such a demand for his trade that two days after his arrival he had set up a forge and was at work. The westward-moving pioneer farmers brought plows with them which worked well in the light, sandy New England soil but were no match for the heavy Midwestern sod. Deere was visiting a friend's sawmill in 1837 when he noticed a broken saw blade. He observed how it was polished bright from sawing, and an idea began to dawn upon him. He asked for the blade, carried it to his blacksmith shop, cut the teeth off, and shaped a moldboard over a log pattern. He then attached the moldboard to a one-piece wrought-iron plow and tested his theory on the farm of Lewis Crandall, near Grand Detour. His new steel plow sliced through the soil without sticking, and the "self-polisher" became an immediate success. His story is chronicled in "The Story of John Deere," by his company.

This is John Deere's Amazon power mill.

John Deere also developed another revolutionary idea that propelled his business into the giant it is today. In the early days blacksmiths built tools for farmers on order. However, Deere began producing his plows in advance, then put them on the market to be sold. By the end of the first decade after he developed the first "self polisher" Deere was producing 1,000 plows a year. Quality steel was difficult to find in the beginning, so Deere ordered a special shipment from England. Getting steel from England to Grand Detour, Illinois, in those days was no small task. In 1848 he moved his operation to Moline, Illinois, in order to take advantage of water power and transportation available there. The first slab of cast plow steel produced in America was made for John Deere's company in 1846 in the mills at Pittsburgh and shipped to the new plant at Moline. The quality of craftsmanship which characterized Deere from the beginning continued in these formative years of his company. He determined that "I will never put my name on a plow that does not have in it the best that is in me." Deere's business was incorporated in 1868 as Deere and Company.

Product research and development were high priorities for the company. Other new and innovative agricultural implements were added along the way by Deere, such as the 1874 two-wheel sulky plow on which a farmer could ride. Deere and Company got into the tractor business reluctantly, however. They developed a couple of experimental models which did not meet their expectations. They finally purchased the Waterloo Boy Tractor Engine Company in 1918. John Froehlich, of Froehlich, Iowa, built a gasoline tractor in 1892. He moved to Waterloo, Iowa, in 1893 and built one of the first companies for the production of gasoline tractors, the Waterloo Boy Tractor Engine Company. They produced the first of their famous Waterloo Boy tractors in 1914. On March 18, 1918, Deere and Company purchased the company for $2,100,000, and they were then formally in the tractor business. The company which began with a moldboard built from a broken saw blade grew into the leading producer of agricultural equipment in the world.

Deere sold a Blue Ribbon Cane Mill which looks much like those manufactured by the Brennan Company of Louisville, and later by the Blymyer Company of Cincinnati, Ohio. This model featured a vertical oil tube which carried lubrication directly to the bottom journals. The gears were cast separate from the journals for ease of replacement and at less expense. The gears were encased for the safety of the operator, and the top plates were made with a wide flange for additional strength. This mill's unique feed guide was reversible and was also divided so the entire surface of the rollers could be utilized without the cane jamming. The shafts were made of selected rolled steel and all boxes had brass linings, making this a light, smooth running mill. Deere offered this mill in five models.

Chart for John Deere's Three Roller Vertical Mills

Model No.	Horsepower	Height of Rollers	Diameter of Large Roller	Diameter of S. Rollers	Juice Per Hr.	Weight	1913 Price
0	One Horse	5½"	10⅛"	6⅛"	40 gals.	430 lbs.	$30.00
1	Reg. 1 Horse	6³⁄₁₆"	11⅜"	6¾"	60 gals.	530 lbs.	$40.00
2	Two-Horse	7½"	13½"	7⅛"	80 gals.	750 lbs.	$60.00
3	Reg. 2 Horse	9¾"	14¹³⁄₁₆"	8"	100 gals.	950 lbs.	$80.00
4	Hvy. 2 Horse	12"	16"	9¹¹⁄₁₆"	120 gals.	1,300 lbs.	$100.00

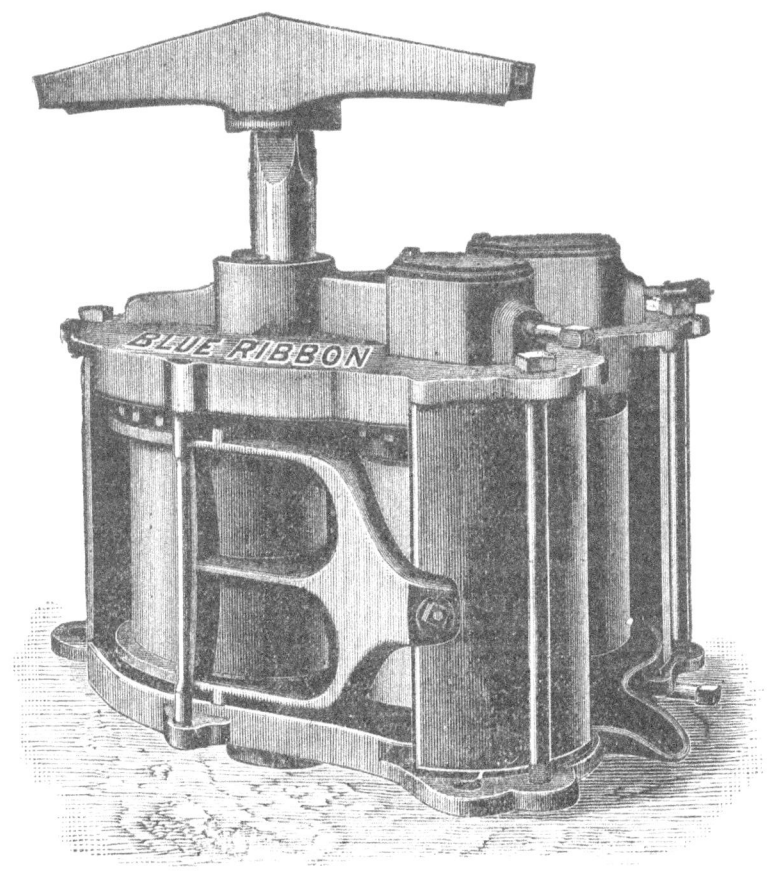

Brennan probably made these mills for Deere.

The Magnolia was a three vertical roller mill (courtesy Tommy Clayton, Hilliard, Florida).

The Blue Ribbon Mill was offered as improved for sorghum or sugar cane and was lauded for economy, safety, strength, simplicity and improved features.

The Magnolia Cane Mill "for sorghum or tropical cane" was also sold by the John Deere Plow Company. The Magnolia Mill had turned rolls, steel shafts, brass bearings and the gearing and rollers were cast separate for ease and economy of replacement. This mill featured oil tubes passing through the rollers to the bottom journals and bearing boxes. An interesting observation of the time is found in Deere's 1913 catalog concerning well oiled journals: "By using fluid lard oil on the upper journals the oil will flow through the tubes and oil the lower journals."

The main rollers were flanged at top and bottom to keep the cane from passing off the rollers either at top or bottom. This mill had a divided feed guide in order to utilize the entire roller surface.

Chart for John Deere's Magnolia Cane Mills

Model No.	Horsepower	Height of Rollers	Diameter of Large Roller	Diameter of S. Rollers	Juice Per Hr.	Weight	1913 Price
0	L. 1 Horse	5⅝"	8¼"	5½"	40–50	400 lbs.	$30.00
1	One Horse	6"	9½"	6⅜"	50–60	500 lbs.	$40.00
2	One Horse	6⅝"	11½"	6¾"	60–75	625 lbs.	$50.00
3	Two Horse	7⅜"	12"	7⅛"	75–90	800 lbs.	$60.00
4	Two Horse	8¾"	13"	7⅛"	90–100	850 lbs.	$70.00
5	Hv. 2 Horse	9¼"	14"	8¾"	100–120	1,150 lbs.	$80.00
6	Ex.H.2 Hor.	11½"	14"	8¾"	120–140	1,250 lbs.	$95.00

Deere claimed that ordinary gray iron test bars would break at an average strain of about 1150 pounds and that they did not use any that would not stand a strain of from 1600 to 1800 pounds, making this one of the strongest mills on the market.

Deere marketed a series of horizontal roller mills in various sizes and configuration. One of these was the Amazon Cane Mill with double back gearing. These mills were claimed to be of the most modern design and of extra strength for grinding "tropical cane." A unique feature of these mills was found in the self-adjusting rollers by means of rubber springs. The rollers were adjustable by means of set screws, but the rubber springs gave the rollers a little extra give in the event they ever became clogged. The main roller was flanged and serrated, making the entire length available for use. Strong, steel shafts were used and the journals ran in brass boxes. The Amazon Cane Mill with double back gearing was offered in four sizes.

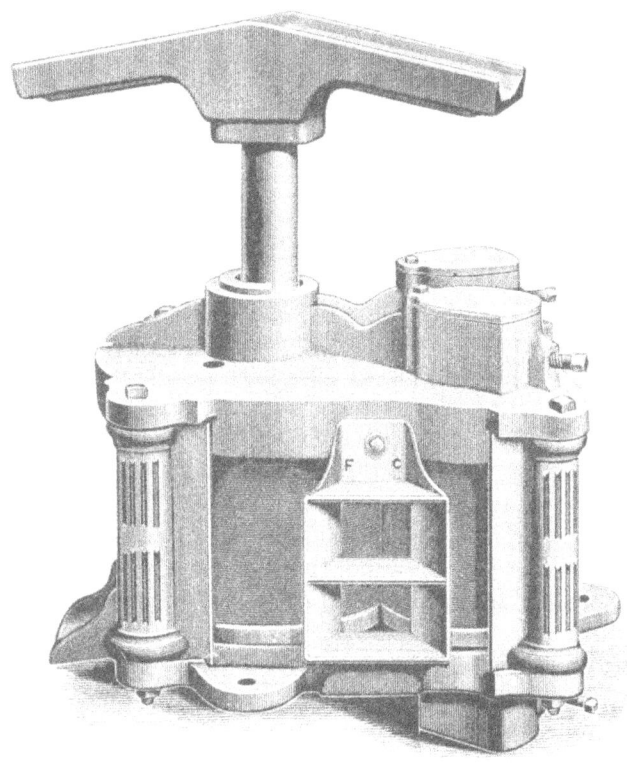

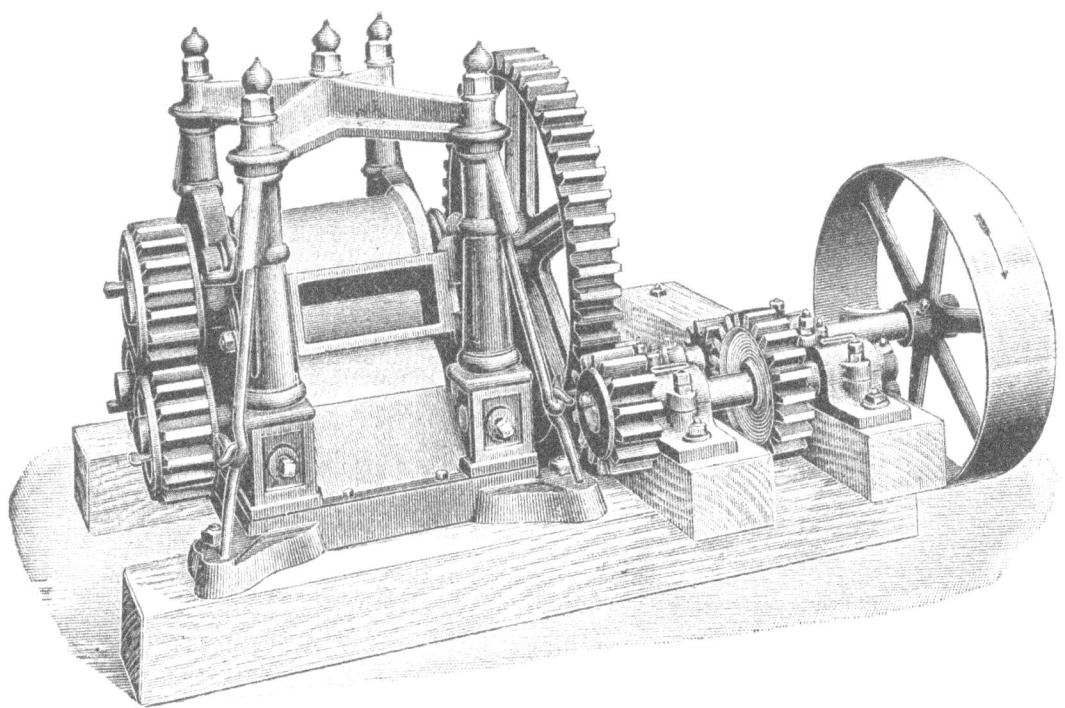

Top: An engraving of Deere's Magnolia mill. *Bottom:* This Amazon is geared for steam power.

Chart for John Deere's Amazon Cane Mills with Double Back Gearing

Model No.	Horsepower Required	Length of Rollers	Diameter of L. Rollers	Diameter of S. Rollers	Weight of Mill	Tons of Cane per 12 hrs.	Gals. of Juice per 12 hrs.
1	1–2	8"	8"	6"	1,250 lbs.	6	810
2	2–4	10"	10"	8"	1,850 lbs.	9	1,250
3	2–4	12"	10"	8"	2,000 lbs.	12	1,600
4	4–6	16"	12"	10"	3,425 lbs.	18	2,400

The pulley shaft on this mill should turn at 80 to 100 rpm which gave the countershaft 40 to 50 rpm and the large roller speed of 10 to 12 rpm. These mills were not geared for the faster speed of gasoline engines and were recommended to be used with steam engines.

However, Deere did offer the Amazon Power Cane Mill with a high ratio double back gearing designed for gasoline engine use. These mills came in four sizes and also featured rubber springs for added insurance against breakage. Steel shafts ran in brass boxes. Gasoline engines run at a much higher speed than steam engines; therefore, it was necessary to increase the size of the gear wheel on the countershaft in order to reduce the speed of the rollers. It was essential to slow the rollers down so the juice would not flow out with the bagasse.

This Amazon has high ratio gearing.

Chart for John Deere's Amazon Power Mill with High Ratio Double Back Gearing

Model No.	Horsepower Required	Length of Rollers	Diameter of L. Rollers	Diameter of S. Rollers	Weight of Main Roll	Weight of Mill	Tons of Cane per 12 hrs.
10	3–5	8"	8"	6"	100 lbs.	1,330 lbs.	5
20	5–8	10"	10"	8"	190 lbs.	2.060 lbs.	8
30	7–10	12"	10"	8"	200 lbs.	2,343 lbs.	10
40	9–12	16"	12"	10"	400 lbs.	3,450 lbs.	16

This mill was offered in larger capacity upon contract with the company. No prices were offered for these horizontal mills in Deere's 1913 Catalog.

An Amazon Cane Mill with Single Back Gearing suited for water power was offered by the John Deere Company. This is the same mill as that shown above, except it has single back gearing instead of double back gearing. Where a mill was wanted for light work the single back gear mill could be used successfully, though the double back geared mill is the more substantial. As with the above mills, this mill came with rubber springs, steel shafts, and brass boxes. This mill was offered in four sizes. It was recommended that the pulley turn at 35 to 40 rpm which would give the large roller a speed of 10 to 12 rpm. The mill was usually furnished with a 24-inch pulley, though other sizes were available.

This horizontal mill is geared for water power.

Chart for John Deere's Amazon Cane Mill with Single Back Gearing

Model No.	Horsepower Required	Length of Rollers	Diameter of L. Rollers	Diameter of S. Rollers	Weight of Mill	Tons of Cane per 12 hrs.	Gals. of Juice per 12 hrs.
1	1	8"	8"	6"	1,000 lbs.	6	810
2	2	10"	10"	8"	1,700 lbs.	9	1,250
3	3	12"	10"	8"	1,850 lbs.	12	1,600
4	4	16"	12"	10"	3,250 lbs.	18	2,400

Bagasse carriers, feed tables, Cook's Stationary Evaporator Pan for a brick arch, Cook's-portable furnaces, furnace doors and grates were also sold by the John Deere Plow Company.

Anthony Demarce Machine Shop and Foundry, Fairfield, Iowa

When the Louisiana sugar industries began to subside in the early 1850s American farmers began looking for alternative sources for sugar production. One promising source seemed to be the new "Chinese sugar cane" introduced into the country in 1853. The origins of sorghum are lost in obscurity, as we have seen earlier, though some believe it originated in eastern Africa 5,000 years ago. One variety, Chinese Amber, introduced into France from northern China in 1851, and then into America in 1853, seemed to hold some promise. However, it was with Leonard Wray's arrival with seeds of fifteen varieties from South Africa that the American sweet sorgho industry began to flourish. In 1861 there were 65,000 gallons of molasses and 3,000 pounds of sugar produced in the area around Fairfield, Iowa. According to *A Fair Field*, by Welty, the future looked promising and a grower's association was formed. In 1863 a wealthy Chicago businessman, L.D. Wilson, invested $30,000 in a Fairfield sorghum mill and sugar refinery. By 1867 nearly a thousand acres of sorghum was grown in the Fairfield area. However, the sugar would not granulate properly, Wilson lost his money and refinery, and farmers had to look to other sources of revenue. By the end of the Civil War the easy shipment of sugar by rail spelled further doom for the sorghum sugar market. Some years later, in 1920 in fact, it was said that Anthony DeMarce "was the only one of the early manufacturers in Fairfield who gained a competence." DeMarce designed a portable cane mill which could be dismantled, carried to the field, reassembled and used to grind the sweet sorghum. For his design he received Patent No. 96,088 on October 10, 1869.

Anthony DeMarce was a man of vision, industry, and fortitude. He established a machine shop in Fairfield in 1857 to which he later added a foundry. It was located then in Ward Lamson's pasture at what is now near the end of South Court Street. DeMarce manufactured steam engines, boilers, and sorghum machinery, remaining in business until the late 1880s. The foundry was only one of DeMarce's numerous industrial enterprises. His fortitude demonstrated itself when he dared to venture his financial resources on a thing called electricity. Because of his vision and willingness to risk personal capital Fairfield became the second city west of the Mississippi River to have electricity.

Gaslights were common in that era, and Fairfield first operated them at busy intersections of the city in September, 1877. When there was no moon they were lighted at dark and turned off after the saloons closed. The good folks of Fairfield got their first glimpse of electrical lighting when a traveling showman named W.W. Cole came to perform in the city. He had two electrical arc lamps, one for his tent and one for his performances. The city

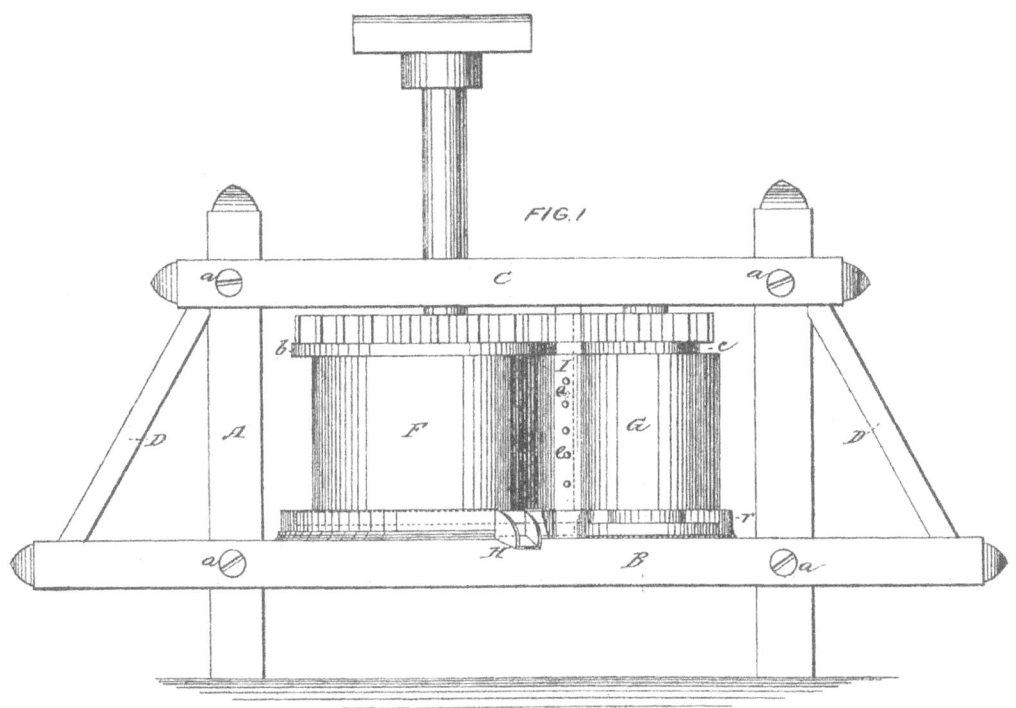

Portability is the key in this DeMarce patent.

fathers of Fairfield saw the possibilities of electrical lighting and erected a 185 foot tall steel-frame tower in the middle of Central Park. On this tower were erected six arc lamps with 1800 candlepower each, enough to light the entire town. Anthony DeMarce personally guaranteed the contract for installation. He owned and operated the 10 ampere brush generator, installed in his foundry building, which provided electricity for the city lamps. After a storm blew the tower down in May 1883 it was rebuilt to a height of 175 feet, and at that time the city bought DeMarce's interest in the electrical system. Because of his vision and boldness, Anthony DeMarce literally put Fairfield, Iowa, on the map. The city's electric lights were such a novelty that excursion trains came from as far as sixty miles away so people could see the lights. The DeMarce Machine Shop and Foundry prospered, and after his retirement Anthony and his wife were able to live out their lives in comfort in Fairfield.

Demorest Foundry and Machine Works, Demorest, Georgia

Habersham County lies in the beautiful hill country of northeast Georgia. Established in 1818, it was named in honor of Joseph Habersham. Habersham served as an officer of the First Georgia Regiment, 1776, and in the Continental Congress, 1785–86. He then served his nation as postmaster general from 1795 to 1801. Among other things, Habersham County is known for Tallulah Gorge and for its beautiful vistas along the Chattahoochee River. Demorest, one of the latest towns formed in Habersham County, was settled by a group of persons from Massachusetts, New Hampshire, Ohio, and Indiana and was named for the famous prohibition speaker, W. Jennings Demorest. A strict morality was imposed upon the infant town, and any person guilty of drinking, gambling, or prostitution would have to forfeit his property.

Demorest began in 1890 under the name Demorest Home, Mining and Improvement Company. The New England influence could be seen in the homes they constructed in those formative years. The town was heavily promoted by northern real estate promoters for its natural beauty, its lake, and its proximity to other north Georgia attractions such as Tallulah Gorge. Mineral springs fed a manmade lake, making Demorest an ideal spot for a health resort. Lake Demorest had a ferry, and the town had several manufacturers—such as the Demorest Engraving Works, which produced photographic equipment, dental chairs, and a wide assortment of other items; the Demorest Foundry and Machine Works, which produced furniture, wagons, and cane mills from 1890 until 1930; Norton and Cooper hoop factory; and a factory which manufactured the Goodrich self-heating, folding bathtub.

The product list of the Demorest Foundry and Machine Works is incomplete, but they presumedly did manufacture several models of cane mills. A model No. 2 three roller mill has been found and is in this writer's collection. The large roller is approximately 12" D × 6" H and the two small rollers are 6" D × 6" H.

Diebert, Bancroft and Ross, New Orleans, Louisiana

John Diebert was born in Tremont City, Ohio, January 4, 1844, the child of a lumber and timber man. He moved to New Orleans in 1870 and entered the lumber business as a grader, a trade he learned from his father. He became an inspector for a Texas cypress lumber company and became a partner with the Lutcher and Moore Cypress Company of Texas and Louisiana in 1891. The Bancroft, Ross and Sinclair Foundry was incorporated in 1904 in New Orleans at the corner of South Jefferson Davis Parkway and Tulane Avenue. In 1912 Diebert became president of the company and the name was changed to Diebert,

This is a rare Demorest Foundry No. 2 mill.

Bancroft and Ross. Diebert was involved in banking and insurance, and held interest in twenty lumber mills in the South. He was also a public minded citizen and the John Diebert Public School is but a token of his numerous, and often unpublicized, philanthropies. John Diebert died in New Orleans on June 5, 1912. Diebert's wife, Eve Butterworth Diebert, was also known for her extensive philanthropies. She was decorated by the king of Italy for founding and equipping the Loyola Unit Base Hospital in Italy during World War I. She donated funds for the John Diebert Tuberculosis Hospital as a memorial to her husband. She also contributed generously to numerous charities and relief agencies and as an Episcopalian was the first non–Catholic woman in the South to receive the *Benemerenti* medal, a papal award recognizing her service to Catholic institutions.

The foundry moved from New Orleans to Amite, Louisiana, in the late 1960s. It was sold in the late 1980s, and after changing hands a couple of times it continued to exist as Amite Foundry until it was purchased by the Atchison Casting Corporation in 1993. Diebert, Bancroft and Ross made a variety of items, even manhole covers for the city of New Orleans. Their cane mills were of the larger sugar mill variety and, so far, a small, backyard type has not been located by the author.

Dyer Company, Cleveland, Ohio

The history of the Dyer Company, 3030 Euclid Avenue, Cleveland, Ohio, goes back to the American Civil War times and to California and its desperate search for a successful method of converting sugar beets into sugar. Shortly after the close of the Civil War, Edward

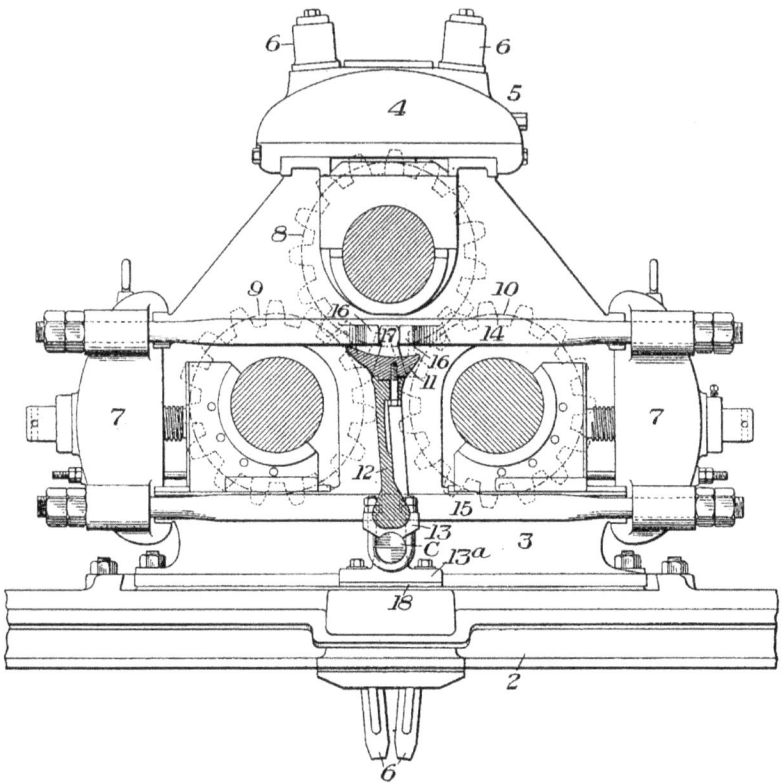

Dyer's patent provided a scheme for adjusting the turn plate.

F. Dyer was busy experimenting day and night for an economical conversion process. He built his first successful mill in Alvarado, California, in 1869. What began with machinery largely discarded from other unsuccessful endeavors, Dyer grew his company forward to become one of the world's largest engineering companies specializing in sugar factory construction. His company was able to design and erect mills from the foundation to the roof, design and build the equipment, and set the plant into operation. The first barrel of beet sugar he manufactured was shipped to United States President Ulysses S. Grant as a signal that a new industry had been born.

Dyer continued his operation in California until 1892, and while searching for a central location for his company, he selected Cleveland, Ohio. The Mormon Church awarded Dyer a contract to build a mill in Utah. When the construction of that project was completed Dyer decided to abandon the manufacture of sugar and concentrate on sugar mill construction altogether. His son, Herrick H. Dyer, succeeded his father as head of the company.

On June 10, 1913, Frank A. Monroe, Jr., and Nicolas A. Helmer, assignors to the Dyer Company, were granted Patent No. 1,064,362 for new and useful improvements in cane grinding mills. Their invention related to the exact and convenient adjustment of the turn plate between the rollers. Their invention provided a means whereby the frame bolts which held the side caps in place could be utilized for securing the adjustment of the turn plate. By adjusting the side cap bolts on a horizontal plane one could adjust the turn plate.

Eastwood Brothers and Carson, McMinnville, Tennessee

T.H. Eastwood, William Eastwood and D.B. Carson were the prime movers for Eastwood Brothers and Carson, Foundry and Machine Works, in McMinnville, Tennessee, and were manufacturers and dealers in "Everything pertaining to the foundry and machine businesses." Located in east central Tennessee, the foundry and machine works produced iron and brass castings, iron columns, fencing, shafting, pulleys, pipe, hollow ware of all kinds, belting and general mill supplies.

They also manufactured the Improved Giant Cane Mill which they claimed to be the "lightest running mill made." Eastwood Brothers and Carson manufactured three sizes of their Giant Cane Mills, the numbers 0, 1, and 2. Four things contributed to the quality of their mills. They were manufactured with great care, made out of the very best materials available by skilled craftsmen, and were closely inspected before leaving the factory. Other features of their mills were steel shafts, steel set screws, and brass boxes which made them light-running. There were also flanges on top and bottom of the main roll, above and below the small rollers, to keep the cane between the rollers. To lessen the possibility of injury, all gears were enclosed. Strong clutches, and not keys, were used to connect the gear wheels and rollers. This design allowed the owner to disassemble the mill with a minimum of trouble. Each mill came with an oil can, full set of bolts, and a wrench.

Chart for Eastwood Brothers and Carson
Improved Giant Cane Mills

Model No.	Horsepower	Main Roller- D × H	Small Rollers- D × H	Juice Per Hour	Weight	Price
No. 0	1 Horse	10" × 5"	5" × 5"	35–40 gals.	325 lbs.	$30.00
No. 1	1 Horse L.	12" × 6"	6" × 6"	40–50 gals.	550 lbs.	$40.00
No. 2	2 Horse L.	14" × 7"	7" × 7"	50–75 gals.	750 lbs.	$60.00

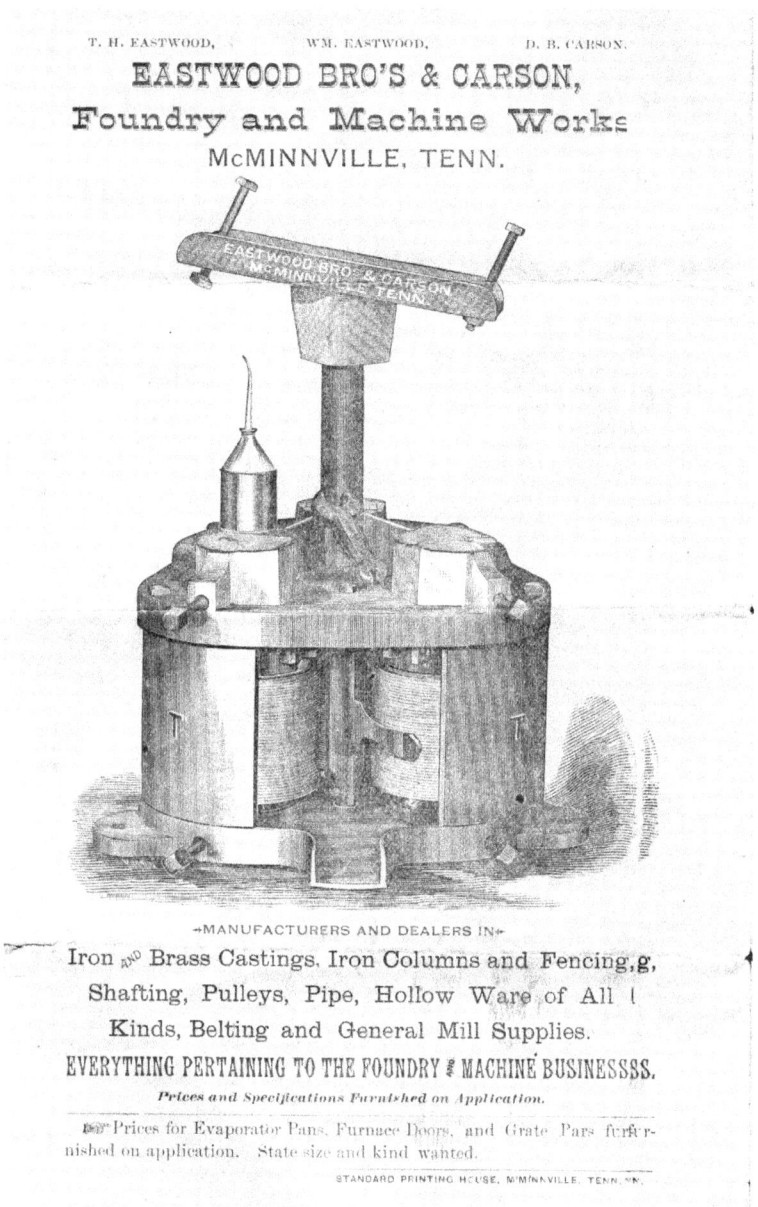

Feed side view from a sales brochure.

The No. 0 was manufactured to meet the needs of the farmer raising only small crops of cane. It was light, convenient, and easy to handle. The No. 1 mill was a popular, well-built mill, and at times the company could not keep up with orders for the $40 mill. It truly was a "Giant." The No. 2 mill was a large two-horse mill designed for large producers.

An early company brochure has this interesting statement on "Directions for Setting Up Our Giant Cane Mill": Set the mill firmly and level on posts or frame. If you place the mill upon posts they should be five or six feet long, and set from two to three feet in the ground. A stiff lever should be used, from 10 to 15 feet long, according to number of mill. Set the feed roll ¼ to ⅜ inch from main roll varying the parallel by adjusting the steel set

Opposite side view from a sales brochure.

screws at top and bottom. Feed the cane butt end foremost and feed regular. Mill should be oiled well before running, and should be kept oiled regularly while in use. Much depends on this, as it will save the mill and power. We would suggest the best Lard Oil be used. Keep a lookout and see that the oil goes into the lower boxes. Our mills are so constructed that no oil can get into the juice, so don't be afraid to oil well.

Parts and repair were also available from Eastwood Brothers and Carson, though they claimed that repairs were "seldom ever necessary."

Eddy, Thompson and Company, Springfield, Missouri

Most of the history of the Eddy, Thompson and Company foundry and ironworks in Springfield has been lost and we have to piece together an account from secondary sources. In an 1874 listing there is a reference to the Eddy, Thompson and Company in Springfield. In 1881, R.S. Eddy was listed as the superintendent of the Springfield Iron Works in the Springfield city directory. In the 1890–91 city directory there is a reference to the Springfield Foundry and Machine Company at 233–247 W. Mill Street. In 1895 Rollin S. Eddy is again referred to as the superintendent of the foundry, and in 1898 he is listed as president of the company. The Thompson part of the company is lost in obscurity, and in 1899 the company was referred to as Eddy Foundry and Machine Company (W.H. Eddy) and disappeared from the records after 1901. Eddy, Thompson and Company manufactured steam engines, boilers, sawmills, gristmills, threshing machinery, and cane mills to meet the growing needs of the Missouri farmers.

Emerson Manufacturing Company, Rockford, Illinois

Ralph Emerson, founder of Emerson Manufacturing Company, Rockford, Illinois, was born May 3, 1831, in Andover, Massachusetts, the son of a Congregational clergyman. After receiving his early education he taught school briefly, then moved to Bloomington to study law. On the advice of Abraham Lincoln, who became a close friend, Emerson redirected his

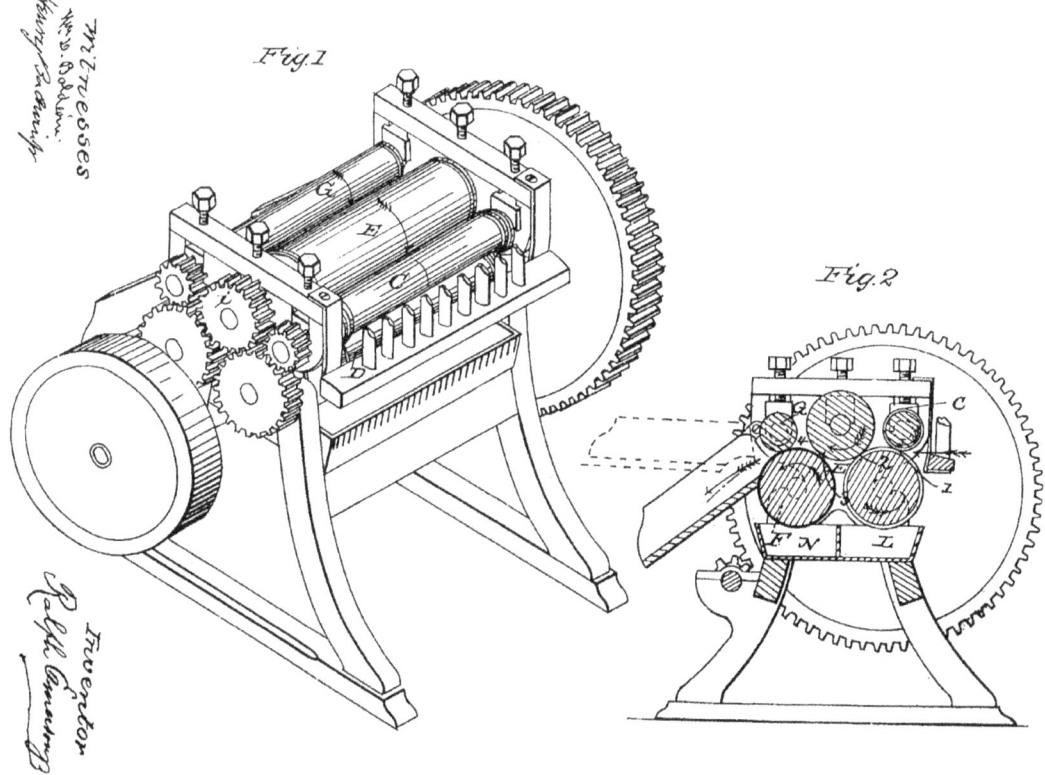

Two juice pans characterize Emerson's mill.

energies to industrial endeavors. His industrial ventures took him first to Beloit, Wisconsin, and then in 1852 to Rockford, where he went into the hardware business in partnership with Jesse Blinn. In 1853, John H. Manny, who had invented a reaper, moved to Rockford. Manny's reapers, which won competitive trials in 1855 in Europe and established their reputation abroad, were manufactured by Clarke and Utter's company and sold through Emerson and Blinn's hardware company.

Wait and Sylvester Talcott became Manny's partners in the spring of 1854, and in the fall Emerson and Blinn also joined the firm now known as Manny and Company. Manny died in 1856. In 1857, Emerson bought out Blinn's share and Emerson and Company, manufacturers of agricultural implements, was formed. Emerson received a patent for a cane mill in 1859 which was unique in its method of separating juice in the squeezing process. His mill was characterized by a series of rollers exerting from light to intense pressure on the cane with the juice flowing into one or the other of two juice pans. Emerson's theory was that the lighter pressure would squeeze out the better juice from the pith, which would flow into one pan. More intense pressure from a second set of rollers would squeeze out the more bitter albuminous juice and coloring matter from the rind, which would flow into the other juice pan.

The company reorganized as Emerson and Talcott in 1876, and reorganized again as Emerson Manufacturing Company in 1895. In 1909, Charles S. Brantingham, a long-time business associate, became a partner and the name changed to Emerson-Brantingham Company with Brantingham as president and Emerson chairman of the board. The factory, which had been relocated, now covered one hundred acres, with Emerson Carriage Company occupying the original site. The Emerson-Brantingham Company owned a chain of factories in other cities, employed 5,000 workers, and shipped their agricultural products worldwide. While reapers had long been their primary product, Emerson-Brantingham expanded their business to include tractors in 1912 with the purchase of Reeve and Company and Gas Traction Company. They manufactured the Emerson-Brantingham L12-20, a large four-cylinder L-head engine rated at 800 rpm and capable of pulling a three-bottom plow. The company was ultimately purchased by the J.I. Case Threshing Company in 1928.

Upon his retirement Emerson devoted his energies to numerous charitable enterprises, but was still involved in several industrial and financial institutions. He was president of the Burson Knitting Company and the Burson Manufacturing Company, director of the Rockford Mitten and Hosiery Company, Nelson Knitting Company and Winnebago National Bank. A man of boundless energies, full of compassion and a genuine desire to help his city and its people, Emerson had investments in lumber, electric lighting and insurance. At his death on August 14, 1914, he was identified with over forty different manufacturing, commercial, financial, educational, and charitable enterprises.

Though successful by every stretch of the imagination, his life was not without loss and sorrow. On Sunday, August 25, 1889, a fire broke out in P.A. Peterson's original Union Furniture factory. When it seemed the fire was out of control efforts turned to saving the adjacent property of Emerson, Talcott and Company, separated from Peterson's only by a narrow alley. Among the first to jump up on the one story blacksmith shop was Ralph Emerson, Jr., a young man in his early twenties. The immense fire drew hundreds of spectators, and Emerson, Sr., watched from the high steps of the old office building. As young Emerson was fighting the fire threatening to engulf his father's business, the hose kinked and bulked, and the pressure threw him off the building onto the tracks below. Word spread through the throng that someone had fallen from an Emerson building and was badly hurt. Compassion and generosity rose in Mr. Emerson and he determined that no mere hospitalization was good enough for someone hurt defending his building. "Take him to my home!" Emerson instructed. There the person would have the housing of his own home, the nursing and care of his own family. Soon a group of strong men tenderly carried the now lifeless body of young Emerson to the foot of the steps. Seeing the injured man, now dead to this world, Emerson exclaimed, "My God! It is Ralph!"

Ralph, Jr., had the reputation of a plain spoken, clean minded, sturdy bodied young man who was full of promise. Rockford held him in such high esteem that at his funeral the leading industries of the city shut down. The church was filled to overflowing and the crowd extended far back into an adjacent park, and the *Rockford Star* carried a moving account of the funeral service. At the conclusion of a long and eloquent eulogy honoring Emerson, his sister and brother-in-law, Mr. and Mrs. William E. Hinchliff, came forward and presented their infant son, Ralph, for Christian baptism, a moving symbol of death and resurrection.

Ralph Emerson, Sr., was a cousin of the poet, Ralph Waldo Emerson, a friend of President Abraham Lincoln, and a friend to all. Dr. Booker T. Washington paid Emerson a marvelous tribute at his death, almost twenty-five years after the death of his son, when he said, "Our race has lost one of its greatest friends, a friend of Lincoln, a friend of the Negro, everyone's friend."

Excelsior Foundry Company, Belleville, Illinois

The Excelsior Foundry Company, 1123 B Street, Belleville, Illinois, has been known for quality castings since 1892, including their famous Excelsior, Favorite and St. Louis cane mills. The company was founded by Eddy P. and George B. Rogers in December 1851 in a building on South Street across from the main factory of the International Shoe Company. The original company manufactured window sash weights, and at this writing is in the fourth generation of the Rogers family. Those early Rogers men built the integrity of their company on reliable products and on-time delivery, a trait which still characterizes the company. This uncompromising quality was also built into their mills. At some point early on the company moved to East B Street at Iowa Avenue and specialized in castings for electric motor housings and appliances, and sorghum cane mills. At this time the company was producing 35,000 tons of castings and 1,500 cane mills annually.

Frank B. Rogers, then president and general superintendent of the plant, was issued Patent No. 1,355,620 on October 12, 1920, for a new method of securing rollers to their shafts. Rogers' design was for hollow rollers with square openings adapted to receive square shafts. Round bearing blocks with square openings set in bearing boxes in the frame of the machine created suitable bearings for the shafts:

Excelsior touted the following characteristics of their cane mills from an earlier catalog in which all the mills had the standard round shafts:

- All our Mills are made of the best materials throughout.
- All shafts being cold rolled steel.
- Large rollers flanged on both ends.
- Small rollers adjustable to accommodate the different sizes of cane.
- All rollers and shafts lathe turned.

Excelsior No. 50 Horizontal Power Cane Mill

The Model No. 50 mill was a double back geared mill, and featured adjustable rollers of extra hard cast iron with shells of more than ordinary thickness. The shafts were of very heavy steel, and were secured in the roller by three heavy steel keys cast into the inner hub

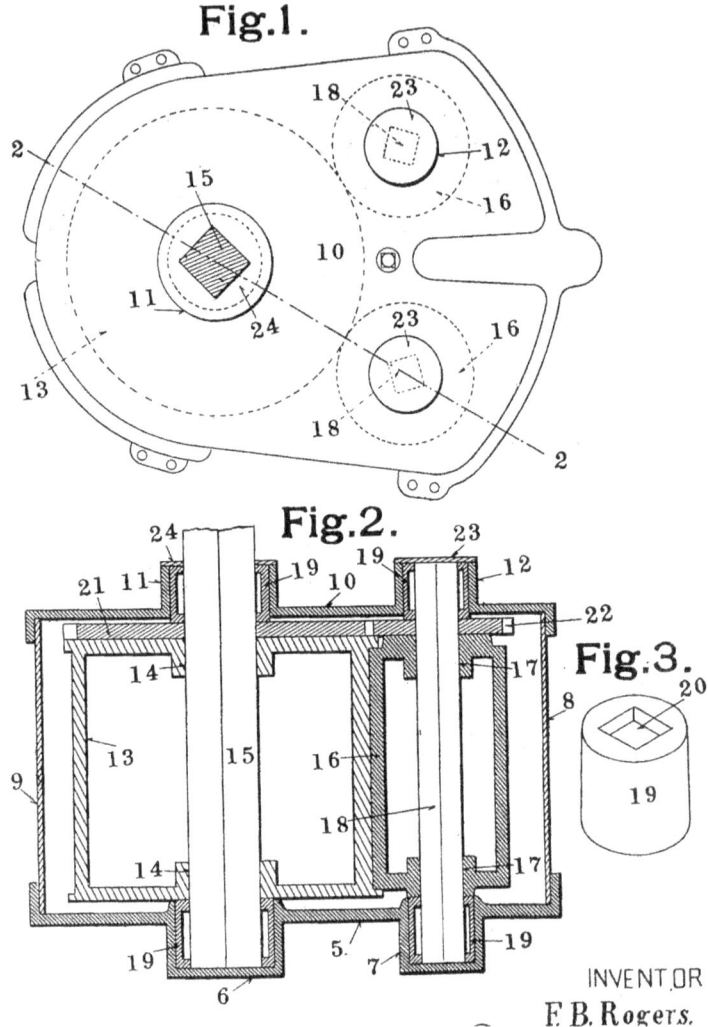

Note the square openings for square shafts that sat in round bearing boxes.

of the roller. The bearings were made of solid bronze. All bolts and screws were extra large, and the spur wheels were heavy, with ribbed arms. The pinions were very strong, and the teeth shrouded up to the pitch line. A scraper was attached to the top plate to keep the top roller clean at all times and to prevent bagasse from clogging.

Chart for Excelsior's No. 50 Cane Mill

Model No.	Horsepower	Main Roller- D × H	Small Rollers- D × H	Cane Per Hour	Weight	Price
No. 50	12 to 15 HP	16" × 15"	10" × 15"	4½ Tons	4,500 lbs.	$675.00

Excelsior Horizontal Power Mills

The No. 44 and No. 45 Excelsior cane mills featured many of the above features, but had babbitt bearings. These mills came with a 24" D × 6" W pulley.

Above: Model No. 50 featured double back gearing for more power. *Below:* This model came with babbitt bearings (both illustrations courtesy Excelsior Foundry Company, Belleville, Illinois).

Chart for Excelsior's Horizontal Power Mills

Model No.	Horsepower	Main Roller- D × H	Small Rollers- D × H	Cane Per Hour	Weight	Price
No. 44	10–12 HP	16" × 12"	10" × 12	3½ tons	2,800 lbs.	$420.00
No. 45	10–12 HP	16" × 18"	10" × 18"	4 tons	3,200 lbs.	$480.00

Excelsior Models 42 and 43 Horizontal Cane Mills

These mills were powerful double back gear mills suitable for gasoline engine power operation. They also came with Excelsior's new device for cleaning the main roller to prevent clogging.

Chart for Excelsior's No. 42 and 43 Power Mills

Model No.	Horsepower	Main Roller- D × H	Small Rollers- D × H	Cane Per Hour	Weight	Price
No. 42	4 Horse	10" × 10"	7" × 10"	1½ Tons	1.250 lbs.	$179.00
No. 43	6 Horse	10" × 16"	7" × 16"	2 Tons	1,450 lbs.	$207.00

The New Excelsior Horizontal Power Mills

The New Excelsior Mill was the same as the No. 42 and No. 43, except that the gears were keyed on to the rollers outside of the side plates, thus making the roller surface two and one half inches longer.

These models were geared for gasoline engine power operation (courtesy Excelsior Foundry Company, Belleville, Illinois).

By keying the gears outside, the rollers were made 2½ inches wider (courtesy Excelsior Foundry Company, Belleville, Illinois).

Chart for the "New Excelsior" Power Mills

Model No.	Horsepower	Main Roller- D × H	Small Rollers- D × H	Cane Per Hour	Weight	Price
No. 42A	4 Horse	10" × 12½"	7" × 12½"	2½ Tons	1,350 lbs.	$203.00
No. 43A	6 Horse	10" × 18½"	7" × 18½"	3 Tons	1,500 lbs.	$225.00

Excelsior Single Back Gear Horizontal Mills

The Excelsior Nos. 40 and 41 were horizontal power mills with single back gearing. The bearings were babbitt, and there was a scraper on the main roller to prevent clogging. The top rollers were stationary with adjustable small rollers.

Chart for Excelsior's Single Back Gearing Power Mills

Model No.	Horsepower	Main Roller- D × H	Small Rollers- D × H	Cane Per Hour	Weight	Price
No. 40	2 to 4 Horse	10" × 10"	7" × 10"	¾ Ton	1,200 lbs.	$171.00
No. 41	4 to 6 Horse	10" × 16"	7" × 16"	1 Ton	1,350 lbs.	$193.00

Excelsior's Wonderful Pony Mill

The Wonderful Pony Mill was produced in response to numerous requests for a small mill which could be operated by a small gasoline engine. This mill carried the same features and quality of the larger mills.

Above: This model featured babbitt bearings and single back gearing (courtesy Excelsior Foundry Company, Belleville, Illinois). *Below:* Excelsior's Wonderful Pony is a neat little mill.

A company engraving of the Wonderful Pony (courtesy Excelsior Foundry Company, Belleville, Illinois).

Chart for Excelsior's Wonderful Pony Mills

Model No.	Horsepower	Main Roller- D × H	Small Rollers- D × H	Cane Per Hour	Weight	Price
No. 39	2½ Horse	8" × 8"	5½" × 8"	¾ Ton	650 lbs.	$93.00

Excelsior's Horizontal Sweep Cane Mill

Excelsior also made a horizontal mill with a top geared sweep. With this gearing the rollers made two revolutions to one of the horse, making the capacity twice that of the vertical mill.

Chart for Excelsior's Horizontal Sweep Cane Mills

Model No.	Horsepower	Main Roller- D × H	Small Rollers- D × H	Cane Per Hour	Weight	Price
No. 30	2 Horse	10" × 10"	7" × 10"	¾ Ton	1,150 lbs.	$138.00
No. 31	4 Horse	10" × 16"	7" × 16"	1 Ton	1,375 lbs.	$165.00

St. Louis Cane Mill

The St. Louis Cane Mill was a vertical three-roller mill offered in seven sizes. This series featured brass bearings, cog wheels cast separate from the rollers and held in place with a clutch. The mills had encased gearing and flanged main rollers.

Above: Excelsior's horizontal mill with top sweep. *Below:* The St. Louis was offered in seven sizes (both courtesy Excelsior Foundry Company, Belleville, Illinois).

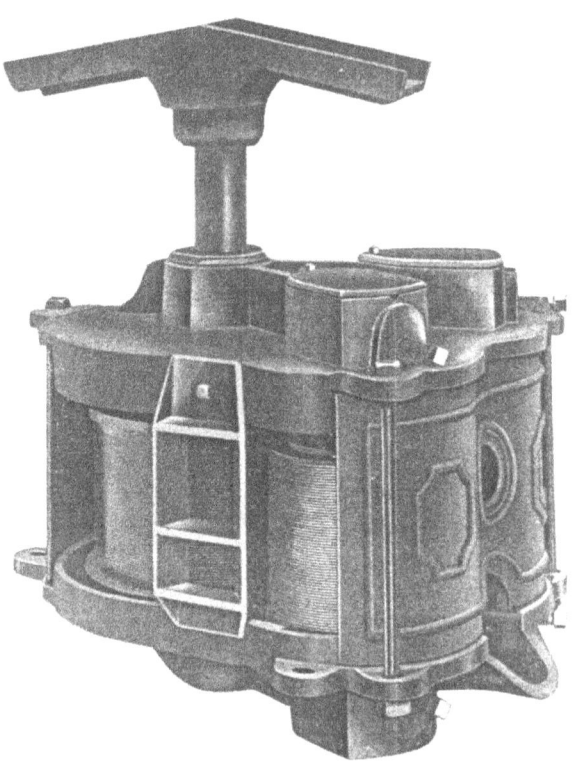

Chart for Excelsior's St. Louis Cane Mill

Model No.	Horsepower	Main Roller- D × H	Small Rollers- D × H	Juice Per Hour	Weight	Price
No. 0	1 Light	8½" × 5¾"	5½" × 5¾"	30–45 gals.	435 lbs.	$43.00
No. 1	1 Horse	10" × 6½"	6" × 6½"	45–60 gals.	550 lbs.	$54.00
No. 2	1 Horse	11½" × 6¾"	6¼" × 6¾"	60–75 gals.	635 lbs.	$62.00
No. 3	2 Horse	13 ⅝" × 7½"	7½" × 7½"	75–90 gals.	900 lbs.	$88.00
No. 4	2 Horse	13 ⅝" × 8½"	7½" × 8½"	90–100 gals.	950 lbs.	$93.00
No. 5	2 Horse	13¾" × 9"	7½" × 9"	100–120 gals.	1,035 lbs.	$101.00
No. 6	2 Horse Heavy	13¾" × 12"	7½" × 12"	120–145 gals.	1,125 lbs.	$110.00

Favorite Cane Mill

Excelsior's Favorite Cane Mill featured four main bolts holding the mill together, gears cast separate from the rolls, brass gear boxes top and bottom; the main roller was flanged top and bottom; a feed guide designed to use the entire surface of the roller was included.

Chart for Excelsior's Favorite Cane Mill

Model No.	Horsepower	Main Roller- D × H	Small Rollers- D × H	Juice Per Hour	Weight	Price
No. 9	1 Horse	8¼" × 5 ⅝"	5½" × 5 ⅝"	40–50 gals.	450 lbs.	$44.00
No. 10	1 Horse	9½" × 6⅜"	6" × 6⅜"	40–60 gals.	575 lbs.	$56.00
No. 11	1 Horse	11½" × 6¾"	6⅝" × 6¾"	60–75 gals.	650 lbs.	$64.00
No. 12	2 Horse	13" × 7⅜"	7⅛" × 7⅜"	75–90 gals.	925 lbs.	$91.00
No. 13	2 Horse Heavy	14" × 9¼"	8¾" × 9¼"	90–100 gals.	1,050 lbs.	$103.00

Excelsior's Favorite had brass gear boxes top and bottom (courtesy Excelsior Foundry Company, Belleville, Illinois).

Bagasse carriers, feed tables, the improved "Cook's" Portable Evaporator Pan And Rocker Furnace, evaporator pans, furnace irons, doors, grates and skimmers were also available. The Excelsior Foundry Company, while no longer manufacturing cane mills, is still in business in Belleville, Illinois, specializing in gray iron, ductile iron, Meehanite, and compacted graphite. The company excels in short-run work, manufacturing such items as water pumps for automobiles, manifolds, transmission cases, and electric motor frames.

Farrel Foundry and Machine Company, Ansonia, Connecticut

F. Farrel served as president of the Farrel Foundry and Machine Company, manufacturers of a variety of iron products, including steam engines, chilled rolls, general rolling machines, portable mills, ore crushers, racks, stone mills, cartridge machines and cane mills.

On August 11, 1891, David R. Bowen, assignor to the Farrel Foundry, received Patent No. 457,395 for a device to take the pressure off the bottom roller and thus eliminate wear and breakage.

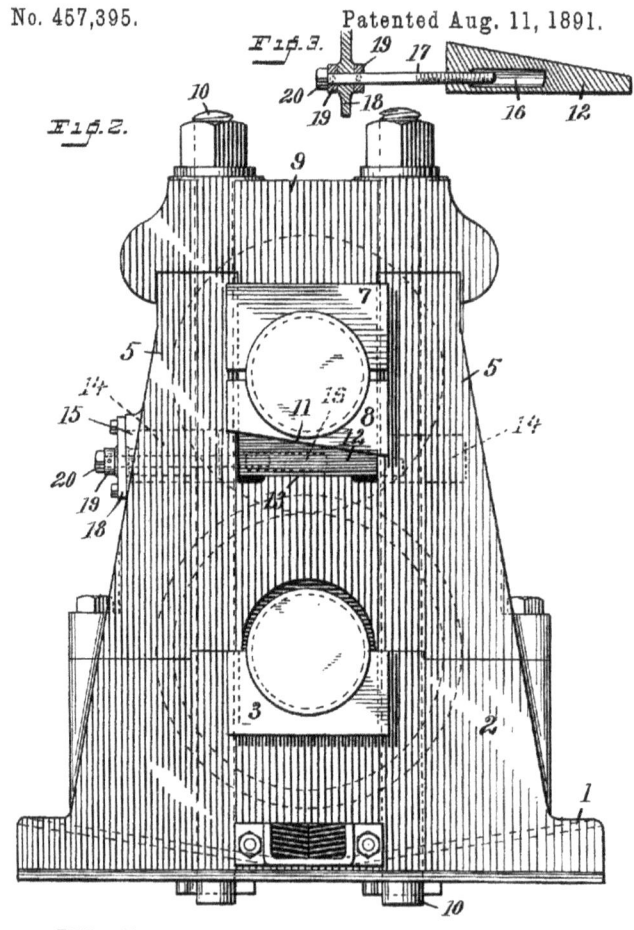

Bowen, of Farrel Foundry, invented a system to take some of the pressure off the bottom roller.

J.A. Field and Company, St. Louis, Missouri

J.A. Field and Company, at the corner of Eighth and Howard streets, St. Louis, was in business with Alexander Magee in 1881. Magee withdrew and established his own company, Alexander Magee and Company, in 1885. Field manufactured the Star cane mills in three sizes. Their No. 1 mill was a three roller horizontal mill with a main roller ten inches in diameter and two six inch diameter lower rollers. This mill weighed 800 pounds. The No. 2 mill also had a ten inch diameter main roller and two six inch diameter lower rollers, and weighed 1,000 pounds. The No. 3 mill had a fourteen inch diameter main roller and two nine inch diameter lower rollers. The front lower roller on the No. 3 was self-adjusting to accommodate variations in cane sizes and irregular feeding. The back lower roller was adjustable and could be held firmly in place. The configuration of the gearing allowed the rollers to make two revolutions for each one of the horses. The company claimed these mills could grind nearly twice as fast as any mill of the same price and were featured in *Farm Machinery*, a monthly journal of agricultural manufacturers, in July, 1887.

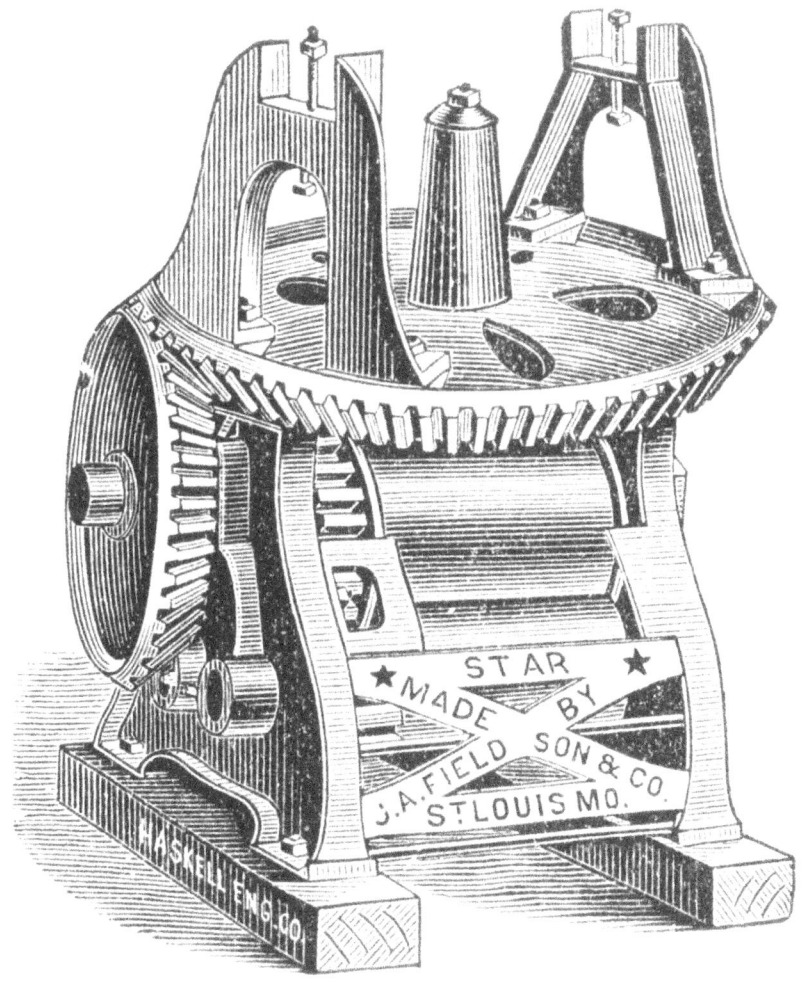

Field cane mill (Special Collections, St. Louis Public Library).

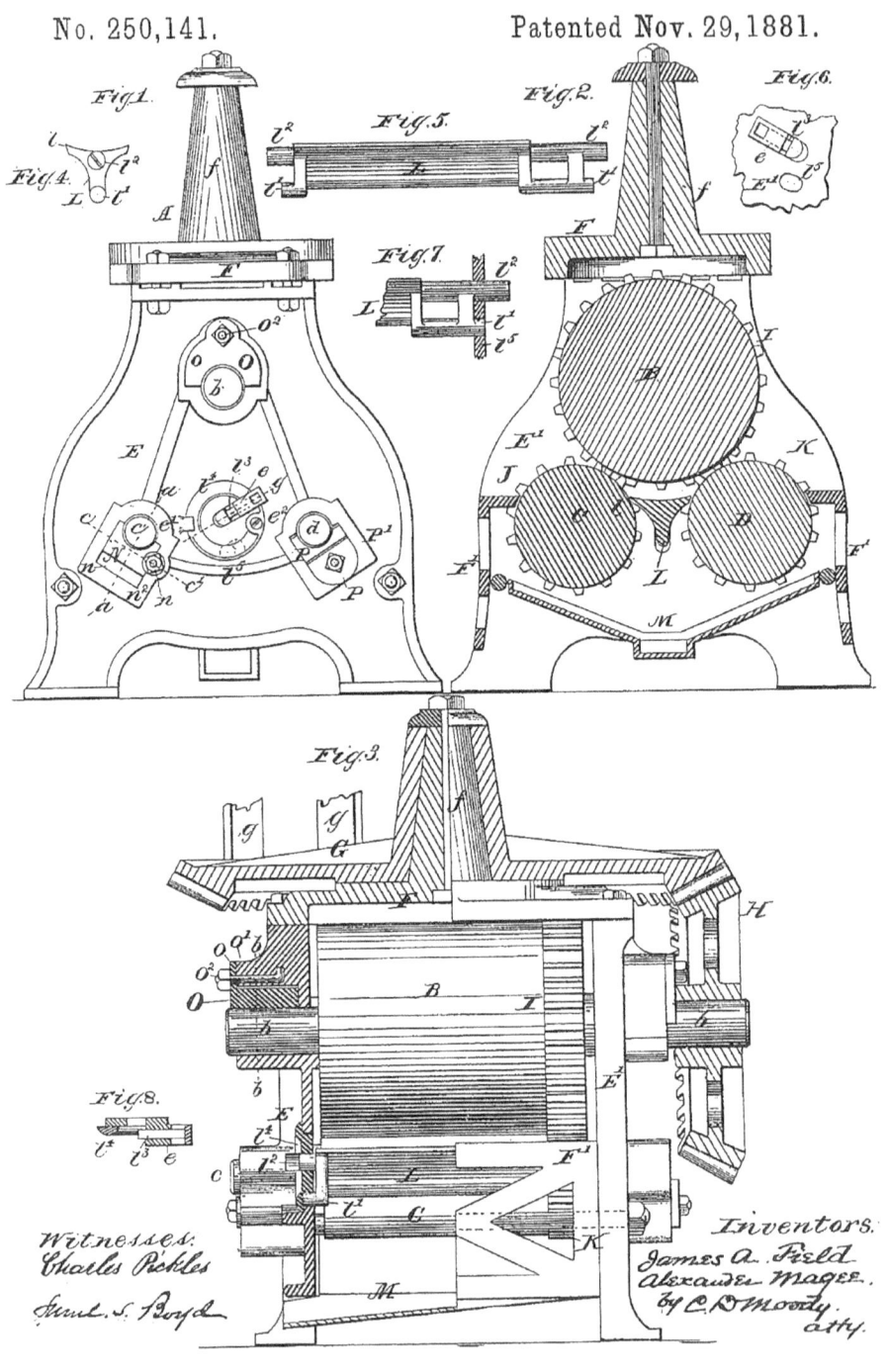

The Field-Magee patent featured an improved knife guide.

Chart for Field's Cane Mills

Model No.	Main Roller Diameter	Small Roller Diameter	Weight
No. 1	10"	6"	800 lbs.
No. 2	10"	6"	1000 lbs.
No. 3	14"	9"	3000 lbs.

On November 29, 1881, James A. Field and Alexander Magee were awarded Patent No. 250,141 for their cane mill, which featured an improved guide knife situated between the lower rollers on their horizontal mill. Their design utilized a spring which kept the guide knife up against the roller.

Robert Findlay Iron Works, Macon, Georgia

One of the keys to the success of the Robert Findlay Iron Works, Macon, Georgia, is found in the fact that Findlay listened to his customers and tried to respond to their needs. Many times a customer would say, "This might work better if done this way." Findlay would listen and attempt to improve his product. Consequently, his steam engines were years ahead of others of that era, but he never applied for a patent for any of his innovations. But this was just like Robert Findlay.

Findlay was born January 17, 1808, in Water of Leith, a textile village now incorporated into Edinburgh, Scotland, and known, interestingly, as Dean Village. He was apprenticed and trained as a cabinet maker. Like numerous others, he joined the long line of Scots seeking a better life in America and emigrated to New York in August 1828. By 1837 he was a naturalized United States citizen living in Philadelphia and was employed by a pioneer locomotive manufacturer. The first steam engines for powering pumps and mills came to the United States, to Philadelphia, in the 1780s, though they were not considered widely practical until around 1800. Locomotive manufacturing was a young industry, and when the great depression of 1837 set in, Findlay moved to Macon, Georgia, to work on one of the South's first railroads. When the depression reached Macon, that company went bankrupt. Findlay left the firm in 1838 and joined a local foundry, which was surviving by building and repairing railroad, mill and plantation machinery.

The Macon Brass and Iron Works began as a carriage and coach factory in 1831. After experiencing several changes of ownership over the next few years, James William Smallwood, Nathaniel Smith, and William John McElroy bought the business in January 1839 and converted the shop into a blacksmith, coppersmith, and boiler-making business. Smallwood dropped out of the business in May 1839. Findlay joined the concern in October 1839, and together the partners formed the Macon Brass and Iron Works and Machine Shop. Smith sold his interest to his partners for $1,000 in May 1840. Findlay bought out McElroy in 1841 to become sole proprietor. By 1854, the Findlay Iron Works was a massive industrial complex touted as the largest south of Richmond, Virginia. Additional foundries were established in Atlanta and Griffin, with another planned for Albany.

Stationary steam engines became Findlay's signature product, but his main business, however, consisted of repairing and producing replacement parts for plows and for machinery built outside the South. The Findlay Iron Works had an impressive product list, including circular, single and gang saws; mill gearing; mill stones; water wheels; cotton gins; cotton presses; gold mining equipment; corn grinding machines; bark mills; stirrups; iron columns; iron tombstones; pulleys; cane mills; syrup boilers; and even a railroad car. Findlay hoped to sell his steam powered cane mills to growers in Louisiana and Mississippi, but found that most of them purchased their mills from manufacturers in the Midwest or New York. However, he did find a ready market for his mills among the cane growers in the southeastern states.

Robert Findlay was a man of fierce integrity who never forgot to be grateful for his adopted homeland and his adopted home of Macon. He was a successful businessman, and served Macon as fire chief, city engineer, and alderman. He was a deacon in the Baptist church, and a member of the local Masonic Lodge. He contracted pneumonia on November 25, 1859, and died five days later. His family continued the ironworks business following his death. During the Civil War his foundry was converted to a cannon factory. The United States Army occupied the ironworks until 1866, and when the family finally took possession of the property again they could not reopen for business until 1868. By then, the concern was faced with debt, worn-out machinery and stiff competition. For a time, the foundry survived by manufacturing lead window sash weights. After several bankruptcies, the Findlays closed their once proud and productive foundry in 1912. A more robust account of this man's life may be found in *Cotton, Fire and Dreams: The Robert Findlay Iron Works and Heavy Industry in Macon, Georgia, 1839–1912*, by Robert S. Davis.

Franklin Iron Works, Philadelphia, Pennsylvania

James T. Sutton and Company were proprietors of the well established and respected Franklin Iron Works of Philadelphia. One employee who rose through the company to distinguish himself in his field was Robert Cartwright. A native of Philadelphia, Robert was born September 2, 1830, received his education in the public schools of the city, and began his apprenticeship at the Franklin Iron Works as a seventeen year old youth in March 1847. Cartwright remained with Franklin until he was "of age," and his story may be found in the *History of the City of Rochester*, by the Post Express Print Company. During this time he fitted out eighteen vessels with their engines and boilers, quite an achievement for such a young man. He also mastered the art of constructing marine, stationary and blowing engines, blast furnaces and rolling-mills of every description as well as sugar mills. Cartwright became a distinguished draftsman and civil and mechanical engineer who was connected in some way with thirty-four gasworks in the United States and Canada.

The most extensive arsenal in the United States was at Bridesburg, Pennsylvania. The facility consisted of elaborate, innovative and effective equipment for the production of ordinances. The engine powering this equipment was built by the Franklin Iron Works in 1852 and was still giving dependable service a decade later. In the late 1850s the proprietors were ready to retire, and in 1859 they advertised their iron foundry and machine shop for sale or rent. The plant consisted of an iron foundry, machine, boiler, smith, patterns and millwright shops, along with the machinery, tools, patterns and fixtures. Fronting three streets, the ironworks sat on a lot 100 feet-1 inch by 245 feet-7 inches. While cane mills did not seem to be the focus of the Franklin Iron Works, they did endeavor to supply growers and sugar producers of that era with the needed equipment.

Frost Manufacturing Company, Galesburg, Illinois

Begun in a little twenty-five by eighteen foot wooden frame building in 1851, the Frost Manufacturing Company eventually became the leading engine and boilermaker in the west. J.P. Frost, an ingenious and skilled mechanic, moved to Galesburg from Whitesboro, New York, and established a little business. A Mr. L.M. Fuller wanted to erect a gristmill on North

Broad Street just south of the old Santa Fe passenger station and contacted Frost to build the mill for him. However, Frost didn't have a metal turning lathe necessary for the job. Fuller supplied the lathe, and Frost paid for it in labor on the gristmill. This humble, cooperative venture was the beginning of manufacturing in Galesburg. And the lathe that began it all was preserved for years by the Frost Company.

Frost built a small wooden shop near Fuller's mill to be near the work. This building was later moved to W. Simmons Street where the company was eventually built. While improvements became the ongoing policy of the company, the original shop was kept intact for years as a reminder of the humble beginning of the great Frost manufacturing industry. The company made other gristmill machinery, and as demand grew began branching out with one or two other items. The first motive power of the company was a horse. It was used to pull Frost's wagon and power his machinery.

In 1855 two young men, Andrew Harrington, a skilled mechanic, and W.S. Bellows, an expert foundry-man, moved to Galesburg from Chleopee, Massachusetts, and joined Frost in his endeavors. These three men formed the J.P. Frost and Company. They built a rather large factory and installed a steam engine to power their machinery. L.C. Field joined the partnership in 1857. In 1867 the company was incorporated with a capital stock of $80,000, and Field was elected the first president. The partnership was disrupted by Bellows' death in 1875, Field's in 1878, and Frost's in 1880. This left Harrington to head the company until his death in 1890.

The Frost mill had exposed cogs characteristic of the day (courtesy Bob McGuire, Lenexa, Kansas, and Bill McGuire, Oregon, Missouri).

The Frost Manufacturing Company became an important industry in western trade. The company made thirty-two different styles of engines, moved with the times and manufactured gasoline engines, brick-making machinery, and grain elevator machinery. In the late 1800s demands were so great that the one hundred employees had to work sixteen hours per day to fill orders. At peak seasons the company shipped out a boxcar of machinery each day. This was quite an accomplishment for the little company which began its lustrous life in a minute 18' × 25' wooden building, and whose record is preserved in *Voices of the Prairie Land*, by Litvin and Churchill.

The Frost Manufacturing Company also made cane mills, but a complete product line has not been discovered by this writer.

Fulton Iron and Manufacturing, St. Louis, Missouri

Fulton Iron and Manufacturing had its beginning in a machine shop established in 1852 by Gerald B. Allen on the banks of the Mississippi River in St. Louis, Missouri, and much information about the company may be found on their website, www.fultoniron.net and from *Fulton Installations*, a publication of the company. Robert Fulton had built the first really successful steamboat, the *Clermont*, in 1807. By 1850 the immense river traffic on the mighty Mississippi offered a lucrative business for manufacturers of steam engines and boilers. In fact, Allen's steam engine business was so successful that in 1879 he named his company Fulton Iron Works in honor of the inventor of the steamboat. By the end of the century the demand for steamboat engines had begun to diminish and Fulton began looking for other markets for their steam power plants. Various presses, mining equipment, and sugar mills were possibilities for Fulton's expertise.

Though their power plants were used by sugar mills much earlier, in 1891 Fulton Iron Works designed and built a revolutionary new cane mill. The Cora Mill was the first mill manufactured which had nine rollers driven by a common gearing system and a single engine.

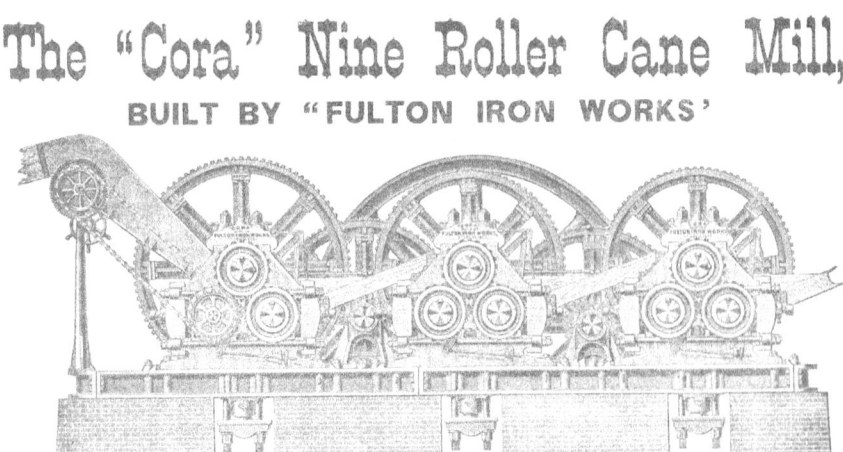

The Cora had nine rollers driven by a common gearing system.

Fulton build exceedingly large sugarhouse mills.

A hundred years later this mill was still in operation after being moved from Louisiana to Columbia and then to Panama. In 1892 Fulton began production of this revolutionary nine roller mill, and other manufacturers were soon to follow. While most of our emphasis has been, and will be, on smaller backyard type mills it is significant to note Fulton's place in the development of significant designs in cane mills. Fulton is still is business in St. Louis designing and building complete sugar factories worldwide. Some larger sorghum syrup producers do use some of their smaller mills.

P.W. Gates and Company, Chicago, Illinois

Philetus W. Gates was an industrious and successful Chicago businessman who was involved in a variety of interests and endeavors, though his initial efforts were ever so humble. He and Hiram H. Scoville bought 1,000 feet of lumber on credit and built a building for their ironworks near the bridge. At the end of the year a foundry and machine shop was built on the corner of Washington and West Water streets. After conducting business for about five years, manufacturing railroad cars on a small scale, Gates purchased Scoville's interest, according to Ancestry.com. In 1848 Gates admitted A.H. Hoge into partnership and before the end of that year George S. Kcknight purchased Hoge's interest and the firm became P.W. Gates and Company. Soon afterwards other men were added to the firm and the manufacture of railroad cars intensified in their already extensive business. The panic of 1857 left the firm $350,000 in debt, and though the company was placed in the hands of an assignee, by 1860 every dollar of its indebtedness was paid off.

The business interests of Mr. Gates included P.W. Gates and Company, Eagle Iron Works and Manufacturing Company, and Gates and McKnight. Of apparent boundless energy and of a creative genius, Gates held numerous U.S. patents. He received a patent for dies for cutting screws on May 8, 1847, and there followed a flood of patents over the next two decades for steam engine gearing, boiler steam valves, quartz crushing machines, stone breakers, stamping machines, brick machines, evaporators and cane mills. His company made the power transmission shafting for an Illinois State Fair, and he even served as a fair judge for the power traction category.

Gates designed a mill with concave rollers to accommodate large cane (courtesy John Kreinbrink, Ludington, Michigan).

A Gates mill built on Hedges' patent.

In the company's early cane mill production they used Hedges' patent, but Gates received patent No. 27,863 for his own mill on April 10, 1860. The uniqueness of Gates' mill consisted in the design of concave rollers circumferentially. This arrangement, Gates alleged, would allow the larger cane to be crushed satisfactorily in the space created by the concave rollers, while the smaller stalks would slide down and be crushed in the narrower space between the cylindric portions of the surface of the rollers. After the sorghum sugar flurry began to subside it seems that the P.W. Gates and Company concentrated on dies for cutting screws and quartz crushers.

S.W. Gleason and Company, Savannah, Georgia

Solomon Wilson Gleason, a native of Massachusetts, moved to Savannah, Georgia, in the mid 1850s. After the American Civil War he opened a foundry and machine shop on St. Julian Street, with the first listing in the *Savannah City Directory* appearing in 1871. Gleason advertised himself as an iron and brass founder, an engineer and machinist. He manufactured sugar mills, sugar pans, gin gear, shafting, pulleys and all kinds of iron and brass castings. He was also a dealer in portable and stationary steam engines, cotton screws, and machinery of various descriptions. Around 1874 James Manning joined the firm and is listed as a partner in the business. Gleason died on October 3, 1876, at age 58, of yellow fever.

45

S. W. GLEASON,

Iron and Brass Founder,

ENGINEER & MACHINIST,

Nos. 193 and 195 St. Julian st.,

SAVANNAH, GA.

Manufacturer of Sugar Mills, Sugar Pans, Gin Gear, Shafting, Pulleys, and all kinds of Iron and Brass Castings.

DEALER IN

Portable and Stationary Steam Engines, Cotton Screws, and Machinery of all kinds.

Gleason included cane mills in its product line (courtesy Live Oak Public Library, Savannah, Georgia).

Goldens' Foundry and Machine Company, Columbus, Georgia

    The Goldens' Foundry and Machine Company, 600 Twelfth Street, Columbus, Georgia, stands today as a glowing tribute to two young men who caught a vision and dared to venture. It is also a tribute to an older entrepreneur who believed in the integrity, abilities, and courage of these young men and dared to share the vision with them. John Poitevent (Porter) Golden and his brother Theodore (Theo) Earnest Golden had hardly gotten over the loss of their mother when their father passed away. Porter was twenty-two and Theo was twenty when their father died—young men with their lives ahead of them. They had seen their father weather some terrific storms in life, and he had instilled in them a sense of value, of courage, and of determination. Less than two years after their father's death Porter and Theo hitched up their trousers, gritted their teeth and took a bold step of faith. They each had inherited two shares in Columbus Iron Works, which they sold to W.R. Brown, president and majority stockholder of the company. Purchasing some tools, hammers, saws, and building equipment from the William Beach Hardware Company on Broad Street, Columbus, Porter and Theo began building a 30 by 100 foot one-story frame building at the

Above: Goldens' Foundry is still open for business in Columbus, Georgia. *Below:* This foundry ad [showing an alternate spelling, "Golden's"] reveals a massive complex.

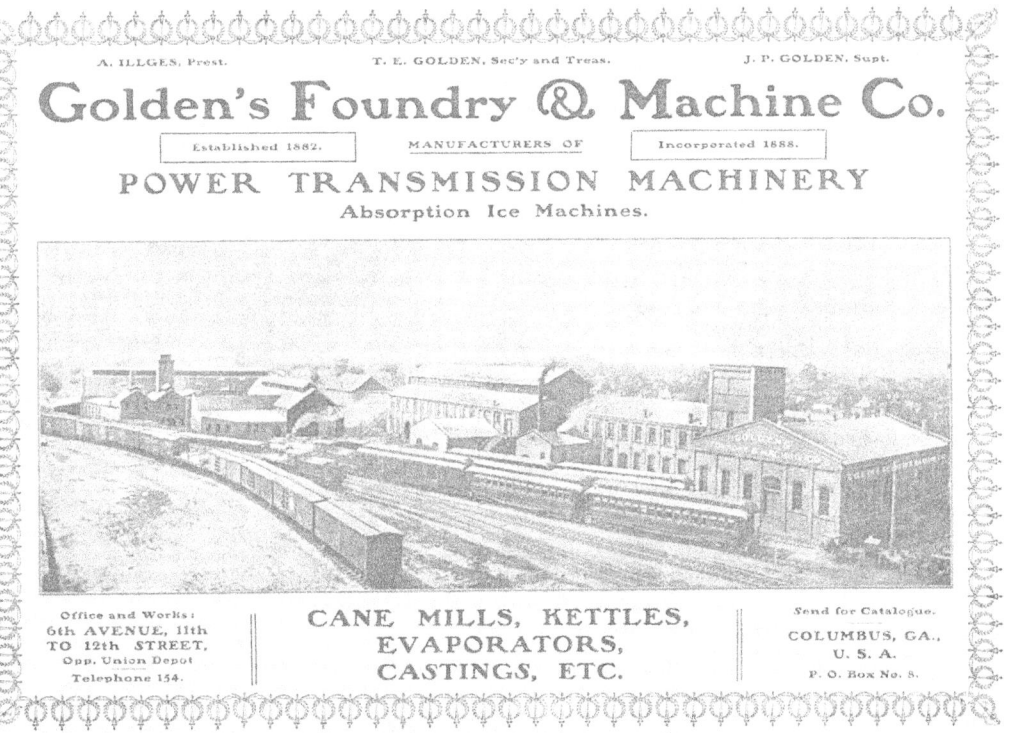

northwest corner of Sixth Avenue and Thirteenth Street. This was the beginning of a foundry and machine shop called Golden Brothers.

The foundry and machine shop business was literally in their blood. Their father, George Jasper Golden, was one of the original incorporators of the Columbus Iron Works and an officer in its predecessor. Born in Spartanburgh (old spelling), South Carolina, on April 18, 1833, George moved to Etowa, Georgia, as a young man. He learned the trade of pattern making at the ironworks of Mark A. Cooper, and at the tender age of sixteen he moved to Columbus where he found work as a skilled pattern maker and superb machinist. After the Civil War, he was one of the five men who reorganized the Columbus Iron Works under its original charter; he served as superintendent until his death in 1880.

Both Porter and Theo found work at the Columbus Iron Works, Porter becoming a pattern maker and Theo, who began work at age eleven, an excellent machinist. But they also observed and learned the foundry business, a knowledge which enabled them to launch Golden Brothers in 1882. Business grew rapidly once their building was completed. By 1884 they were making hanger collars and pulleys; alums cotton screws; evaporators with either copper or galvanized bottoms; couplings and shafting; hot polished shafting; engines and boilers; syrup kettles of the shallow pattern; and cane mills which could be run by steam or horsepower. Quite a feat for two young men who had not yet reached their thirtieth birthdays.

Within the next few years another individual would come into their lives and would give them support and guidance and establish a partnership and develop a lifelong friendship. This man was Abraham Illges, a successful Columbus businessman and entrepreneur. Born in Lancaster County, Pennsylvania, on April 7, 1830, Abraham Illges left school at thirteen and moved to Columbus to live with his brother and help him in the grocery business. He prospered in literally everything he tried, becoming a successful businessman and serving on the board of directors of numerous businesses. Somewhere along the way he and the Golden brothers came together and incorporated Golden Brothers on February 15, 1889, and he became a partner with them. He was elected president of the company, and the name was changed to Goldens' Foundry and Machine Company. Abraham Illges served as president of the company, without compensation, until he died on February 23, 1915, just short of his eighty-fifth birthday.

A meeting of the stockholders was called on June 3, 1890, to arrange means for increasing the capacity of the old building, and to proceed with building a new plant. On January 23, 1891, their plant was destroyed by fire. They had seen how their father had persevered after the Columbus Iron Works was burned during the Civil War, and the brothers, too, were determined to build a new plant. They succeeded and business was so good that in 1904 arrangements were made for further plant expansion.

In the president's report of January 9, 1925, however, it was noted that their cane mill sales were the poorest since the company had begun manufacturing them. The company offered a wide range of sizes and power applications, they had a large market, the mills were excellent in quality of workmanship and castings, and the company had seven cane mill patents. These were Patent No. 778,410 of December 27, 1904, for an improved scraper to eliminate the loss of juice normally carried off in the bagasse; Patent No. 783,428 of February 28, 1905, for feed boxes for horizontal mills to prevent the back-squirting of juice regardless of the size of cane being fed into the mill; Patent No. 799,326 of September 12, 1905, for an improved three-roller vertical mill featuring an enlarged juice cavity and discharge spout, an improved roller mounting, improved means for keeping the mill clear, and improved mill casting; Patent No. 799,327 of September 12, 1905, for an improved two-roller vertical mill with an improved mounting on the driven roller and improved arrangements for the juice-receiving cavity, along with other features; Patent No. 809,440 of January 9, 1906, for improved feed boxes to avoid juice loss on entry of cane, and to make the box reversible; Patent No. 848,025 of March 26, 1907, for improved gearing on horizontal mills to economize in space and protect the gears; and Patent No. 1,485,386 of March 4, 1924, for improvements in the guide knife on three-roller mills.

Now these patents were about to expire, and no doubt some competitors began to adopt some of the same features in their mills, thus increasing the competition. Another cause for declining sales lay in the fact that producers began using new methods for processing cane in the sugar regions of south Florida, Louisiana, and the Caribbean. The old mills were not capable of competing with the new type machinery. The company now made another bold step and decided to move into modern products, and cane mills became a minor part of their business. Sensing the change in industrial machinery, Goldens' Foundry and Machine Company began producing V-belt pulleys, replacing the flat belt pulleys which had been a mainstay of their business for years. They began manufacturing ball bearing units to replace the old babbitt-metal bearings, and in relation, began manufacturing housing for ball bearings, which was another bold step toward the future. But then this spirit had characterized Goldens' from the beginning, as characterized by J.P. Golden II in *The First Hundred Years, 1882–1982*.

"The Golden Mill" which made Goldens' famous (photograph by Tommy Clayton, Hilliard, Florida).

Goldens' began manufacturing cane mills in 1882. Prior to 1904, their mills were called "The Golden Mill." These were "flat-top" models with four fluted corner posts. During the year 1904, and subsequently, they manufactured and marketed their "New Model Mill."

Their transitional mills in 1904 were marked with a plate stating "Patent Applied For."

Goldens' regular two- and three-roller mills were painted brick red, and were known as "The Red Mill." Their extra-heavy duty mills were painted green, and their export models were blue.

In their 1911 catalog, Number 35, they offered numerous mills in various sizes and power applications. In the standard vertical three-roller horsepower mills, like the New Model above, Goldens' offered four models.

Chart for Goldens' Three Roller Vertical Mills

Model No. and Horsepower	Main Roller D × H	Feed Roller D × H	Discharge Roller D × H	Juice Per Hour	Weight	Price
No. 1, 1 light	10" × 5³⁄₁₆"	4⅝" × 5"	5" × 5"	35 gals.	375 lbs.	$30.00
No. 2. 1 heavy	12" × 6³⁄₁₆"	5⅝" × 6"	6" × 6"	45 gals.	570 lbs.	$40.00
No. 3, 2 light	14" × 7³⁄₁₆"	6⅝" × 7"	7" × 7"	65 gals.	770 lbs.	$60.00
No. 4, 2 heavy	16" × 8³⁄₁₆"	7⅝" × 8"	8" × 8"	100 gals.	1,100 lbs.	$80.00

Top left: "The Golden Mill" side view. It is still in service. *Top right:* Goldens' "New Model," which appeared in 1904. *Below:* New Model engraving from a company catalog (courtesy Dennis Parker and the Goldens' Foundry and Machine Company, Columbus, Georgia).

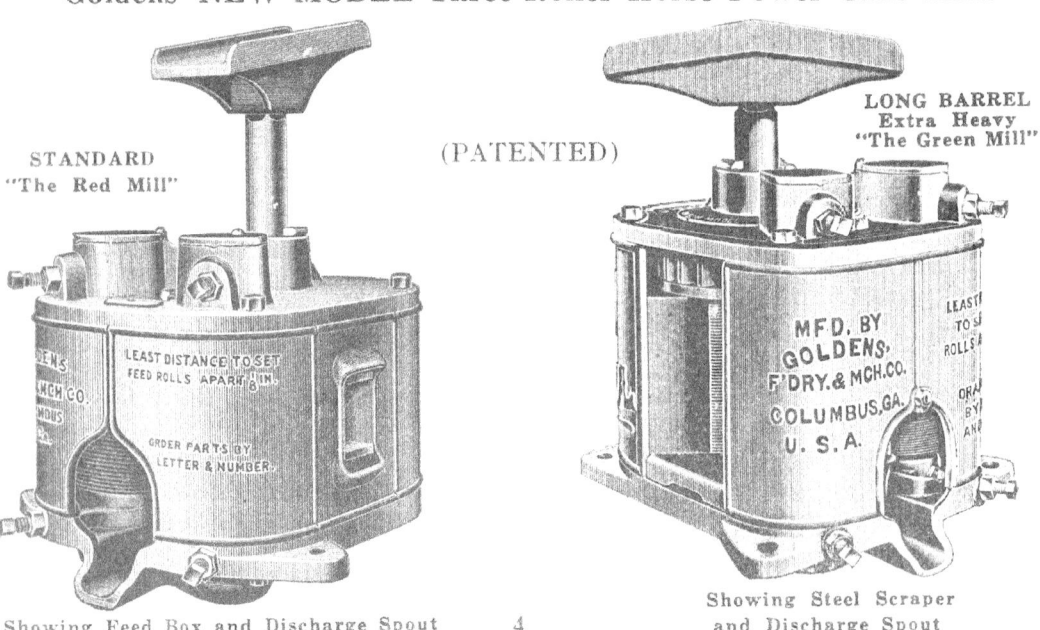

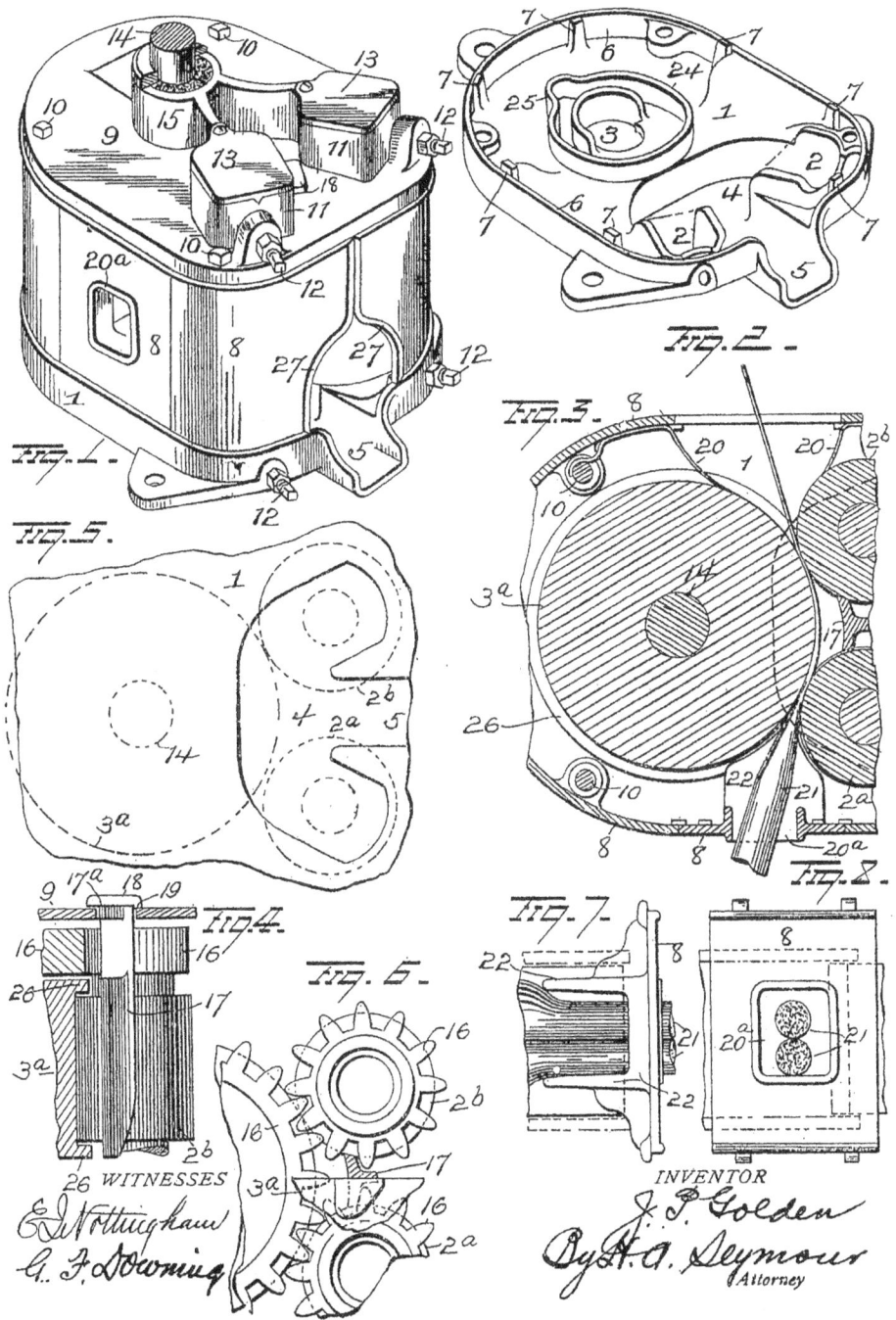

Goldens' three roller mill patent.

"Patent Applied For" plate from 1904.

Goldens' X Series

Goldens' manufactured vertical "X" three-roller horsepower mills, like this No. 4 X, which were of the same general design, but the rollers, guide knife and feed box were fifty percent longer than the standard mills.

Chart for Goldens' "X" Three Roller Cane Mills

Model No. and Horsepower	Main Roller D × H	Feed Roller D × H	Discharge Roller D × H	Juice Per Hour	Weight	Price
No. 1X, 1 Medium	10" × 7^{11}/$_{16}$"	4⅝" × 7½"	5" × 7½"	52 gals.	450 lbs.	$40.00
No. 2X, 1 Heavy	12" × 9³/₁₆"	5⅝" × 9"	6" × 9"	67 gals.	680 lbs.	$52.00
No. 3X, 2 Medium	14" × 10^{11}/$_{16}$"	6⅝" × 10½"	7" × 10½"	97 gals.	930 lbs.	$77.00
No. 4X, 2 Heavy	16" × 12³/₁₆"	7⅝" × 12"	8" × 12"	150 gals.	1,300 lbs.	$100.00

Goldens' XX Series

The "XX" series of vertical three-roller mills was a series of extra heavy duty mills specially designed with long barrels for grinding hard stubble and tropical cane. These mills were of the same general design as the other mills, but they had larger journals for the larger rollers. They came with solid brass bearings and heavy brass linings for the small rollers. The large roller gear was bored and attached to the roller. The rollers were 50 percent longer than the standard mill.

Chart for Goldens' "XX" Three Roller Cane Mills

Model No. and Horsepower	Main Roller D × H	Small Roller D × H	Discharge Roller D × H	Juice Per Hour	Weight	Price
No. 2XX, 1 Heavy	12" × 9³/₁₆"	5⅝" × 9"	6" × 9"	67 gals.	730 lbs.	$80.00
No. 3XX, 2 Med.	14" × 10^{11}/$_{16}$"	6⅝" × 10½"	7" × 10½"	97 gals.	990 lbs.	$105.00
No. 4XX, 2 Heavy	16" × 12³/₁₆"	7⅝" × 12"	8" × 12"	150 gals.	1,395 lbs.	$135.00

Goldens' Horsepowered Horizontal Cane Mills

Goldens' manufactured a series of horizontal power mills including one model designed for horsepower. This model was called a Self-Contained Three-Roller Horizontal Horse Power Cane Mill. The rollers were held in rigid housings, with adjustable boxes for jour-

Left: The X models were heftier models. *Right:* The XX models were even heftier still.

nals. The housing was mounted on a heavy bed plate with a ribbed extension containing a babbitted bearing for driving shaft journals. The upper end of the shaft was supported by a yoke which attached both top boxes for roll and shaft bearings in one rigid piece which was bolted to the housing. The rollers were driven by beveled gears with a proportion of one and one-half to one, which gave a faster surface speed of the rollers than where the drive shaft is attached directly to the roller, as is the case in vertical mills.

Chart for Goldens' Horse Powered Horizontal Cane Mills

Model No.	Horsepower	Large Roller D × L	Feed Roller D × L	Discharge Roller D × L	Juice Per Hr.	Weight	Price
No. 8	2 Extra Heavy	9" × 12⁵⁄₃₂"	5⁶⁄₁₆" × 12³⁄₃₂"	6¹⁄₁₆" × 12³⁄₃₂"	125 gals.	1350 lbs.	$203
No. 9	2 Extra Heavy	12" × 15⁵⁄₃₂"	7⁷⁄₁₆" × 15"	8¹⁄₁₆" × 15"	176 gals.	2370 lbs.	$350

Goldens' Horizontal Power Mills

Goldens' manufactured a series of horizontal power mills as well. Probably one of the most popular and often found on the farm was the model No. 27, an all around outstanding mill. However, they did manufacture other larger sizes.

Chart for Goldens' Horizontal Power Mills

Model No. and Horsepower	Main Roller D × L	Feed Roller D × L	Discharge Roller D × L	Juice Per Hour	Weight	Price
No. 27, 4–6 hp	9" × 12"	5½" × 12"	6" × 12"	125–175 gals.	1,650 lbs.	$175.00
No. 36, 6–8 hp	12" × 15"	7½" × 15"	8" × 15"	175–225 gals.	2,750 lbs.	$275.00
No. 45, 8–12 hp	15" × 20"	9½" × 20"	10" × 20"	225–325 gals.	4,700 lbs.	$450.00
No. 54, 15–20 hp	18" × 25"	11½" × 25"	12" × 25"	400–550 gals.	7,900 lbs.	$750.00
No. 63, 25–30 hp	21" × 30"	13½" × 30"	14" × 30"	550–650 gals.	13,000 lbs.	$1,350.00

Above: Goldens' made horsepowered horizontal mills, the No. 8 and No. 9 (courtesy Dennis Parker and the Goldens' Foundry and Machine Company, Columbus, Georgia). *Below:* The No. 27 is one of Goldens' more popular models.

Above: Goldens' also made "The Golden Mill" in two roller models. *Below:* This is a two roller mill in the "New Model" series.

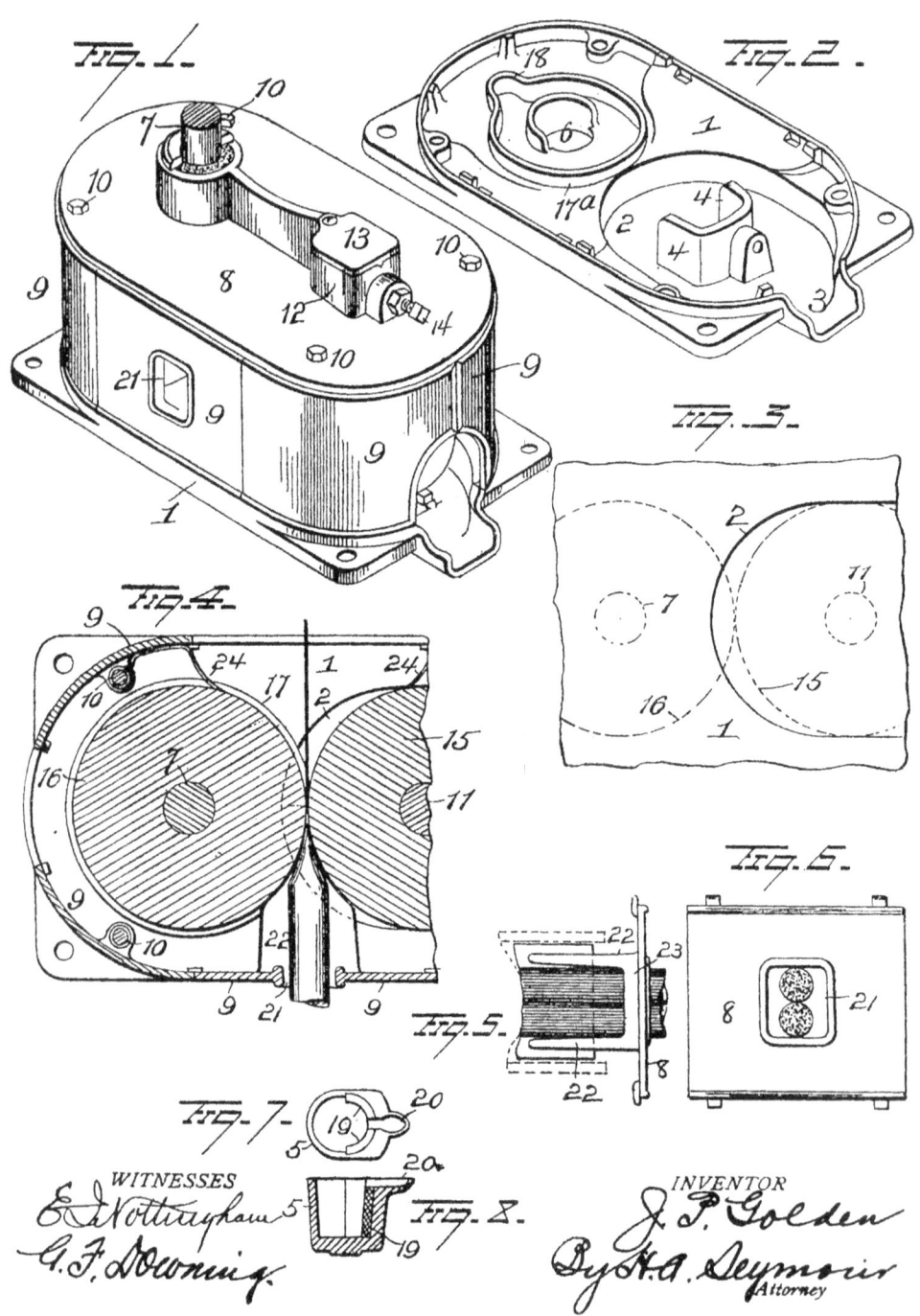

Goldens held a patent for a two roller mill also.

Goldens' Standard Two-Roller Horse Power Cane Mills

A series of two-roller horsepower cane mills was also produced by the Goldens' Foundry and Machine Company. These were offered in the Standard, X and XX models.

Chart for Goldens' Standard Two-Roller Cane Mills

Model No.	Horsepower	Roller Size- D × H	Juice Per Hour	Weight	Price
No. 12	1 Horse Heavy	12" × 6³⁄₁₆"	45 gals.	605 lbs.	$44.00
No. 14	2 Horse Light	14" × 7³⁄₁₆"	70 gals.	835 lbs.	$66.00
No. 16	2 Horse Heavy	16" × 8³⁄₁₆"	100 gals.	1,160 lbs.	$88.00

Goldens' Two-Roller Horse Power X Cane Mills

Goldens' manufactured a series of long barrel two-roller horsepower cane mills that were built extra heavy, while having the same general design and patented features of the Standard two-roller mills. The rollers were built 50 percent longer than the Standard rollers, the journals were made extra large, the gears were bored to fit the shafts and had heavy, strong, wide faces and the boxes for the long journal roller were solid brass and cast-iron boxes with heavy brass liners on the short journal.

Chart for Goldens' Two-Roller "X" Cane Mills

Model No.	Horsepower	Roller Size- D × H	Juice Per Hour	Weight	Price
No. 12 X	1 Horse Heavy	12" × 9³⁄₁₆"	67 gals.	730 lbs.	$58.00
No. 14 X	2 Horse Medium	14" × 10¹¹⁄₁₆"	105 gals.	1,010 lbs.	$84.00
No. 16 X	2 Horse Heavy	16" × 12³⁄₁₆"	150 gals.	1,395 lbs.	$110.00

Goldens' Two-Roller Horse Power XX Cane Mills

To meet the demand of some of their customers for an extra heavy two roller mill, Goldens' designed and manufactured two models in a XX series. These mills were considered in a class by themselves, with all the parts doubled extra heavy. The top was connected between the bearings with two ribs instead of one, with extra wide side braces on box bearings. The adjustment screws were extra large and the brass bearings were extra long. The bolts tying the frame together were doubled from four to eight to meet the increased strain due to the large diameter rollers and extra length of the rollers.

Chart for Goldens' "XX" Two-Roller Cane Mills

Model No.	Horsepower	Roller Size- D × H	Juice Per Hour	Weight	Price
No. 18 XX	4 Horse Light	18" × 13¹¹⁄₁₆"	125–175 gals.	2,300 lbs.	$225.00
No. 20 XX	4 Horse Medium	20" × 15³⁄₁₆"	150–200 gals.	2,930 lbs.	$285.00

In the Goldens' Foundry and Machine Company catalog for 1928, Number 52, the standard two and three-roller mills were referred to as "The Red Mill," the long-barrel two- and three-roller mills were called "The Green Mill," and the extra heavy duty export models were advertised as "The Blue Mill." Goldens' also sold all type accessories, such as steam boilers, bagasse carriers, cane carriers and feed tables, kettles, gearing to adapt a horse drawn mill

Above: The two rollers came in the X Model as well. *Below:* Stronger still were the XX Models (courtesy Dennis Parker and the Goldens' Foundry and Machine Company, Columbus, Georgia).

to a power mill, and two-roller mills without frames. The 1X, 2X, 3X and 4X three-roller mills had been discontinued by 1928, along with the 2XX, 3XX and 4XX three-roller mills, the 12X, 14X, 16X, 12XX, 14XX and 16XX two-roller mills.

Rollers without frames were manufactured by Goldens' as well.

Goldens' Rollers without Frames

These rollers were produced for those who wanted to economize and make their own frames, even though Goldens' felt their mills were already so inexpensive that it was not economical to do so. However, to satisfy their customers who wanted to make their own frames, the foundry produced rollers for the standard size cane mill for the X series and also for the XX series. These came with top and bottom boxes with square sides to accommodate wedges used to regulate space between the rollers. As steam and gasoline engine power became more and more common on the farm, Goldens' produced a number of power combinations by which one could convert their horsepower mill into a belt driven power mill.

Goldens' Combination Mill

These mills adapted the 18XX and 20XX

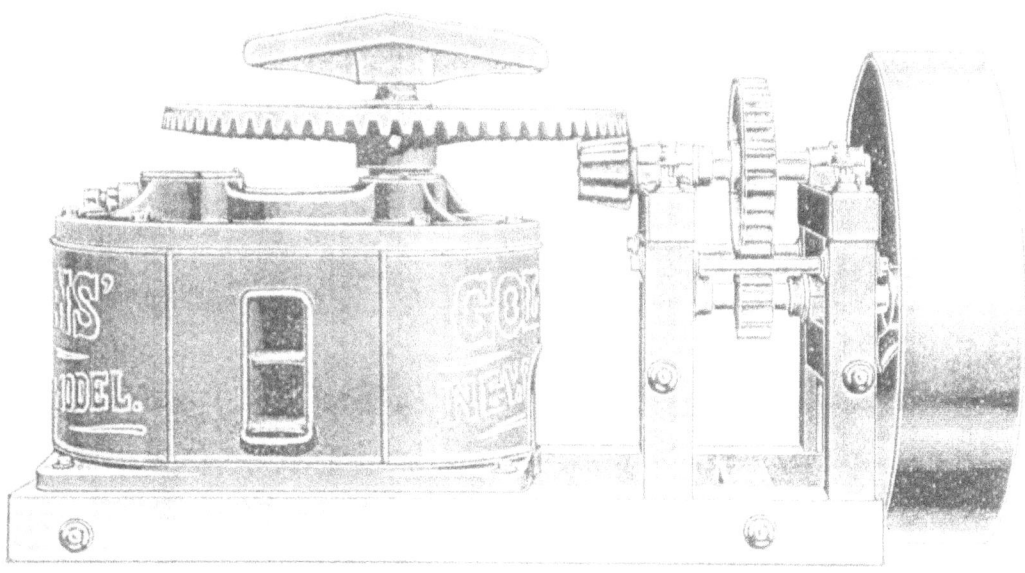

Top: Goldens also manufactured rollers without frames. *Bottom:* Combination mills were offered by the company, this one with double gearing (both courtesy Dennis Parker and the Goldens' Foundry and Machine Company, Columbus, Georgia).

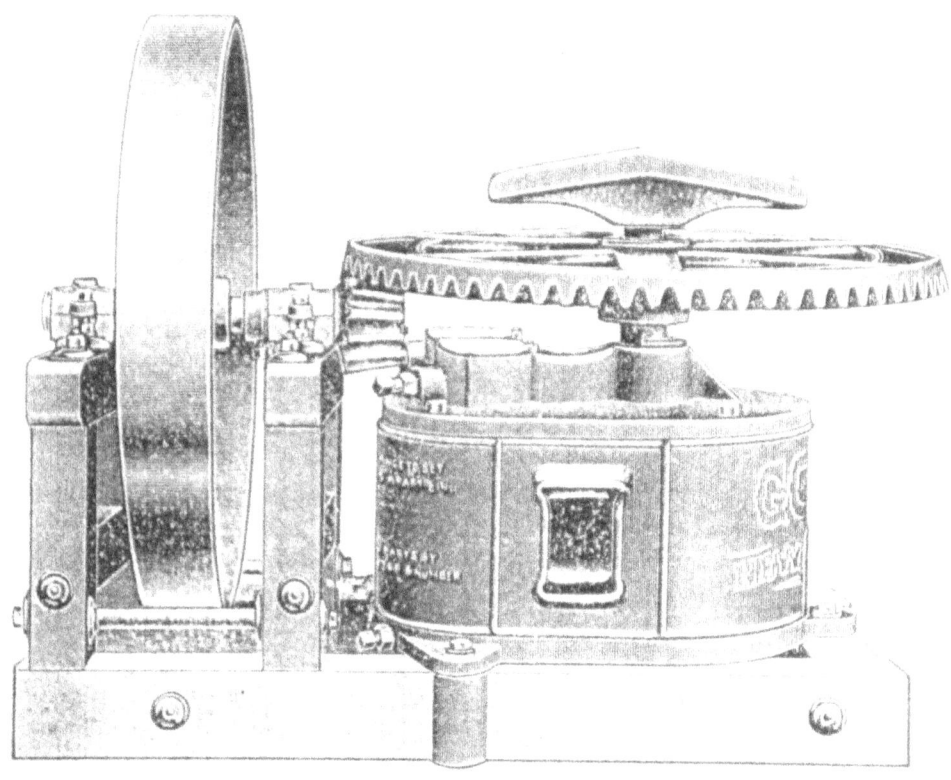

Above: A combination mill with single gearing (courtesy Dennis Parker and the Goldens' Foundry and Machine Company, Columbus, Georgia). *Below:* A combination mill mounted on a hay baler.

to belt driven steam power. A turn cap was also provided, however, in the event it was necessary to use animal power. The mills were offered in single and double gearing.

Gearing for adapting the standard 2, 3 and 4, and the 2XX, 3XX and 4XX mills to steam power was available from Goldens' as well. These combinations were available in single and double gearing. It was recommended that surface speed of the rollers should be 27 feet per minute.

Numerous accessories were manufactured by the Columbus firm, such as bagasse carriers, Golden-Cook Evaporators, furnace doors, grates, steam coils, steam collectors, and kettles. Faced with keen competition from other manufacturers, the decline in the popularity of sugar cane table syrup, and the changing technology in the sugar industry, Goldens' gradually discontinued their cane mill line. The foundry is still alive and well in the city of Columbus and to this day still receives requests for spare parts and information on their cane mills. The step of faith of Porter and Theo Golden back in 1882, and the confidence Abraham Illges had in these brothers, still pays dividends in the city of Columbus. Presently Goldens' Foundry and Machine Company offers a complete pattern shop, foundry, laboratory, heat treating and machining facilities. Today, as it has been since 1882, Goldens' Foundry stands as a symbol of dependability and quality.

G.H. Grimm Manufacturing Company, Hudson, Ohio

The G.H. Grimm Manufacturing Company of Hudson, Ohio, advertised cane mills and fruit dryers in its 1895 catalog. However, no specifics or mills have been located by this writer.

Harris Manufacturing Company, Janesville, Wisconsin

Janesville manufacturer and industrialist James Harris was born in Kingston, Ontario, on September 13, 1833. He moved to Watertown, New York, as a young man and there he worked as a machinist apprentice. Having learned his trade well, he began his pilgrimage westward in 1853, working briefly in Milwaukee before settling in Janesville. His first employment in the city was as a machinist at the Novelty Works. In 1859 he entered into a partnership with Zebediah Guild, R.R. Angell, and Leonard Tyler and established the Rock River Iron Works on S. Franklin Street, where they became the first manufacturers of agricultural implements in Janesville. They began manufacturing reapers but soon branched out into numerous other farm items, including mills to grind the recently imported "Chinese cane," or sweet sorghum, as their specialty. This partnership was ideally composed, with each man contributing his specialty—one a machinist, one a molder, and two with related trades. From their plant, consisting of a warehouse, office, wood shop, three-story machine shop, foundry, and blacksmith shop, came the Sweepstakes Separators, Little Champion Reapers, Champion Threshing Machines, cast iron columns, castings of various kinds, and cane mills.

Harris and Elbridge G. Fifield, who operated the first lumber yard in Janesville, assumed controlling interest of the company in 1868 and established Harris, Fifield and Company. This concern was incorporated as Harris Manufacturing Company in 1869 with Harris, Elbridge G. Fifield, Leavett Fifield and Horace Dewey as stockholders. On April 16, 1875, a fire severely damaged the plant and in order to rebuild Harris took Allen P. Lovejoy as a new partner. They reorganized the company as the Janesville Machine Company in 1881.

Harris withdrew from active participation in the company in the early 1870s and formed a partnership with D.P. Smith for the manufacture of a patented safety lamp. In 1882 Harris and Smith bought the license and business of Fish and Connell, manufacturers of barbed wire, of Joliet, Illinois, and moved the machinery to Janesville. They built the necessary factories and began manufacturing barbed wire under the name of Janesville Barb Wire Company. Smith sold his shares in 1886 and Arthur Harris, son of the founder, was taken into partnership. Later, wire nails and woven fence were added to the product list of the factory. By 1921 they were producing a line of steel fence posts and the company was renamed The Janesville Fence and Post Company. In 1938 it became a hardware and appliance retail store.

The Thomas Manufacturing Company of Springfield, Ohio, purchased the mowing machine operations of the Janesville Machine Company but the parent company continued to produce farm implements until it was purchased by General Motors in 1918. By the early 1900s farming was moving toward mechanization, and General Motors wanted its share of the tractor market. The Ford Company had literally dominated the automobile market with its Model T, and was poised to do the same with its Fordson Tractor. William D. Durant, chairman of General Motors at the time, was determined, however, this would not happen with the tractor industry. They merged the Janesville Machine Company with the Samson Tractor Company of Stockton, California, which they had purchased in 1917. General Motors built a large factory in Janesville and on May 1, 1919, began producing Samson Tractors. Their Model M was designed by GM engineer Arthur Mason, but for some reason it did not suit the chairman of the board. Durant had his tractor division secure Jim Dandy's Motor Cultivator, which he sold as the Samson Iron Horse. The name was quite fitting since reins were actually used to steer the tractor. Unfortunately, the endeavor was a complete failure and General Motors repurchased many of the tractors for scrap and parts. The Janesville facility was converted to a Chevrolet assembly plant in 1922 and General Motors "plowed under" their tractor venture.

James Harris was issued Patent No. 49,998 on September 19, 1865, for his design of a cane mill with adjustable rollers by means of a spring or elastic attachment to the bearings. One design shows a set of leaf springs pressing a plunger upon the bearing boxes. While constant pressure was applied, the crushing roller could move under a heavy load of cane, thereby reducing the risk of breakage. Another design shows an elastic material, such as rubber, between the setscrews and bearing boxes, allowing the crushing roller to move under heavy pressure. Harris received the Second Premium for his cane mill at the 1865 Wisconsin State Fair in the "Apparatus Complete" category. While E.W. Skinner and Company of Madison won First Premium, not everyone concurred with the decision. In reporting on sugar mills at the state fair, on October 3, 1865, the *Janesville Gazette* wrote: "We presume not one man in a hundred who looked at the operation of the mills on exhibition at the Fair Grounds, had a doubt that the machinery of the James Harris and Company, of this city, would receive the First Premium. It certainly worked the freest, seemed to be the most efficient, and we understand the committee admitted that the best syrup was produced by it, and yet the committee recommended that a Second Premium be given it.... We do not know the names of the gentlemen comprising the committee on sugar mills, but their decision in this instance cannot fail to elicit a smile from those who gave much attention to the Sorghum Camp."

Mr. Harris was a creative and industrious man who held several other United States patents, including one for a cultivator, an evaporator, and a harvester. To his credit he enjoyed the reputation of being "a man of simple ways and firm and unyielding integrity." Up to the time of his death on March 15, 1912, he was busy and actively involved in the industry of Janesville as president of the Janesville Barb Wire Company, vice president and director of the Janesville Machine Company, president of the Forks Logging Company, and president of the Slack Mining Company.

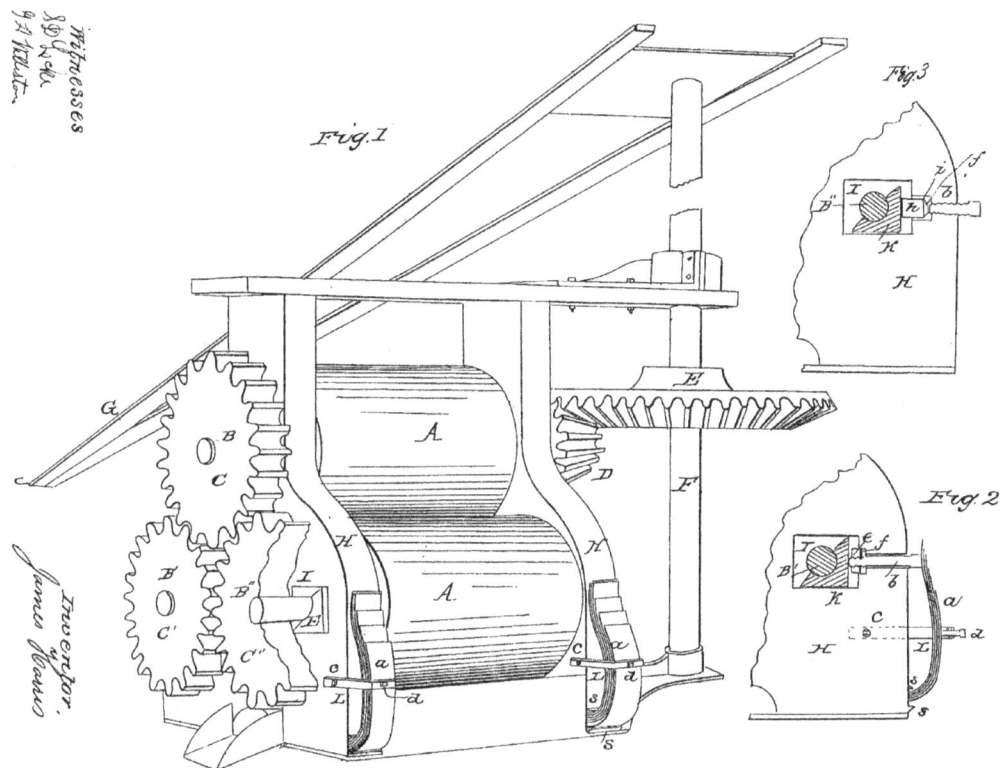

Harris' patent. Notice the leaf springs applying pressure to the roller.

Hartford Foundry and Machine Company, Hartford, Connecticut

An announcement in *The Manufacturer and Builder* of March 1874 stated that the Hartford Foundry and Machine Company had leased the foundry and machinery of the late Woodruff and Beach Iron Works and had secured the control and right to use its vast collection of patterns, perhaps the largest in New England. Through this acquisition they were prepared to fill orders for a variety of machinery, including steam engines of all sizes; pumping engines and pumps; feed pumps and safety valves; powder, paper, and flour mill machinery; cider mills; clothiers' screws; builders' screw jacks; hydraulic presses; various shafting, couplings, pulleys and flywheels, and cane mills. From additional advertisements in 1875 and 1876 it seems that the company continued as Woodruff Iron Works, 223 State Street, Hartford. One series of advertisements referred to Woodruff Iron Works as "successors to Woodruff and Beach Iron Works" and stated that "the Woodruff and Beach Iron Works and the firm of Woodruff and Beach are both dissolved."

Hartford Sorghum Machine Company, Hartford, Connecticut Branch Manufactory, Bellows Falls, VT

The earliest mention of the Hartford Sorghum Machine Company in the *Hartford, Connecticut, City Directory* is 1866, when the business was located at 148 State Street. In 1869

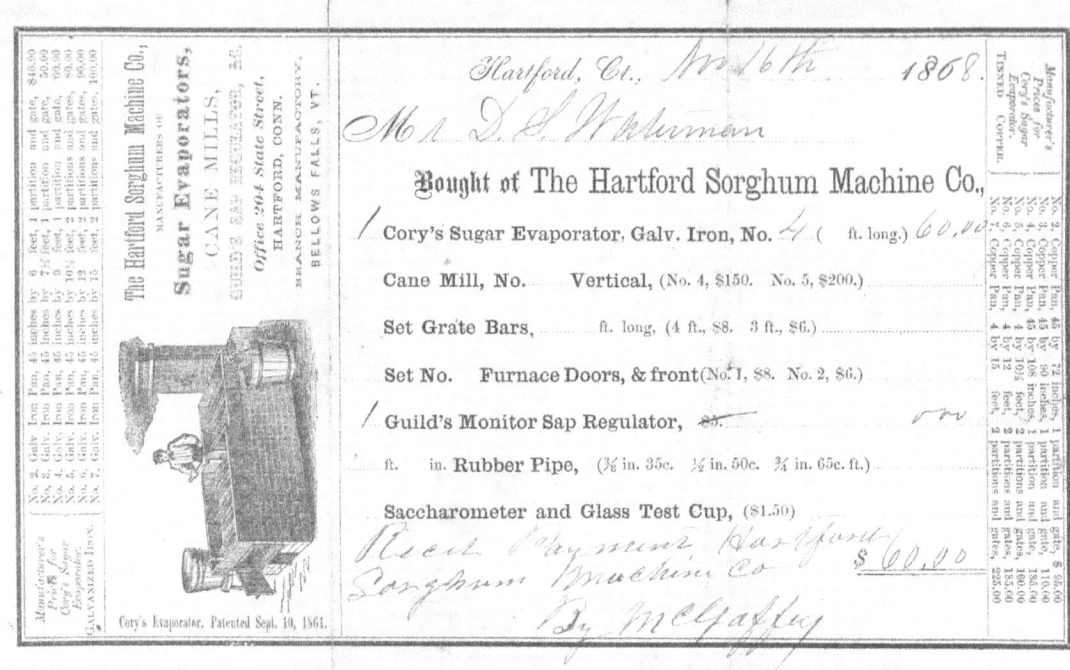

Both cane mills and evaporators are listed on this invoice.

they relocated to 228 Main Street and by 1871 the company disappeared from the city directories altogether. During their apparent brief existence the Hartford Sorghum Machine Company manufactured the Cory's Evaporators, patented September 10, 1861, in both galvanized iron and tinned copper, grate bars, furnace doors and fronts, and Guild's Monitor Sap Regulators. They also manufactured vertical roller cane mills in at least two sizes. In a bill of sale dated November 16, 1868, their No. 4 mill listed for $150 and their No. 5 mill listed for $200.

On June 29, 1869, James B. Williams, of Glastenbury, Connecticut, assignor to the Hartford Sorghum Machine Company, received patent No. 91,890 for an evaporator pan with a corrugated bottom which was manufactured and sold through the company.

James L. Haven Company, Cincinnati, Ohio

The James L. Haven Company of Cincinnati, Ohio, was founded in 1844 and continued under Haven's leadership for almost half a century. Originally begun as an iron foundry, Haven continued to diversify their product list and expand their facilities until they covered a sizable tract from Elm to Plum streets, and from Second to Commerce streets in Cincinnati. James Haven, a member of the Cincinnati Board of Trade and Transportation, purchased all the tools, patterns, and machinery of Sechler and Haven, who were the successors of Sechler and Porter and Hedges, Free and Company, who were pioneers in the manufacture of sweet sorghum machinery.

An 1879 catalog advertised hardware and farm implements and their company is mentioned in *The City of Cincinnati and Its Resources*. By 1883 their catalog had grown to include agricultural implements, sorgo machinery, Haven's IXL cider mills, cutting boxes, corn shellers, Little Giant corn crushers, portable hay presses, and farm and church bells. While the company was most noted for the manufacture of high services steam and hydraulic passenger and freight elevators, they also manufactured hardware items, piano and organ stools, school desks, and sugar cane mills.

The Economist Cane Mill

This mill was introduced by Haven's predecessors in 1865 and was designed as an inexpensive mill for working a small crop. One improvement which Haven made to the pattern was a feed box with sloping partitions to prevent overcrowding the lower part of the rollers and to save juice by having it run back into the mill rather than down the drooping canes. This was a two-roller mill with exposed gears meshing above the top plate.

Chart for Haven's Economist Cane Mill

Roller Size-D × H	Juice Per Hour	Weight	1879 Price
8" × 9"	50 gals.	365 lbs.	$35.00

The Pioneer Cane Mill

The Pioneer Cane Mill was made with wrought iron shafts, turned bearings, and rollers. The gearing was cast separate from the rollers The journals turned in brass boxes, and a patented design prevented clogging.

Chart for Haven's Pioneer Cane Mill

Model No.	Main Roller- D × H	Small Rollers- D × H	Weight	Juice Per Hour	Price
No. 00	10" × 6"	6" × 6"	350 lbs.	50 gals.	$40.00
No. 1	12" × 7"	8" × 7"	550 lbs.	70 gals.	$55.00
No. 2	16" × 8"	8" × 8"	750 lbs.	105 gals.	$72.00
No. 3	16" × 12"	8" × 12"	1,000 lbs.	134 gals.	$90.00

Champion Horizontal Mill

Chart for Haven's Champion Horizontal Cane Mill

Model No.	Horsepower	Main Roller- D × H	Small Rollers- D × H	Juice Per Hour	Weight	1879 Price
No. A	1 Horse	9" × 6½"	6" × 6½"	60 gals.	550 lbs.	$50.00
No. B	1 or 2 Horse	9" × 10½"	6" × 10½"	75 gals.	660 lbs.	$75.00
No. C	2 Horse	9" × 12"	6" × 12"	100 gals.	825 lbs.	$100.00
No. D	2 or 3 Horse	9" × 14"	6" × 14"	125 gals.	833 lbs.	$125.00

Haven's Champion Mill was a three-roller horizontal mill which came with wrought iron shafts, flanged rollers, babbitted boxes and feed boxes. The James L. Haven Company pointed out that their mills were not to be judged by their looks, but by their strength and by the size of their rollers. Buyers were reminded that the capacity of a mill depended on the diameter and length of the main roller, and not on how imposing a mill appeared to be.

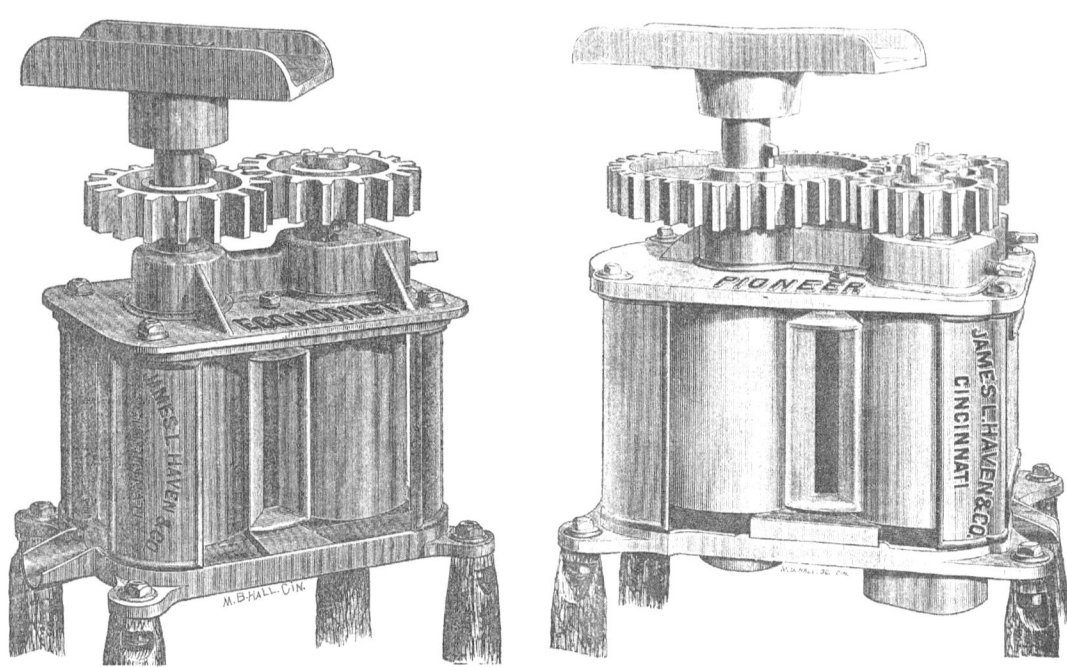

Left: Haven's Economist mill. *Right:* Haven's Pioneer mill. *Below:* Haven's Champion mill (all from the Collection of The Public Library of Cincinnati and Hamilton County).

Hedges, Free and Company, Cincinnati, Ohio

Hedges, Free and Company were not only makers of farm implements, but also were on the cutting edge of experiments done with a revolutionary new plant recently introduced into the United States. Their treatise on sugar making, *Experiments with Sorghum Sugar Cane*, included testimonials and research done with Chinese Sorgho and African Imphee canes. In spite of the "cold, backward, and disagreeable" growing season of 1857 the results of the experiments with these new canes were most encouraging. Samples of syrup made with these new canes were "as transparent and pleasant almost as honey." An added bonus was that these new canes were capable of producing sugar, from the "darkest brown to the finest loaf." That this new sugar cane, Chinese Sorgho and African Imphee, could be grown in the middle and northern states of the United States opened new and exciting economic possibilities.

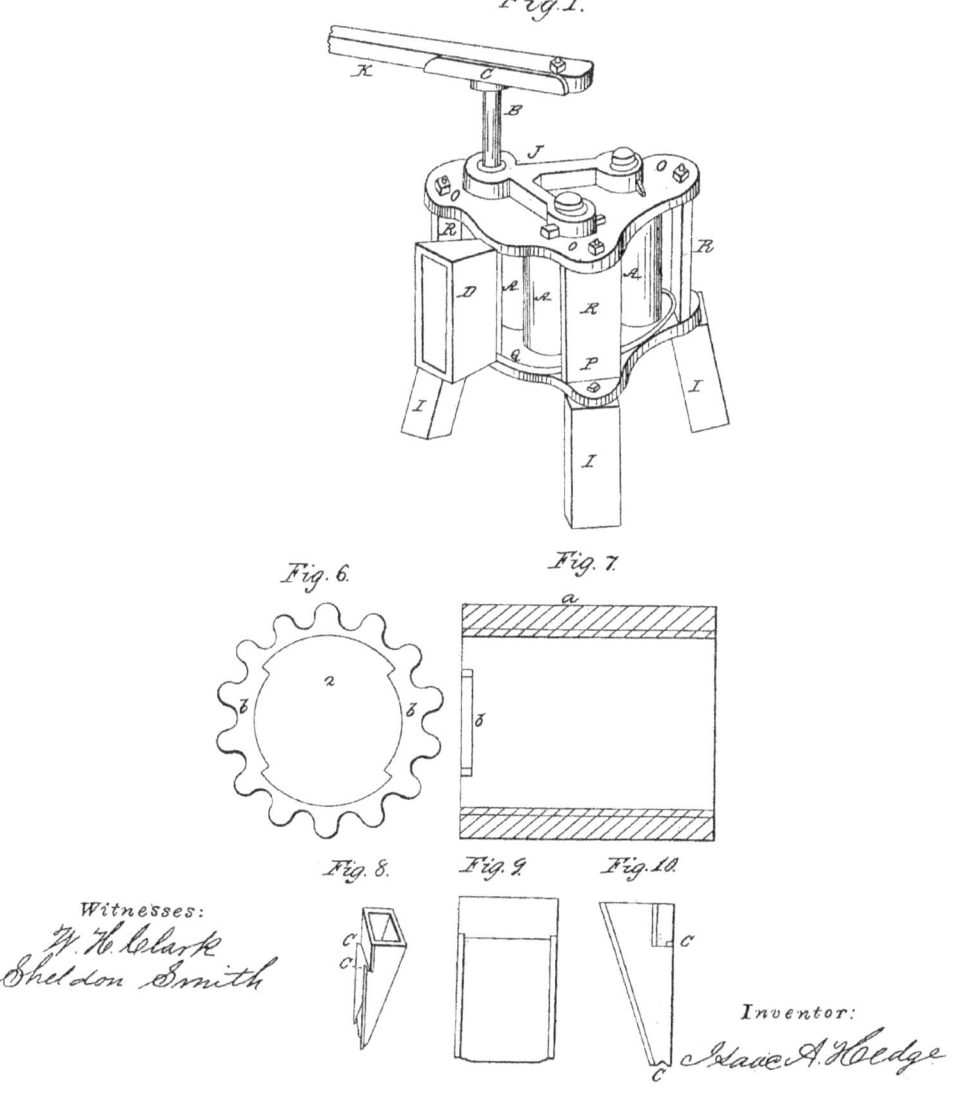

Hedges was a pioneer in the sweet sorghum industry, and this is his patent.

HEDGES' IMPROVED SUGAR MILL.

Above: This image shows Hedges' "improved" cane mill (courtesy Bill Outlaw, Tallahassee, Florida). *Below:* Hedges recommended this setup for pressing "Chinese" cane.

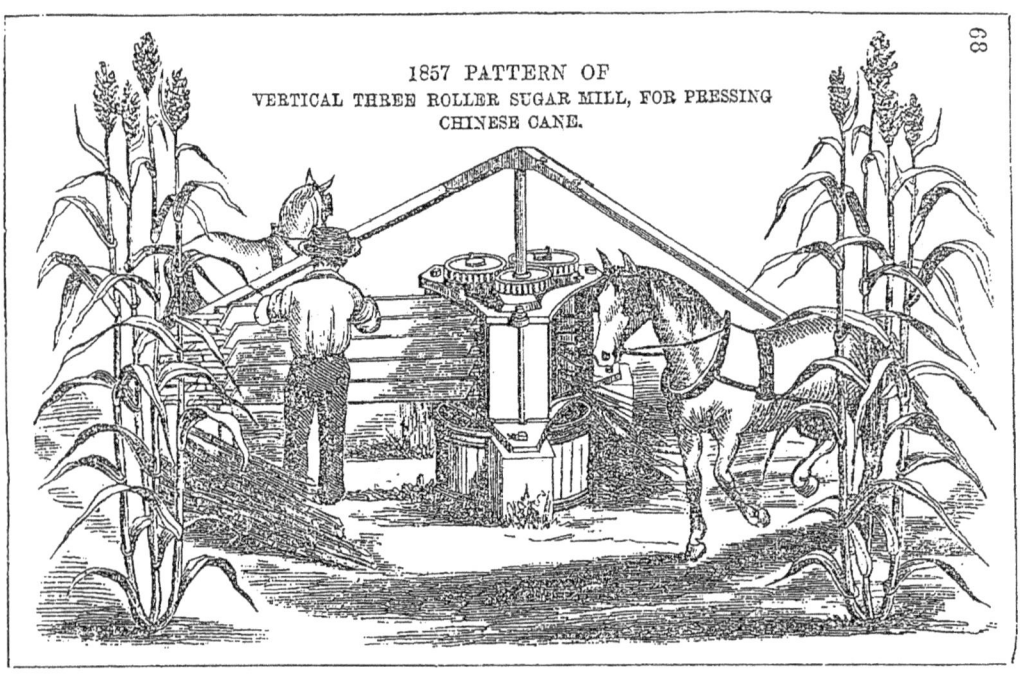

While promoting the cultivation of sweet sorghum, Hedges, Free also manufactured and sold farm implements. Their catalog included corn and cob crushers, with a treatise on the value of the cob as a nutrient; steam boilers and a treatise advocating cooking cattle feed; a kitchen mill for grinding coffee, cornmeal, flour or spices; the Tom Thumb Grist Mill; a sugar crushing mill for crushing loaves of sugar; India-rubber plantation belts; and cane mills.

By special arrangement Hedges, Free and Company sold plows manufactured by James F. Dane and Company, as well as Male's Improved Convertible Cider Mill; Sanford's Straw Cutter; Berea Grindstones; and Cook's Evaporators.

Hedges, Free and Company gives us such a wonderful glimpse into a turning point of history in their 1859 catalog. In it is a statement on the superiority of iron mills over wooden mills. The company asserts that wooden mills might serve for experimental purposes, but unless a farmer was willing to lose 33 to 50 percent of his cane juice because of an ineffective mill, they should not be relied upon. Three attributes were claimed for the Hedges, Free and Company mills: (1) as near perfection as possible, (2) reliability of construction, and (3) a price based on the "live and let live" principle.

Hedges offered a single geared vertical roller mill.

Single-Geared Vertical Mill

Five models were offered in their Single-Geared Vertical Mills. These mills consisted of three iron rolls enclosed in cast plates top and bottom, antifriction boxes, and keys for convenient adjustment. The sweep cap was fitted to the shaft of the master roll, supplying a direct application of power.

Chart for Hedges' Single-Geared Vertical Cane Mills

Horsepower	Juice Per Hour	Acres of Cane	Weight	1859 Price
One-horse	35–45 gals.	1 to 5 Acres	675 lbs.	$56.00
One-horse	40–50 gals.	4 to 6 Acres	675 lbs.	$60.00
One-horse Stout	50–60 gals.	5 to 7 Acres	700 lbs.	$65.00
Two-horse	70–85 gals.	8 to 12 Acres	1,125 lbs.	$100.00
Four-horse	100–125 gals.	10 to 20 Acres	1,300 lbs.	$135.00

Double-Geared Vertical Mill

The company produced a double-geared vertical mill with rollers the same size as those of the one-horse mills, but by means of the double-gearing they made two revolutions for each revolution of the horse-team. Because of the loss of power necessary to turn the double-gearing, its output was not more than 50 percent greater than the single-geared mill. The double-geared mill came with wrought iron shafts and brass boxes. It was capable of grinding 60 to 70 gallons of juice per hour, weighed about 1,050 pounds, and sold for $85.

Left: Hedges had a double geared vertical roller mill as well. *Right:* Hedges horizontal mills were offered in two sizes, one horse and two horse.

Horizontal Mill with Vertical Shaft

A horizontal mill with a vertical shaft for horsepower was manufactured by Hedges, Free and Company. By means of a beveled wheel and vertical shaft the farmer could hitch his horses to a sweep and power the mill in the same manner as with a vertical mill.

Chart for Hedges' Horizontal Mill with Vertical Shaft

Horsepower	Juice Per Hour	Weight	1859 Price
Two-horse	60–80 gals.	1,300 lbs.	$100.00
Two-horse	60–70 gals.	1,200 lbs.	$90.00

Horizontal Back-Geared Mill

There was a horizontal back-geared mill adapted for steam, water, or wind power produced by the company. This mill had wrought iron shafts, brass boxes, and a flat belt pulley. It came in five sizes, with larger sizes available upon contract with the company.

Chart for Hedges Horizontal Back-Geared Cane Mill

Horsepower	Acres of Cane	Weight	1859 Price
Four-horse	15 to 25 Acres	1,200 lbs.	$125.00
Six-horse	15 to 25 Acres	1,675 lbs.	$165.00
Eight-horse	25 to 40 Acres	1,800 lbs.	$200.00
Ten-horse	40 to 60 Acres	2,300 lbs.	$265.00
Twelve-horse	50 to 75 Acres	2,500 lbs.	$300.00

D.M. Cook, of Mansfield, Ohio, patented a portable, adjustable, and self-contained evaporator that was revolutionary in its day. Cook's Evaporator featured a set of rockers which enabled the operator to control the flow of juice in evaporation. Hedges, Free and Company investigated the merits of the evaporator, made arrangements to manufacture it in their plant and offered it for sale. The Cincinnati company produced other syrup and sugar making implements, such as sugar molds, drain pots, brass wire skimmers, test cups, furnace doors, grates, corrugated evaporator pans, juice tanks, coolers, clarifiers, and both round and oval union boiling pans. The company offered arrangements through which one could get the rights to use Hedges' improvements along with valuable information in reference to patterns, different modes of construction in order to make the work profitable at the established price and at the same time offered to the farmer a quality machine. P.W. Gates, of Chicago, was a manufacturer who produced mills based on Hedges' patent. Through the fascinating catalog of Hedges, Free and Company, and their treatises on various subjects, we get an interesting glimpse into the changing face of American agriculture. Hedges, Free and Company was predecessor of the James L. Haven and Company of Cincinnati, Ohio.

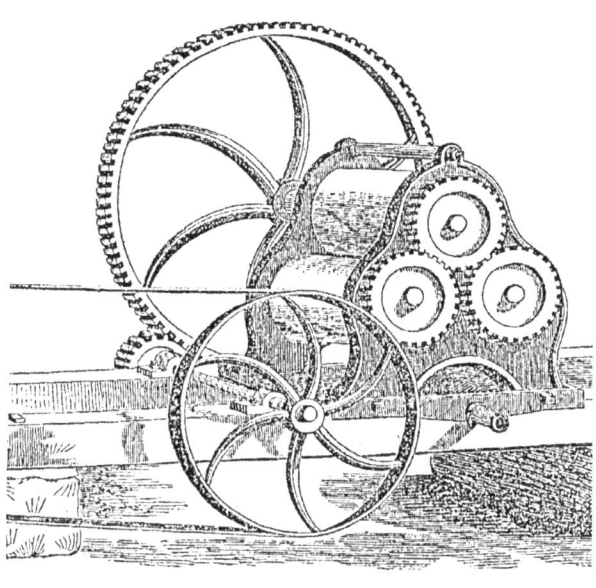

Hedges also offered a horizontal back-geared power mill in five sizes.

W.S. Henerey and Company, Charleston, South Carolina

W.S. Henerey & Co. was founded in Charleston around 1855 by its namesake, W.S. Henerey, and while our knowledge of the company is limited much of what we know is found in *The Journal of Southern History*. Originally established at 318 Meeting Street near Line Street in Charleston, at some point the business was relocated to 314 Meeting Street. The company manufactured steam engines, boilers and various kinds of machinery, including improved corn mills, crank pestles, the McCarthy Cotton Gin, and vertical and horizontal cane mills, along with horsepower units to operate them. The company did iron and brass castings and made sawmill and rice mill equipment to order.

Hewes and Phillips, Newark, New Jersey

An 1869 advertisement in the *Scientific American* of September 11, 1869, extolled the first-class machinery manufactured by Hewes and Phillips, of Newark, New Jersey, which was sold through D.P. Davis, 46 Cortlandt Street, New York City. The foundry and machine shop of Hewes and Phillips manufactured high and low pressure steam engines and boilers; mining machinery; engine and hand lathes; drill presses; shaping and slotting machines; planing and bolt cutting machines; punching, shearing, and drop presses; railroad car axel lathes; gear cutters, shafting; pulleys and hangers; and machinists' tools of all kinds. Though no models have been found by this writer, the company manufactured cane mills and joined other companies of the northeast in producing sorghum syrup and sugar refining machinery.

F. Holtz Company, Evansville, Indiana

The lineage of the F. Holtz Company reaches back to 1865, when a group of mechanics established a foundry and machine shop on First Street at Third Avenue in Evansville. In those formative years the company was known as Mechanics Foundry and Machine Shop. About 1867, a group of eight mechanics, including Augustus Schultz, Charles Human, John Human, Alex Jack and M. Becker, bought Mechanics Foundry and established it as Schultz, Human & Company. This was an energetic team that soon became known for its promptness, thoroughness, and superior workmanship. The men succeeded because they were conscientious about their work and were men of integrity. In 1907 Ferdinand Holtz, a German emigrant, purchased the company and incorporated it as F. Holtz Company. The foundry and machine shop specialized in boilers, steam engines, repairs, sawmill machinery, iron and brass castings, doctor pumps, pipe and pipe fittings, steel shafting, mill supplies, steamboat machinery and, according to *The Evansville Courier*, "Southern" cane mills. Mr. Holtz passed away on October 28, 1907 after a long illness.

E.J. Horn, Addison, New York

The cane mill designed and manufactured by E.J. Horn, of Addison, New York, was reputed to be the cheapest, most compact, and simplest arrangement of a mill ever devised, and was featured in *Scientific American* on September 17, 1859. The mill featured adjustable boxes to regulate space between the rollers. The top roller was smaller than the bottom two rollers, but the mill was so geared that they turned at the same speed. A large-geared drive wheel was mounted on top to a vertical arbor. Two brackets were fixed to this wheel so a sweep could be securely attached. Two friction rollers bore down on the upper surface of the drive wheel to keep it meshing securely with the gears below it. Horn manufactured various sizes of his mill extensively, with 1859 prices ranging from $15 to $50.

Horn's mill was reputed to be the most simple and least expensive.

Hudson Machine Works and Iron Foundry, Hudson City, New York

Frederic Cook II and McClelland were the proprietors of Frederic Cook and Company, operators of the Hudson Machine Works and Iron Foundry, Hudson City, New York. The foundry specialized in contract casting for railroads, bridges, buildings, gas pipes, posts, water pipe, cast iron ornamental floors and cannon. However, they did manufacture steam engines and boilers, both in high and low pressure models; Cornish lifting and forcing pumps for mines; stamps, mortars and mining machinery; Superior hydraulic pumps and presses, and machinists' tools made to order. Special attention was given to contract manufacture of patent machines. The Hudson Machine Works and Iron Foundry made sugar mills, and though advertised in *Scientific American* no particulars concerning the mills have been found.

Hunt, Dake and Company, Indianapolis, Indiana

Hunt, Dake and Company, of Indianapolis, Indiana, were manufacturers of Dake's cane mill, for which he received patent No. 20,124 on April 27, 1858, and which was featured in *Scientific American* on June 19, 1858. The mill designed by Frederick E. Dake featured a bed plate and two beveled rollers revolving around it. When cane was fed into the hopper it passed under the rollers and was crushed against the bed plate. The genius of this mill was that it was simple, inexpensive, required no gearing, was compact and portable, and in use the rollers exerted uniform pressure upon the cane.

Thomas E. Hunt, Dake's partner, received a patent for a cane mill, patent No. 23,287, on March 15, 1859, for a similar mill. Hunt's mill, however, had a large beveled central stationary cone around which four beveled rollers turned. The sides of the central cone rose at exactly 60 degrees and the beveled rollers stood upon the sides of the cone at 30 degrees. A gum spring gave the mill some elasticity to the rollers to keep them from being damaged. Dake and Hunt's mills were similar in concept but differed in how the concept was applied.

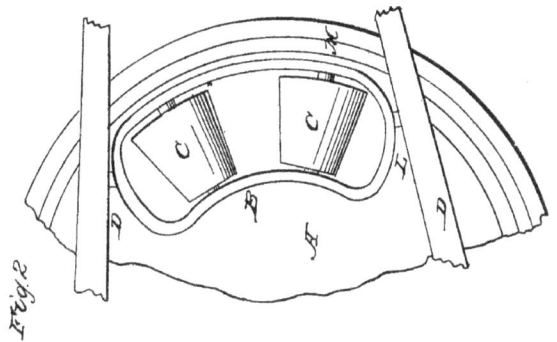

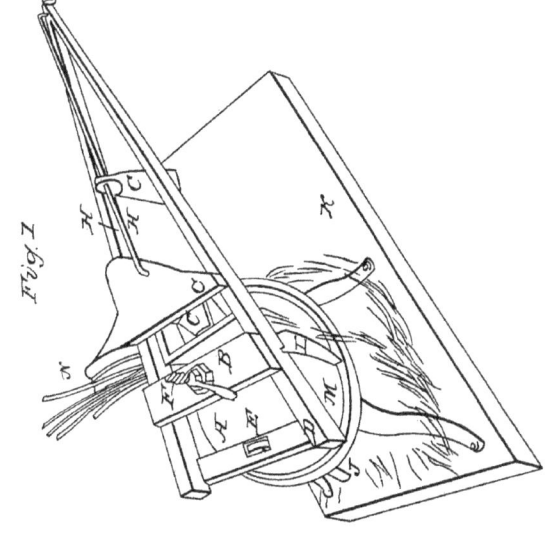

Hunt and Dake's patent featured a mill with beveled rollers.

Huntsville Foundry and Machine Works, Huntsville, Alabama

The state of Alabama was established as a separate territory in 1817 and officially became a state in 1819. One of the Southern states which

Above: Dake conceived another mill in which everything rotated around a stationary roller. *Below:* An early photograph of the Huntsville Foundry (courtesy Huntsville-Madison County Public Library, Huntsville, Alabama).

seceded from the Union and joined the Confederate States of America, Alabama was to experience a devastating aftermath, both politically and economically. Recovery was slow after the ravages of the Civil War. Cotton was king, but a new South began to emerge. Pig-iron production began to accelerate in the 1880s, and by 1900 Alabama was one of the more highly industrialized of the Southern states, Huntsville making a significant contribution.

Huntsville was originally named Twickenham by Leroy Pope after the home of his beloved kinsman, the English poet Alexander Pope. In 1811 it became the first community in Alabama to be granted a city charter from the territorial government, and it was then renamed Huntsville after John Hunt, the Virginia Revolutionary War veteran who first settled in the area. The city played an important role in the political climate of Alabama, serving briefly as the state capital and the site of Alabama's first constitutional convention. However, it was in agriculture and industry that Huntsville excelled. By 1900 the north side of the city was booming with new and expanded industry. In fact, the local newspaper, *The Weekly Mercury*, reported that "North Huntsville resembles a western boom town."

One of those industries was the National Manufacturing Company, owned by Nolen and Jones, which received a complete renovation in 1899–1900. At some point between 1900 and 1905 the business became known as the Huntsville Foundry and Machine Works, and was located on North Church Street. An ad in a city directory gives some insight into the product list of the company. The foundry and machine works, operated by Nolen and Jones, founders, machinists and manufacturers, produced swing saws, gang edgers, veneer wringers, pulleys, fire dogs, hangers, cane mills, couplings, grate bars, cultivators, tuyere irons, tire benders, swage blocks, saw mandrels, furnace doors, pillow blocks, furnace grates, lumber trucks, emery grinders, fireplace grates, and shoelasts and stands.

In 1911–12 a Mr. J.R. Jones became associated with the company, and in 1913 Mr. C.M. Grace, who joined the firm in 1902, became president. The company was still in operation in 1916, and advertised as founders, machinists, manufacturers dealing in oxy-acetylene welding and cutting, Ohio Valves, injectors, lubricators and belting. Unfortunately, a record of the models of cane mills manufactured by the Huntsville Foundry and Machine Works has not been found.

An early Huntsville Foundry ad listed cane mills for sale (courtesy Huntsville-Madison County Public Library, Huntsville, Alabama).

International Harvister see *McCormick-Deering*

Jefferson Foundry, Steubenville, Ohio

The first foundry established west of the Allegheny Mountains was the Steubenville Foundry, Steubenville, Ohio, founded in 1816 by Arthur M. Phillips and Robert Carroll. Phillips, a native of Carlisle, Pennsylvania, moved to Steubenville in 1807, where he began work as a blacksmith. He was an industrious man with an aptitude for metalwork and soon learned the machinist trade that was to insure him a prosperous future. In the early days his foundry made hollowware and grate castings. His first steam engine was made for a steamer being built by "Bezaleer Wells," and despite some difficulties on its maiden voyage, orders started coming in for engines and machinery for boats being built in Steubenville (Ohio) and Wheeling (West Virginia) and points beyond. A newspaper advertisement of April 9, 1828, announced the reopening of the old Steubenville Foundry by Arthur M. Phillips. Apparently Phillips had moved to Wheeling, for the advertisement reads, "The subscriber having returned from Wheeling, to his old establishment in Steubenville, takes this method to inform his friends and old customers that the establishment is in complete operation." Another advertisement of the same date announced the opening of a new foundry in Steubenville, the Jefferson Foundry, by James Means, "where all kinds of castings can be had." Evidently James Means had run the Steubenville Foundry in Phillips' absence, and his advertisement reads, "He respectfully tenders his thanks to the public for the encouragement he received while conducting the old Steubenville Foundry, and begs of his friends and former customers to give him a call." At some point James Means purchased the Steubenville Foundry, and the Jefferson Foundry name was then changed to James Means and Company. The *Steubenville Herald-Star Centennial Edition, 1906*, stated that James Means and Company operated the business as the Steubenville Foundry and Machine Works.

The foundry and machine works were developed and enlarged, primarily by Means' sons, Joseph, James and John P., and their business was known later as the Means Brothers. The foundry was located on the banks of the Ohio River between Dock and North streets, and on the C & P Railway, with spur tracks to every part of the vast complex. James Means and Company did extensive business in the United States and Canada, and their product line included sewer pipe presses, pipe tile, brick dies, clay grinding and tempering pans, pug mills, blast furnaces, rolling mills, coal mine machinery, glass works, steam engines, bolts, nuts, architectural iron work, sugar mills, and iron, brass and bronze casting of all kinds. In addition to being the first foundry west of the Allegheny Mountains the old Steubenville Foundry had another claim to fame. William McKinley, Sr., father of President William McKinley (1897–1901), was employed as a blacksmith and molder with the foundry in the early 1820s. A new company, organized by a group headed by C.J. Davis, purchased the foundry on December 31, 1898.

Kehoe Iron Works, Savannah, Georgia

One of the leading industries and most extensive manufacturers in Savannah in the late 1890s was Kehoe's Iron Works, located on Broughton Street, from Reynolds to Randolph streets, the successor to the Phoenix Ironworks. The Iron Works consisted of founders, machinists, blacksmiths and boilermakers, with special attention given to repair work. While they made engines, boilers, injectors, steam gauges, governors, lubricators, water gauges,

KEHOE'S IRON WORKS,

Broughton Street, from Reynolds to Randolph Streets, Savannah, Ga.

TELEPHONE 268.

FOUNDERS, MACHINISTS, BLACKSMITHS —AND— BOILERMAKERS. Special attention to repair work. Estimates promptly furnished.

Engines, Boilers, Injectors, Steam Gauges, Governors, Lubricators, and Water Gauges, Steam Fittings and Machinery of all kinds.

Sugar Mills and Pans

OF THE LATEST AND MOST APPROVED STYLES.

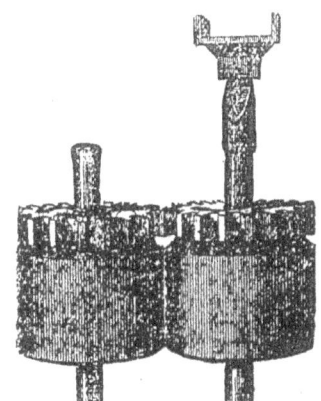

A GREAT REDUCTION IN PRICES.

The great number of SUGAR MILLS and PANS manufactured and sold by us is evidence of their superiority, and the general satisfaction given by them has induced us to make them our leading specialty. We do not hesitate to say that a careful examination of the material and workmanship will warrant the assertion that they are the best on the market. Having unsurpassed facilities, we guarantee our prices to be as low as any offered. A large stock always on hand for prompt delivery.

N. B. The Name "Kehoe's Iron Works" Is cast on all our Mills and Pans. Beware of the light Sorghum Mills now being offered. Buy only Mills that are fully warranted to grind heavy, matured cane.

Knownles Pumps, Excelsior and Penberthy Injectors.
Shay Locomotive Repairs a Specialty.

WILLIAM KEHOE & CO.

Kehoe's Iron Works specialized in mills and kettles (courtesy Live Oak Public Library, Savannah, Georgia).

steam fittings and machinery of all kinds, their specialty was sugar mills and pans of the latest and most approved styles. They advertised that "The great number of SUGAR MILLS and PANS manufactured and sold by us is evidence of their superiority, and the general satisfaction given by them has induced us to make them our leading specialty."

William Kehoe, president of the company, was one of Savannah's most prosperous citizens and served his community on the board of county commissioners. He was born in Ireland in 1842 and immigrated to Savannah while just a child. His first experience in metals came during the War Between the States when he served as a molder and caster at the Confederate national armory in Selma, Alabama, where George Peacock was superintendent (see

Above: Here's a pair of Kehoe's rollers. *Below:* This is a Kehoe stamping on one of its kettles.

Peacock's mill). Following the war he returned to Savannah and began working with James Monahan. After Monahan's death, Kehoe purchased Mrs. Monahan's share and established William Kehoe and Company. Don Kehoe was vice president, S. Kehoe was treasurer, and J. Kehoe was secretary. It is said that Mr. Kehoe's favorite product was the cane mill, and much of his business came from the sale of mills and kettles. By 1900 he was employing 150 men and doing about $250,000 in business annually across the deep South. The business apparently closed its doors in 1932.

Kilby Manufacturing Company, Cleveland, Ohio

The Kilby Manufacturing Company, 4623 Lakeside Avenue NE, was established in Cleveland, Ohio, in 1889 and grew to be one of the nation's largest manufacturers of sugar machinery. While the company manufactured other items, such as pulp drying machinery, gas washers, heavy gray iron castings, steel tanks, pattern work, machine shop items, and all kinds of heavy castings and machinery to the buyer's specifications and blueprints, their specialty was sugar making machinery. The foundry and machine shop were housed in a plant occupying 105,000 square feet covering six acres. After sixty years of successful business in Cleveland, the Kilby Manufacturing Company was sold at public auction to the Cleveland Twist Drill Company on December 17, 1948. Some of Kilby's former employees started a new company, Sugar and Chemical Machinery, Inc., in January 1949, for the manufacture of sugar machinery and to position themselves to supply replacement parts for machinery made by the former company.

Kingsland and Douglas Manufacturing Company, St. Louis, Missouri

The Kingsland and Douglas Manufacturing Company of St. Louis, Missouri, manufactured numerous farm implements, including sugar cane mills designed similar to the standard horizontal mill of the day, according to *The City of St. Louis and Its Resources*, published by the *St. Louis Star*. With offices at 1521 N. Eleventh Street and a factory covering two blocks on Mullanphy Street, Kingsland and Douglas became one of Missouri's greatest enterprises and one of the largest in the world in its time. The company was established in 1844 by George Kingsland and

Top: Here is an impressive nameplate of a Kingsland and Douglas mill. *Bottom:* Kingsland and Douglas of Louisville, Kentucky, made this mill (both photographs by Jimmie Barnes, Paragould, Arkansas).

D.K. Ferguson for manufacturing farm machinery, agricultural implements and sawmill machinery of the highest quality.

Kingsland died in 1874 and his son, L.D. Kingsland, succeeded him in the business. Kingsland and Ferguson Mfg. Co. was incorporated in 1885 and continued until 1887, when Ferguson retired. E.W. Douglas, a large stockholder, then joined the firm. The product list of the company included threshing machines, gristmills, machines for husking and shelling corn, corn crushers, cob crushers, machinery for ginning and baling cotton, sawmilling machinery and complete sawmill outfits, agricultural and farm machinery, steam engines and boilers, general foundry work, and cane mills. All of these were made under patents held by the company.

Lawrence D. Kingsland was born September 15, 1841, in St. Louis and was educated at the private academy of Edward Wyman and at the Military Institute of Nashville. During the Civil War he fought on the Confederate side and gained the rank of captain. He joined the firm as a bookkeeper and at the 1885 incorporation became vice president. When Ferguson retired he became president of the prosperous company. He was known throughout St. Louis for his numerous activities for the welfare of St. Louis. E.W. Douglas came to St. Louis from Pittsburgh in 1865 and was connected with the firm from that time.

The company employed from 300 to 400 workers and their shop was a model in regard to machinery, facilities, skilled workers, and organizational and systematic division of their labor pool. This mill was similar in construction to the Improved Gold Basis manufactured by Manny and Company, also of St. Louis. This mill was patented on April 6, 1880.

Krajewski-Peasant Company, New York, New York

The Krajewski-Peasant Company, located at 32 Broadway, New York City, was a manufacturer of sugar cane machinery primarily for the sugar industry. On September 21, 1886, Thomas F. Krajewski received Patent No. 349,503 for a machine designed to break and cut cane in preparation for milling. The uniqueness of the Krajewski crusher lay in fourteen or fifteen sets of more or less sharp teeth running in a zigzag pattern the length of the rollers. These teeth would intermesh, but not touch each other. The rollers would grip and crush the cane and at the same time cut it into small pieces. This type of crusher became such a standard in sugar mills that crushers with longitudinal zigzag grooves made by other manufacturers were referred to as "Krajewski" crushers. This is not a mill in the truest sense, but a device for preparing cane for milling. However, since it was such a trendsetter it is included in this work.

C. Kratz Foundry, Evansville, Indiana

Christian Kratz moved to Evansville in 1847 along with his brother-in-law, William Heilman. Together they established a small ironworks shop on Pine Street. Using two blind horses to power their machinery the two men set about supplying the machine and foundry needs of the community. Through intensive labor and wise decisions their business grew to the extent that within three years they had to expand their facilities. A large brick shop was built and a steam engine installed to power their machinery. Their first portable engine was built in 1854, and in 1859 they produced their first thresher. Christian Kratz resigned from the firm in 1864 and received $100,000 for his interest in the business. By 1869 he was in business again, operating the Southern Machine Works at the corner of First and Pine and Second and Elm streets.

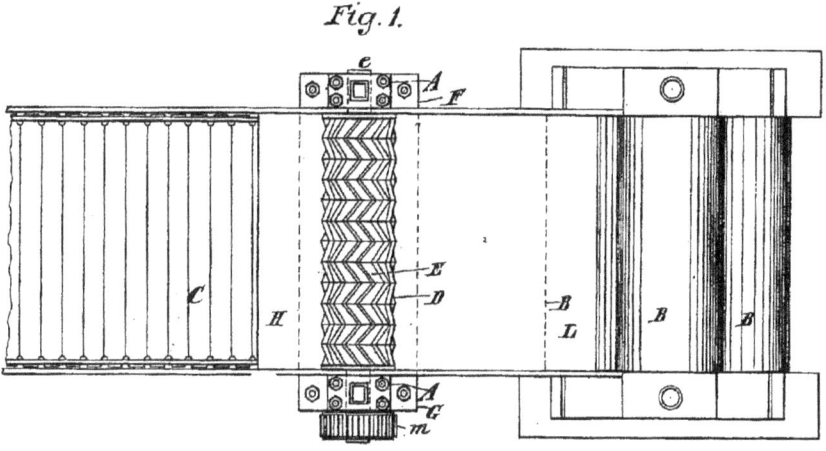

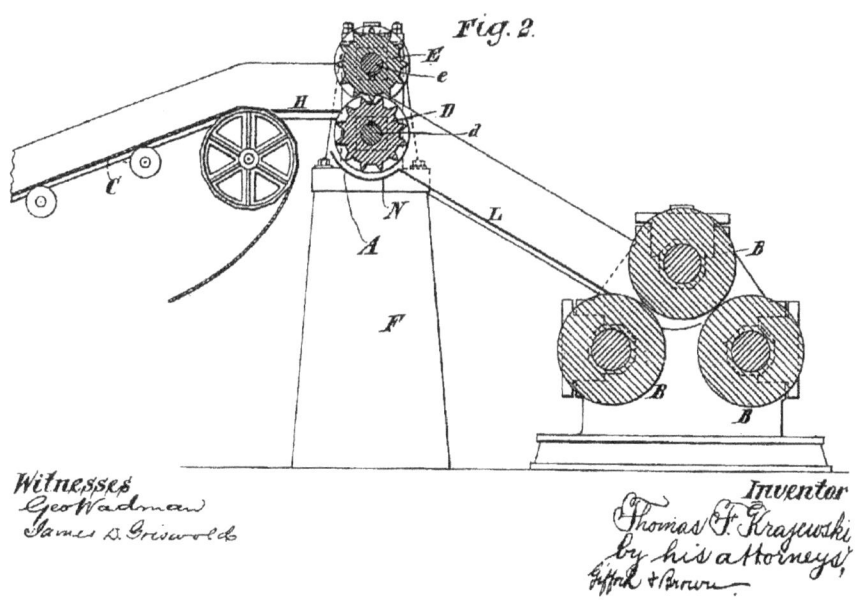

This is a patent for a Krajewski-Peasant Company crusher.

Kratz advertised himself in the *Evansville Daily Journal* as C. Kratz, Founder and Machinist: Builder of portable engines, portable circular sawmills, sugar cane mills, corn shellers, improved steel amalgam and composition bells for farms, shops, engine houses, churches and schools. Machinery, castings, plate and sheet ironwork of every description was made at the Southern Machine Works. Kratz was also the proprietor and agent of the territory for a patent drive tubular well. At a time when many steam engines operated at 125 to 150 pounds pressure per square inch, Kratz discovered a way to successfully reduce the pressure to 60 to 80 pounds pressure per square inch. This was a less dangerous level and more economical in saving fuel. He made another interesting discovery, that sorghum skimmings mixed with sharp sand, molding sand and sawdust made excellent cores for casting. He asserted that they were cheaper, stronger and less likely to "blow" than cores made with flour. Kratz offered his discovery to other foundrymen through the *Scientific American* in 1867. By 1870 his foundry was shipping mills as far away as Texas. Southern Machine Works produced boilers for steam engines and in 1869 built the boilers for the steamboat *Clara Scott*. Though Christian Kratz was a wealthy man he was known as "a workman among his men," and appreciated by them. To show their esteem his employees presented him with a gold-headed cane on Christmas of 1870.

The changing times which spelled doom for numerous foundries in this era impacted the C. Kratz Foundry as well. The foundry, an entire city block on First between Pine and Ingle, was purchased by George L. Mesker at a sheriff's sale in June 1900, for about $10,000. This ended the existence of one of the oldest foundries in southern Indiana, and one of Evansville's great old business institutions.

Leeds Foundry and Machine Shop, New Orleans, Louisiana

The Leeds Foundry and Machine Shop originated with a small repair shop in New Orleans known as the New Orleans Foundry. In 1825, Jedechal Leeds saw the possibilities of the shop and became the sole proprietor in 1826; it remained in the Leeds family for over sixty years. From this humble beginning Leeds grew the foundry forward to occupy ten or twelve buildings, employing a constant workforce of one hundred fifty men, with as many as four hundred needed for some jobs. Two large engines were used for powering turning lathes and smith and boiler work. The shop was equipped with a large steam hammer and modern machinery for heavy work. Leeds' Foundry and Machine Shops produced sugar mills, kettles, clarifiers, vacuum pans, centrifugal machines, draining machines, sawmills, gin gearing, cotton presses, steam boilers, and smith work of various kinds. Their products were used throughout the South.

While no record of Leeds' vertical mills has been found, a rather brief summation of their sugar mills from the late 1840s has been discovered. Apparently they made large mills for the sugar industry in five sizes.

Chart for Leeds' Cane Mills

Diameter in Inches	Length	Price
25	Four feet	$3,200
27	Four feet	$3,500
27	Four feet, Six inches	$3,650
28	Five feet	$4,000
28	Five feet, Six inches	$4,200

John H. Lester, New York, New York

While John Lester maintained an office at 192 Fulton Street, New York City, his factory and foundry were located at Hastings-upon-the-Hudson, some 20 miles from the city. In 1857, his business had relocated to 57 Pearl Street, Brooklyn, three blocks above Fulton Ferry. Lester manufactured Woodworth's Planing Machines; steam engines and boilers; slide lathes; and iron planing machines as well as iron and brass castings of every description which he advertised frequently in *The Scientific American*. Though he kept planning machines of all sizes and with the latest up to date improvements on hand at all time she was able also to make custom orders on short notice. In the late 1850s he added shuttle sewing machines to his inventory.

Lester's ironworks factory not only manufactured sugar mills but also all the shafting and machinery needed to set up a mill. This part of his 1850 business would have been directed to the Southern sugar cane industry, since sweet sorgho had not yet arrived in the United States.

Logan Foundry and Machine Shop, Logan, Ohio

The town of Logan, Ohio, is located on a beautiful plateau two miles by three-quarters of a mile wide in the center of the rich mining districts of the Hocking Valley. The rich mineral deposits, fertile fields and beautiful setting made Logan a choice location. The Logan Foundry & Machine Company, Logan, Ohio, manufacturers of steam engines, hot blast pipes, coal cars, plows, iron railings, fire fronts, grates and cane mills, was one of the oldest and most prosperous industries in the Hocking Valley. Founded in 1848 by Raymond Belt, it was the city's first steam powered plant, and the first industry to employ large numbers of personnel. Belt's grandfather, Humphries Belt, emigrated to the Chesapeake Bay area from County York, East Riding, England, according to the *History of Hocking Valley*. Belt's father, John, emigrated to Ohio, settling on a farm in Licking County near Newark. There Raymond, the youngest of ten children, was born on March 4, 1819. He received his early education, worked on a farm, and at age twenty-three began working as a carpenter in the small village of Van Attasburg, Ohio. A foundry in Van Attasburg made plows and agricultural implements needing wooden handles and stocks, and there Raymond Belt excelled in his craft. In the spring of 1846 he moved his plow-stocking business to Logan, Ohio. Since there was no foundry in Logan, Belt had to import from other foundries all the iron parts necessary for his plows. In 1848 Belt and Robert Van Atta successfully built the first foundry and machine shop in Logan, with Belt becoming the sole owner in 1860. He enlarged the manufacturing capacity of the company and began producing machinery of every description. During the Civil War, especially, he manufactured great numbers of cane mills.

The frame buildings housing the main machine shop and a portion of the foundry were destroyed by fire in 1873 and then rebuilt on an even more comprehensive scale. This time the foundry and machine shop were built more permanently of stone, brick and iron and equipped with the most modern machinery available at the time. The machine shop operated out of a building fifty by seventy-five feet, two stories high, to which an annex was added at a later date. The foundry was twenty-five by one hundred twenty-five feet, two stories high, a part of which served as pattern storage. Because of Raymond Belt's invincible spirit, dynamic energy, and creative mind, the Logan Foundry & Machine Shop grew to be one of the largest industries of its kind in southern Ohio. After forty-four years in the business, Raymond Belt sold the entire plant to J.P. Henderson, who continued to manufacture a combination plow, self-lubricating car wheels, coal cars, columns and iron fronts for buildings and boiler fronts. He became an agent for the American Boiler Company of New York and Chicago and began to specialize in heating systems for homes and commercial properties. After changing hands several times, the Logan Clay Products Company purchased the property in 1952, including a part of the original brick structure. One of the R. Belt Cane Mills is on display in their museum.

A Raymond Belt mill manufactured by the Logan Foundry (courtesy Hocking County Historical Society Museum, 64 N. Culver St., Logan, OH 43138).

Lombard Iron Works, Augusta, Georgia

The Augusta Machine Works, Eleventh Street, Augusta, Georgia, was incorporated in 1850 by William M. D'Antignac, John M. Adams, Lambert Hopkins, James M. Poe, and William Turpin, Jr. The incorporation papers stated that the machine works were to be operated by water power and that a site had been secured on the Augusta Canal. Much of what we know about the company comes from the *Memorial History of Augusta, Georgia*, by Charles C. Jones, Jr. In 1870, George R. Lombard and Co. assumed controlling interest in the company and developed the facilities into an immense complex of long sprawling buildings with an elaborate drafting room upstairs. The Lombards were to maintain ownership of the ironworks for the next seventy-seven years.

Known also as Lombard Iron Works, the manufacturer did extensive millwork for several mills in the vicinity. They also operated a foundry, using iron ore from north Georgia, and a boiler shop where they built and repaired boilers. When the firm made a machine on order, the name of the customer's name was stamped into the piece. However, when the Augusta Iron Works made the whole machine, its own name was stamped proudly on the product. Their ornate railing work was popular and celebrated for its neatness. They manufactured hitching posts, corner pieces and grill work, as well as sawmills, gin ribs and gear, band saws, gristmills, stamping mills and sugar cane mills.

McCormick-Deering Company, International Harvester Company, Chicago, Illinois (Works at Chattanooga, Tennessee)

The International Harvester Company had its origin in fierce competition. Robert McCormick, the father of Cyrus, had tried for thirty years to develop a reaper practical enough to help farmers harvest their grain crops. After thirty years of failure he gave up. His son, Cyrus, then began the effort, and six weeks later he had a machine which would successfully cut grain. A demonstration was given on John Steele's farm in Virginia in July 1831. However, at the same time, Obed Hussey was also developing a reaper. Subsequent demonstrations and competitions were held to try to ascertain which had the best invention. Cyrus McCormick's machine was not the first invented or patented, but it was the first practical reaper manufactured and sold on a large scale.

It was competition which led to the founding of the International Harvester Corporation in the summer of 1902. Five fierce competitors came to realize that their strength lay in unity and not competition. Those companies were the McCormick Harvesting Machine Company, Deering Harvester Company (which had purchased the Marsh twine binder), Warder, Bushness and Glessner Company (which made Champion machines), Plano Manufacturing Company, and Milwaukee Harvester Company. These companies incorporated in the summer of 1902 and became the international giant International Harvester Company. The book *150 Years of International Harvester*, by Wendel, is an excellent resource here.

For many years the John Deere Company made plows and the International Harvester

This is a McCormick-Deering (IHC) vertical mill (photograph by Tommy Clayton, Hilliard, Florida).

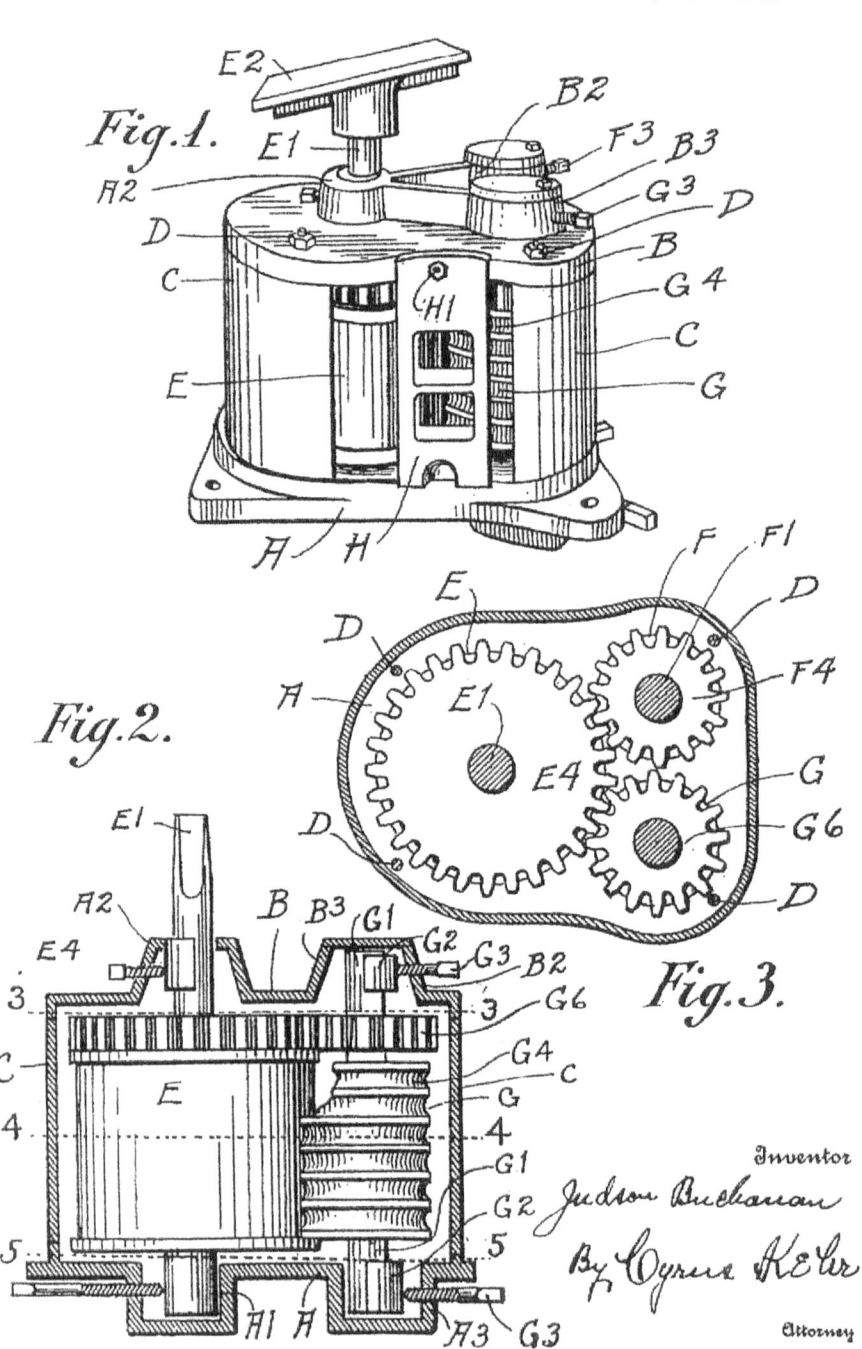

A McCormick-Deering patent.

Company made harvesters and the two companies resisted going into direct competition with each other. However, when the John Deere Company broke ground for a new harvester plant in East Moline, Illinois, in 1912 the International Harvester Company knew the time had come for them to offer a well-rounded line of agricultural implements. On May 7, 1919, the International Harvester Company announced the purchase of the Parlin and Orendorff Company of Canton, Illinois. This was the oldest and one of the largest plow companies in the nation, and had an outstanding reputation for manufacturing excellent plows. The Chattanooga Plow Company, of Chattanooga, Tennessee, was purchased by International Harvester a few months later. Chattanooga Plow produced a line of excellent chilled plows of the highest quality. The purchase of these two plow companies gave International Harvester a full product line of essential agricultural implements. A part of the Chattanooga Plow line was a series of cane mills (Please see the section on Chattanooga Plow for a more detailed account of the Chattanooga Plow line.). There seems to be no record that International Harvester Company produced cane mills before their purchase of Chattanooga Plow. After absorbing the company into their corporation, several cane mills were discontinued and several others were added. The No. 16 two-roll mill was introduced in 1905 and discontinued in 1920. The No. 34 three-roll two-horse mill was introduced in 1913 and discontinued in 1920. The No. 70, a three-roll horizontal power mill, was introduced in 1908 and discontinued in 1928. The No. 71, another three-roll horizontal power mill, was introduced in 1915 and discontinued in 1927. The Nos. 109 and 112 three-roll horizontal power mills were introduced in 1915 and discontinued in 1921 and 1922 respectively.

Some of the mills introduced into the International Harvester line after the purchase of Chattanooga Plow included Nos. 111, 112, 113, and 114, three-roll mills with fluted feed rolls which were introduced in 1925. The 44A, 144A, 45A, 145A, 171, 192, and 192A three-roll horizontal power mills were all introduced into the line in 1927. Belt power attachments for Nos. 22, 23, 122, and 123 vertical animal-powered mills were offered in 1927.

An IHC horizontal power mill (photograph by John Dean, Hartford, Alabama).

Have your House painted by McKenna & Hanley.

| First Premium Awarded South Georgia Fair, at Thomasville, | First Premium, Silver Medal, at Agricultural and Mechanical, at Savannah, Ga., 1872-'73. |

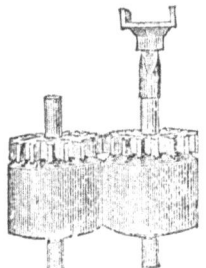

SUGAR MILLS AND PANS.
McDonough & Ballantyne,

MACHINISTS
IRON AND BRASS FOUNDERS,
Savannah, - - - Georgia.

D. FERGUSON, Funeral Undertaker, 137 Broughton Street, Savannah, Ga.

We would inform our patrons that we have a full stock of our popular **Sugar Mills and Pans**, which are recommended by all who have worked them.

ARCHITECTURAL IRON WORK

We have made a specialty of, and are prepared to fill orders for IRON FRONTS for Stores and Dwellings, Verandahs, Office and Cemetery Railings, of the latest designs, at Northern Prices. All kinds of Iron and Brass Castings made at short notice.

Go to Jas. S. Silva's for Brooms and Brushes, 142 Congress St.

This McDonough & Ballantyne ad featured mills and kettles (courtesy Live Oak Public Library, Savannah, Georgia).

One of the most popular of the Chattanooga Plow line was a small mill known as the "Old Red Mill." It was a simple, inexpensive one-horse mill capable of grinding about 25 gallons of juice per hour. On the upper end of Chattanooga Plow's line was the model 92, a three-roll horizontal power mill weighing 2,750 pounds, and capable of producing 250 gallons of juice per hour. This was a double-geared mill with two 8" D × 12" L small rollers and a large 12" D × 12" L main roller. The No. 92 was classified as a 12 horsepower mill. The Nos. 45 and 71 were two of the more popular horizontal power mills, though the No. 71 was discontinued in 1927.

The International Harvester Company continued to offer cane mill and syrup making accessories, such as waterpower connections, Bagasse carriers, feed tables, juice pumps, evaporators (until 1929), and brick and stone furnaces.

McDonough and Ballantyne, Savannah, Georgia

The McDonough & Ballantyne Company was located on East Broad Street in Savannah and had one of the finest plants in the South. John J. McDonough was born in 1849 and died in 1926 at seventy-seven years of age. He was mayor of Savannah from 1891 to 1895, and in addition to his ironworks he had one of the South's largest lumber operations. Late in life he served as harbormaster for Savannah. The *City Directory of Savannah, Georgia, 1871*, gave McDonough quite a write-up. Thomas Ballantyne was a director of the Chatham Bank, and was connected to numerous Savannah businesses, including the ironworks. The company consisted of a foundry, machine shop, blacksmiths, and boilermakers. They manufactured stationary and portable engines, the popular vertical and top running corn mills and kept shafting and pulleys in stock. A good reputation was enjoyed by the company for filling special orders quickly. McDonough & Ballantyne manufactured well known and immensely popular syrup pans and cane mills. Their products were stamped "McD. & B." The company last appears in the city directory in 1923.

Alex. Magee and Company, St. Louis, Missouri

In the early 1800s Alexander Magee was in business with J.A. Field and Company, manufacturers of feed mills and agricultural implements in St. Louis. The Alexander Magee and Company, 1902 Walnut Street, first appears in 1885. In 1887 he was joined in business by Daniel J. Lattimore, and the name was shortened to Alex. Magee and Company, manufac-

A Magee mill (Special Collections, St. Louis Public Library).

turers of woodworking machinery. Magee, Lattimore and LaBerge Manufacturing Company emerged in 1889, which became Lattimore Machine Company in 1890, with Alexander Magee listed as a "fitter."

Alex. Magee and Company manufactured the St. Louis Cane Mill, a heavy, three horizontal roller mill which was featured in *Farm Machinery* in July 1887. Several features were peculiar to this mill. The shaft boxes of the lower rollers rested upon load bearing bars supported by heavy bolts and rubber cushions. These bolts also served as set screws to set the pressure of the rollers against the main roller. If one wanted a rigid mill rather than a flexible mill, wooden blocks were available. The removable and replaceable guide knife was also attached to the bearing bars, allowing it to stay in close constant contact with the front rollers. The main bolts extended down to the bed plate of the mill, thus distributing the pressure on the bolts and castings. The St. Louis model was available in both single back and double back gearing, and was also adaptable for belt power or tumbling rod.

Manny and Company, St. Louis, Missouri

Manny and Company was established in St. Louis at 1248 Broadway in 1867 by Abraham J. Manny, and was a manufacturer and dealer in agricultural implements and machinery. In 1875 George R. Oyler joined the firm, and in 1879 George K. Oyler became one of the owners. Charles Bauer became associated with the company in 1881, and the name was changed to Manny and Bauer Manufacturing Company. Abraham J. Manny continued to serve as president and Bauer was vice president. This relationship apparently didn't last long, and by 1883 the name was again changed to Manny Manufacturing Company. By 1891 the company had completely changed hands or ceased to exist, and Manny Manufacturing Company disappeared from the St. Louis city directory.

Manny was a creative individual and received United States patents for a cultivator, Patent No. 50,018, which could be directed from the seat, and a harvester, Patent No. 51,203. On July 31, 1883, he was awarded Patent No. 282,339 for a three roller animal powered horizontal cane mill which featured a large crushing roller on the bottom with smaller feed and delivery rollers on top, all arranged in triangular form, the Improved Gold Basis.

The Improved Gold Basis

Power was delivered by a bevel wheel on the upright shaft and a bevel pinion on the crushing roller. The rollers had juice disks, the crushing roller had flanges at the ends, the feed plate and discharge plate were interchangeable, and there was an improved juice basin. The mill was so geared that it made three revolutions to every one of their vertical mills. Oil tight boxes, wrought iron shafts, babbitted bearings, turned rollers, and heavy end gearing were features which made this an outstanding mill. The Improved Gold Basis horizontal mill was finished nicely with red and green paint and bronze ornaments.

Chart for Manny's Improved Gold Basis Horizontal Cane Mill

Model No.	Horsepower	Main Roller- D × L	Small Rollers- D × L	Juice Per Hour	Weight	1880 Price
Model A	1 Horse	9" × 6½"	6" × 6½"	60 gals.	560 lbs.	$70.00
Model B	1 or 2 Horse	9" × 10½"	6" × 10½"	75 gals.	660 lbs.	$80.00
Model C	2 Horse	9" × 12"	6" × 12"	100 gals.	845 lbs.	$100.00

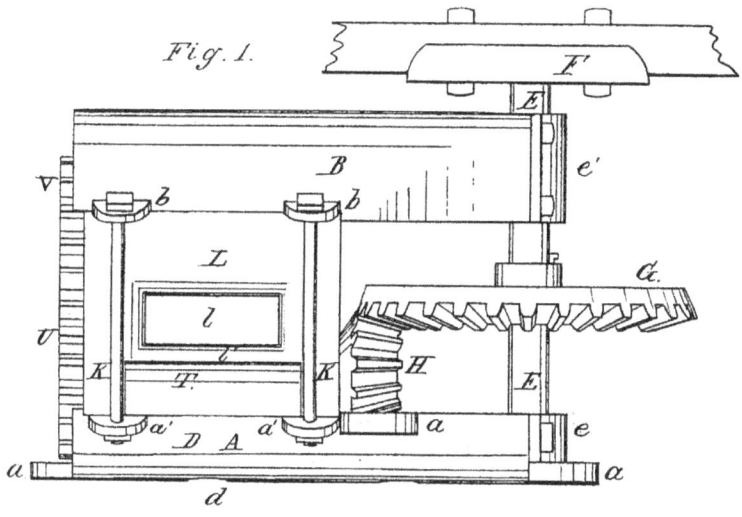
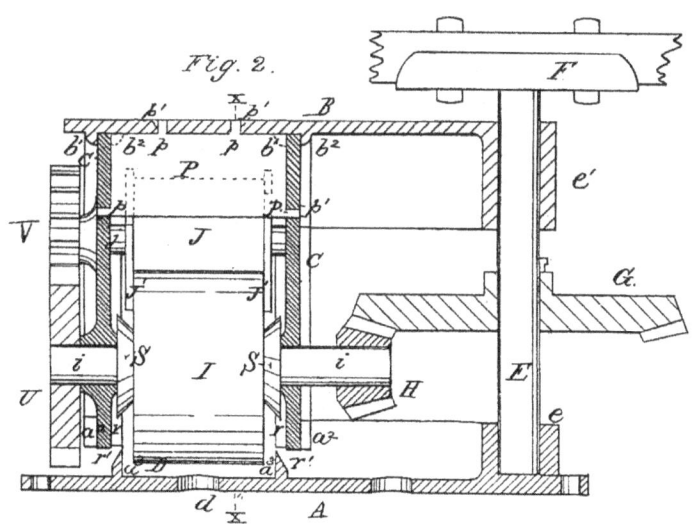

Manny's patent of a familiar looking horizontal animal powered mill.

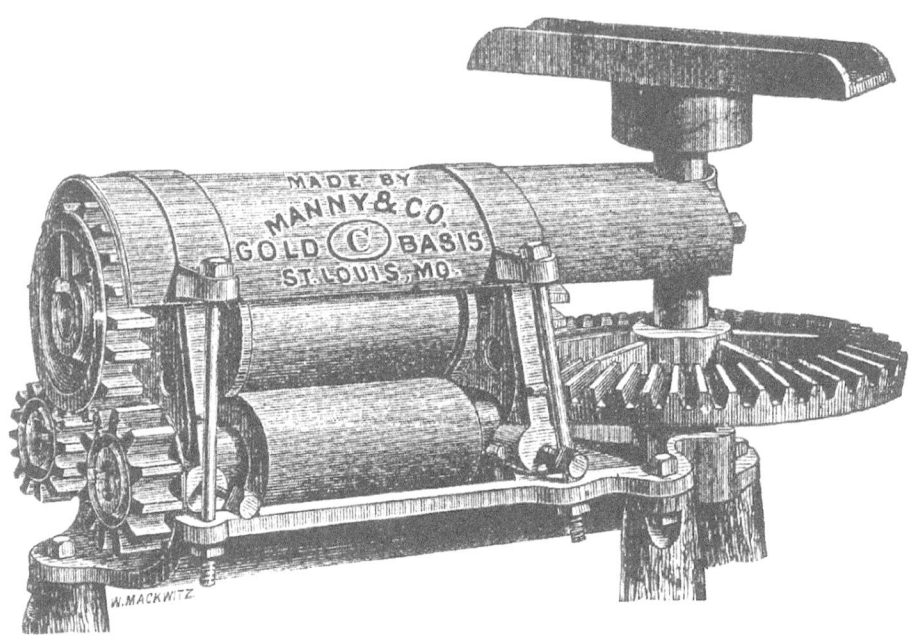

The Improved Gold Basis mill by Manny.

THE PIONEER VERTICAL ROLLER MILL. Another mill manufactured was the Pioneer, a vertical three roller mill which was top geared, had a patented bridge, wrought iron shafts, turned bearings and lathe turned rollers. This model featured their new patented feed box which allowed the juice to run downward inside the mill rather than drain outward.

Chart for Manny's Pioneer Three-Roller Vertical Cane Mill

Model No.	Main Roller D × L	Small Rollers D × L	Acres of Cane	Weight	1880 Price
No. 00	10" × 6"	6" × 6"	2 to 8 Acres	350 lbs.	$44.00
No. 1	12" × 7"	8" × 7"	4 to 5 Acres	550 lbs.	$65.00
No. 2	16" × 8"	8" × 8"	5 to 8 Acres	750 lbs.	$80.00
No. 8	16" × 12"	8" × 12"	8 to 18 Acres	1000 lbs.	$100.00

THE GREAT SOUTH-WESTERN. The Great South-Western was another three vertical roller mill manufactured by the St. Louis company. The Great South-Western was advertised as having ample strength to crush ribbon cane or sorghum. The bearing boxes were oil tight, the mill had a movable sweet cap, cleaning scrapers, wrought iron shafts, turned rollers with serrated faces, flanges on the main rollers, a clutch on the driving gear to minimize damage, brass boxes and turned bearings. The gear and rollers were cast separately for easy dismantling, and the gear was encased for safety. Manny noted that his mill rollers were not filled with sand to increase weight without adding strength.

Opposite—top: **Manny's pioneer mill came in three sizes.** *Bottom:* **The Great South-Western was made in five sizes.**

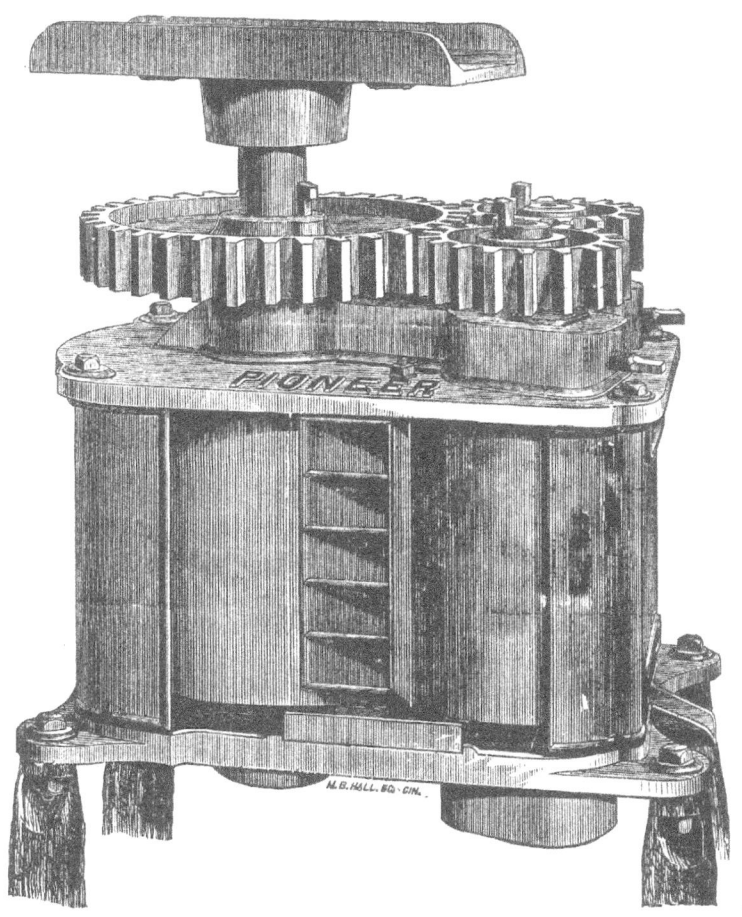

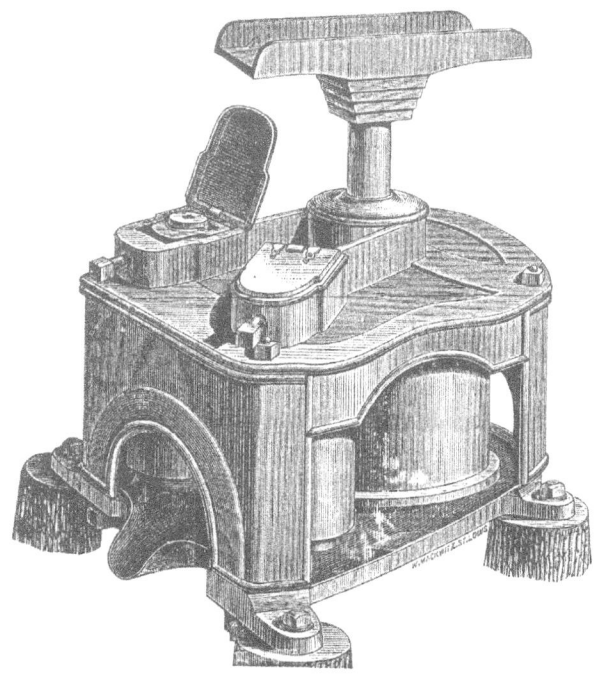

Chart for Manny's Great South-Western Cane Mill

Model No.	Horsepower	Main Roller- D × L	Small Rollers- D × L	Juice Per Hour	Weight	1880 Price
No. 0	Large 1 Horse	9" × 5"	6" × 5"	30–40 gals.	375 lbs.	$55.00
No. 1	Reg. 1 Horse	10" × 6¾"	7" × 6¾"	40–50 gals.	475 lbs.	$70.00
No. 2	Heavy 1 Horse	12" × 6½"	7" × 6½"	60–70 gals.	575 lbs.	$85.00
No. 3	Reg. 2 Horse	14" × 7½"	8" × 7½"	80–90 gals.	825 lbs.	$100.00
No. 4	Heavy 2 Horse	16" × 9½"	8" × 9½"	90–110 gals.	935 lbs.	$115.00

Manny's 1880 General Catalogue of Cane Mills makes this interesting observation for skilled and careful operation: "In supplying any machine at the very low rate charged for the mechanical part, it cannot be undertaken to furnish the BRAINS to operate it also."

Mansur and Tebbetts Implement Company, St. Louis, Missouri

Alvah Mansur established the first wholesale agricultural implements company west of the Mississippi River, at Kansas City in 1870, which was featured in *Mercantile, Industrial and Professional St. Louis*, by Kargau. The firm opened under the name of Deere, Mansur and Co. Mansur had learned the agricultural implement business through his earlier association with John Deere's celebrated steel plow factory in Moline, Illinois. In 1874 another implement business was opened in St. Louis, and L.B. Tebbetts, a brother-in-law of Mansur, became associated with that company. In 1890, Deere purchased Mansur's interest in the Kansas City firm and Mansur purchased Deere's share in the St. Louis business. At that

The side plates of a Mansur and Tebbetts cane mill (courtesy of Bill Outlaw, Tallahassee, Florida.

time the Mansur and Tebbetts Implement Co. was organized, with Alvah Mansur serving as president, L.D. Tebbetts as vice president and treasurer, and his son, G.S. Tebbetts, as secretary.

At Mansur's death in 1898, the general supervision of the company fell into the hands of L.D. Tebbetts, assisted by his more than capable son, G.S. The implements manufactured and sold by the Mansur and Tebbetts Implement Co. spanned a wide spectrum of agricultural endeavor; carried their business into all the United States, Mexico and South America. A subsidiary, the Mansur and Tebbetts Carriage Manufacturing Co., did an extensive business, with branches in Dallas, Texas, and Nashville, Tennessee.

According to a February 1904 dealer's list, Mansur and Tibbetts Implement Company offered the following mills for sale:

No. 2 Hildago	$27.50
No. 3 Hildago	$42.50
No. 1 Rio Grande	$52.00
No. 3 Rio Grande	$80.00
No. 1 Forest King	$9.00
No. 1 New Amber	$22.50
No. 1 Star Sweep	$39.00
No. 2 Star Sweep	$48.00
No. 1 Star Single Back Gear	$55.00

Miller and Marsden, Brooklyn, New York

Miller and Marsden, 343 First East D, Brooklyn, New York, were known as coppersmiths, according to the *New York State Business Directory and Gazetteer, 1870*, but also were manufacturers of sugarhouse machinery. However, no specifics have been located by this writer thus far.

Mobile Pulley and Machine Works, Mobile, Alabama

The people of Mobile have a hard winter freeze to thank for the industry which was to become the Mobile Pulley and Machine Company. William Edgar, an emigrant from Manchester, England, saw great possibilities for financial gain in the American South. In the 1880s he and his family settled in the vicinity of Sanford, Florida, where he purchased several orange groves with the intention of going into the fruit business on a large scale. However, a hard freeze one winter wiped out his crop and led him to see how uncertain weather could impact his venture. Looking for something more dependable, Edgar moved to Mobile, Alabama. At that time Mobile was one of the leading industrial cities in the South and through its cotton exports was well known to British commerce. Edgar saw a new industry emerging in the Deep South. Lumber camps were springing up as crews began cutting the vast stands of southern pine, and lumber promised to be a substantial market force. In 1892 Edgar purchased a foundry on Royal Street in downtown Mobile, established Edgar Foundry, and began producing stoves, pans, skillets and cooking utensils to meet the needs of the lumber camps.

The next few years were so good for the foundry that Edgar had to relocate in order to expand his business. On March 13, 1897, he purchased a site in rural Mobile, on Ann Street, for $250 and set himself for future growth. His business continued to prosper and he soon added other items for sawmills, such as flat belt pulleys and gears. Within a few years his foundry was again taxed to the limit and Edgar Foundry needed new equipment to meet the growing demand. He looked to English investors for financing and the business was incorporated as Mobile Stove and Pulley Manufacturing Company in 1904. Arthur J. Parsons was sent from England to oversee the new investments, and he became president of the company. With a good working relationship, he and Edgar led the company in steady growth, making pulleys, gears, and castings for the lumber industry. So successful were they that they opened a branch in New Orleans to supply lumber mills in Mississippi and Louisiana.

During this 1904 time frame the company decided that their name should reflect the diversity of products they manufactured, so the name was changed to Mobile Pulley and Machine Works, and the company's history is recorded in *Mobile Pulley & Machine Works, Inc., 1892–1992*. The following few years were critical years for the foundry and William Edgar had to once again demonstrate his adaptability. By 1910 most of the timber had been cut over and the needs of the foundry radically shifted. They began manufacturing artillery shells and by 1912 they were a major supplier of shells for target practice. Mobile Pulley and Machine Works was one of only three American shell producing factories when the United States joined World War I in 1917. C.S. Latshaw was the navy representative assigned to the foundry to oversee its work. He so impressed Mr. Parsons that he was offered a position with the company, an offer which he later accepted. Latshaw went on to become president and part owner of Mobile Pulley.

When the war was over and the demand for shells ceased, the foundry was once again faced with finding new markets. In 1923 Mobile Pulley purchased a war surplus electric furnace which enabled them to produce steel, and subsequently the ability to produce marine and shipyard castings. This led once again to a new direction for the foundry. About that time the Florida land boom began, and much land being developed required dredging. Here Mobile Pulley found an immediate market and its future. From that point Mobile Pulley

While dredging equipment was Mobile Pulley's main product, the company did manufacture cane mills (courtesy Tommy Clayton, Hilliard, Florida).

became a supplier of dredging equipment, from the small dredges in Florida to equipment for the U.S. Army Corps of Engineers' fleet of dredges.

However, manufacturing dredging equipment wasn't enough to sustain the company during the Great Depression and the company had to diversify once again. They produced cast iron furniture, lighthouse clocks, casting for shipyards and paper mills, even cast iron bunnies for lawn decorations. Supplying steam cargo winches and anchor windlasses to shipyards on the West Coast was Mobile Pulley's contribution to the World War II effort. Since these items were machine-intensive, a new facility had to be erected on the east side of Ann Street. On May 12, 1943, the new facility opened and has since contributed greatly to the success of the company. Following World War II the company concentrated on the pulp and paper industry, and by 1958 that accounted for nearly all the its production. Once again, when building and expansions were complete, the work vanished and Mobile Pulley fell on such hard times that it even resorted to building its own machine tools. Then, in the late 1950s and early 1960s some federal government policies were changed and dredging operations were turned over to private industry. With its previous history of manufacturing dredging equipment, Mobile Pulley quickly adapted its facilities and moved successfully into this new field. Large contracts followed, and the manufacture of dredging equipment became, and remains today, the primary business of Mobile Pulley and Machine Works. Though a complete product history of the company has not been located, they were also known to have manufactured cane mills, several of which are still in use.

Monahan and Parry, Savannah, Georgia

Monahan and Parry was the predecessor company of Rourke's Iron Works. Please see Rourke's Iron Works for a more detailed account of this company.

William Montgomery and Company, New York, New York

William Montgomery and Company maintained an office at 219 Broadway, New York City, while their products were manufactured at the Yonkers Machine Works, Westchester County, New York. Montgomery manufactured portable upright steam sawmills which embraced Lund's patents. The 1857 prices for those mills were $1,650 and $2,000. The company manufactured gristmills, shingle machines, steam engines, boilers, and sugar mills, along with all the pulleys and shafting needed for installation. Though they advertised in *Scientific American*, no details were given about the size and models of their mills.

Montgomery Manufacturing Company and Iron Works, Montgomery, Alabama

Joseph Samuel Prince Winter came from a long line of influential, creative and productive Americans. His grandfather, Joseph Winter, of New York City, was secretary of the committee of safety on Washington's staff and a member of the provincial congress. Winter was chosen by the congress as one of the two delegates to number and sign the paper currency issued by the congress on March 5, 1776. He was also chosen to read the Declaration of Independence to the residents of New York City on July 18, 1776. The British coat-of-arms was torn from the front of city hall at that time.

This mill shows the Montgomery Iron Works stamping.

We learn more about the Winter family from the *History of Alabama and Dictionary of Alabama Biography*, by Thomas Owen. Winter's father, John Gano Winter, was also a prominent and industrious man. After moving from New York to Georgia, he became one of that state's greatest promoters and financiers. He was a member of the Warren County, Georgia, court from 1825 to 1831, a prominent banker of Augusta, and a banker and industrialist in Columbus. After moving to Montgomery, Alabama, he became a promoter of plank roads and the founder of the famous Winter Iron Works. He designed and manufactured an engine which received gold and silver medals at the Crystal Palace World's Fair in New York in 1854. That engine became one of the most famous engines of its day and was used for many years in New England. While a complete product list is incomplete, it is known that in 1851 the Montgomery Manufacturing Company and Iron Works manufactured steam engines and boilers; Reuben Rich's cast-iron center vent waterwheel and iron scrolls, complete; sawmills; gristmills; iron and brass castings of numerous kinds; and cane mills, though no details of specific models have been located. Joseph Samuel Prince Winter was educated in Georgia and New York. He became involved in his father's businesses, especially the Winter Iron Works and the Montgomery Gas Company. He began a mercantile business in Montgomery in 1823 and then a bank, the J.S. Winter Company. The Winter Building at 2 Dexter Avenue in downtown Montgomery is of historical significance. It was built in 1841 by John Grindrat to house the Montgomery Branch of the Bank of St. Mary's. Grindrat willed it to his daughter, Mary Elizabeth, wife of Joseph Winter, in 1854. Confederate Secretary of War Leroy Pope Walker sent a telegram from the second floor of the building, from the offices of the Southern Telegraph Company, on April 11, 1861, authorizing Confederate General P.G.T. Beauregard to fire on Fort Sumter. The subsequent bombardment of the fort

This is a Montgomery Iron Works two roller mill.

was the first military action of the War Between the States. The telegram which began the Civil War stated:

> Do not desire needlessly to bombard Fort Sumter. If Major Anderson will state the time at which, as indicated by him, he will evacuate, and agree that in the meantime he will not use his guns against us unless ours should be employed against Fort Sumter, you are thus authorized to avoid the effusion of blood. If this or its equivalent be refused, reduce the fort as your judgment decides to be most practical. L.P. Walker, Sec. Of War, CSA.

The Winter Iron Works was sold for $175,000 in February 1854, and Joseph began studying law under Judge Keyes in Montgomery. He served in the Confederate army as captain of Co. F, Third Alabama Infantry Regiment, and commanded the troops when ordered to Fort Barrancas. He practiced law in New York for five years following the war, then returned to Montgomery to continue his practice. Winter was also a planter and inventor. He introduced Johnson grass to the Deep South and promoted it as a pasture grass. He spent the last years of his life working on the invention of a car axle, but he died before he had developed its full potential.

Monument Iron Works, Baltimore, Maryland

The Monument Iron Works of Baltimore, Maryland, was owned and operated by A.W. Denmead and his son; they were manufacturers of stationary and marine steam engines, boilers and tanks. Their product list was more extensive than this, however, and they did manufacture machinery for iron furnaces; rolling mills; flour mills; distilleries; pumps for mines; portable gristmills; shafting and pulleys; bridge bolts, and castings of all kinds to order. The Monument Iron Works advertised in *Scientific American* in 1868 that they manufactured sugar mill machinery.

Morgan Iron Works, New York, New York

The Morgan Iron Works, located at 814 East Ninth Avenue in New York City, were manufacturers of steam engines, boilers, and sugar cane machinery. The company was founded in 1838 under the leadership of T.F. Secor, Charles Morgan and William H. Caulkin. These men, trading as T.F. Secor and Company, purchased eight lots at the foot of 9th Street and the East River, and established an engine building works. Numerous engines are documented, but not their mills.

Henry G. Morris, Philadelphia, Pennsylvania

Henry G. Morris was a mechanical engineer in Philadelphia in the late 1800s and early 1900s who established a business about 1876 at 229 Pear Street, then relocated to the Drexel Building at the corner of Fifth and Chestnut streets in 1889. He entered into a partnership with Pedro G. Salom in 1899 and the company was called Morris and Salom, with locations in the Drexel Building and at the Philadelphia Bourse. By 1902 Morris was again the sole proprietor of the company located at the Bourse. He relocated his business to 333 Walnut Street in 1904 and the last listing for the company is in the 1912–1914 city directory. While a complete product list is unavailable, there is a listing stating that the Henry G. Morris Company manufactured sugar cane machinery. Mr. Morris also invented an atmospheric elevator which was described in *The Manufacturer and Builder* of May 1884.

Morven Foundry and Machine Works, Morven, Georgia

Morven, Georgia, in northern Brooks County, was named for an estate in the area, which in turn was named for Mount Morven in Scotland. The Morven Foundry and Machine Works were founded in 1898 by J.W. Hitch, who also served as mayor of the thriving young town. Robert Mathis, a skilled artisan from Scotland, was foreman of the foundry, which manufactured engines, boilers, cane mills and all manner of iron products. Numerous Movren Mills can be found scattered across south Georgia.

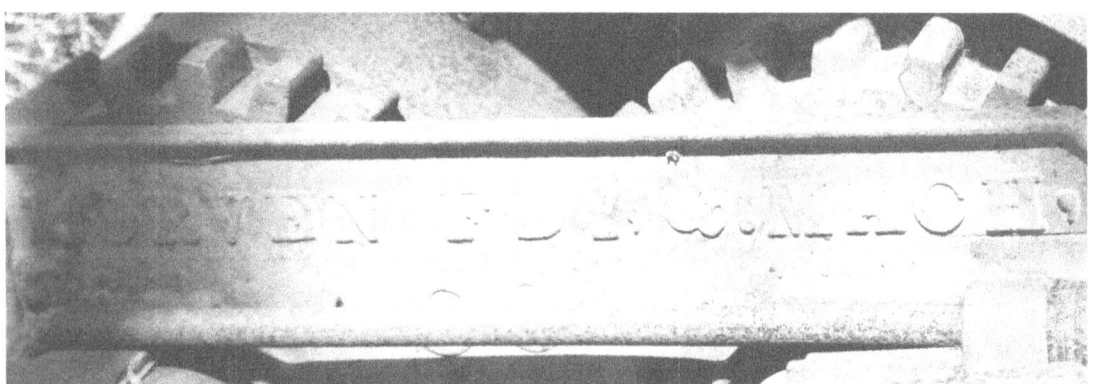

A rare Morven Foundry nameplate.

Above: An early photo of the Morven Foundry and workers (courtesy Bonnell Holmes and the Brooks County Historical Society, Quitman, Georgia). *Below:* This is a Morven Foundry cane mill similar to others made in southeast Georgia.

Mount Airy Iron Works, Mount Airy, North Carolina

The Mount Airy Iron Works were located at the northwest corner of East Oak Street and Riverside Drive in Mount Airy, North Carolina, according to a brief history in the Mount Airy Museum of Regional History. In 1900, J.E. Spraugh, a veteran of North Carolina's 21st Regiment Infantry, operated a foundry at that location. The building, a one-story brick industrial building with stepped parapet ends, had been altered to accommodate the foundry. A gristmill was located just to the east of Spraugh's foundry. The origins of the company seem to have been lost, but about 1910 the business became known as the Mount Airy Iron Works. The establishment was purchased by John D. Minick in 1915 and operated by him for a number of years thereafter.

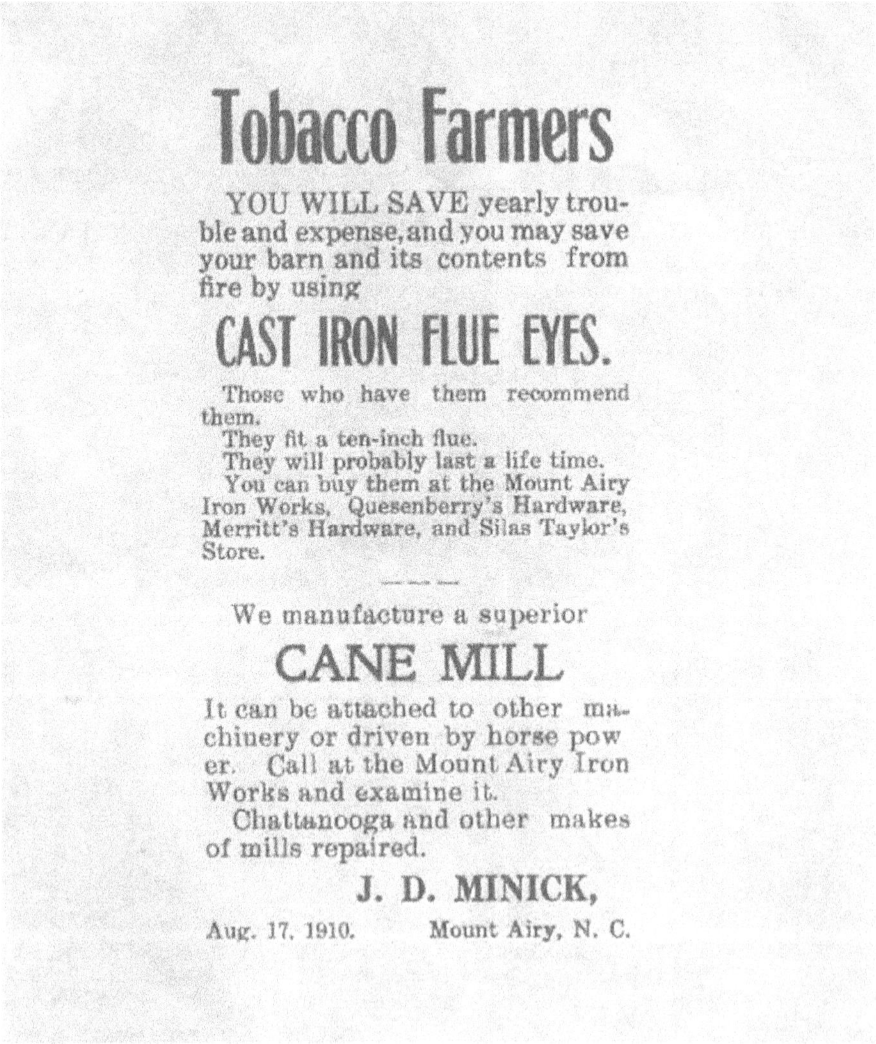

Tobacco Farmers

YOU WILL SAVE yearly trouble and expense, and you may save your barn and its contents from fire by using

CAST IRON FLUE EYES.

Those who have them recommend them.
They fit a ten-inch flue.
They will probably last a life time.
You can buy them at the Mount Airy Iron Works, Quesenberry's Hardware, Merritt's Hardware, and Silas Taylor's Store.

We manufacture a superior

CANE MILL

It can be attached to other machinery or driven by horse power. Call at the Mount Airy Iron Works and examine it.
Chattanooga and other makes of mills repaired.

J. D. MINICK,

Aug. 17, 1910.   Mount Airy, N. C.

This Mount Airy Iron Works ad calls attention to its cane mills (courtesy Ken Christison, Conway, North Carolina).

Minick was a native of Franklin County, Pennsylvania, and was of German and Scottish stock. After a brief tenure teaching school he returned to college and obtained his master's degree in Latin from Bucknell University in Lewisburg, Pennsylvania. Following graduation he moved south to become president of Davenport College, a small Methodist College in Lenoir, North Carolina. In 1899, he and Mrs. Minick moved to Mount Airy, where he entered the bark business. Shortly after that he purchased the Spraugh Grist Mill and Foundry. Both Mr. and Mrs. Minick were ardent Methodists and loyal supporters of their adopted hometown.

Among the agricultural implements manufactured by the Mount Airy Iron Works were animal powered and engine powered "Giant" cane mills. A 1910 ad claims, "We manufacture a superior cane mill. It can be attached to other machinery or driven by horsepower."

This is a Mount Airy Iron Works mill (photograph by Rick Lance, Winston-Salem, North Carolina).

N.O. Nelson Manufacturing Company, St. Louis, Missouri

N.O. Nelson was a man of great industrial vision, social conscience, and initiative. Repulsed by the callous attitude of management toward workers he experienced as an arbitrator in an 1886 railroad strike, he was determined to seek a better solution to conflicts within his own St. Louis company. At the time, the N.O. Nelson Manufacturing Company manufactured plumbing goods, fire hydrants, and, among other things, cane mills. Earnestly seeking to make a difference in management/worker relations, Nelson decided in 1888 to relocate his manufacturing facility to a rural location. In 1890 he found some property in Illinois, across the Mississippi River from St. Louis, that satisfied his requirements, and there he built a "company town." He named his town Leclaire in honor of the Frenchman, Edmund Leclaire, who was an advocate of profit sharing. In the 1930s the town was annexed into the city of Edwardsville. Manufacturing ceased in 1948 though the company continued to operate as a wholesale distributor of plumbing products. After changing hands several times and working through bankruptcy, Primus, Inc., bought the Nelson company in 1958, and today, under the parent name Winholesale, there are over four hundred branches specializing in municipal waterworks products. The history of the company and some of their products may be seen at www.firehydrant.org.

The Star was one of the cane mills made by the N.O. Nelson Manufacturing Company. This was a horizontal three-roller mill designed so that it could be powered by attaching a belt pulley for steam power, or by an attachment for horsepower.

Neosho Manufacturing Company, Neosho, Missouri

Neosho lies in the southwest corner of Missouri between Springfield and Tulsa, Oklahoma. This is the general area of the state which gave birth to the great American agricultural chemist, agronomist and relentless experimentalist, George Washington Carver. The seat of Newton County, Neosho was founded in 1839, and its name is an Osage Indian derivation meaning "clear and abundant water." This is probably a lucid and accurate characterization of the town's nine flowing springs within the city limits. The town is situated in the Ozark Mountains, and the city square seems to have been built over a large cave which runs beneath the city. In addition to the early agricultural crops the area became known for its mineral deposits of lead and zinc.

The business leaders of the young city recognized the need for a foundry and machine shop to meet the needs of the growing agricultural and mining economy of their area. The first railroad built in America, the Baltimore and Ohio, was chartered in 1827. As the railroad began expanding westward the city fathers could see the potential of a foundry and machine shop to meet growing steam power needs. Twenty thousand dollars was raised for capital, and the Neosho Manufacturing Company was organized. The site selected for the company was the Alexander Planing Mill and Lumber Yard. Col. C.W. Thrasher was selected president and James E. Vickery, secretary, with J.E. Alexander, George N. Walbridge, George S. Likens, and J.T. Washburn as directors. Alexander was made general manager of the new enterprise. The company was founded on June 20, 1870, began operations five days later, and opened for business on October 2, 1870. By January 1871, it was ready to supply the area farmers with plows and agricultural implements. In those formative months the company manufactured steam engines, sugar cane mills, cider mills, flour mill machinery, pony pumps, and horsepowers for mining operations. They began smelting operations on August 14, 1871.

J.E. Alexander withdrew from the firm in 1872 to begin his own company. (Please see Alexander & Son Plow Works.) The Neosho Manufacturing Company struggled for a few years and finally went into the hands of a receiver. Charles Van Riper and his son-in-law, John A. Rogers, both of Joplin, Missouri, leased the business for several years and purchased the property on April 10, 1883. The name was then changed to Neosho Foundry, Machine Shop and Iron Works. With new capital and new contacts the new owners built such a large and profitable business that they were able to build a new 40' × 70' brick building in 1888. John Rogers sold the foundry to Warren Heaton in January 1905, and on March 8, 1907, it was consolidated with Alexander's company and the name changed to Neosho Foundry and Plow Works. The company produced plows, mining equipment, heavy foundry products and stoves. Due to a shortage of raw materials the foundry was forced to close during the early years of World War II.

Newburgh Steam Engine Works, Newburgh, New York

The Newburgh Steam Engine Works of Newburgh, New York, was owned and operated by Corwin, Stanton and Company, and joined one of several companies of Newburgh manufacturing cane mills. While the company had a varied product list it seems that circular saws of all sizes, with solid iron or heavy wood frames, "suitable for the Southern market," comprised their largest business. However, they also manufactured steam engines and boilers, both stationary and portable; brick machinery; mill gearing; various iron and brass castings; an 1865 advertisement in *Scientific American* stated they manufactured both vertical roller and horizontal roller cane mills.

Niles Works, Cincinnati, Ohio

James and Jonathan Niles left their home state of Connecticut and moved to Cincinnati in 1845 to establish a boat repair company on the Ohio River. Their business, the Niles

Works, a large machine shop at 222 East Front Street, flourished. Soon the brothers were designing and building their own power plants for riverboats and general industrial use. It was this step which led them to design and build steam-powered cane mills which they shipped by riverboat to the booming sugar plantations in Louisiana. In their Cincinnati shop they did general millwork and built steam engines, steamboat engines, locomotive engines, and heavy sugar machinery. By 1853 their business had so prospered that the Niles Works

NEWBURGH STEAM-ENGINE WORKS.
ESTABLISHED 1824.

Adjustable Slide-Valve Cut-Off Engine.

Horizontal Tubular Boiler.

Portable Engine on Wheels.

Portable Hoisting Engine.

FIRST-CLASS ENGINES AND BOILERS A SPECIALTY.

Improved *STATIONARY ENGINES*, either plain, slide-valve, adjustable slide-valve cut-off, or automatic cut-off. *BOILERS* of all kinds. PORTABLE HOISTING ENGINES, and the celebrated *AMES PORTABLE ENGINES*. Also Saw and Grist-Mills, Turbine Water-Wheels, Shafting, Gearing, &c.
We are making *a specialty* of the above, carry a large stock, and are able to sell at low prices. *Send for our Catalogue.*

HAMPSON, WHITEHILL & CO.,
38 Cortlandt Street, New York.

Above: Steam engines were a specialty at Newburgh Steam Engine Works. *Below:* This Newburgh Steam Engine Works ad also lists cane mills.

CIRCULAR SAW-MILLS. — THE UNDERSIGNED are now manufacturing Circular Saw-mills of all sizes, with solid iron or heavy wood frame, suitable for the Southern market. Also, Sugar Mills, vertical or horizontal; Steam Engines and Boilers, stationary or portable; Brick Machinery; Mill Gearing, and Iron and Brass Castings of every description.
 Sample of our Saw-mill may be seen at our N. Y. Agency, with JOHN ASHCROFT, No. 50 John street.
 For particulars address
    CORWIN, STANTON & CO.,
17 4*   Newburgh Steam Engine Works, Newburgh, N. Y.

was a major employer in Cincinnati, employing between four hundred and five hundred workers. Their work was also diversified. In addition to the large steam engines and cane mill equipment they manufactured sawmills, draining machines, sugar refining equipment, boilers, tyre-lathes, boring mills, planing machines, oil presses for cotton seed, and heavy castings of numerous applications.

During the Civil War, when materials were scarce, the Niles Works needed one or two new lathes but couldn't get their order filled. The brothers commissioned two of their excellent machinists to build one. George A. Gray, Jr., a Scotsman, and Alexander Gordon, an Irishman, who had worked together on numerous other projects, set about designing and building the needed lathes. They produced such an excellent lathe that soon other industries wanted to purchase them. In 1866, Mr. James Gaff, a wealthy distiller from Aurora, Illinois, became interested in Gray and Gordon's work and proposed a new company. The firm of Gaff, Gray and Gordon was organized and named the Niles Tool Works. They bought out the Niles brothers' Niles Works, and that part of the industry lapsed into oblivion. The Niles Tool Works went on to become the largest machine-tool company in the world for a period of time, and is chronicled in *Sketches and Statistics of Cincinnati in 1859*, by Charles Cist. In all probability the Niles Mill manufactured by the Blymyer Company was of this company's pattern.

Norris Works, Norristown, Pennsylvania

Andrew Ingles, Richard R. Corson, and John West were the proprietors of Ingles, Corson, and West, Iron and Brass Founders, of Norristown, Pennsylvania. Service provided by the Norris Works included machine shop work, boiler making and steam engine building. They manufactured improved Cornish Pumping Engines of any capacity for mines and waterworks; mining machinery; propeller engines for canal boats; and all heavy machinery required in the engineering business in general. An August 23, 1856, advertisement in *Scientific American* stated that the Norris Works manufactured sugar mills. However, no specifics about models were given.

North Alabama Engineering Company, New Decatur, Alabama

The North Alabama Engineering Company, Moulton Road, New Decatur, Alabama, was a short lived company in one of the business ventures of Robert Dyas. New Decatur, Alabama, was originally named Albany. When a street was built connecting Albany and Decatur, Alabama, Albany became New Decatur and Decatur was referred to as Old Decatur. The two northern Alabama communities have so grown together that today they are simply known as Decatur. On January 7, 1901, Robert Dyas purchased from the Decatur Land Company a tract of land and the facilities of what was known as the old Ivens and Son Machine Company in New Decatur. A rather detailed inventory of equipment is listed in the deed, including several Gleason lathes, planers, milling machines, drills, pipe cutters, a cotton press machine, benches, vises, wood lathe, cranes, wood mortising machines, blacksmith tools, cupola winches, three stationary engines, ladders, pulleys, shafts, hangers, and assorted patterns and equipment. While the North Alabama Engineering Company has been listed as a manufacturer of cane mills, in all probability they were from patterns of the Ivens and Son Machine Company. The company ran into some financial difficulties and the iron works were sold to W.C. Stubbs for $4,000 on July 29, 1907.

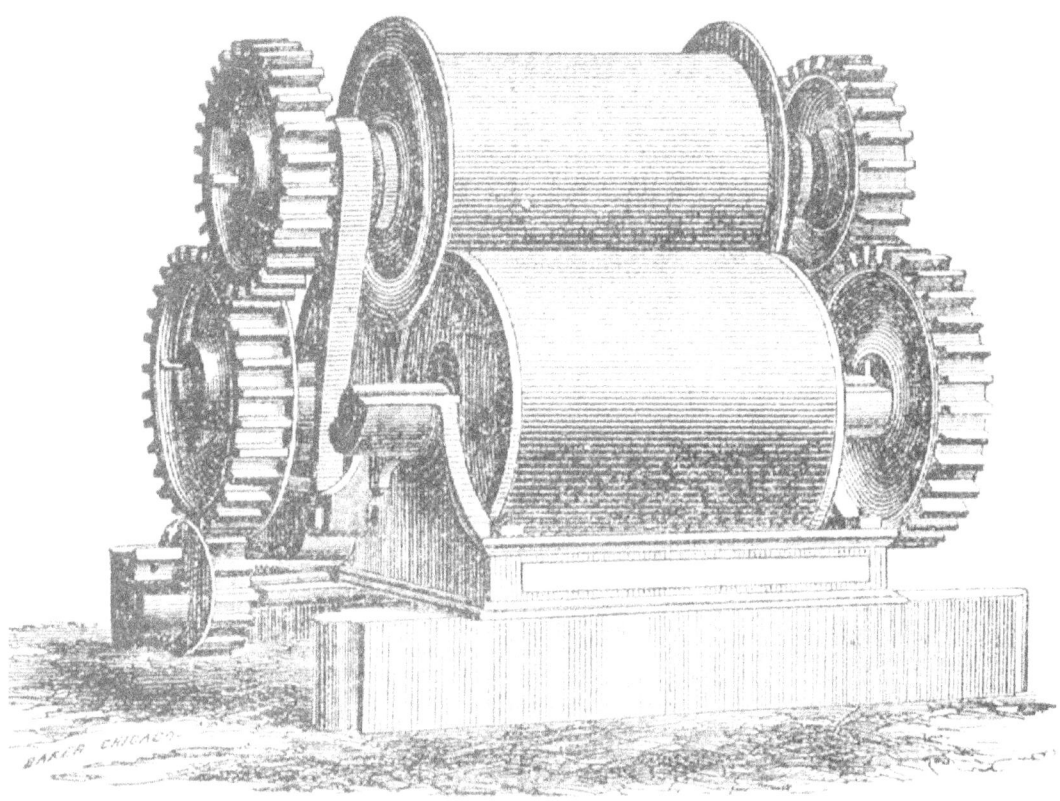

Other than this mill, not much is known about the Northwestern Sorgho Company.

Northwestern Sorgho Company, Chicago, Illinois

Claiming to be "the most justly celebrated Sorgho machinery manufacturers of the country," Northwestern Sorgho Company, Chicago, Illinois, manufactured several styles and varieties of mills. Their line spanned from machinery for the small farmer to equipment capable of producing from one hundred to five hundred gallons of good syrup per day for larger operations. Their mills were warranted to be stouter and better, and their evaporators to do more and better work per fuel required, than that of any other manufacturer' in the United States. At the 1865 Wisconsin State Fair the company took second place for their Sweep Sugar Mill, with an accompanying award of $5.00.

The Novelty Iron Works, New Orleans, Louisiana

To meet the growing needs of the cotton and sugar industries of the Deep South, the Novelty Iron Works was begun in 1853 by two gentlemen named McKewen and Patterson. In 1865, William Golding became the sole proprietor of the company and expanded its productivity. Golding was born in Liverpool, England, in 1838 but settled in New Orleans at an early age. A trusted businessman, Golding was also a creative genius. He invented a number of significant improvements in cotton presses at a time when cotton was king in the South. He was the manufacturer of all the bridge work for the New Orleans & Pacific Railroad. While the Novelty Iron Works produced horizontal and vertical steam engines, sugar mills, cotton presses, and iron and brass castings of all descriptions, their specialties were heavy forging and cotton presses. They also had facilities for marine repair. The ironworks used a twenty-five horsepower engine to drive the machinery used by twenty skilled mechanics. The Novelty Iron Works' trade area included all of the Southern United States, Mexico and Cuba.

George K. Oyler Manufacturing Company, St. Louis, Missouri

The George K. Oyler Manufacturing Company, 515 and 517 Elm Street, St. Louis, Missouri, manufactured both two and three vertical roller mills, and three roller horizontal mills. The Oyler cane mills were warranted to be well made of good materials and any defective part was replaced free of charge. Each mill listed a suggested capacity based on reports from Mexico and Florida in the south to Manitoba in the north, but it could not be guaranteed. Oyler suggested using a stiff sweep 12 to 13 feet long, "and if the mill is a small one, let the left end project so as to partially balance the weight of the other."

The Economist

The smallest mill carried in Oyler's 1884–85 catalog was the Economist. This was a small, vertical two-roller mill manufactured for those looking for a good, but cheap, mill. It featured lathe turned rolls, and wrought iron shafts which turned in chilled iron and brass boxes. The Economist had a patented juice plate, and their newly designed feed plate prevented overcrowding while allowing the juice to run down the inside of the mill rather than down the drooping stalks of cane.

Chart for the Economist Cane Mill

Model No.	Roller Size-D × H	Juice Per Hour	Weight	1884 Price
No. 0	8" × 9"	50 gals.	365 lbs.	$35.00

The Pioneer Cane Mill was a vertical three-roller mill with exposed gearing above the top-plate. The mill was designed to be powered by horses and carried a large, sturdy sweep bracket on the crushing roller shaft. A large gear was keyed to this shaft which in turn powered the two smaller rollers. This mill was so constructed that the lower journals required no oil, but were lubricated by the juice. It had similar structural refinements to the Economist.

Chart for the Pioneer Cane Mill

Model No.	Main Roller- D × H	Small Rollers- D × H	Juice Per Hour	Weight	1884 Price
No. 00	10" × 6"	6" × 6"	50 gals.	350 lbs.	$40.00
No. 1	12" × 7"	8" × 7"	70 gals.	550 lbs.	$55.00
No. 2	16" × 8"	8" × 8"	105 gals.	750 lbs.	$72.00
No. 3	16" × 12"	8" × 12"	134 gals.	1,000 lbs.	$90.00

Oyler's Western Sugar Cane Mill was made with separate gearing encased within the mill. The gears had two clutches on each wheel which fit into two corresponding ones in each roller, doing away with all keys and enabling the mill to be taken apart by removing

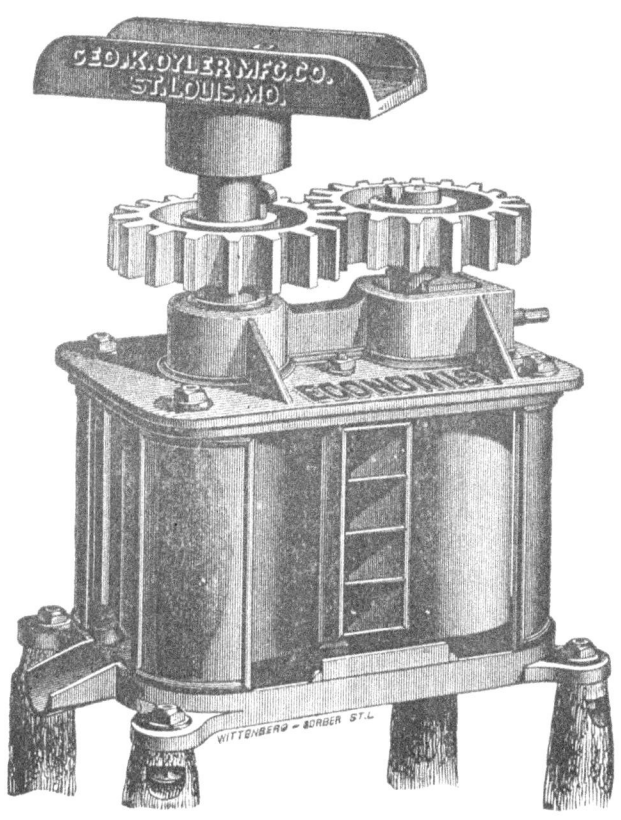

Above: Oyler's Economist cane mill came in only one size. *Below:* Oyler's Pioneer mill cane in four sizes.

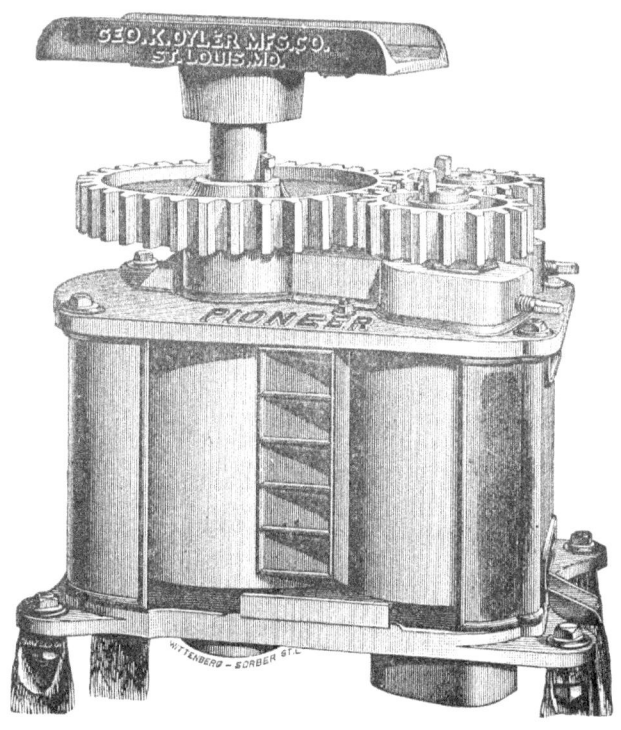

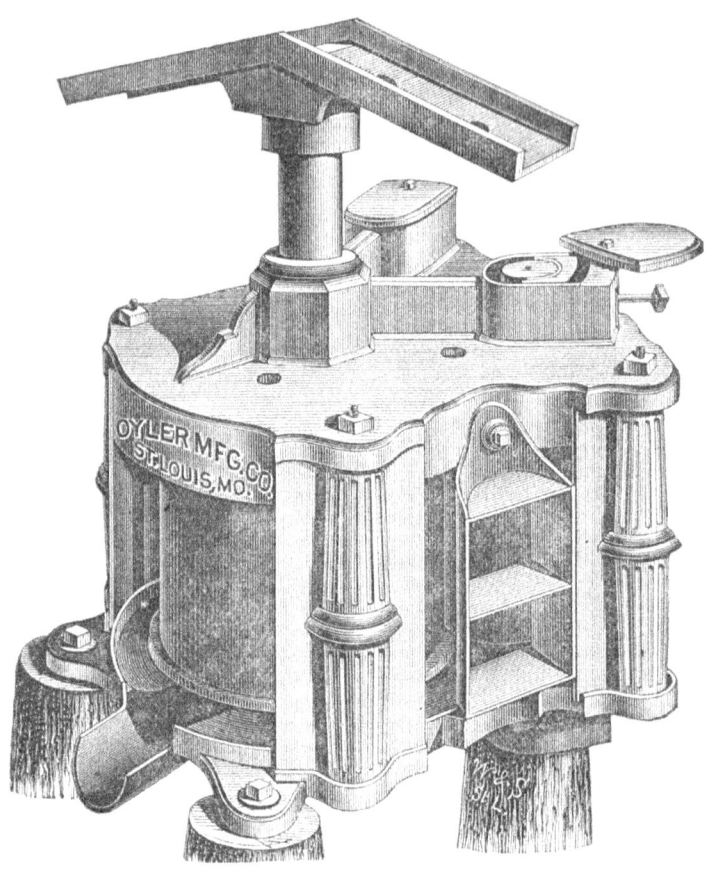

The Western model came in five sizes and had gears encased within the mill.

four bolts. The main rollers were flanged, top and bottom, and lathe turned with serrated faces. The cold rolled iron shafts ran in brass bearings. The Western carried an angling sweep cap doing away with the need of a bent sweep as is necessary with a flat sweep cap. The Oyler Company warned against mills manufactured with sand in the rolls to give them extra weight but no extra strength.

Chart for the Western Cane Mill

Model No.	Horsepower	Main Roller— D × H	Small Rollers— D × H	Juice Per Hour	Weight	1884 Price
No. A	One Light	9½" × 6"	6⅜" × 6"	40–60 gals.	450 lbs.	$45.00
No. B	One Regular	11½" × 6⅝"	6¾" × 6⅝"	60–75 gals.	600 lbs.	$60.00
No. C	One Heavy	13" × 7⅜"	7⅛" × 7⅜"	75–90 gals.	725 lbs.	$75.00
No. D	Two Regular	14" × 9¼"	8¾" × 9¼"	90–100 gals.	1,075 lbs.	$95.00
No. E	Two Heavy	14" × 11½"	8 3¾" × 11½"	100–125 gals.	1,200 lbs.	$115.00

Gold Medal Horizontal Sugar Cane Mill

The Oyler Gold Medal horizontal mill came in three sizes, and was manufactured first class in style and finish. This mill featured lathe turned rolls, wrought iron shafts which turned in chilled boxes with babbitt bearings, and a main roll flanged to prevent clogging. Oyler claimed this mill could grind cane and leave the bagasse dry enough to burn. The boxes were constructed so as to prevent oil from getting into the juice. The sweep cap had a square eye and sat on the top shaft without keys so it could easily be removed. It was geared to make three revolutions to every one the horses made. The patented feed box kept the mill from choking no matter how fast it was being fed. Every part was made in duplicate so it could be taken apart and repaired without taking it to the shop. Each mill came painted and varnished, and was in every respect a first-class horizontal mill.

Chart for the Gold Medal Horizontal Cane Mill

Model No.	Horsepower	Main Roller- D × L	Small Rollers- D × L	Juice Per Hour	Weight	1884 Price
No. A	1 Horse	9" × 6½"	6" × 6½"	60 gals.	600 lbs.	$55.00
No. B	1 or 2 Horse	9" × 10½"	6" × 10½"	75 gals.	700 lbs.	$70.00
No. C	2 Horse	9" × 12"	6" × 12"	100 gals.	900 lbs.	$85.00

Plantation Power Horizontal Sugar Cane Mill

Oyler offered the Plantation model, which was a power horizontal mill adaptable to either thresher engine, steam, or waterpower. This mill came with either single back or double back gears, and regular or extra heavy mills. A feature of the Plantation Mill was adjustable rolls and elastic bearings. The feed roll was adjustable to accommodate uneven feeding or different sizes of cane. It could be made rigid by removing the elastic bearing and replacing it with a piece of metal or hard wood. The discharge roll was adjustable to

The Gold Medal mill came in three sizes. (photograph by Ken Christison, Conway, North Carolina).

The Gold Medal was first class in style and finish.

get all the juice out of the bagasse. The gears were set inside the mill for service and protection.

Chart for the Plantation Cane Mill

Model No.	Gearing	Main Roller- D × L	Small Rollers- D × L	Juice Per Hour	Weight	1884 Price
No. 1	Single	10" × 10"	6" × 10"	100 gals.	700 lbs.	$125.00
No. 1	Double	10" × 10"	6" × 10"	100 gals.	800 lbs.	$150.00
No. 2	Single	10" × 16"	6" × 16"	160 gals.	850 lbs.	$150.00
No. 2	Double	10" × 16"	6" × 16"	160 gals.	950 lbs.	$200.00

Oyler offered an extra heavy Plantation Power Mill built larger and stronger for large sugar plantations. The specifics for these mills are as follows:

Chart for the Plantation Power Cane Mill for Large Plantations

Model No.	Horsepower	Main Roller- D × L	Small Rollers- D × L	Cane Per Hour	Weight	1884 Price
No. 3	8–10	16" × 12"	10" × 12"	2 Tons	2,500 lbs.	$350.00
No. 4	12–15	16" × 18"	10" × 18"	3½ Tons	3,000 lbs.	$450.00

Plantation Mill with Sweep Below

Oyler offered the Plantation mill rigged with a seven foot shaft and a sweep below. Some advantages of the sweep below were: in such an arrangement the mill is more steady; the

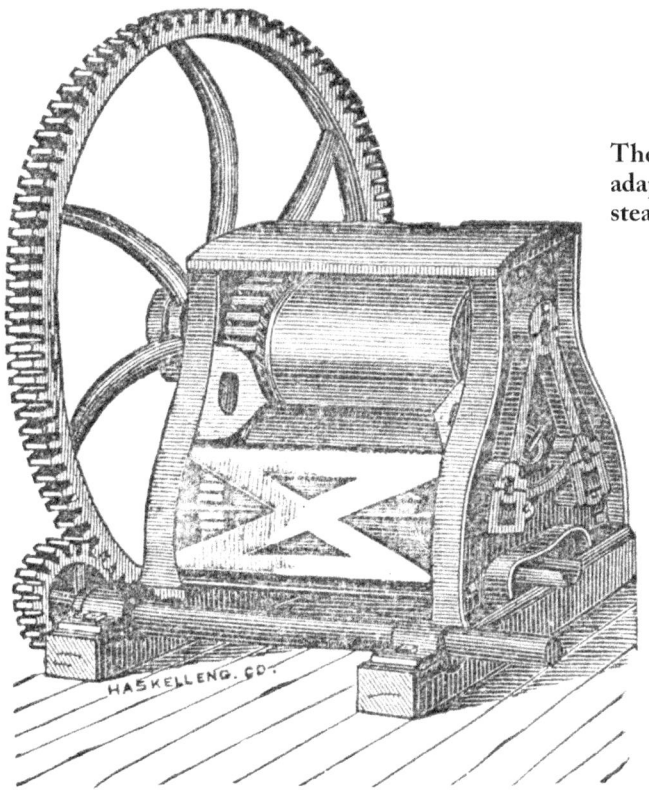

The Plantation mill was adaptable to thresher engine, steam power or water power.

The Plantation mill with shaft below came rigged with a seven foot shaft.

horses and cane do not interfere with each other; the bagasse is more easily removed; and the juice can flow downward to the evaporator.

Chart for the Plantation Cane Mill With Sweep Below

Model No.	Horsepower	Main Roller- D × H	Small Rollers- D × H	Juice Per Hour	Weight	1884 Price
No. 1	2 Horse	10" × 10"	6" × 10"	80 gals.	1,000 lbs.	$150.00
No. 2	4 Horse	10" × 16"	6" × 16"	125 gals.	1,200 lbs.	$175.00

The George K. Oyler Manufacturing Company manufactured all kinds of accessories for cane mills, such as evaporators, fire doors, grates, feed tables and bagasse carriers. Their catalog did not carry any kettles in 1884. They did, however, manufacture all kinds of farm machinery, including buggies, carriages, and spring wagons.

Parlin and Orendorff Company, Canton, Illinois

Located midway between Chicago and St. Louis in an agricultural and mineral rich part of Illinois is the city of Canton. The city was founded by Isaac Swan in 1825 and named Canton because he believed it to be the exact geographical opposite of Canton, China. One of the first businesses in Canton was Swan's sawmill on Big Creek, a mill which prospered by providing building materials for a developing, growing city. Canton was incorporated in 1837. Three years later, in 1840, a mechanical genius, William Parlin, settled in Canton. Parlin built one of the largest manufacturers of agricultural implements in the nation, but when he arrived in Canton he had three hammers, a leather apron, and twenty-five cents in his pocket. He began work as a journeyman in Robert Culton's Diamond Plow Company, which manufactured a plow with a wooden moldboard and iron share. Parlin later purchased a foundry and began his own plow business. In 1842 he produced Canton's first steel plow and over the next decade the demand for it was greater than he could produce. It was at that time, in 1852, that Parlin took his brother-in-law, William J. Orendorff, into partnership. The company, William Parlin and Company, was incorporated as Parlin and Orendorff in 1860. The company first advertised their Clipper Plows in 1865 but also produced Parlin's Cultivator, a cornstalk cutter, a disc harrow, and a double plow known as the "lister." By 1900 Parlin and

"P&O Co., Canton, Ill" is visible on this old stalk cutter footrest.

Orendorff employed about 1,000 workers and was one of the three largest manufacturers of agricultural implements in the nation. More about the city may be found at www.cantonillinois.org.

A 1903 wholesale sales brochure lists the following mills:

Cane Mills

No. 0 New Canton Vertical Mill	400 lbs.	$17.00
No. 1 New Canton Vertical Mill	600 lbs	$20.50
No. 2 New Canton Vertical Mill	800 lbs.	$28.00
No. 3 New Canton Vertical Mill	1000 lbs.	$36.00
No. 4 New Canton Vertical Mill	1300 lbs.	$49.00
No. 0 Climax Vertical Mill	440 lbs.	$13.25
No. 1 Climax Vertical Mill	540 lbs.	$17.50
No. 2 Climax Vertical Mill	750 lbs.	$27.00
No. 3 Climax Vertical Mill	1000 lbs.	$37.00
No. 4 Climax Vertical Mill	1300 lbs.	$47.00

The Improved Three-Roll Kentucky Cane Mill

No. 0 Kentucky Light 1-Horse	400 lbs.	$14.00
No. 1 Kentucky Regular 1-Horse	500 lbs.	$19.00
No. 2 Kentucky Heavy 1-Horse	725 lbs.	$28.00
No. 3 Kentucky Regular 2-Horse	900 lbs.	$38.00
No. 4 Kentucky Heavy 2-Horse	1200 lbs.	$47.50
No. A New Clipper Horizontal Mill	650 lbs.	$23.00
No. B New Clipper Horizontal Mill	700 lbs.	$30.00
No. C New Clipper Horizontal Mill	900 lbs.	$35.00
No. 1 Imperial or Cont'l Power Mill	1000 lbs.	$62.50
No. 2 Imperial or Cont'l Power Mill	1400 lbs.	$81.25
No. 3 Imperial or Cont'l Power Mill	1700 lbs.	$100.00
No. 4 Imperial or Cont'l Power Mill	3100 lbs.	$187.50
No. 3 Eclipse Power Mill	2800 lbs.	$132.00
No. 4 Eclipse Power Mill	3200 lbs.	$182.50

The International Harvester Company purchased the company in 1919. Canton IH became one of the nation's defense factories during World War II, producing shell clips for stopping shell containers. When the war was over the company returned to producing agricultural implements. The International Harvester Company closed the doors of the Parlin and Orendorff factory in 1983.

Pascal Iron Works, Philadelphia, Pennsylvania

The Pascal Iron Works had its beginning in Philadelphia, Pennsylvania, in 1821 when Stephen P. Morris began manufacturing stoves, grates, and miscellaneous iron castings. Two significant things happened for the company in 1835. One, Henry Morris and Thomas T. Tasker, Sr., became associated with Stephen P. Morris in his business, and two, gas was introduced to Philadelphia. The Pascal Iron Works moved quickly to begin manufacture of gas pipe. As this business grew they added gas fittings and gas fitters' tools. Next came the manufacture of machinery for generating, washing, purifying, and storing illuminating gas. Pipes for other purposes followed, including tubes for conveying water, lap-welded boiler tubes, boiler water fittings, hot water heaters and ventilation equipment. By 1873 Pascal Iron Works was manufacturing all the equipment needed to light, heat, ventilate, and plumb a building for water. From this inauspicious beginning, the Pascal Iron Works grew to a plant covering twelve acres of land, employing thousands, and producing items valued in millions of dollars each year. A branch office was opened at No.15 Gold Street in New York City. The 1873 plant facilities included twelve boilers and seven steam engines capable of generating one thousand horsepower. A duplication of all machinery was kept on hand in the event of breakage or other mechanical problems, and the factory could be back on line within twenty-four hours. The business by this time was carried on by Tasker's sons. They employed 1,600 workers, kept the pipe mills in constant operation, day and night, opened a branch at Newcastle, Delaware, and were featured in *The Manufacturer and Builder* in November 1873.

In the early 1870s, the Pascal Iron Works of Morris, Tasker, and Company was recognized as one of the oldest machine shops in the United States and at one time was the largest. While pipes and tubes seemed to be the product upon which their success was built, and which sustained them through the years, they did manufacture other items as well, including cane mills. An 1877 advertisement in *The Manufacturer and Builder* announced the sale of "Improved Sugar Machinery."

Payne and Joubert, New Orleans, Louisiana

Payne and Joubert, 423 Carondelet, New Orleans, Louisiana, manufactured sugar cane machinery for the large sugar industry of Louisiana. No specifics of their machinery have been found by this writer.

Peacock Foundry, Selma, Alabama

America's fledgling iron and foundry business was remarkably dependent upon expertise from abroad. The same held true for what was to become Peacock Foundry in Selma, Alabama. George Peacock was born on a farm near Stockton-on-Tees, in the county of Durham, England, on May 5, 1823. When George was seven his family moved to the town

George Peacock was a genius in iron molding.

A close-up of one of Peacock's mills at Rikard's Mill Park, Monroe County, Alabama).

of Stockton, where he was apprenticed, at age fourteen, to the Potrick Lane Iron Works. Over the next seven years he mastered the trade of iron molding. Following his apprenticeship he secured employment at one of the largest ironworks in Liverpool, England. When a job offer from Ericsson's in the United States of America fell through, George Peacock found employment with Townsend's Foundry and Machine Shops in Albany, New York. The Peacock family subsequently emigrated to America in 1848. George became known as an expert in iron works, and became renowned as a manufacturer and inventor. His services were in great demand, and he had served as superintendent in several ironworks in various places, such as Coller, Sage and Dunhams in West Troy, New York, by the time of the Civil War. There he enabled the company to increase its output of cast-iron pipe from ten tons per day to fifty tons per day. He next worked for Ashcraft, McCammon and Company in Cleveland, Ohio, where he built a plant that produced the pipe for the city water system. From Cleveland, George went to Louisville, Kentucky, where he built the city waterworks and opened a new foundry. From Louisville Peacock moved to Natchez, Mississippi, to manage the C.B. Churchill and Company Iron Works. America was soon to be a nation at war as the Confederate states made their stand. Churchill's was one of the first companies to manufacture munitions of war, and with the fall of lower Mississippi in 1862, the company relocated in Columbiana, Alabama. By a special act of the Confederate congress, a confederate foundry, a naval cannon factory, was established at Selma, Alabama, and Peacock became its superintendent in 1863. By this time he was already known for his creative genius with a long list of inventions, and he brought to the foundry a system of core making for shells which tripled its production. Much of what we know about Peacock is recorded in the *Memorial Record of Alabama*. Other industries sprang up along the banks of the Alabama River, and at one time there were 10,000 industrial workers in Selma in such businesses as

Above: Peacock's mill at a distance. *Below:* A close-up of Peacock's rollers.

Central City Iron Works, Central City Foundry, Dallas Iron Works, Alabama Factory, Phelan and McBride Iron Works, Campbell's Foundry, Selma Shovel Factory, and Selma Iron Works. The factories covered fifty acres along the banks of the river, and at least 6,000 persons were employed by the Confederate government alone in its war effort. Selma became a thriving manufacturing center, and by 1863 only Richmond exceeded it as the largest in the Confederacy.

Following the war, George Peacock established his own foundry in Selma in 1865 and continued to produce numerous innovations. He discovered the first coal in Alabama useful for making coke, so essential in the foundry industry. His faithfulness to his customers, his skill, and his attentiveness to detail brought such business that his establishment had to be enlarged. He manufactured railroad car wheels on an extensive scale, and the "Peacock railroad car wheel" was sold all across the nation. He invented and produced a "self-oiling" railroad car wheel. Though his father had been struck and killed by a New York Central train while visiting Selma in 1851, George continued to improve the locomotive industry with his creative designs. He did, however, design and produce some agricultural implements, such as cotton presses, plows, and cane mills. One of his mills is on display at Rikard's Mill Park, part of the Monroe County Heritage Museums, near Beatrice, Alabama. Peacock's mill as displayed and utilized at Rikard's Mill is an interesting example of emerging technology. Rather than being simply set in a frame of heavy timbers, Peacock's mill is designed to be mounted between two sets of timbers.

Above: Note how the flanges direct the juice downward. *Below:* The juice pan is bolted beneath the mill.

Space between the rollers is regulated by the use of four long bolts running side to side, top and bottom. Vertical alignment of the rollers is attained by adjusting the cross-timbers and securing them with shims and wedges. The journals are set in metal bearing boxes. The bottom of the rollers are surrounded by metal flanges which spiral downward in order to channel the juice into the reservoir bolted beneath the timbers. This is the only Peacock mill this writer has been able to locate and is a wonderful example of combining wood and metal into a functional piece of equipment.

Pearson, Aikin and Company, Louisville, Kentucky

Elisha A. Pearson, William Aikin, and William Drummond were proprietors of the Pearson, Aikin and Company, founders and machinists, located on Main Street between Twelfth and Thirteenth according to the *1867–1868 Louisville City Directory*. The company operated a variety foundry and produced agricultural implements. While the origins of the company are somewhat obscure, there is some historical record from the time Drummond joined the firm (*The History of Kentucky*, Vol. 4). In 1865, William W. Drummond left his position as superintendent of Aimslee, Coehens and Company and bought one-third interest in Pearson and Aikin, and the name was changed to Aikin and Drummond.

William W. Drummond was born in Scotland and emigrated to America with his family in 1849, when he was nine years old. With his parents he returned to Scotland in 1850, only to return to the United States in 1851. Settling first in Troy, New York, William, a lad of 18—with his parents, four brothers and two sisters—moved to Louisville on July 4, 1858. He went to work with Aimslee, Coehens and Company for 50 cents per day, but with a determination to learn the machinists' trade. Six years later, when he left the company, he had been promoted to superintendent with an annual salary of $3,000. Aikin and Drummond also operated the Louisville Axle Works. They developed a round molding machine which was awarded medals at the World's Fair in Paris in 1878. In 1880, Drummond purchased all other interests and organized the Drummond Manufacturing Company.

On January 19, 1869, William Aikin and William Bennett, administrators of the estate of the late J.R. Gates, assignors to J.F. Pearson and William Aikin, received a United States patent, No. 85,984, for an improved cane mill. W.W. Drummond was one of the witnesses on the patent application. The uniqueness of this mill was in its simplified construction, provisions for adjustable, good bearings for the rollers, and for facilities for lubricating and repairing the bearings. The mill featured removable journals, adjustable set screws, a yielding scraper which kept the rollers clean, and a new means for retaining grease in the lower journals. Pearson and Aikin marketed their mills as the Great Western Premium Sugar Mill. In that a No. D has been found one could assume they manufactured several size models.

A Pearson, Aikin mill from the front (courtesy Jeff and Lisa McClain, Martinsville, Indiana).

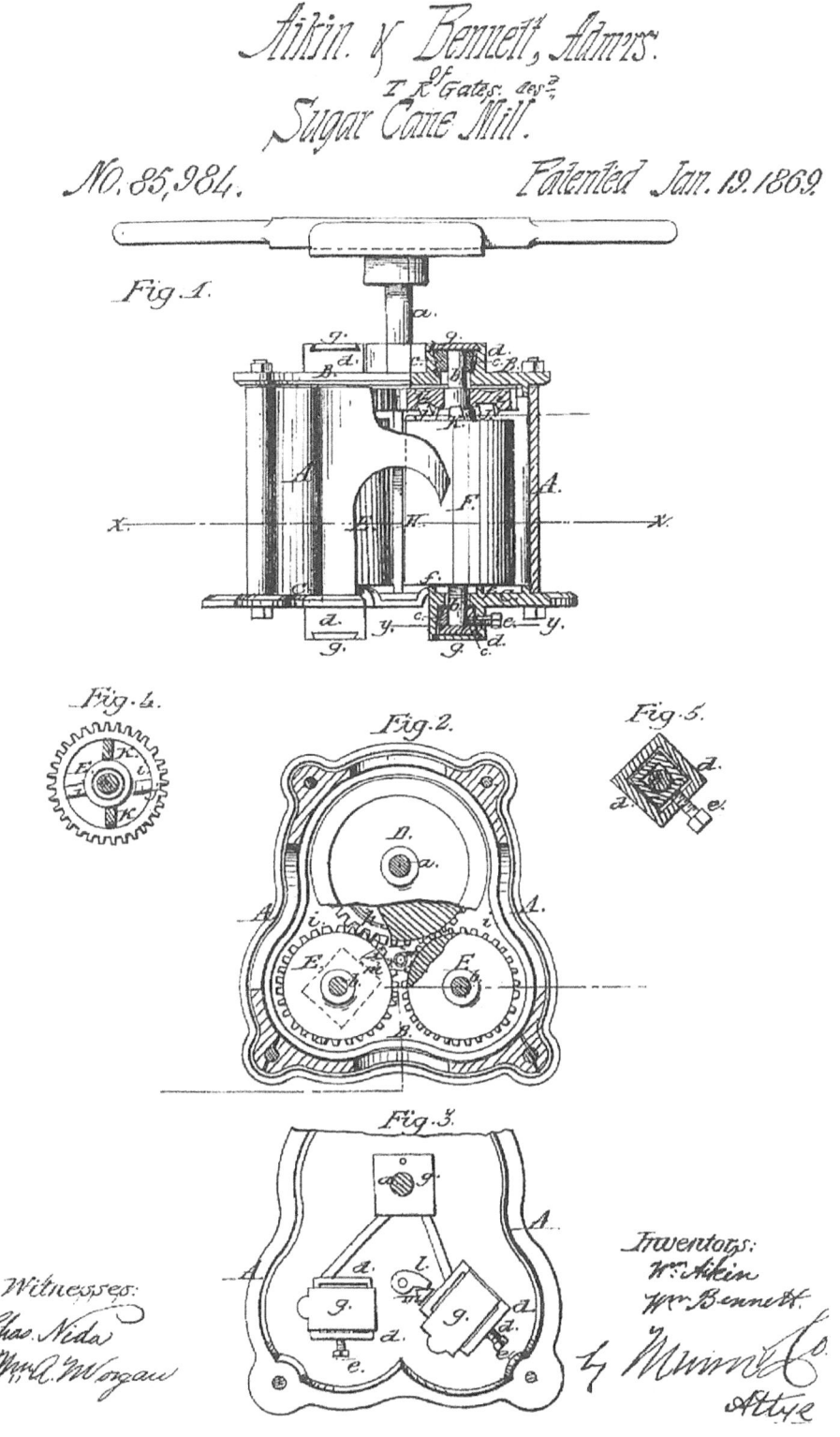

The patent of a Pearson, Aikin, and Co. mill.

A close-up of the front of the Pearson, Aikin mill.

A side view of the beautiful Pearson, Aikin mill.

Phoenix Foundry and Manufacturing Company, Ripley, Ohio

To name his foundry the Phoenix Foundry seems more than appropriate for John P. Parker, for, indeed, it rose from the ashes of his old life and developed into a long and significant new life. To own a thriving business, hold three U.S. Patents, and be a man of means and influence seems improbable for a little eight year old biracial boy being marched from Norfolk to Richmond, Virginia. Born in 1827, the son of a black slave woman and a white father, John P. Parker was taken from his mother and sold into slavery. From Richmond, a gang of slaves, including young Parker, were chained and marched to Mobile, Alabama. In Mobile, Parker was purchased by a kindly physician whose sons slipped him books and helped him learn to read and write.

By his own testimony, Parker was treated well by the physician, who encouraged the young man to learn a skill. However, Parker chaffed at the injustice of the slavery system and fought against it at every opportunity. After a failed runaway attempt he was sold to a widowed patient of the doctor for $1,800. Parker persuaded the widow to let him work and pay her for his freedom. Having learned the skill of an iron molder, and with the possibility of buying his freedom, Parker plunged himself into his work. Finally, in 1845, at age eighteen, he paid the widow and was a free man. He made his way to the ironworks of New Albany, Indiana, where he found work. Soon he moved on to Cincinnati, where he met and married Miranda Boulden. The two of them moved to Ripley, Ohio, in 1849, where he became engaged in the foundry business. While in Cincinnati Parker had become involved in helping slaves escape their Southern slavery. In Ripley he worked at the foundry by day and was a conductor on the Underground Railroad by night. More about this remarkable man can be found in his autobiography, *His Promised Land*, published by W.W. Norton.

With his partner, William Hood, Parker established the Phoenix Foundry in 1854. By 1865 their business had grown so much that they needed more spacious facilities. They purchased the Buckeye Foundry on Front Street and employed twelve to fifteen hands in producing steam engines of ten- to twenty-five horsepower; sugar mills, pans and evaporators; wine screws; machinery for woolen factories; Dorsey's Patent Reaper and Mower; and castings of

> 100
> **SUGAR MILLS,**
> All Sizes and Prices,
> —OF THE—
> Latest Improvements
> —WITH—
> Wrought Iron Shafts.
>
> Made and Warranted by
> PARKER & HOOD.
> And for Sale by
> MANKER,
> CHASE &
> MOCKBEE.
> **RIPLEY, OHIO.**
>
> We will keep on hand a stock of
> Sugar Pans, and Evaporators,
> At Manufacturer's Prices.
>
> MANKER,
> CHASE &
> MOCKBEE
> July 5, 1865.

An ad for mills manufactured by Parker and Hood of the Phoenix Foundry, Ripley, Ohio (courtesy Union Township Public Library, Ripley, Ohio).

J. P. PARKER,

—MANUFACTURER OF—

STEAM Engines — Threshing Machines!

Sugar Mills and Dorsey's Patent Reaper and Mower. Also, Portable Engines for Threshers and Mowers.

Saw Mills, or any of the various uses which they are adapted to, cheaper than any other establishment in this section. Also, manufacturer of Cider Mills and Cutting Boxes.

Above: Another advertisement of J.P. Parker's work (courtesy Union Township Public Library, Ripley, Ohio). *Below left:* One of Parker's Phoenix Foundry mills. *Right:* Another view of this fascinating mill (both photographs by Alison Gibson for John P. Parker Historical Society, Ripley, Ohio).

every description. They also manufactured Parker's patented Clod Pulverizer and Tobacco Presses. Despite two devastating fires, by 1890 Parker had built the Phoenix Foundry into the largest ironworks facility between Portsmouth and Cincinnati. It is interesting to note that his will forbade any of his children to carry on their father's business. He wanted them to enter the learned professions, and they did not disappoint him. Of his three sons, one became a lawyer, one a schoolteacher and another a school principal. His three daughters all studied music.

With sweet sorghum becoming a promising new crop, the Phoenix Foundry advertised sugar mills and sugar pans as early as March 27, 1858. They offered one-, two-, and four-horse mills the following year. In 1865 advertisements they announced the manufacture of the Great Centre Draft Mill.

Chart for the Phoenix Vertical Cane Mills

Model Number	Gallons Per Hour	Price
No. 1	40 gals.	$60.00
No. 2	60 gals.	$85.00

Chart for the Phoenix Horizontal Cane Mills

Model Number	Gallons Per Hour	Price
No. 1	85 gals.	$120.00
No. 2	100 gals.	$130.00

Phoenix Foundry's 1871 product list included sugar mills, "of our own make, warranted to be the best and cheapest in the market," steam engines of several sizes, new and used steam boilers, Ralston patent Star Threshing Machine, Superior portable engines, reapers, plows, corn crushers, iron frames for schoolhouse seats, and iron weights. At the Fourteenth Annual Fair of the Industrial Association held at Ripley, September 26–29, 1871, John P. Parker won First Premium for his cider mill, sugar mill, portable sawmill (crosscut), and corn-cob crusher.

John P. Parker, a man born into slavery who rose to be a successful businessman, a creative genius who held three U.S. patents, and a conductor on the Underground Railroad who helped over 1,000 slaves find a life of freedom, died in 1900, leaving a significant legacy for his family and nation.

Phoenix Iron Works, Savannah, Georgia

The Phoenix Iron Works, Savannah, Georgia, did typical foundry and machine shop business, including cane mills and syrup kettles. In the late 1870s the foundry was operated by James Monahan, an Irish foundryman, at the corner of Broughton and Randolph streets. Monahan first worked as a machinist for the A.N. Miller Foundry but left to establish the Phoenix Iron Works in 1873. William

PHŒNIX IRON WORKS.

J. MONAHAN
IRON AND BRASS FOUNDER.
Blacksmith, Shipsmith and Pattern-maker,
COR. BROUGHTON and RANDOLPH STS., E. END BROUGHTON,
SAVANNAN, GA.

SPECIAL ATTENTION GIVEN TO SHIP WORK.

An ad from the Phoenix Iron Works of Savannah, Georgia (courtesy Live Oak Public Library, Savannah, Georgia.)

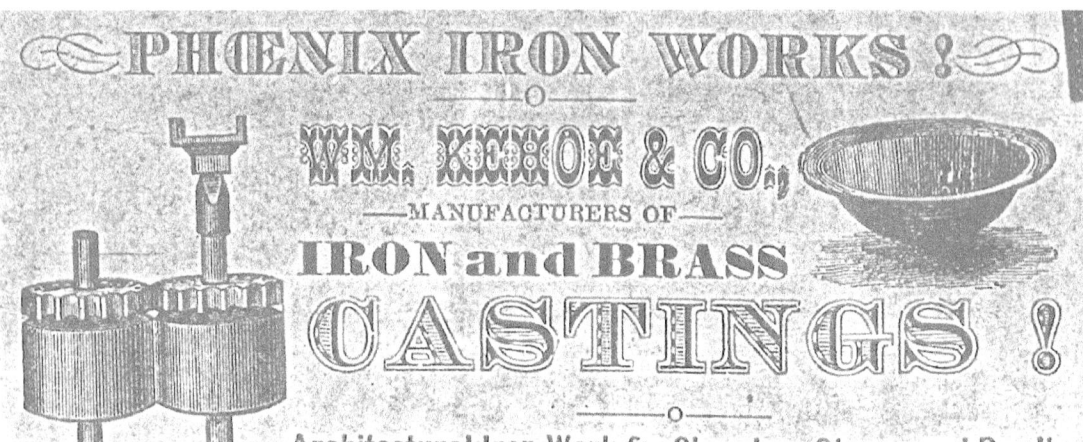

Above: This ad announces the manufacture of cane mills and kettles (courtesy Live Oak Public Library, Savannah, Georgia.) *Below:* These rollers were made by the Phoenix Iron Works of Savannah, Georgia.

Kehoe and John Rourke, two men who were destined to become ironworking giants in Savannah, were employed by Monahan. Monahan died in 1878, leaving his business to his wife and Kehoe. In the early 1880s Mrs. Monahan's share was purchased by Kehoe and the foundry operated under a dual name for about three years. In an ad in the *Savannah City Directory* of 1881 the foundry advertised architectural ironwork for churches stores, and dwellings; cemetery, veranda, garden, and balcony railings; plow castings; with sugar mills and pans a specialty. After the Phoenix name was dropped, the foundry was known as Kehoe's Iron Works.

Pioneer Iron Works, Brooklyn, New York

Incorporated in 1866, the Pioneer Iron Works, 151 William, Brooklyn, New York, were manufacturers of stationary and marine engines, boilers, oil stills, tanks, sheet ironworks and shafting. Their specialties included sugar mill machinery, flour mills, grain elevators, tools for paving and road-making equipment. The various departments of the ironworks were housed in a multistory facility, 200 by 200 feet along 149–163 William Street and 144–158 King Street in Brooklyn. The very latest tools, equipment and machinery produced excellent results at the hands of one hundred fifty skilled workers, according to *Half-Century of the City of Brooklyn*, by Maurice Blumenthal.

A widespread workers' strike crippled the ironworking industry of the greater New York City area in May 1886. The workers wanted ten hours' pay for nine hours' work, and when their employers refused, most of them walked off the job. About a week later many of the companies relented and promised ten hour's pay, but when the men received their paychecks on Saturday they discovered they were only given one-half cent per hour raise. The May 1886 pay scale for the various trades were, for boilermakers, $2.85; machinists, $2.85; blacksmiths, $3.00; and pattern makers, $3.50. When the beginning whistle blew on Monday morning not a single worker showed up for work. The Pioneer Iron Works and some of the other concerns managed some work by hiring men from Scranton, Pennsylvania.

Alexander Bass, president of Pioneer Iron Works, patented a portable iron railroad on June 8, 1875. The railroad was quite popular with contractors, miners, and plantation owners. A four-alarm fire, which originated on the third floor of the plant, completely destroyed the ironworks on September 16, 1906. During its years of productivity the Pioneer Iron Works was highly regarded for its superior workmanship, quality of materials, superb finish, efficiency, and general excellence.

Pusey and Jones Company, Wilmington, Delaware

Established as a machine shop on Walnut Street in Wilmington, Delaware, in 1848 by Joshua L. Pusey and John Jones, the Pusey and Jones Company had a long, varied, and interesting history. In 1851 Edward Betts and Joseph Seal joined the firm and it became Betts, Pusey, Jones and Seal. Later the ironworks company was known as Pusey, Jones and Betts, and by 1859 they called themselves the Wilmington Iron Works, "engineers, machinists, iron boat builders and boiler makers." By 1860 it was once again the Pusey and Jones Company.

The plant expanded their facilities during the Civil War as they received numerous government contracts. In 1863 they built thirteen wooden ships and three iron ones for the North's navy. In the period after the Civil War, Wilmington produced more iron ships than the rest of the country combined, and the Pusey and Jones Company was among the largest builders, with well equipped facilities along the Christina River at the foot of Lombard Street. From their modest beginning in 1848 the company grew to 900 employees by the 1880s. They produced papermaking machinery, boilers, cotton presses, machine tools, and machinery for sugar plants. However, shipbuilding was their strength and "The Delaware Story," by John A. Munroe, is helpful here.

One boat was special. The company built a large steamboat which was launched on February 6, 1928, and named the *President Warfield*. She crossed the Atlantic in 1943, and on D-Day was an on-station ship for harbor control at Omaha Beach. At the end of the war she was purchased by a group of Baltimore Jews who renamed her the *Exodus* and sent her to France in 1947. Though built for 540 passengers, the *Exodus* carried 4,554 displaced Jews from Marseilles to Haifa, Israel, and became the inspiration for Leon Uris' best selling novel of the same name.

However, Pusey and Jones did have other interests. They manufactured papermaking machinery and exported it to Great Britain, Austria, Switzerland, Russia, and Japan, as well as to numerous sites in the United States. They manufactured the anchors for the Brooklyn Bridge. Each anchor weighed twenty-three tons and had to be carried by ship directly from the foundry to the bridge site. One of the last important contracts filled by the company was for the manufacture of the 288-foot legs for the Texas towers installed in the Atlantic Ocean as radar stations for the air force. After this 1957 contract was filled other contracts were harder to obtain and the company went into receivership, then bankruptcy.

Quitman Machine Works, Quitman, Georgia

In the absence of accurate historical records of the Quitman Machine Works the following is offered by a local historian. Apparently the Underwood family purchased the Morven Foundry and Machine Works in Morven, Georgia, moved the equipment to Quitman,

Above: This invoice is from the Quitman Machine Works of Quitman, Georgia. *Below:* A Quitman two roller cane mill.

and named the business Southern Machine Company. At some later date the name was changed to F.C. Underwood, successor to Southern Machinery Company. At some still later date, with F.C. Underwood, Jr., serving as president of the company, the name was changed again, this time to Quitman Machine Works. You will observe that the Morven Mill, the SM Co. Mill, and the Quitman Manufacturing Company Mill are identical. The Winship Mill is also built on the same pattern and these mills may be found all over south Georgia.

Reading Iron Company, Reading, Pennsylvania

The first large ironworks established in Reading, Pennsylvania, was the Reading Iron Company, according to *The History of Reading, Pennsylvania*, compiled by Morton L. Montgomery. The concern was founded in 1836 by Benneville Keim, George M. Keim, James Whittaker and Simon Seyfert and became known as the Reading Iron and Nail Works. The extensive facilities were located on the southern part of town between the railroad and canal so shipment could be made easily by rail or water. The company made bar-iron in large quantities and twenty-six nail machines produced vast quantities of cut nails. The company name was changed to Seyfert, McManus and Company in 1846, then, when incorporated in 1862, it was changed again to Reading Iron Works. The business failed in 1889, and the Reading Iron Company was organized and incorporated the same year. The new company purchased all the plants of the former company, improved them, and launched an extensive ironworks business. The four tube works were among the largest in America, producing an extensive line of various kinds of pipe. Their five blast furnaces produced a superior grade of pigiron. Five rolling mills produced beams, channels and rails of every description. The foundry produced cotton presses, sugar mill machinery, blast furnace engines, rolling mill work, tools, boilers, tanks, ordinance and projectiles. The steam forge produced heavy forging for marine and engine work. At one time this vast ironworks employed between 3,000 and 4,000 workers.

Richmond Foundry, Richmond, Virginia

Beginning with the attack on Fort Sumter on April 12, 1861, and ending with General Robert E. Lee's surrender at Appomattox Court House on April 9, 1865, were four dismal, horrible years in America's history. During this time 200,000 soldiers were killed in battle or died of wounds, and another 413,000 died of disease, accidents and other causes. Great deprivation was widespread across the South, as families, homes and farms were lost in the cause. During this unfortunate epoch Richmond, Virginia, became a significant center. On May 20, 1861, the Confederacy voted to move its capital from Montgomery to Richmond. Subsequent battles around the city drained its already over-taxed resources. Refugees flooded into the city, and by the second year of the war they equaled if not surpassed Richmond's resident inhabitants. Local foundries and machine shops turned out a vast supply of valuable arms and weapons of warfare, but its inhabitants were suffering. One woman observed that she had "never known such a scarcity of food—such absolute want of the necessities of life." Extortion was prevalent, and what food existed most people could not buy because the price was so high. Many had a daily diet of sorghum syrup and cornbread. The situation reached a breaking point when, on April 2, 1863, the women of Richmond marched through the streets protesting the rising cost of bread. The mayor read the riot act to the women, but they ignored him and started looting shops. They were finally dispersed when President

Davis threatened to order the militia to fire upon them. Richmond was growing tired, rusty, dilapidated, and war-torn.

Thomas Samson, James Pae, John G. Andrew, and A. Scott formed Samson, Pae and Company, which operated the Richmond Foundry at the corner of Byrd and Fifth streets in Richmond during this period. In J.W. Randolph's 1864 publication, *Experiments with Sorghum Sugar Cane*, the revised edition of one published by Hedges, Free & Co., they announced the manufacture of iron and brass castings, mill and machine gearing, improved bark mills, sorghum cane mills and syrup boilers. In a very touching, and perhaps insightful, comment they stated: "We will supply the above in exchange for Provisions or Forage. We offer great inducements to those who may favor us with their orders, in the large assortment of patterns of the most improved kind which we have made during the last thirty years."

"In exchange for Provisions or Forage": Understanding the economic climate in Richmond in 1864 we understand this offer today.

Rockford Iron Works, Rockford, Illinois

The Rockford Iron Works first made its appearance in Rockford, Illinois, as the Rockford Well Drill Company. In the 1900–01 city directory D.E. Trahern is listed as president, H.H. Gerber as vice president and superintendent, and M.F. Thayer as secretary and treasurer. As early as 1874 the Trahern family was involved in ironwork, and W.D. Trahern operated a machine shop and foundry in Rockford. In 1909 the name was changed from Rockford Well Drill Company to Rockford Iron Works, and the same men continued to serve their respective offices. In addition to well drilling equipment, the Rockford Iron Works manufactured riding cultivators, broadcast seeders, sugar cane mills, sorghum mills, and general agricultural machinery, and was the successor company of the Utter Manufacturing Company.

Rost and Heiny, Sullivan, Indiana

The sorghum sugar enterprise had begun to subside by 1884, though there were foundries which continued to manufacture cane mills. By this time there were several thriving industries in Sullivan, Indiana, which depended upon the services of ironworks and machine shops, and we draw our information from Binford's *History of Greene and Sullivan Counties, State of Indiana*. There were several flour mills, including those operated by George Bauer and Son, Jetson, Eaton and Parks. Sullivan also had two factories making attractive, durable, and dependable carriages, namely, E.J.C. Hilderbrand and J.H. Welling. Their ironwork needs were met by Rost and Heiny, manufacturers of stationary and portable steam engines, mill machinery, coal shaft machinery, reapers, mowers, threshers, gas and steam pipe fittings, general repairs, cane mills and related equipment.

John Rourke Iron and Brass Works, Savannah, Georgia

The sky was aglow over Savannah, and burning embers hurling upward in the heated draft put on an astoundingly colorful display. Within minutes an estimated crowd of 10,000 persons lined the streets to watch the spectacular fire, according to the *Savannah Morning News*. It was no joyous celebration, however, for when the sun rose on Sunday, October 4, 1903, all the things for which John Rourke (rhymes with Duke) had worked across the years lay in ruins. The fire might have destroyed the largest boiler shop and foundry south of Baltimore, the John Rourke Iron and Brass Works, but it did not destroy the spirit of John Rourke. Rourke was no stranger to adversity. Born in the County of Cork, Ireland, in 1837, John knew difficult times from childhood. Most of the peasants in Ireland subsisted mainly on potatoes. The potato blight ruined the crop in 1845 and again in 1846. Starvation was widespread after another failure in 1847, and a "road fever" plague was also claiming numerous lives. It is estimated that 729,033 lives were lost during the famine. Thousands of others decided to emigrate and many came to America. John and his parents were among the masses which chose America as their new homeland. As a young man John followed his father, Arthur, as a molder at an iron foundry.

At the outbreak of the War Between the States, Rourke joined the Confederate army, was recruited into the Irish Jasper Greens and was stationed at Thunderbolt Battery. The responsibility of the Irish Jasper Greens was to keep the Yankee fleet from attacking the city by way of the Wilmington River. In 1862 he was promoted to captain and in 1864, while en route to Charleston, he was captured and

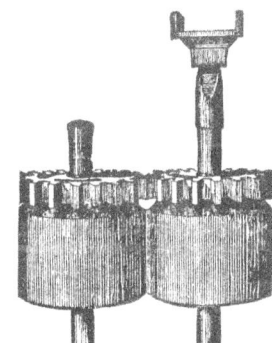

¶ The ever increased demand for our Mills and Pans is a guarantee of their superiority.

¶ See that our name is cast on your Mill and pan and you will have no trouble.

Rourkes Iron Works
SAVANNAH, GEORGIA

Above: Rourke's ad touts the superiority of its mills. *Below:* Rourke's two roller mill has hefty rollers.

Rourke's mills were built to last (photograph by Carl Arndt, Savannah, Georgia).

spent the remaining days of the war as a prisoner at Fort Pulaski. After the Civil War John joined the firm of Monahan and Parry as a molder and became a full partner in 1870. Known for his aggressiveness and indefatigable perseverance, Rourke was able to buy Monahan's share of the company in 1876, and the company became known as John Rourke Iron and Brass Works. Later, when his sons joined the company the name was changed to John Rourke and Sons Iron Works.

From a small single building John Rourke built the company into an impressive complex. The plant was located in a hollow on the Savannah River, 602 to 665 Bay Street, East, the corner of East Broad, and with wharves on the river. The second floor, street level, held the stockrooms, patterns, drawings, drafting department, brass fittings, leather belting, some lathes, other metal-working machines and machine shop material. The lower floor contained the largest lathe in the South along with machinery for shipbuilding and repair. Along the wharf was a boiler shop and a marine railway. Rourke's wide experience as a mechanic and builder, his industry, and his untiring labors made John Rourke Iron and Brass Works the widest known firm in Savannah. Having begun business in 1876 while just a young man, by 1902 Rourke had built the largest ironworks south of Baltimore and had become known as the "Iron Master of Savannah."

The headlines of the *Savannah Morning News*, Sunday, October 4, 1903, read, "Rourke's Iron Works in Ruins. Largest plant south of Baltimore wiped out by fire." However, John Rourke was no quitter. In just a few days his crews were back at work repairing ships, and he built another foundry and machine shop as quickly as possible. Among the items they manufactured were cane mills and syrup pans. In fact, his mills and pans had an outstanding reputation for quality throughout south Georgia.

After John's death in 1932, James, his son, managed the company until his death in 1942. The company then remained in operation until 1953, when it was sold to the Savannah Machine Shop. The business is no longer in operation, the mills are silent, the fires have gone out, thus ending the long and successful industry of the John Rourke Iron and Brass Works.

L.M. Rumsey Manufacturing Company, St. Louis, Missouri

L.M. Rumsey and Company was founded around 1865 by two Rumsey brothers, L.M. and Moses. This St. Louis factory manufactured lead pipe, sheet and bar lead, pump chains,

L. M. Rumsey Mfg. Co's

NET PRICES

AND

SPECIAL DISCOUNTS

APPLYING TO

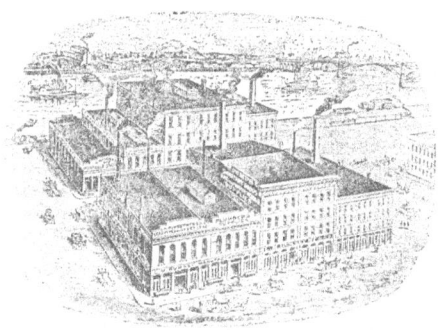

Lawn Mowers, Cultivators, Haying
Tools, Garden Tools, Pumps,
Cane Mills, Thresher
Supplies, Etc.

CATALOGUE No. 130

All Lists, Net Prices and Discounts Subject to Change Without Notice.

ST. LOUIS, MARCH 1st, 1910

Rumsey produced several cane mill models in its factory (courtesy Missouri Historical Society, St. Louis).

This Rumsey No. 2 was manufactured by the St. Louis company (photograph courtesy Butch Tindell, Elm Mott, Texas).

and numerous agricultural implements, including cane mills. Their facility was an enormous complex including a large five story main building, a factory, a warehouse, and a branch which covered an area equal to an entire city block. The parent factory was located at Seneca Falls, New York, where heavy machinery and fire engines were made. In 1877 another large factory was built in north Indianapolis, where harvesting and light agricultural implements were manufactured. Insight into this growth is given to us by Dacus and Buel in *A Tour of St. Louis*. The St. Louis branch manufactured lawn mowers, haying tools, pumps, sowers, corn shellers, horsepowers, cultivators, garden tools, thresher supplies, corn planters, gristmills and cider mills. Rumsey produced cane mills in several models. The Rival was a two roller mill with a 1910 cost of $14. The Hero came in six models, the Nos. 50, 51, 52, 53, 54 and 55, ranging in price from $18.75 to $55. The Rumsey came in model Nos. 1, 2, 3, and 4 and ranged in price from $21 to $44. The Victor was offered in seven models, including Nos. 0, 1 Jr., 1 Heavy, 2, 3, 4, and 6 and cost between $16.25 and $80. The Mohawk came in models A, B, and C and cost between $26.50 and $39.50. Rumsey manufactured the Star and Tiger in top and back geared mills, and offered the Tiger in model Nos. 3 and 4. The hardware giant also sold bagasse carriers and feed tables, evaporator pans, furnace parts, doors and grates.

Salem Iron Works, Winston-Salem, North Carolina

The foundry, the Salem Iron Works, Winston-Salem, North Carolina, was founded in 1873 and was a significant contributor to the industrial development of the city. By 1884, when C.A. Hege operated the company, they employed eight blacksmiths and manufactured farm implements. However, the ironworks continued to grow with the growing industrial city. Under the leadership of W.T. Spaugh, who had become president, treasurer, and general manager, farm implements were shipped throughout the Southern states, from Virginia to Texas, and the workforce grew to 60–75 skilled mechanics. The company developed an extensive export business and opened a branch office at 68 Broad Street, New York, New York. A part of the company's success can be attributed to the quality of workmanship and attention to detail, with every machine being inspected carefully before it was shipped out of the plant. The Salem Iron Works of Winston-Salem were manufacturers of corn mills; cob grinding mills; feed grinding mills; French buhr grinding mills (millstones); and steam, water, and animal power cane mills. They manufactured Hustler Saw Mills; Hustler Peanut Pickers; Hustler Continuous Process Dyeing Machines; and castings of various kinds as well. The company, as the Salem Iron Works, last appeared in the city directory in 1923. An interesting account of the company may be found in an article in the booklet *Winston-Salem, North Carolina, City of Industry*.

Savannah Iron and Brass Foundry and Machine Works, Savannah, Georgia

Monahan, Manning and Company operated the Savannah Iron and Brass Foundry and Machine Works at the eastern wharves in Savannah, Georgia. An 1870 advertisement in the

SAVANNAH IRON AND BRASS FOUNDRY AND MACHINE WORKS, EASTERN WHARVES.
MONAHAN, MANNING & CO.
HIGH AND LOW PRESSURE ENGINES AND BOILERS, SAW MILLS, GRIST MILLS, AND ALL OTHER MACHINERY manufactured to order.
CASTINGS, OF IRON OR BRASS,
Of any size or pattern, executed in the best possible manner and without delay.
SUGAR MILLS, GIN GEARING, AND PORTABLE ENGINES,
Of the most approved styles, on hand or can be furnished.
Can do Repairing and Finishing with Greater Facility than any other Establishment in the City.

Savannah Iron and Brass foundry listed cane mills, gin gearing and portable engines (courtesy Live Oak Public Library, Savannah, Georgia.)

Savannah City Directory states that they were manufacturers of steam engines and boilers, sawmills, gristmills, general machinery, cane mills, gin bearings, and portable engines. For more on Monahan, please see Phoenix Iron Works, Savannah, Georgia.

Savannah Iron Works, Savannah, Georgia

The *1877–1878 Savannah City Directory* listed the Savannah Iron Works at the Lumber corner of Pine Street, with Daniel Harris and Thomas Mulligan as proprietors. The ironworks manufactured machinery of various kinds, railings for cemeteries and porches, plows, cane mills and syrup kettles. In 1882, the proprietors are listed as J. and T. Mulligan. Thomas Mulligan, one of Savannah's numerous Irish ironworkers, was trained by yet another Irishman, James Monahan. When Monahan moved his facility to Randolph and East Broughton streets in the mid 1870s, he left Mulligan in charge of the facility at Bay and Randolph streets. On March 10, 1874, Mulligan received recognition for his supervision of the casting of the iron columns for Savannah's new cathedral, which was one of the largest jobs ever done by a Savannah foundry. Apparently, shortly thereafter he and Harris opened their business at Lumber and Pine streets. In February 1877, he, James Mulligan and W.B. Ballantyne, invented a hand truck known as "Mulligan's Iron Cotton Truck." The hand trucks came in three sizes and were exhibited at the Thomasville Fair in October 1877.

DANIEL HARRIS.   THOMAS MULLIGAN.

SAVANNAH IRON WORKS,

Lumber Corner of Pine Street,

SAVANNAH, GA.

Machinery, House work, Cemetery and Verandah Railings, Plows, Sugar Mills and Pans, Patent Warehouse Trucks (something new), on hand or to order, at prices to suit the times. Also general jobbing work. Orders attended to with promptness. Satisfaction guaranteed.

HARRIS & MULLIGAN.

Savannah Iron Works manufactured machinery of various kinds (courtesy Live Oak Public Library, Savannah, Georgia.)

Thomas Mulligan was an active member of the community for many years, serving as an officer in the Excelsior Lodge as well as chairing the Workers' Protective Union Society. He died on August 24, 1909, at the age of 64 while residing at the Little Sisters of the Poor Home for the Aged in Savannah.

Savannah Locomotive Works and Supply Company, Savannah, Georgia

The Savannah Locomotive Works & Supply Company was one of the several business interests of John Joseph McDonough, one of Savannah's leading citizens. McDonough owned and operated a large lumber business, McDonough and Ballantyne Iron Foundry,

This ad, from a convention brochure, lists "sugar mills and pans."

several machine shops, and the Savannah Locomotive Works & Supply Company. McDonough was also active in the political life of Savannah, having served as an alderman for four years and then as mayor of the city from 1891 until 1895. It was said of his first term that he was a "bold and fearless" leader, and his second term was marked by even greater success. Upon his retirement from office, the city council adopted a resolution which stated that he had "presided over that body with dignity, fairness, and impartiality, and was entitled to the thanks of each and every member of the board for the faithful and impartial manner in which he had discharged his duty as presiding officer and as the chief magistrate of the city." McDonough was appointed harbormaster in January 1925, and he served in that capacity until his death on November 28, 1926. Though born in Augusta, Georgia, McDonough lived most of his life in Savannah.

In addition to the needs of the

Above: A Savannah Locomotive roller up close (photograph by Laurie Parsons, courtesy of Ronnie and Marie Malphrus, Ridgeland, South Carolina). *Below:* A set of Savannah Locomotive rollers found in South Carolina.

locomotive industry, the Savannah Locomotive Works And Supply Company also manufactured cane mills and syrup kettles.

Savannah Machine Works, Savannah, Georgia

Please see S.W. Gleason and Company.

Thomas Scantling and Son, Evansville, Indiana

Thomas E. Scantling was born in Lexington, Kentucky, on August 9, 1814, and moved with his family to Gibson County, Indiana, when he was six years old. He and his father operated a tin shop, which gave Thomas the early training for his life's work. He moved to Evansville in 1834 and opened a tin shop on Water Street which eventually grew into a foundry. By 1866 his son, James M., had joined him in the business and the company became known as Thomas Scantling and Son. Having expanded beyond the limits of a tin shop, the foundry now manufactured stoves, castings, grates, plain and fancy tinware, agricultural implements and sugar machinery.

Thomas moved to Evansville as a young man and lived to become the oldest man in town. He passed away on Friday, January 19, 1912, at the age of ninety-seven. When his wife preceded him in death they had been married for seventy years. Scantling remembered as a youth seeing Col. Robert Evans throw the first shovelful of dirt out of the old Wabash-Erie Canal. Scantling built the first three-story building in Evansville, on Sycamore Street, and produced the first cast-iron storefront. His foundry was destroyed by fire on April 3, 1884, but was rebuilt and continued in business. After Thomas retired, the foundry continued as a family business, incorporating as the Scantling Foundry on June 26, 1891, with Thomas S. Scantling as president and James M. Scantling as secretary-treasurer. The company listing disappeared from the city directory early in the 1900s.

While there seems to be no record of specific cane mills made by Thomas Scantling and Son it has been noted that they manufactured sugar mill machinery. On May 12, 1870, Scantling showed his portable sugar evaporator and heating apparatus at the Louisiana State Fair. Perhaps one day we can find the record of his cane mills as well.

J.S. Schofield and Son, Macon, Georgia

John Shepley Schofield and his brother, Joshua, were born in Glossop, England, in 1820, and it was there as boys they learned the machinist trade. Glossop is near Manchester, the great iron manufacturing center, and ironworks influenced that whole area of Britain. The Schofield brothers immigrated to Georgia about 1844. Apparently they opened a small foundry that Joshua operated while John was employed as a locomotive engineer on the state's first two railroads leading out of Macon. Macon became their adopted home, and it was there they raised their families and founded in 1850 what was to become a thriving industry. John noticed that the brass bearing boxes on the locomotives wore out quickly and proved unsatisfactory. He purchased a piece of property on Fifth Street and opened a small foundry in order to improve the brass bearings for his trains. His bearings proved to be substantially better and became in such demand that in 1852 he quit his engineer's job to fill all the orders for them. The great Schofield industry began with only a small shack and small cupola, according to *The Macon Telegraph*. Joshua joined the Macon Volunteers during the Civil

Top: A Schofield Iron Works nameplate on one of its mills. *Bottom:* Schofield's Iron Works in 1876 (courtesy Middle Georgia Archives, Washington Memorial Library, Macon).

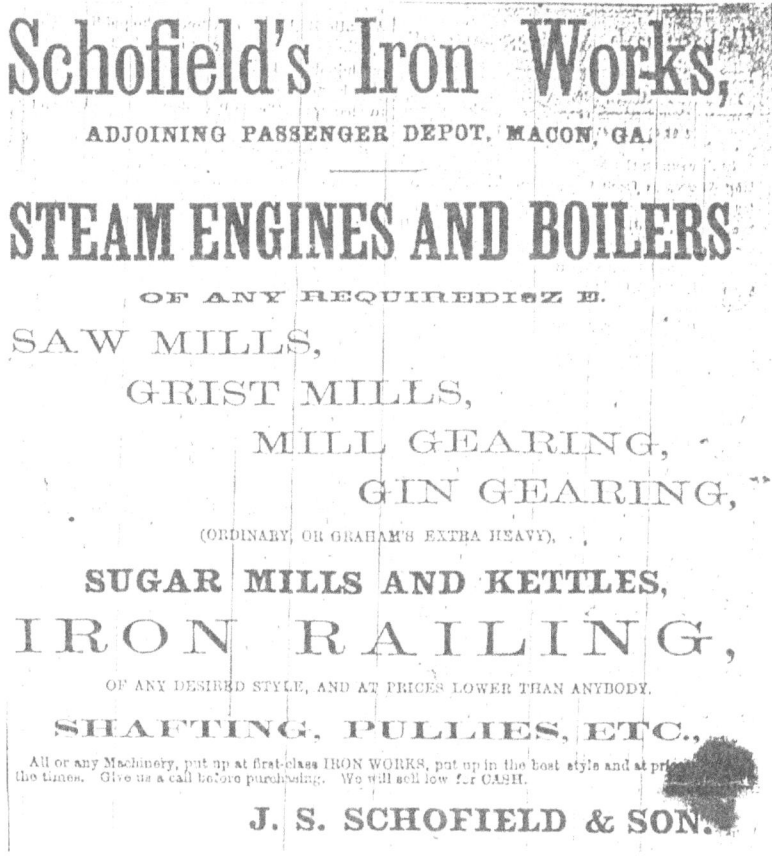

This Schofield ad lists its cane mills and kettles.

War and went to the front, leaving his brother to look after his family and their business interests in Macon. Four years later he came home, only to die from wounds and exposure he sustained serving in the Confederate army. One of John's sons, A.D. Schofield, became a partner in the business and the firm was established as J.S. Schofield & Son. From the early days of a little log blacksmith shop, small capital, and about a half-dozen employees, Schofield built a business which shipped its products all over the South, from North Carolina to Arkansas and Texas. The amount and variety of machinery produced by J.S. Schofield was immense and embraced almost everything which could be produced by a foundry and machine shop. Their product list was extensive and included steam engines, stationary engines, portable engines, upright engines, engines on wheels, engines on skids, sawmills, circular saws, stave machines, Judson Governors, ratchet head blocks, screw head blocks, shafting, pulleys, hangers, boxes, mill spindles, gearing, couplings, waterwheels, millstones, sills, lintels, storefronts, store grating, railings, newels, bridge and truss bolts, builders' jacks, rubber belting, leather belting, rubber packing, hemp packing, iron castings, engine repair, steam boilers, upright boilers, return tubular boilers, cylinder boilers, locomotive boilers, flue boilers, marine boilers, grate bars, plain and grate bars patented, boiler tubes, boiler rivets, iron pipe, pipe fittings, tap and dies, pipe tongs, pipe wrenches, boiler fronts, smokestacks, tanks, steam tank pumps, Hancock Inspirators, steam jet pumps, babbitt metal, files, portable forges, flue cleaners, elbows, T's, unions, nipples, couplings, bushings, brass castings, cotton presses, cotton presses for steam, cotton presses for horse, cotton presses for hand, cotton presses, wrought and cast, cotton gins, cotton gin gearing, Faught Deering Gin gearing, corn mills, wheat mills, wheat fans, wheat threshers, wheat separators, artesian well pipe, artesian water gauges and glasses, oil cups, oil cans, whistles, lubricators, monkey wrenches, combination wrenches, saw gummers, wrought forgings and mill repair. Schofield's first steam boiler was a vertical one which he mounted on a wagon; it became known as "the Rocket." Schofield's produced cane mills, syrup kettles, syrup evaporators, and copper for evaporators. Later he could look back and see that his first cane mill was a "crude two roller" mill. He received United States Patent No. 206,622, July 30, 1878, for a two-roller cane mill which featured a unique iron frame and means by which the pressure on the rollers could be adjusted. One of the unique features of the mill was in the way the tension between the rollers was

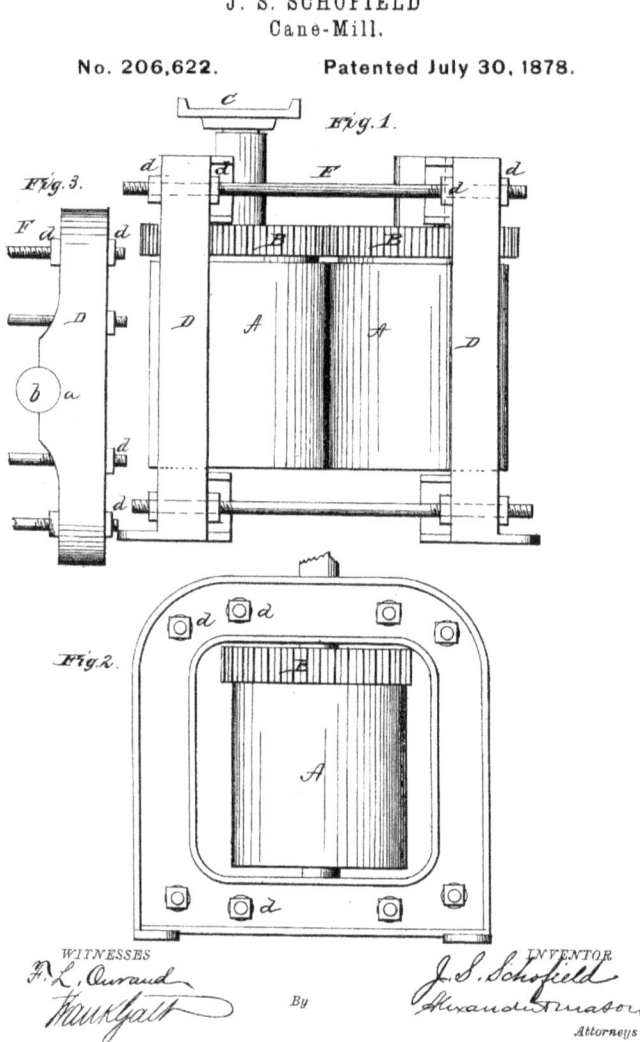

Above: The Schofield patent featured a simple iron frame. *Opposite, top*: A Schofield two roller mill. *Bottom left:* Schofield's mill had a unique wedge for increasing pressure on the rollers. This is from the wedge side. *Right:* This is from the tightening side—the tighter the bolt, the more pressure on the rollers.

attained. Rather than a set screw set at 180 degrees to the bearing box, pushing straight in, a wedge was set at 90 degrees and was regulated by a bolt and nut from the opposite side. As the nut was tightened the wedge was pulled inward, decreasing the space between the two rollers.

John Shepley Schofield, founder of one of Macon's great industries, died in 1891. By July 1933 the company had become bankrupt and the bank foreclosed on the properties. This action was contested. However, a judge ruled that the property would be sold to the highest bidder at public auction. On September 3, 1933, the Taylor Iron Works and Supply Company bought the Schofield property for $40,000.

Schultz, Thuman and Company, Evansville, Indiana

The ironworks company of Schultz, Thuman and Company, First Street and Third Avenue, Evansville, was begun in 1867 by eight mechanics who had a practical knowledge of ironwork and how it could meet the needs of their growing community. Known originally as the Mechanics' Foundry and Machine Shop, the men began with a capital of $8,000 and a willingness to work. Through their industriousness and wise business practices, their company began to prosper. Three of the original eight left the company at some point leaving Charles Thuman as general business manager; Alex Jack, foreman of the machine shop; Augusta Schultz, foreman of the molding shop; M. Becker, foreman of the blacksmith shop; and John Schultz, foreman of the pattern shop. Soon the works became known as Schultz, Thuman and Company, as chronicled in *The City of Evansville*.

A twenty-five horsepower steam engine supplied the power to their machinery, and the company operated out of two buildings approximately the size of a quarter of a city block. Promptness and integrity of the work of their twenty-five skilled employees assured a good reputation and increasing trade. Schultz, Thuman and Company manufactured steam engines; boilers; circular sawmills; gristmills; cane mills; tobacco screw gumming machines; distillery equipment; mining machinery; malt mills; corn shellers; house fronts; cellar grates; and steamboat machinery; they specialized in iron and brass castings of every description. They advertised "Machinery of all kinds made and repaired," and had workmen who could go to all parts to make on the job repairs. In addition the company was a dealer in belting, fire bricks, steam gauges, and wrought iron pipes.

Sears, Roebuck and Company, Chicago, Illinois

Richard Warren Sears, the founder of the great Sears empire, was born in Stewartville, Minnesota, in 1863. In his teens he learned telegraphy, and this led to his ultimate employment with the railroad. While serving as station agent at North Redwood, Minnesota, a local jeweler refused a shipment of watches, a seemingly insignificant act which was to have a great impact on the nation's economy, as told in *Sears, Roebuck and Co. Consumers Guide, Fall 1900*. The shipment was subsequently offered to Sears on consignment. Sears sold the watches so quickly and so profitably that he ordered another shipment, which he planned to resell through other station agents. This side-line business grew so rapidly that he quit the railroad in order to set up a full time mail order business in Minneapolis. The moonlighting initiative now became the R.W. Sears Watch Company. In order to take advantage of a more central location for his business, and to better utilize the transportation facilities, Sears moved his business to Chicago in 1887. One of his immediate needs was for a watch repairman. Within a month a slender young man from Hammond, Indiana, responded to a help wanted ad and applied for the job. That man was Alvah Curtis Roebuck.

Though this youthful business prospered, Sears sold his Chicago operation in 1889 and returned to Minneapolis. Roebuck, now a partner, moved to Toronto to oversee their branch operations there. This was only the beginning of several twists and turns for the fledgling company. Back in Minneapolis, Sears established the Warren Company, a watch and jewelry business. Once again he built a highly profitable company and subsequently sold it to his partner, Roebuck, in 1891. At Sears' urging, Roebuck renamed his company the A.C. Roebuck Company. However, this was not the last of Sears. Almost immediately he talked Roebuck out of a half interest and in 1893 the name of the company changed once again. This time it became the world famous Sears, Roebuck and Company. A Chicago office was opened in late 1893, and by January 1895, the company moved to its permanent home in Chicago.

Roebuck retired and sold his shares in the company in August 1895. Sears, the consummate businessman, lined up two new investors and with a capital of $150,000, he, Aaron Nussbaum and Julius Rosenwald as one-third partners, continued the venture. Sears continued as company president until 1908. This new organization was most advantageous for the company. Sears had attained an excellent reputation among the people of rural America from which he sprang. With the addition of the Chicago businessmen, Nussbaum and Rosenwald, he now had a strong financial base with which to revolutionize mail order selling. Under his leadership the company was formed and grew to a million dollar giant in only twelve years.

The first A.C. Roebuck Company catalog was published in 1891. This was a thirty-three page edition featuring watches, but with an eight-page insert offering jewelry and sewing machines. The 1892 catalog grew to well over one hundred pages. Testimonials and company materials took up a third of these pages, and only a dozen or so pages offered merchandise not related to watches or jewelry. The Sears, Roebuck and Company catalog made its debut in 1893. This edition offered two hundred pages of a much wider variety of merchandise, and an institution was born. As the nation continued to grow so did the size and circulation of the now famous Sears and Roebuck Catalog. Among the numerous items sold by Sears, Roebuck & Co., "the cheapest supply house on earth," was the Acme cane mill. Sears claimed their Acme cane mill was the best mill on the market. It featured turned rolls, steel shafts,

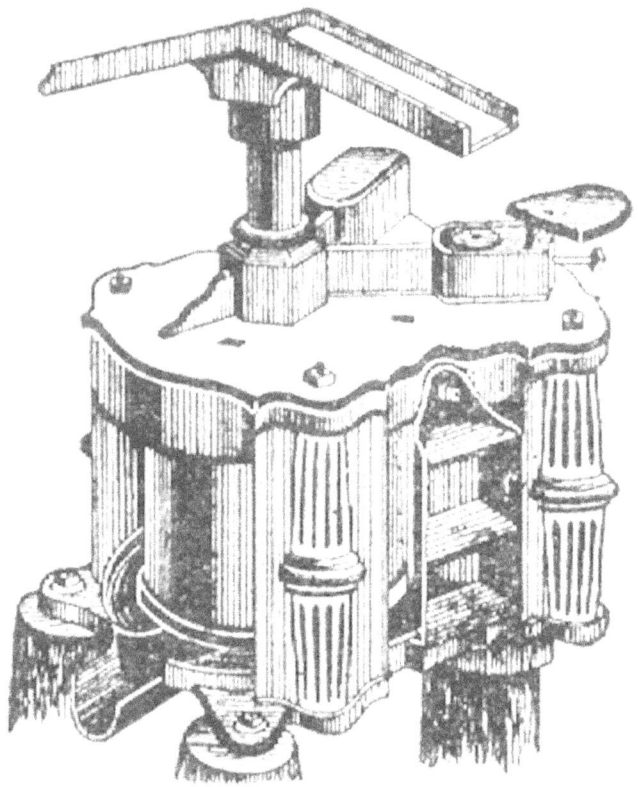

While Sears didn't manufacture mills, it sold several models. This is the Acme cane mill.

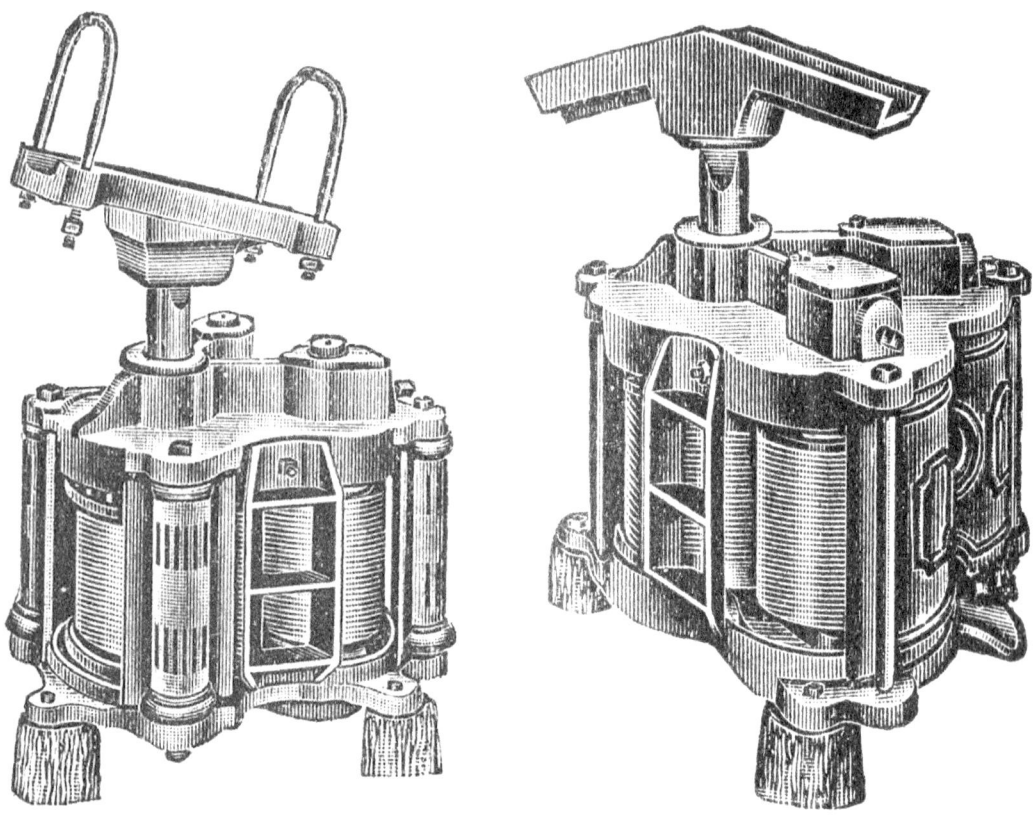

Top left: This is Sears' Champion vertical roller mill. *Top right:* Sears' Defiance vertical roller mill. *Below:* The Little Giant was also sold by Sears.

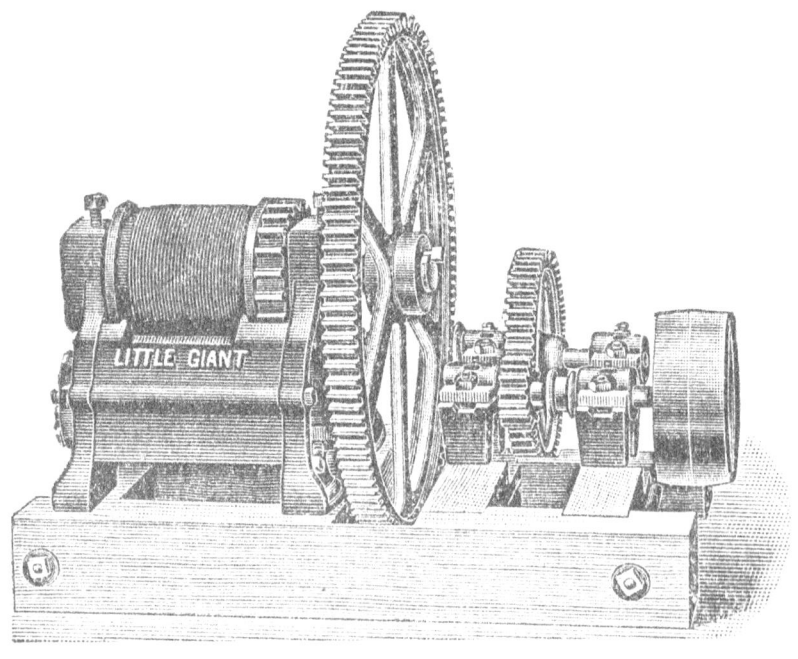

brass bearings, the very best cast steel gears and rollers. The cog gears were cast separately from the rollers and had two clutches on each wheel to minimize breakage. This also permitted easier dismantling for repairs or moving. The rollers were turned and serrated, with the main roller flanged at top and bottom. The 1897 Sears, Roebuck & Co. Catalog offered the Acme mill in the following models:

Chart for Sears' Acme Cane Mills

Model No.	Horsepower	Juice Per Hour	Weight	1897 Price
No. 18087	One Horse	40–50 gals.	400 lbs.	$16.00
No. 18088	One Horse	50–60 gals.	495 lbs.	$20.00
No. 18089	Two Horse	60–75 gals.	625 lbs.	$25.00
No. 18090	Two Horse	75–90 gals.	800 lbs.	$31.00
No. 18091	Two Horse	90–100 gals.	850 lbs.	$35.00
No. 18092	Two Horse Heavy	100–20 gals.	1,150 lbs.	$40.00
No. 18093	Extra Heavy 2 Horse	120–140 gals.	1,250 lbs.	$48.00

Who made these mills for Sears? The Acme Mill displayed in their 1897 catalog is identical to the Perfection Mill pictured in the Spotless Catalog and was most probably made by the C.S. Bell Company of Hillsboro, Ohio. Their 1908 Kenwood Cane Mill was manufactured in southwest Illinois, probably by Excelsior. By 1916 Sears was purchasing their mills from the Excelsior Foundry in Belleville, Illinois. The Champion Horse Power Mill shown is Excelsior's Favorite Mill; their Defiance "Three-post" Mill is Excelsior's St. Louis Mill; their Little Giant Horizontal Mill is Excelsior's Wonderful Pony Mill; and their Invincible Heavy Duty Horizontal Mill is the Excelsior Horizontal Power Mill with Double Back Gearing.

The Invincible was a larger power mill.

Austin Seward and Son, Bloomington, Indiana

The tragedy of Austin Seward's early life, as told in *The Indiana Magazine of History*, September 1908, seems to have impacted him tremendously and melted and molded him into a compassionate, gentle and generous man. His forebears emigrated from England and settled in Surry County, Virginia. John, his father, married Mary Daniel, the daughter of a prominent family of the area. To that union there was born two children, Austin, on November 22, 1799, and a sister, Almira, two years later. While they were but young children their mother died. John later remarried, and his new wife was the proverbial wicked stepmother who mistreated the children beyond imagination. The cruelty exacted upon the children included depriving them of enough to eat, and both Austin and Almira remembered that a beloved colored "Mammy" would feed them from her meager fare in her own cabin. One day while the stepmother was away, an aunt took Almira to her home and raised the child as her daughter.

When Austin was about ten years old his father moved to Richmond, Kentucky. Austin was apprenticed to learn blacksmithing and one day while shoeing an ornery horse he was injured, causing a slight limp which he carried the rest of his life. He found his niche in edge-tool making, a skill he learned from Anderson Wood, of Richmond. On May 18, 1817, he married Jane Irvin and set up a blacksmith shop at Hay's Ford on Silver Creek, about seven miles from Richmond. After about a year of labor there Austin and his wife moved back to Richmond, where he began working as an edge-tool maker with Argo and Caldwell. Some of Seward's family had moved to Bloomington, Indiana. Austin paid them a visit in 1821, saw possibilities, and moved his wife and two children to Bloomington in September of that year. He built a log blacksmith shop, which he used until he built a one-story brick building with four rooms on the east side of Walnut Street in 1825. During these initial years he made his tools on the forge only. When a foundry was installed in his shop in 1843 it enabled him to make all kinds of castings. He enlarged his shop, built a foundry, and added more forges. Horse power was used until 1854 when a steam engine was installed to power his equipment. Seward's business flourished, and he became a noted worker in metals. He was an excellent blacksmith, a foundry-man, an extraordinary gunsmith who made every part of a firearm, but he excelled as an edge-tool maker. His axes, especially, enjoyed an extensive reputation. His son, W.B. Seward, said he had known of men who traveled over one hundred miles to purchase an axe from his father. In addition to the foundry, Seward had a woodworking department where wagons were built, plows stocked, and other essential items provided.

All of his sons, and he had a number of them, were proficient in the ironworking industry as well. John was a born machinist and edge-tool maker; James and Robert were blacksmiths; W.B. was a pattern maker, Irvin a machinist and Bricen a gunsmith. Needless to say, they all became involved in their father's business. Consequently, the name of the company went through several changes: Seward and Son; Seward and Sons; Seward Brothers; and Seward and Company. While a complete product list is impossible, it is evident the company manufactured adzes, augers, braces, bits, bells, scythes, files, guns, knives, axes, sickles, shears, plows, wagons, carts, horseshoes, horseshoe nails, threshing machines, stoves, skillets, sugar kettles, pots, and cane mills.

Austin was baptized into the Episcopal Church, but married into a family of Presbyterians and joined that denomination. A deeply spiritual man, Seward set up an altar in their home and had family worship. In fact, the first Sunday school in Bloomington was held in their cabin. The Sewards were also musicians. Austin organized and was leader of the first band ever organized in Bloomington. He even built, at his own expense, a house for band rehearsals.

Above: Note the beautiful stamping on this Seward mill. *Below:* A Seward mill, beautifully restored by Clayton Ralph (both courtesy Clayton Ralph, Greenhood, Indiana).

Out of the tragedies of his early childhood, Seward developed a deep sense of compassion and felt it his Christian duty to help the helpless. No one was turned away from his door hungry. His workers, especially the apprentices, ate at his table, sat by his fireside, and slept in his beds. Mrs. Seward always set two extra plates on the table just in case someone came in unexpectedly. His son, John, once said of his father that if he had one plow for sale and two men came for it, one with money and one without, the man without the money would get the plow. When one of his sons told his father that someone was stealing corn from their crib, Seward rigged a trap, and sure enough, caught the man. Seward released the man from the trap, filled his basket with corn and told him to come back for more when he needed it. When Austin Seward was approaching death, an old friend, Dr. Andrew Wylie, said, "This community can better spare any man in it, or the college every professor, than it can spare Mr. Seward." It was said by someone who knew him well: "He was by birth a Virginian, by trade a blacksmith, by nature a gentleman, and by grace, a Christian; if more need be said, he was a genius." Austin Seward died October 27, 1872.

While specifications for all models of Seward's mill are not available, the 1866 mill pictured here has a 13" D × 7" H main roller, 6¾" D × 7" H small rollers and weighs 550 pounds.

Shakespeare Iron Works, New Orleans, Louisiana

Joseph A. Shakespeare was a prominent citizen of New Orleans and served his community as mayor of the city. Shakespeare, along with A. Smith and S. Swoop, established Shakespeare, Smith & Co., which was proprietor of the Shakespeare Iron Works, one of the oldest and best known industries in the South during the 1880s. Their large and spacious business was located on Girod Street, between Baronne and Dryades, and was equipped with the most modern and efficient foundry and machine shop equipment available. Shakespeare maintained a large force of skilled workers and guaranteed the satisfaction of their products and workmanship. Consequently, their business extended not only across the city of New Orleans, but across the Deep South.

Shakespeare Iron Works specialized in steam engines, boilers, sugar mills, sawmills, draining and centrifugal machines, mill and gin gearing, grate bars, storefronts, columns of different kinds, ventilators and blacksmith work of every imaginable description. The company was well known for its reliability and product dependability. Examples of their cane mills have not been located at this writing.

E.W. Skinner and Company, Madison, Wisconsin

The E.W. Skinner Company had its beginning in Madison, Wisconsin, in 1851 in a foundry on the corner of State and Gorham streets. The facility was sold to W.S. Hutington in 1859 and subsequently to Andrews and Company in 1864. A building which was constructed by Gorham for a steam sawmill was purchased and converted into a foundry by I.E. Brown. P.H. Turner bought the property in 1859. E.W. Skinner next purchased the property, added O.S. Willey and S.D. Hastings as partners, and established E.W. Skinner and Company.

According to *Madison, a History of the Formative Years*, by David V. Mollenhoff, Madison became the center of Wisconsin's newly founded sorghum industry in the late 1850s and early 1860s. From 1863 to 1866 it hosted the annual state convention of sorghum producers, processors, and manufacturers of sorghum equipment. An industry periodical, *Northwestern Sorgho Journal*, was published in Madison, but like the industry, it was short-lived. From the

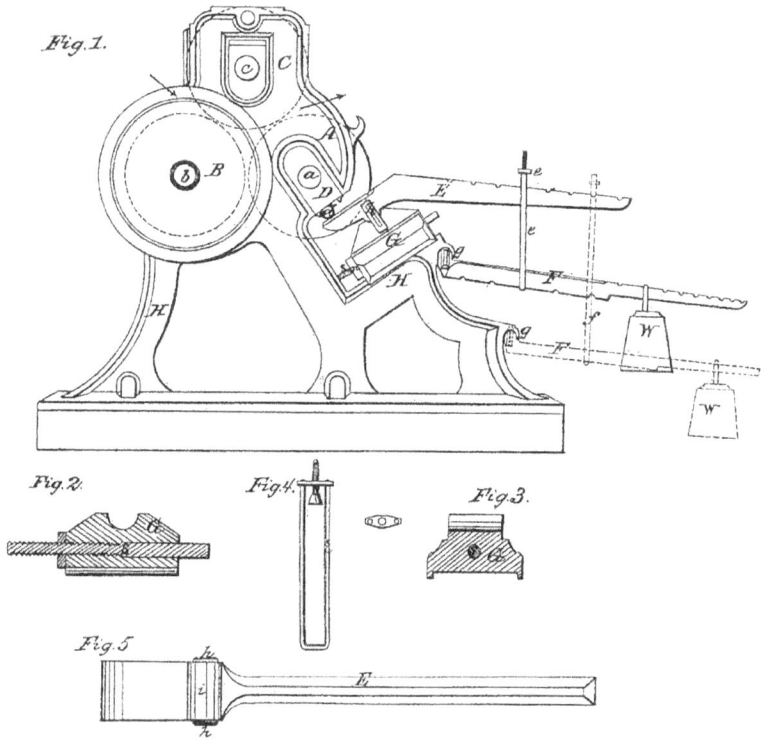

Skinner's mill, based on Porter's patent, featured levers for adding pressure to the rollers.

minutes of the January 1866 state convention, it is evident that Skinner, Willey and Hastings were also involved in growing sorghum as well as manufacturing sorghum equipment. The minutes indicate the men promoted early planting, recommended pure Chinese Sorghum seed, early cutting, finishing syrup quickly as possible; they believed sugar from sorghum would become common as syrup.

E.W. Skinner and Company's first cane mill, the Climax Adjustable Sugar Mill, was manufactured in 1861. In 1862 they produced eleven mills, and increased their output to one hundred in 1863. By 1865 they were manufacturing more than five hundred per year, employing 50 men, with jobbers all over the Northwest. At the 1865 Wisconsin State Fair E.W. Skinner and Company received the following recognition:

- Best Apparatus Complete, First Premium, Silver Medal and $20.
- Best Geared Sugar Mill, First Premium, Diploma.
- Best Sweep Mill, Diploma.
- Best Plantation Sugar Mill, First Premium.

On June 5, 1866, Skinner was awarded Patent No. 55,379 for a mill with a turn knife situated between the lower two rollers in a horizontal mill, and cups situated directly beneath

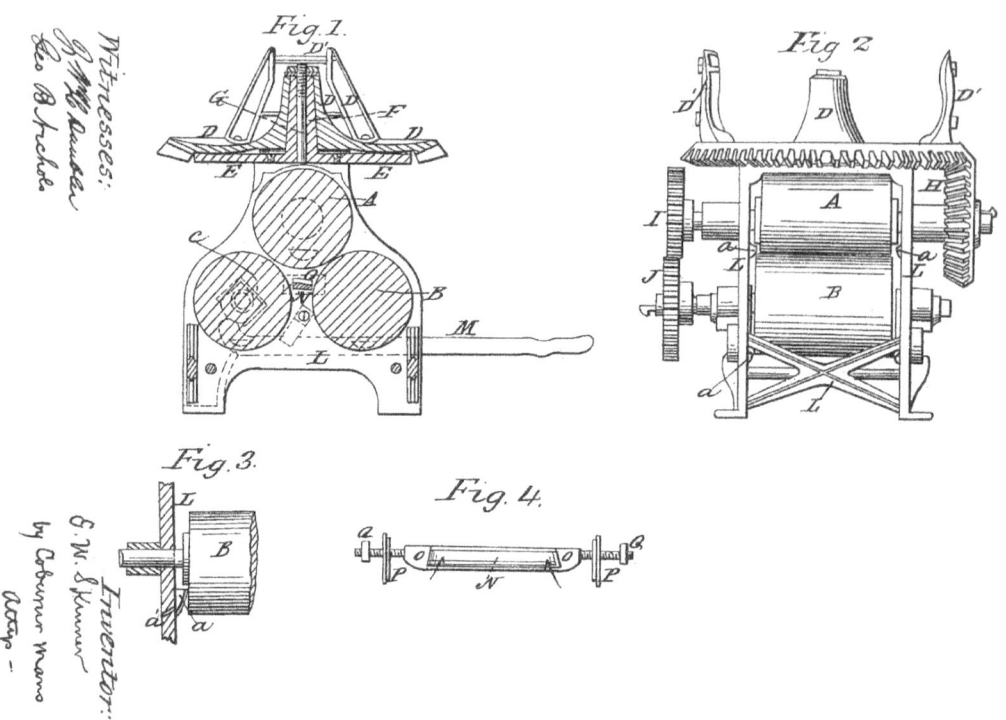

Above: **This Skinner patent featured a turn plate between the lower rollers.** *Below:* A rendering of how Skinner's mill looked.

each of the bearings of the rollers to catch any lubricating oil from the bearings which might otherwise fall into the juice. Skinner's mills were on display at the 1866 Wisconsin State Sorghum Convention.

Luther E. Porter, of Lake Mills, Wisconsin, assignor to the EW. Skinner and Company, received patent No. 41,265 on January 12, 1864, for a mill (above) so designed that pressure on the rollers was regulated by weights set on levers at various positions. This arrangement of a sliding fulcrum also allowed for elasticity so the rollers could yield under heavy strain. E.W. Skinner received a patent, No. 55,379, on June 5, 1866, for a mill with an especially designed turn plate between the lower two rollers to keep the cane from dropping down between them.

Since the short Wisconsin summers did not allow sorghum to mature adequately, and because of the difficulties in getting sugar to crystallize properly, the sorghum industry began to wane. When E.W. Skinner and Company, a leading manufacturer of agricultural implements, began to phase out their cane mills they shifted to reapers and mower production.

Southern Machinery Company, Inc., Quitman, Georgia

Cane mills stamped SM Co. were made by the Southern Machinery Co. Inc., East Foundry Street, Quitman, Georgia, founders and machinists, manufacturers and dealers in

> ESTABLISHED 1905   INCORPORATED 1922
>
> **SOUTHERN MACHINERY CO. INC.**
>
> FOUNDERS and MACHINSTS
>
> Manufactures and Dealers In
>
> **LOCMOTIVES AND MACHINERY**
>
> **MILL SUPPLIES IN STOCK**
>
> **IRON AND BRASS CASTINGS**
>
> ANNUAL CAPACITY 4,680,000 LBS.
>
> **PHONE 59**
> **QUITMAN**
> IN
> **Brooks County Georgia.**

A newspaper ad for the Southern Machinery Company of Quitman, Georgia (courtesy Bonnell Holmes and the Brooks County Historical Society, Quitman, Georgia).

Above: Invoices from the Southern Machinery Company showing periodic change. *Below:* A Southern Machinery Company mill in Quitman, Georgia.

locomotives and machinery. The company prided itself in making high grade castings in brass and iron, as well as keeping a staff of competent machinists, blacksmiths and boilermakers. F.C. Underwood served as president and general manager, while F.C. Underwood, Jr., served as vice president of the company. Underwood was a creative individual who invented a railroad coupling but was denied a patent because of a similarity to another coupling already patented. He also invented an agricultural sprayer which he called "Boll Weevil Destroyer."

In the absence of accurate historical records the following is offered upon the recollection of a local historian. It seems that the Underwoods purchased the Morven Foundry, moved the equipment to Quitman, and named the business Southern Machinery Company. At some later date the name was changed to F.C. Underwood, Successor to Southern Machinery Company. At still some later date, with F.C. Underwood, Jr., serving as president of the company, the name was again changed, this time to Quitman Machine Works. You will observe that the SM Co. mill and the Quitman Manufacturing Company mills are identical.

Southern Plow Company, Columbus, Georgia

The Columbus Iron Works, of which the Southern Plow Company was a subsidiary, was incorporated in 1856 after being part of an informal alliance with several other manufacturers for three or four years. During the Civil War all the resources of the foundry were turned to the war effort. Cannons, steam boilers, and two gunboats poured forth from the foundry. Following that dismal period in our nation's history, agricultural implements were in great demand. In 1877, the Southern Plow Company was created to meet those demands, while the Columbus Iron Works continued to produce gears, pulleys, and shafts which helped rebuild the textile industry of Columbus. Southern Plow made steel and cast-iron plows, cotton planters, cultivators, sawmills, and, yes, cane mills and syrup kettles in its extensive complex north of the railroad trestle in Columbus, Georgia.

Two series of vertical three-roller mills, four sizes of a vertical two-roller mill, two models of a horizontal mill and heavy rolls for wood frames were produced by Southern Plow, along with horse- or steam-power attachments.

Standard Three-Roller Cane Mills

WITH SOUTHERN PLOW PLATE. These mills are identical to the mills produced by the parent company, Columbus Iron Works, and can still be found bearing a plate with the model number and "Southern Plow Company, Columbus, GA." The specifics and prices come from an early undated Southern Plow Company Catalogue, but after the company

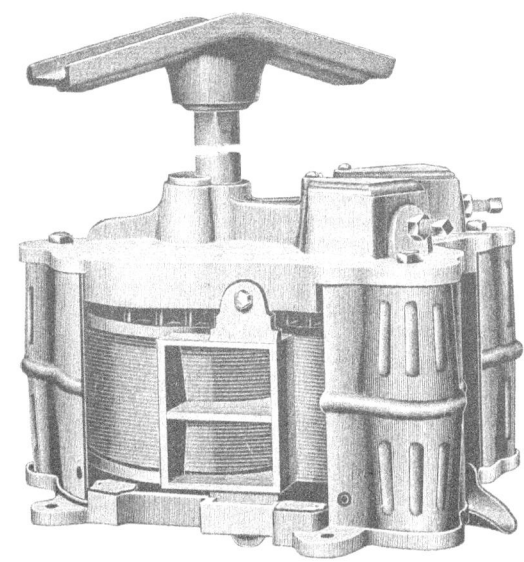

An engraving of the Southern Plow Standard Mill.

Above: A Southern Plow Standard mill. *Below:* The Southern Plow old design nameplate.

began manufacturing the Improved Columbus mills. The rollers of these mills were perfectly balanced and the turned shafts were made of extra quality steel. Bearing boxes were fitted with removable brass bearings and the mill featured amply large feed boxes. These mills were sold throughout the world where cane is grown and they had the reputation of dependability and satisfaction.

Chart for Southern Plow's Standard Three-Roller Cane Mills

Model No.	Horsepower	Main Roller- D × H	Small Rollers- D × H	Juice Per Hour	Weight	Price
No. 0	1 Horse	10⅛" × 5½"	6⅛" × 5½"	40 gals.	410 lbs.	$45.00
No. 1	1 Regular	11⅜" × 6³⁄₁₆"	6¾" × 6³⁄₁₆"	60 gals.	550 lbs.	$65.00
No. 2	2 Horse	13⅛" × 7½"	7⅛" S 7½"	80 gals.	740 lbs.	$90.00
No. 3	2 Regular	15³⁄₁₆" × 9¾"	8" × 9¾"	100 gals.	1,125 lbs.	$130.00

Improved Columbus Three-Roller Cane Mill

The intention of the new, improved version of the Southern Plow mill was to combine strength, simplicity and neatness. The bottom plate is flat on the bottom with four elevated lugs at the corners for ease in handling. The sockets into which the lower bearings fit are cast onto the inside of the bottom plate, and are ribbed and strengthened so as to make them durable and impossible for the oil or grease and juice to mix. The upper gears are so designed that the greater the strain on the mill the tighter the gears press down, making slipping impossible. Other features made the Improved Columbus a durable and dependable mill in its day.

A Southern Plow new design nameplate.

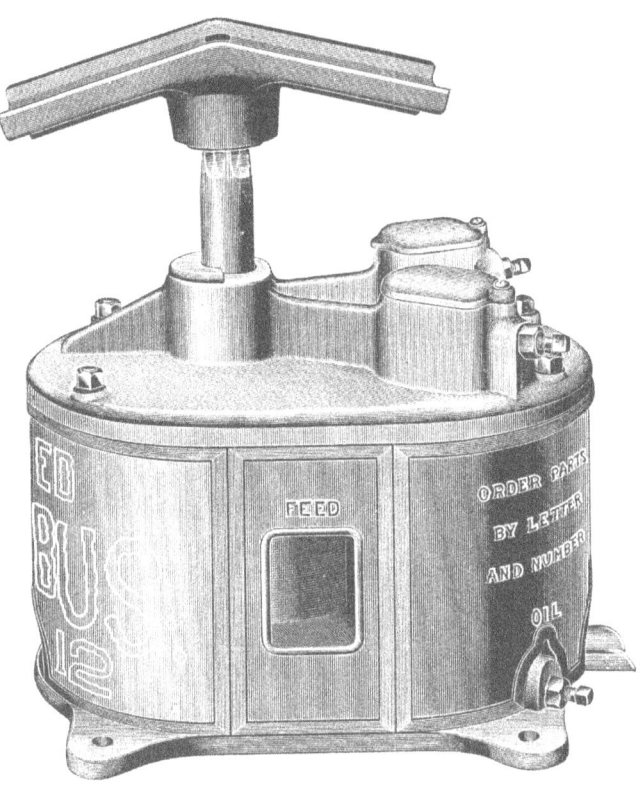

Above: An engraving of the "Improved Columbus" mill. *Below:* This is a Southern Plow No. 14 mill.

Chart for the Improved Columbus Three-Roller Vertical Cane Mills

Model No.	Horsepower	Main Roller- D × H	Small Rollers- D × H	Juice Per Hour	Weight	Price
No. 11	1 Horse	10⅛" × 5½"	6⅛" × 5½"	40 gals.	540 lbs.	$45.00
No. 12	1 Regular	11⅜" × 6³⁄₁₆"	6¾" × 6³⁄₁₆"	60 gals.	626 lbs.	$65.00
No. 13	2 Horse	13⅛" × 7½"	7⅛" × 7½"	80 gals.	855 lbs.	$90.00
No. 14	2 Horse Reg.	15³⁄₁₆" × 9¾"	8" × 9¾"	100 gals.	1,310 lbs.	$130.00
No. 15	2 Horse Heavy	16" × 12"	9¹¹⁄₁₆" × 12"	120 gals.	2,000 lbs.	$220.00

Two-Roller Cane Mills

FOR ANIMAL POWER. The two-roller mills were made in a heavy iron frame, complete and ready to use. Bearings were large and made of babbitt metal. Notice wedges were used to regulate the space between the rollers.

Chart for Southern Plow's Two-Roller Vertical Cane Mills

Model No.	Horsepower	Roller Size- D × H	Juice per Hour	Weight	Price
12	1 Horse	12" × 8½"	50 gals.	900 lbs.	$90.00
14	1 Horse Heavy	14" × 9¼"	60 gals.	1,090 lbs.	$105.00
16	2 Horse	16" × 9½"	80 gals.	1,280 lbs.	$125.00
18	2 Horse Heavy	18" × 12"	100 gals.	1,620 lbs.	$165.00

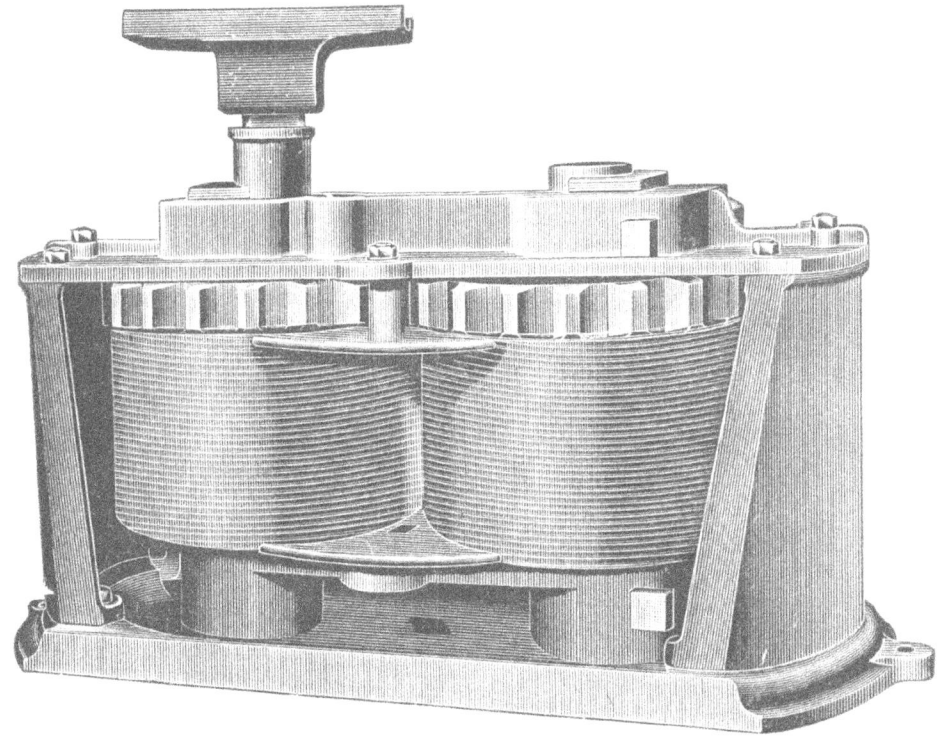

An engraving of the Southern Plow Standard two roller mill.

Above: One of Southern Plow's two roller mills. *Below:* Southern Plow's small horizontal mill, the No. 5 (photograph by Tommy Clayton, Hilliard, Florida).

Above: An engraving of Southern Plow's large horizontal power mill. *Below:* A Southern Plow No. 20 power mill.

Southern Plow made heavy rollers for wooden frames in 12, 14, 16, and 18 inch sizes ranging in weight from 450 to 975 pounds.

Horizontal Three-Roller Belt Power Cane Mills

The No. 5 is not listed in the material available to me, therefore I cannot give any specifics of this mill. Southern Plow's horizontal three-roller belt power mills had an entirely newly designed bed plate which combined strength, solidity and durability without unnecessarily adding weight to the mill. Gears were machine cut and gave a ratio of 16 to 1. They were situated outside the mill so no oil could get into the juice. Extra long bearings, gear covers, flanges on the rollers and scrapers to keep the rollers clean made this an exceptionally efficient and dependable mill.

Chart for Southern Plow's Horizontal Power Cane Mills

Model No.	Horsepower	Main Roller- D × L	Small Rollers- D × L	Juice Per Hour	Weight	Price
No. 18	5 HP	14" × 9"	14" × 6"	175–200 gals.	1,980 lbs.	$300.00
No. 20	6 HP	12" × 12"	12" × 8"	200–250 gals.	2,590 lbs.	$375.00

The pulley on the No. 18 was 20" × 6" and turned a recommended 150 to 160 revolutions per minute. Pulley size for the No. 20 was 24" × 8" and turned 130 to 150 revolutions per minute.

The Southern Plow Company also manufactured Improved Columbus Belt Power Vertical Cane mills, in models 11, 12, 13, and 14.

Improved Columbus Belt Power Cane Mills

When less capacity and a less expensive belt power mill than Southern Plow's horizontal mill was needed, the company recommended the Improved Columbus belt power vertical roller cane mills.

Chart for the Improved Columbus Belt Powered Three-Roller Vertical Cane Mills

Model No.	Large Roller- D × H	Small Rollers- D × H	Pulley Size	Juice Per Hour	Weight	Price
No. 11	10⅛" × 5½"	6⅛" × 5½"	30" × 6"	80 gals.	800 lbs.	$125.00
No. 12	11⅜" × 6³⁄₁₆"	6¾" × 6³⁄₁₆"	30" × 6"	120 gals.	945 lbs.	$165.00
No. 13	13⅛" × 7½"	7⅛" × 7½"	30" × 6"	160 gals.	1,130 lbs.	$210.00
No. 14	15³⁄₁₆" × 9¾"	8" × 9¾"	30" × 6"	200 gals.	1,380 lbs.	$240.00

The Standard three-roller, belt power vertical cane mills which came down from Columbus Iron Works were offered in models 0, 1, 2, and 3.

Standard Three-Roller Belt Power Cane Mills

The design of this mill overcame almost all of the constant friction incurred by the worm gearing. The mill itself was built along the same design of the other standard three-roller mills for animal power. However, with the belt attachment the mill could be used with engine power.

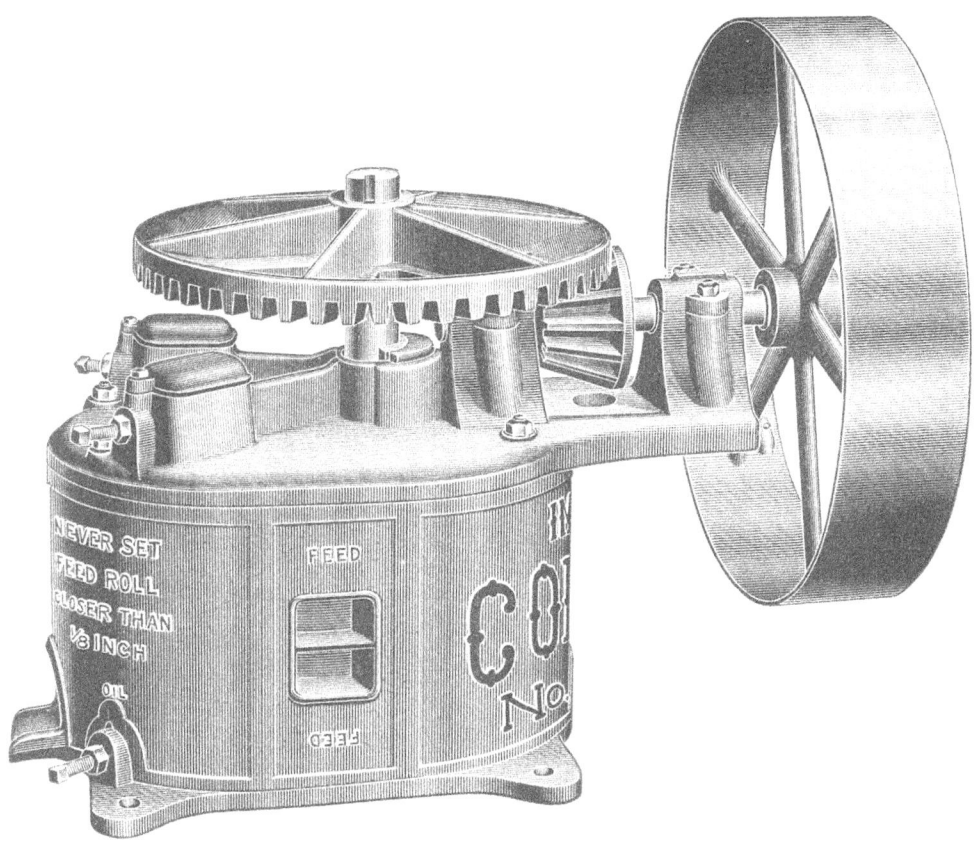

Above: An engraving of a Southern Plow belt powered mill. *Below:* A Southern Plow belt powered mill.

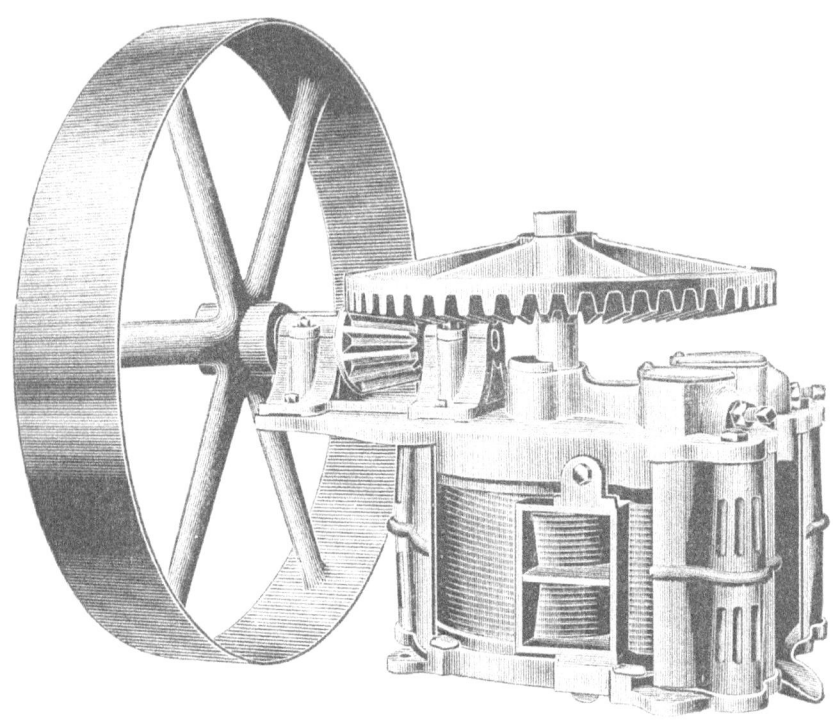

Above: An engraving of Southern Plow's Standard three roller belt powered mill. *Below:* Southern Plow's Standard three roller belt powered mill.

Chart for Southern Plow's Standard Three-Roller Belt Powered Mills

Model No.	Main Roller- D × H	Small Rollers- D × H	Pulley Size	Juice Per Hour	Weight	Price
No. 0	10⅛" × 5½"	6⅛" × 5½"	30" × 6"	80 gals.	728 lbs.	$125.00
No. 1	11⅜" × 6³⁄₁₆"	6¾" × 6³⁄₁₆"	30" × 6"	120 gals.	868 lbs.	$165.00
No. 2	13⅛" × 7½"	7⅛" × 7½"	30" × 6"	160 gals.	1,050 lbs.	$210.00
No. 3	15³⁄₁₆" × 9¾"	8" × 9¾"	30" × 6"	200 gals.	1,610 lbs.	$240.00

Two-Roller Belt Power Vertical Cane Mills

The two-roller belt power vertical cane mills in the 12-inch, 14-inch, 16-inch and 18-inch models were also offered by the company.

Chart for Southern Plow's Two-Roller Cane Mills

Model No.	Roller Size	Pulley Size	Rev. Per Min.	Juice Per Hour	Weight	Price
No. 12	12" × 8¼"	30" × 6"	65–75	110 gals.	1,410 lbs.	$175.00
No. 14	14" × 9¼"	36" × 6"	55–65	150 gals.	1,600 lbs.	$200.00
No. 16	16" × 9½"	36" × 6"	50–60	180 gals.	1,700 lbs.	$230.00
No. 18	18" × 12"	48" × 8"	50–60	210 gals.	2,130 lbs.	$265.00

After the 1902 death of the longtime president and prime mover of Columbus Iron Works, William Brown, the Teague family of Montgomery assumed primary control of the

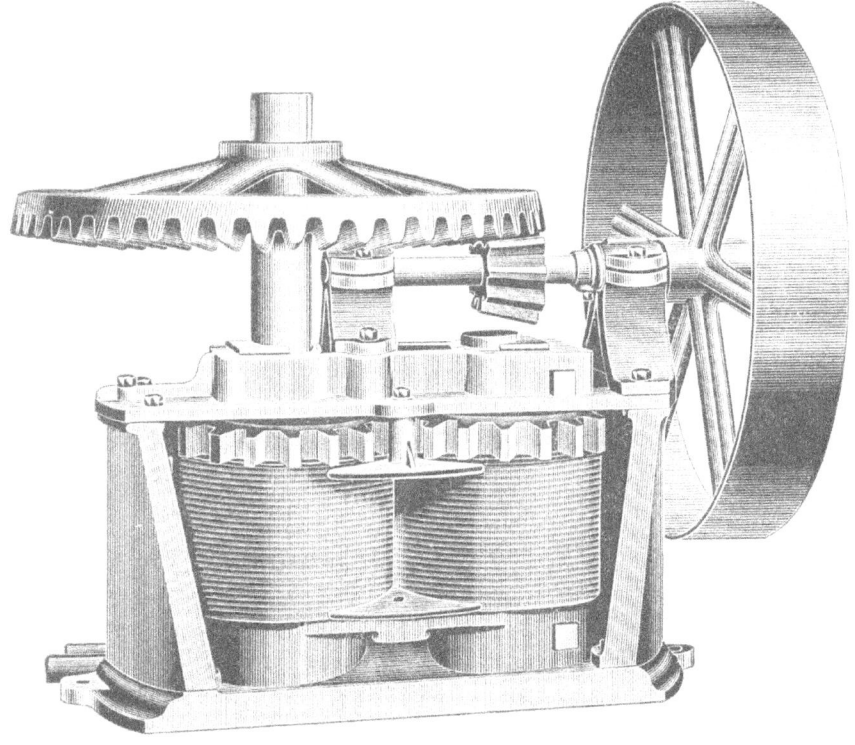

An engraving of Southern Plow's two roller belt powered mill.

Southern Plow's two roller belt powered mill (photograph by John Dean, Hartford, Alabama).

company and continued lines compatible with their hardware interests. W.C. Bradley, a longtime stockholder and prominent Columbus businessman, purchased controlling interest of the company in 1925. Several factors came into play in the demise of the company's long line of productivity. The Great Depression cut sales drastically, rural electrification hurt sales of wood burning stoves and heaters, and the consolidation of farms and the emergence of farm tractors hurt the sale of agricultural implements. In the late 1940s the company began experimenting with barbeque grills, and eventually moved the business with its new product line north of the city, where the W.C. Bradley Company continues to produce Char-Broil Grills.

Southern Sorgho Machine Company, Nashville, Tennessee

The Southern Sorgho Machinery Company manufactured sorghum machinery, but other than this announcement in a trade journal no specifics have been found.

Speedwell Iron Works, Speedwell (Morristown), New Jersey

While the Speedwell Iron Works did indeed manufacture cane mills during the height of the Northern sugar cane industry, that was not how Judge Stephen Vail's foundry distinguished itself. Judge Vail had two sons who became associated with Speedwell Iron Works (located in Speedwell, New Jersey, and later absorbed into Morristown): George, who operated the ironworks and to whom we'll return later, and Alfred. Alfred intended to become a Presbyterian minister, but when he was unable to complete his studies his life took an entirely different turn.

While a student at the University of the City of New York he became deeply interested in electric magnet experiments being made by Professor Samuel F.B. Morse, who taught there. Young Alfred became an apprentice to the American inventor of the telegraph and devoted himself to developing Morse's plans. A special design and experimental room was set up at the Speedwell Iron Works which was kept under constant lock and key. An experienced and trusted employee, William Baxter, became Vail's assistant. When the factory was later remodeled this room was preserved in its original state as a tribute to the significant contribution. Stephen Vail's *Early Days of the First Telegraph Line* gives us much history of this era.

To prove to his still skeptical father that the apparatus he designed and built would work, Alfred offered to send any message his father wished. Judge Vail took a scrap of paper and wrote, "A patient waiter is no loser." On January 6, 1838, Alfred sent the message and it was perfectly received. Alfred became a full partner with Morse and developed the apparatus and secured the patent, yet Morse once pridefully referred to him as "my mechanical assistant." He later apologized for the comment and attitude. Rightfully so. Though Morse will long be remembered as the inventor of the telegraph, the truth is, Alfred Vail took Morse's basic idea and developed an entirely different machine and alphabet, and should forever stand on equal status with him.

George, Judge Vail's other son, associated with the foundry, operated the ironworks factory and was recognized for his outstanding steam engines. Apparently the company had an agency for its products at George Vail and Company, 9 Gold Street, New York City. Around 1851, a Mr. Logan joins the firm and the Gold Street concern becomes Logan, Vail and Company. Their rather extensive product line included Bogardus' celebrated horsepower, cranks, balance wheels, pitmans or noodle-heads, stirrups, feed hand, saw grate slides and rods, wrag wheels, gudgeons, mill bars, saw gummers, shafting for sawmills, smut machines, gearing and shafting for iron waterwheels for flouring mills, paper cutters, Kay's calendering apparatus for continuous sheets for paper mills, screws for lathes and presses, jack screws, heavy forging, cotton gin gear, screws, bolts and nuts, portable sawmills, steam engines, gearing and shafting for large or small industries. At this time cane mills and kettles had not been added to their product line. Under George's leadership, portable and stationary steam engines in the four to eight horsepower category manufactured by the Speedwell Iron Works won a Silver Medal at the Fair of the American Institute, and a Premium and cash of $100 at the Maryland State Fair held in Baltimore in October 1853.

Other changes occurred in Speedwell's listing in 1857. John H. Lidgerwood and Company was listed as their agent at 9 Gold Street though Vail's Speedwell Iron Works was still listed at Morristown. And "Sugar and Chinese Cane Mills and Sugar Pans" were added to their product list. Probably most of us have never heard of a Speedwell Cane Mill or kettle. However, all of us have heard of the telegraph. Who would have ever guessed that they came from the same factory—Vail's Speedwell Iron Works, Speedwell, New Jersey?

Spotless Company, Richmond, Virginia

The Spotless Company, Richmond, Virginia, advertised itself as "The South's Mail Order House." It had its office and warehouse at 1010 Cary Street, with three retail stores in Richmond and a branch retail store in St. Petersburg, Virginia. The General Catalog No. 28 of the Spotless Stores featured over 6,000 items. Buying directly from the manufacturer in large quantities then selling to the user for cash enabled the company to save their customers money. The company operated at a low expense on a large volume much like that of the Sears, Roebuck & Company.

The Spotless Company sold two models of cane mills under their brand, namely the Perfection Cane Mills and the Jumbo Power Mill.

Perfection Cane Mills

The Perfection Cane Mills were three-roller vertical mills in five sizes. These mills featured brass bearing boxes, all steel shafts, and serrated faces on the rolls; the large roll had flanges at top and bottom. The gearing was encased for safety, and the gears were cast separately from the rolls so repairs would be less expensive and less time consuming. A catalog from the late 1920s offered the following mills:

Chart for the Perfection Cane Mills

Model No.	Horsepower	Juice Per Hour	Weight	1897 Price
No. 400	One Horse Light	40–60 gals.	400 lbs.	$30.90
No. 401	One Horse	50–60 gals.	495 lbs.	$35.75
No. 402	One Horse Heavy	60–75 gals.	720 lbs.	$42.45
No. 403	Two Horse Light	75–90 gals.	775 lbs.	$56.85
No. 404	Two Horse	90–100 gals.	800 lbs.	$61.95

This was a high grade mill offered at money saving prices shipped directly from a southern Ohio factory.

Jumbo Power Mill

The Spotless Company's three-roller horizontal mill was called the Jumbo Power Mill. This mill had babbitted bearing boxes, grooved rollers, and adjustable set screws to accommodate large or small cane. The drive pulley was 18" × 6" and was adaptable to either automobile or tractor power. This mill required from three to five horsepower to operate and was capable of grinding from four to six tons of cane every twelve hours. The Jumbo Power Mill weighed 700 pounds and cost $62.75. It, too, was manufactured "in a southern Ohio factory," most probably by the C.S. Bell Company of Hillsboro, Ohio.

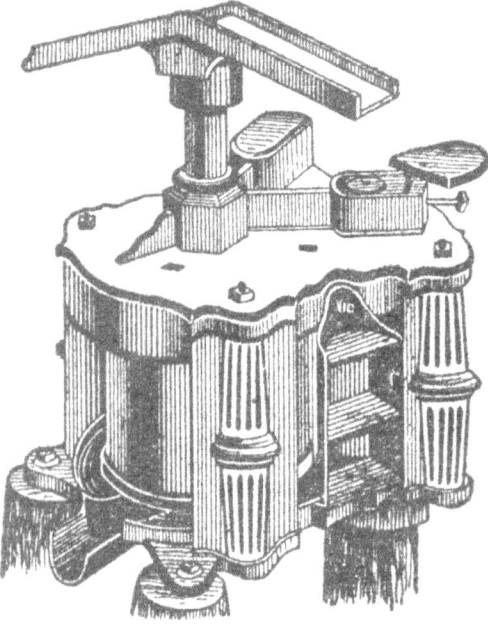

Left: **Spotless Perfection cane mill.** *Right:* **Spotless Jumbo No. 88 nameplate.**

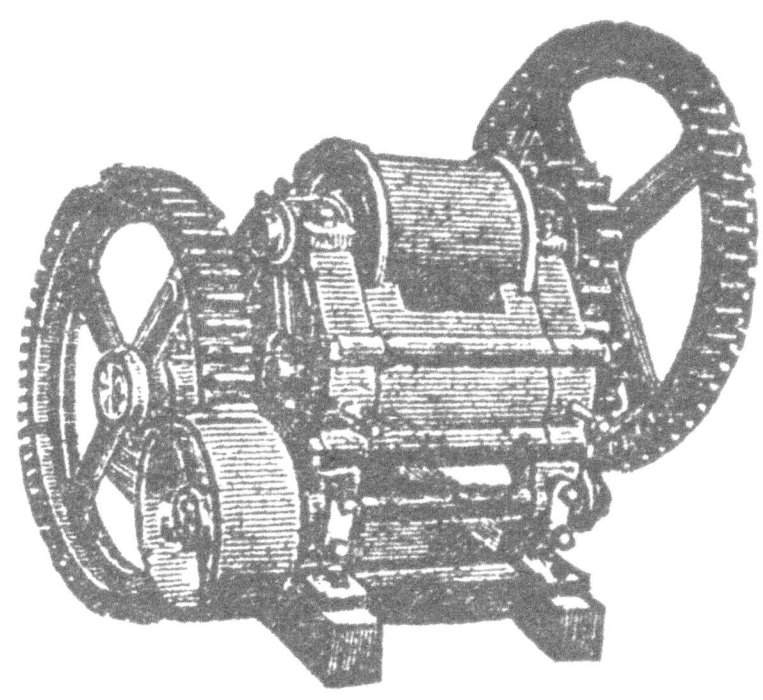

Above: Spotless Jumbo ad extolling its features. *Below:* The Spotless Jumbo weighed 700 pounds.

George L. Squier Manufacturing Company, Buffalo, New York

George L. Squier was born at Lanesboro, Berkshire County, Massachusetts, a descendant from the old Puritans of that name who emigrated from England in 1622. After graduation from Williams College in 1845, George then studied law. He passed the bar

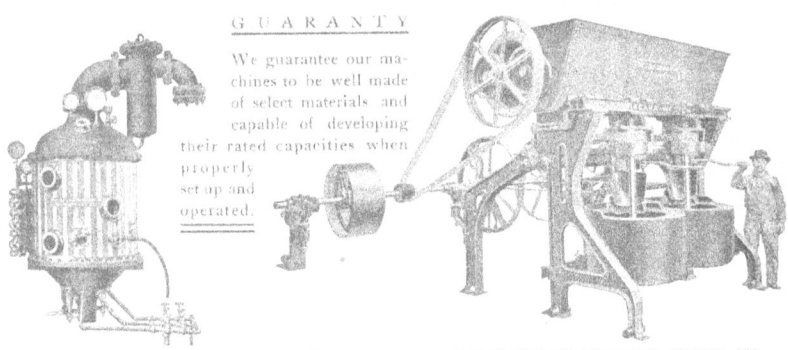

"NIAGARA" VACUUM PAN   "NIAGARA WESTON" CENTRIFUGAL PLANT, WITH MIXER FRAMING, ETC.

The "Cuba" Three Roller Mill combined with Zig-Zag Crusher shown here is exceptionally heavy and powerful and is designed for operation either by steam or water power. The improved type of crusher distributes the cane uniformly between the grinding rolls and makes possible a greater extraction than obtained from the three roll mill. In many instances we can point out a saving of 15% due to this device.

"CUBA" 3 ROLLER MILL COMBINED WITH 2 ROLLER ZIG-ZAG CRUSHER

You should be interested in syrup making plants. If so, let us hear from you. We can make you an interesting proposition.

Write us concerning anything you need in plantation machinery

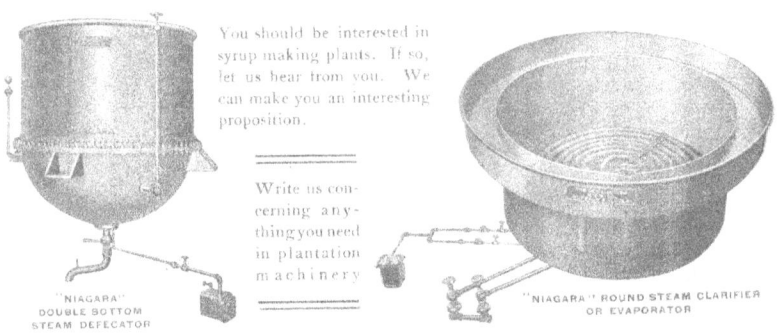

"NIAGARA" DOUBLE BOTTOM STEAM DEFECATOR   "NIAGARA" ROUND STEAM CLARIFIER OR EVAPORATOR

GEO. L. SQUIER MFG. CO., Buffalo, N. Y., U. S. A.

An ad from the Geo. L. Squier Mfg. Co. advertising sugar equipment.

examination after three years' study and was admitted to the bar in Springfield, Massachusetts, in 1848. He then began a law practice in Chicopee Falls. This career didn't last long, and he joined the firm of Whittemore, Squier & Co., manufacturers of agricultural implements. Moving to Buffalo, New York, in 1857, he and D.M. Osborn, of Auburn, New York, founded the Buffalo Agricultural Machine Works on Scott Street near Washington Street. There they introduced, manufactured and marketed the Kirby mower and reaper for twelve

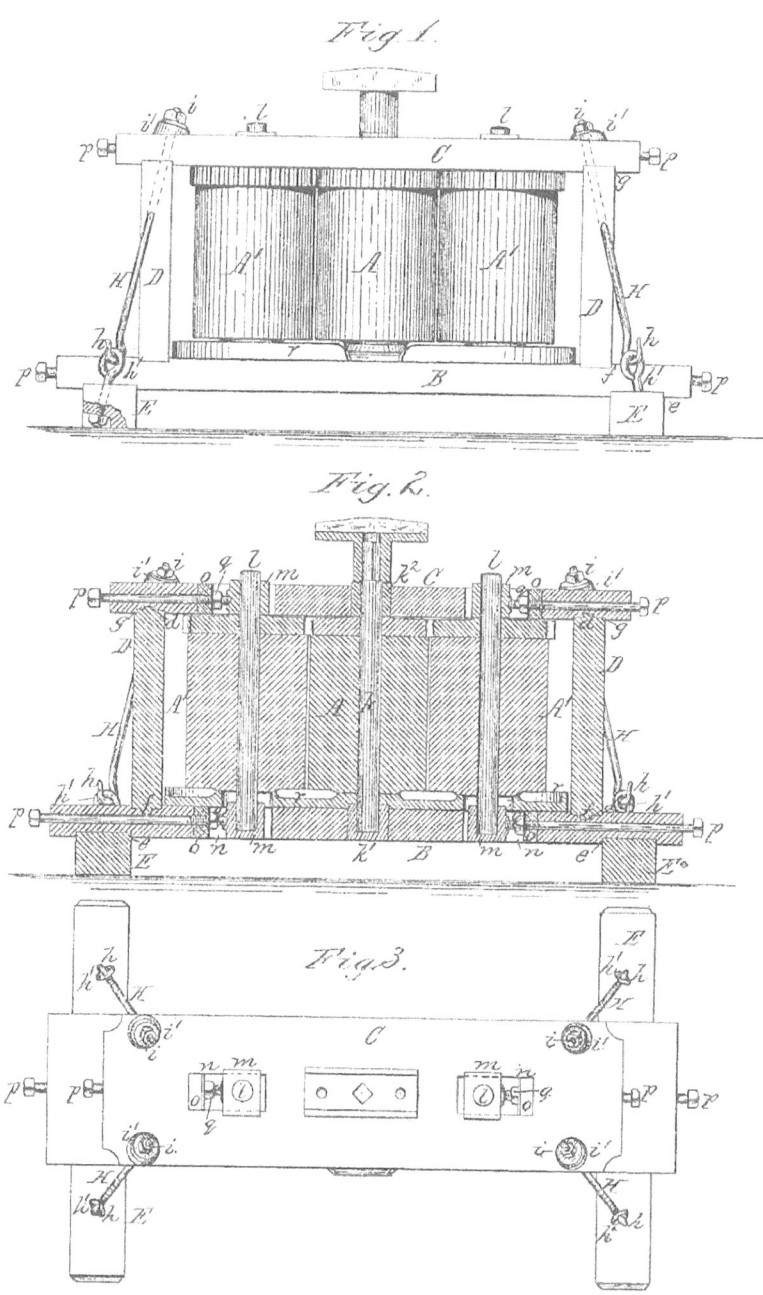

A patent for a mill with three straight-line rollers.

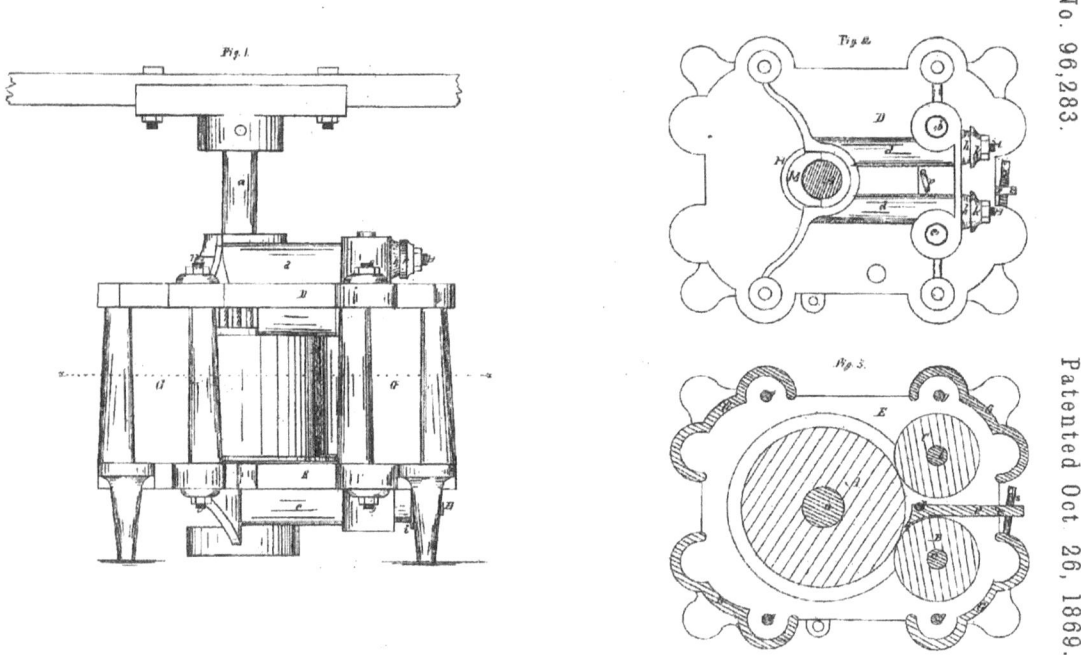

Top: A Squier patent for a mill with rubber bushings. *Below:* A closer view of the cushions used to ease pressure on the rollers.

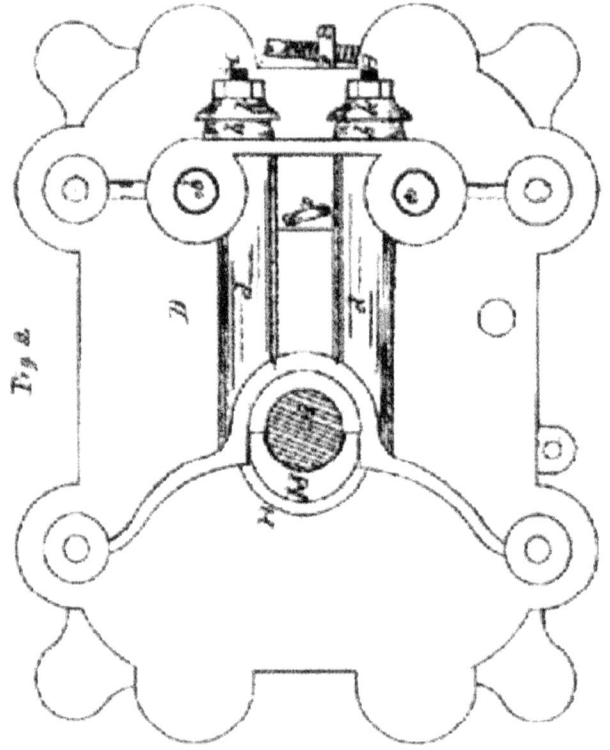

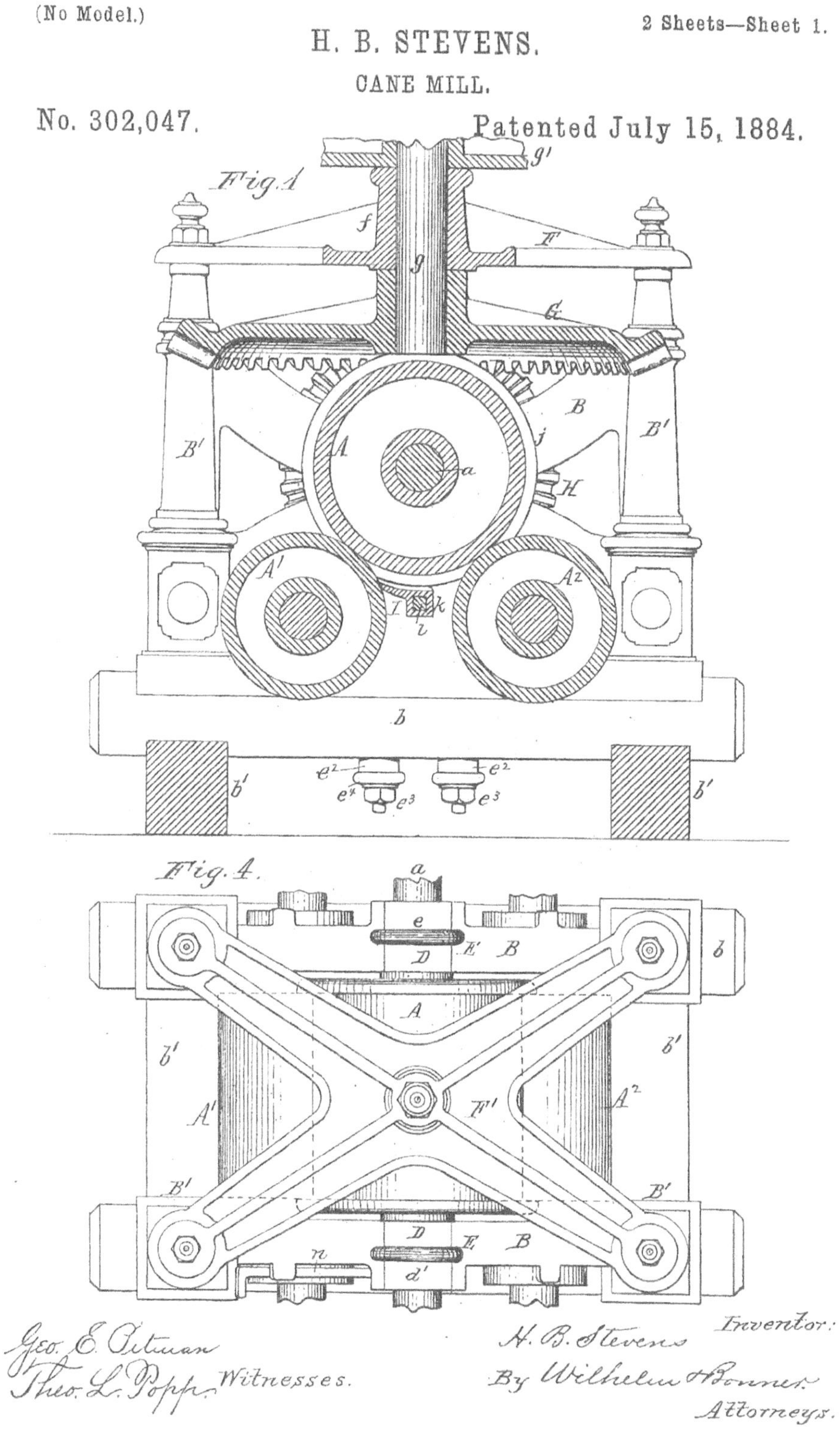

George L. Squier

(No Model.)   2 Sheets—Sheet 1.

H. B. STEVENS.
CANE MILL.

No. 302,047.   Patented July 15, 1884.

Fig. 1

Fig. 4

Geo. E. Pitman
Theo. L. Popp   Witnesses.

H. B. Stevens   Inventor:
By Wilhelm & Bonner
   Attorneys.

Mills built to this patent became a Squier standard for years.

years before Osborn bought rights to the machine and the company dissolved. Squier however, acquired the rights to the patents of the sorghum mills and evaporators they had begun producing a few years before.

George Squier's younger brother, Henry, joined him in establishing a company for the manufacture of the sorghum mills. This company was called Geo. L. Squier & Bro., and was located at 53 Carroll Street. They found a ready market in the sugar producing regions of Cuba and Mexico. They also developed machines to clean rice and coffee, which were in demand on the foreign market as well. Henry died in 1882 and George continued their work for another two years. Then, in December 1884, he formed a stock company with a capital of $200,000 under the name of Geo. L. Squier Manufacturing Company. The purchase of the oldest and best established agricultural implement business in New York City, the R.H. Allen Company, Water Street, manufacturers of farm wagons, city wagons and potato-digging plows, which was founded in 1843 and then run by Higganum Manufacturing Corporation, placed the Squier Manufacturing Company at the head of the agricultural implement houses of the United States, with business in forty-eight foreign countries. While Squier's machinery was used in every tropical country and island in the world, they were especially well known throughout Mexico and Central and South America where they established their largest trade. They had a representative traveling the tropics studying the wants and needs of their customers in order to better serve them. Their huge catalogs were printed in English, Spanish and Portuguese and they corresponded with their customers in these languages.

Weber and Scovell's *The Northern Sugar Cane Manual with Descriptions of the American Sugar Machinery* gives keen insight into the machinery manufactured by George L. Squier. The company owned over one hundred patent claims and they made several hundred different mills. On January 9, 1883, Squier's H.B. Stevens received Patent No. 270,502 for improvements in a mill with three vertical rollers set in a straight line. The mill featured improved frame assembly, set screws for adjusting pressure on the rollers, and a spring to allow the rollers to give under heavy pressure. Earlier, on October 26, 1869, Stevens and D.J. Powers received Patent No. 96,283, for a three vertical roller mill designed with strap bolts around the bearings of the rollers, India-rubber washers on those bolts to give elasticity, and a free removable scraper.

On July 16, 1884, Stevens was awarded patent No. 302,047 for a horizontal animal powered mill. This mill seems to have become the standard for the company for many years. The company's slogan was "From Cane to Sugar Bag," and they offered machinery to accomplish each step of the process. A May 1947 report says, "In the 90 years the Geo. L. Squier Co. has been operating in Buffalo and shipping its tools and machines to the four corners of the world, it has never had a layoff of men."

Squier's company became a part of the Buffalo Forge Company in 1902 and they continued to produce sugar related machinery. In 1963 the company built a crusher weighing more than ten tons for the Iberia Sugar Corp. in New Iberia, Louisiana. Squier experienced a hostile takeover in the 1980s and an out-of-state corporation took over controlling interest. The long and meaningful history of this illustrious company finally came to an end. The last mention of a Squier Corporation in the Buffalo city directory was in 1967.

The Pioneer

To meet the need of a good hand powered mill to test various loads of cane and experiment with various varieties of cane Squier developed the Pioneer. This mill came in

The Pioneer was a manual mill designed for family use.

two sizes, which were even suitable for small family use. By putting a pulley on the No. 2 Pioneer it could be converted to a small power mill and do sufficient work for small operators.

Chart for the Pioneer Cane Mills

Model No.	Roller Number and Size	Weight
No. 1	Two Rollers, 4" × 4"	170 lbs.
No. 2	Three Rollers, 5" × 5"	270 lbs.

Diamond No. 1

For years Squier refused to make an inexpensive vertical roller mill, though there was always a demand for such a mill. There came a time when the price of iron dropped sufficiently that they made a less expensive mill, the Diamond No. 1. Though this was a less expensive model, Squier claimed that they had built into the mill as much strength and capacity as any mill on the market. Many of the features of their Samson Model, which they claimed was the strongest mill of its size made, were built into this mill, making it an outstanding model. Unfortunately no engravings or specifics were given of the Samson mill in this particular catalog.

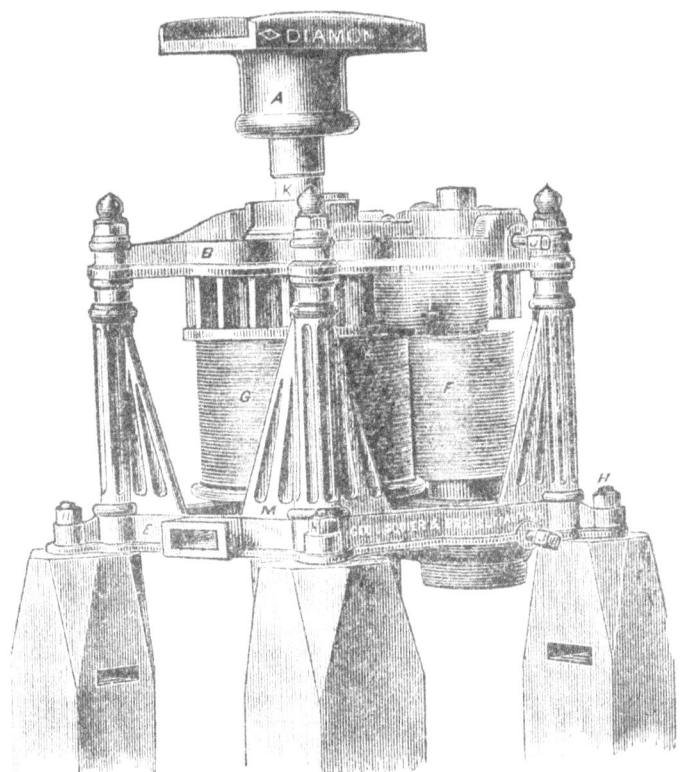

The Diamond No. 1 was one of the less expensive models.

Chart for the Diamond No. 1 Cane Mills

Model No.	Main Roller Size	Weight
No. 1	10" × 7"	500 lbs.

Diamond Mills

These models of the Diamond Mills were designed and manufactured for those needing an extra heavy and strong vertical mill capable of grinding large cane. The forged wrought iron shafts were much larger and stronger than ordinary mills of the same size, and they ran in brass boxes. These mills had Squier's patented rubber springs, which enabled the mill to be self-adjusting, and the feed roller had a set screw so the mill could be adaptable to any size cane.

Chart for the Diamond Cane Mills

Model No.	Main Roller Size	Weight
No. 2	12" × 8"	700 lbs.
No. 3	14" × 10"	1,000 lbs.

The Pearl Cane Mill

The Pearl was a horizontal, self-adjusting, animal-power mill offered in four sizes which were of the same design but larger than Squier's popular Croncher Mill. Extra heavy and strong gears were used and strap bolts took the pressure off the rollers.

Left: Diamond mills Nos. 2 and 3 were designed extra heavy and strong. *Right:* The Pearl was a self-adjusting animal powered mill.

Chart for the Pearl Cane Mills

Model No.	Main Roller Size	Weight
No. 1	8" × 8"	800 lbs.
No. 2	10" × 10"	1,200 lbs.
No. 3	10" × 12"	1,400 lbs.
No. 4	12" × 16"	3,000 lbs.

The Ruby Cane Mill

The Ruby Mill was very similar to the Pearl mill, but had the sweep for animal power below. These mills had Squier's self-adjusting springs, wrought iron stay bolts, heavy wrought shafts, and brass boxes.

Chart for the Ruby Cane Mills

Model No.	Main Roller Size	Weight
No. 1	8" × 8"	900 lbs.
No. 2	10" × 10"	1,300 lbs.
No. 3	10" × 12"	1,500 lbs.
No. 4	12" × 16"	3,200 lbs.

The Texas Cane Mill

Squier claimed that the Texas Mill was the largest, heaviest, and strongest animal power cane mill on the market. The model shown above could use a sweep above or below, or could be adapted for steam power.

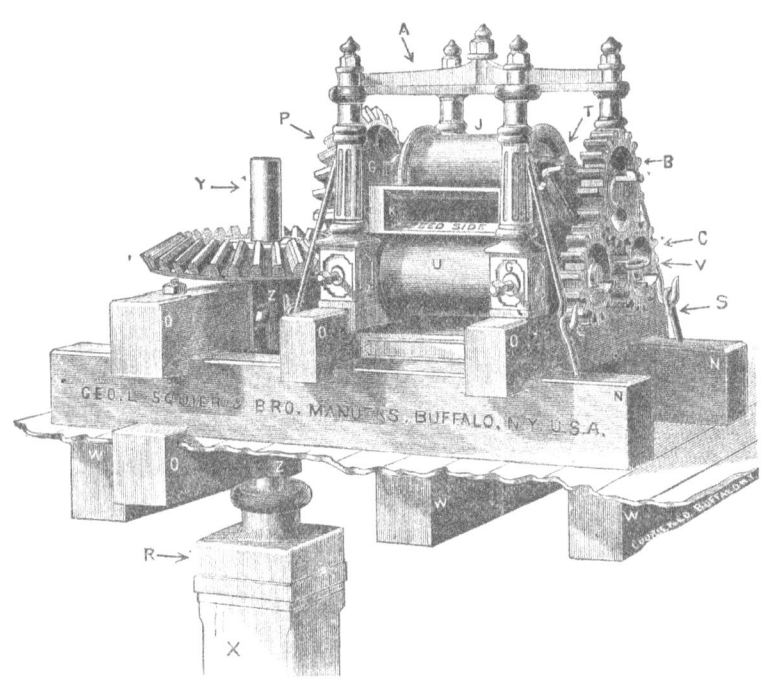

The Ruby had a sweep below for animal power.

Chart for the Texas Cane Mills

Model No.	Main Roller Size	Weight
No. 0	12" × 15"	2,000 lbs.
No. 1	12" × 20"	3,500 lbs.
No. 2	12" × 20"	4,100 lbs.
No. 3	16" × 24"	6,600 lbs.
No. 4	20" × 30"	13,150 lbs.

The Gem Cane Mill

The Gem was the smallest steam- and water-powered mills that Squier manufactured and featured extra large shafts, brass boxes, and Squier's patented rubber springs.

Chart for the Gem Cane Mills

Model No.	Main Roller Size	Weight
No. 2	10" × 10"	1,100 lbs.
No. 3	10" × 12"	1,300 lbs.
No. 4	12" × 16"	2,500 lbs.

The Florida Cane Mills

The Florida Mills were designed to use water power, horsepower, or a small steam engine and were intentionally designed to grind the larger Southern, or tropical, cane. These mills were constructed with Squier's new style of heavy arched housing, and with heavy wrought iron stay bolts to take the strain off the rollers.

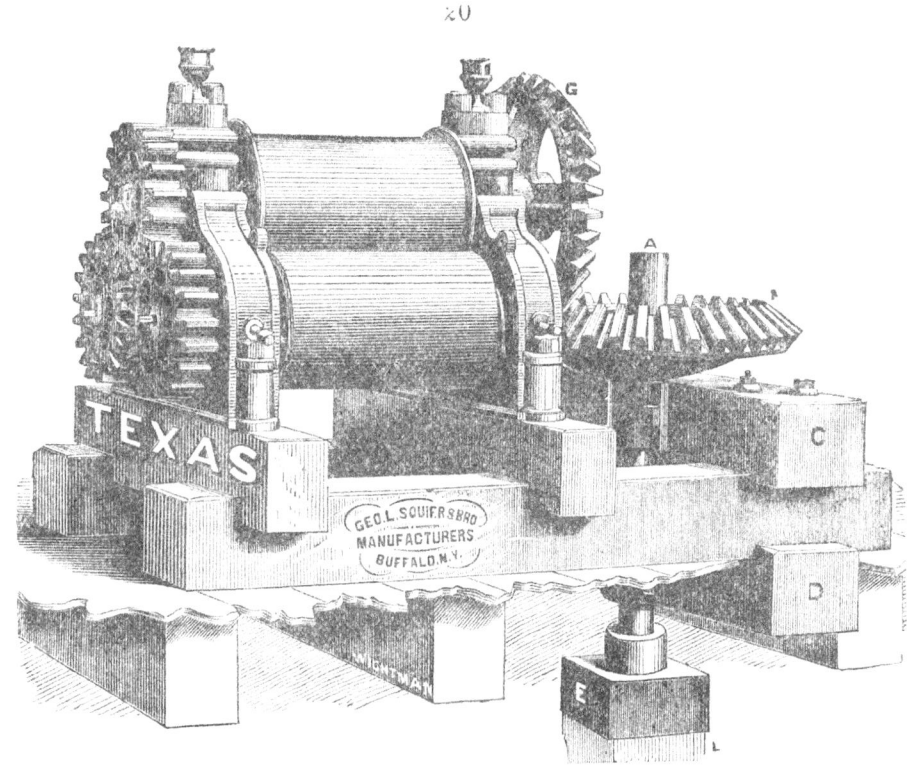

Above: The Texas was claimed to be the heaviest and strongest on the market. *Below:* The Gem was the smallest water powered and steam powered mill Squier made.

Above: **The Florida cane mill was intentionally designed to grind Southern sugar cane.** *Below:* **Squier's Louisiana mill was designed for medium power.**

Chart for the Florida Cane Mills

Model No.	Main Roller Size	Weight
No. 1	12" × 16"	1,400 lbs.
No. 2	12" × 20"	3,000 lbs.

The Louisiana Mills with Iron Bed-Plate

The Louisiana Mills were designed as medium steam or water powered mills and were touted as the cheapest mills on the market in proportion to the size and capacity of the rollers. The iron bed plate was popular in areas where wood was subject to decay or termites.

Chart for the Louisiana Mills with Iron Bed-Plate

Model No.	Main Roller Size	Weight
No. 1	16" × 24"	4,600 lbs.
No. 2	20" × 30"	10,500 lbs.

Louisiana No. 2 with Cane Carrier

In addition, cane carriers were available from Squier for this model mill.

The American Mammoth Cane Mills

The American Mammoth came with Squier's patented rubber springs, which apparently proved beneficial in larger mills, which were under enormous strain. This mill's design, strength, and weight were placed appropriately and in a ten year span there had been very little breakage or damage reported.

This engraving shows a Louisiana No. 2 with a cane carrier.

The American Mammoth sustained very little breakage.

Chart for the American Mammoth Cane Mills

Model No.	Main Roller Size	Small Roller Size	Weight
No. 1	24" × 30"	20" × 30"	16,000 lbs.
No. 2	24" × 36"	20" × 36"	18,000 lbs.

The George L. Squier Manufacturing Company manufactured the American Evaporator, the American Evaporator with a portable furnace, an American Deep Evaporator, steam evaporators, sugar centrifugals, the Samson Horse Power, the Buffalo Post Engine (a small steam engine which could be mounted on a post and with appropriate shafting and pulleys could power a cane mill), the American Vertical Steam Engine, Hercules Engines, and locomotive boilers.

Stauffer, Eshleman and Company, New Orleans, Louisiana

When New Yorker Augustus Whiting settled in New Orleans, it was an infant city. It was so young, in fact, that when he opened his wholesale hardware store at the corner of Chartres and Customhouse streets in 1810 it would be two years before the first steamboat would dock in the city and five years before Andrew Jackson would defeat General Pakenham at Chalmette—so young that Louisiana had not yet been admitted to the Union and beads for the Indians were a part of the store's inventory. But Whiting positioned his business to meet the needs of a growing city and developing southland. Needing additional help, he took a young Englishman, Robert Slark, as a partner and the business continued to prosper. Needing larger facilities the business was moved to new quarters at Magazine and Canal streets.

In 1835, I.H. Stauffer, a twenty-two year old "gentleman of sterling honor and integrity" from Lancaster, Pennsylvania, joined the firm as an apprentice and began the long association of the Stauffer name with the company. Augustus Whiting retired in 1840 and returned to New York. James I. Day had joined the firm and it now became known as Slark, Day and Stauffer and Company. Stauffer sent back to Pennsylvania for his nephew, B.F. Eshleman, in 1850, and here began another long association with the hardware company. As business continued to prosper the company again needed larger facilities and moved to 511 Canal Street in 1850. The name was changed several times during the years as partners

Stauffer's Saville mill looks identical to the Southern Plow (photograph by Walter J. Vaughn, Baton Rouge, Louisiana).

joined the firm then subsequently retired, but in 1890 it was given the now long-standing name, Stauffer, Eshleman and Company. The company incorporated in 1904. Stauffer, Eshleman and Company was known for its fair prices, its willingness to help struggling businesses succeed, and its financial impact in the development of Louisiana and adjacent Southern states. Its domestic sales reached across the Deep South and its export business reached into Central and South America. In an excellent article about the company, *The Item-Tribune* of New Orleans noted that the company was celebrating its one hundred twenty-first anniversary in 1931.

Being a wholesale hardware business, Stauffer, Eshleman and Company did not manufacture cane mills, but like others have done, sold one over their name. The Saville, shown above, is consistent with the Improved Columbus mills manufactured by Southern Plow of Columbus, Georgia.

Isaac Straub and Company, Cincinnati, Ohio

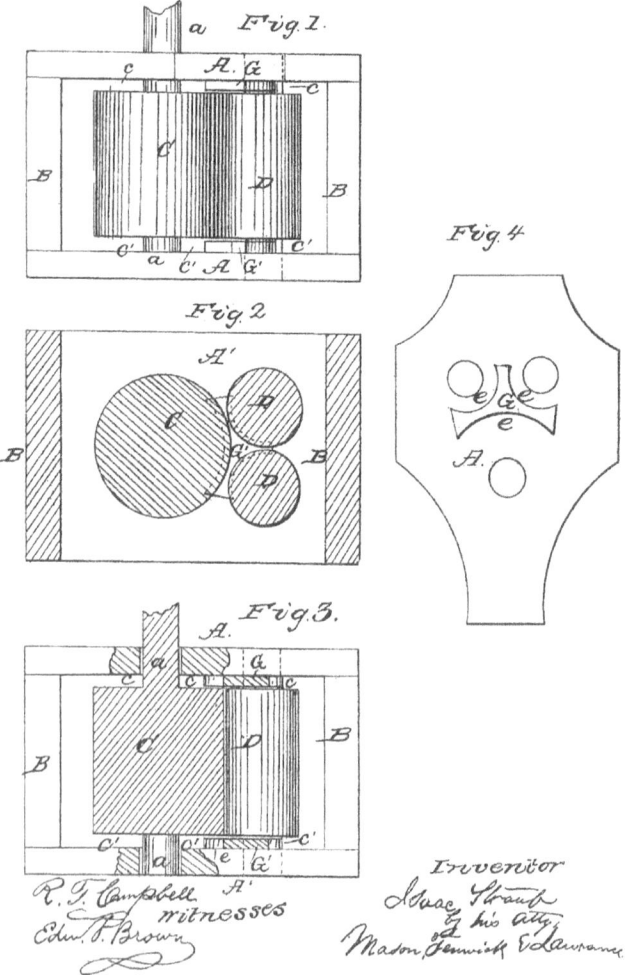

Straub's patent featured fenders to guide the cane through the mill.

In 1840 Isaac Straub was a machinist in Cincinnati with an establishment at West Row and John streets where he manufactured portable mills of various kinds. By 1861 he advertised corn, wheat and sawmills, with an office at 19 W. Front Street and a factory at John and Front streets. He entered into a partnership with Joseph Smith, Jr., Robert Simpson, A.W. Winall, and Joseph Wilder, and by 1870 they were listed as part of the company in the city directory. Robert Simpson became president by 1874, George E. Gault was secretary, and Straub was not listed in the leadership of the company. In 1875 the company name was changed to Straub Mill Company; they manufactured portable wheat, corn and stock feed mills.

Isaac Straub was issued Patent No. 39,182 on July 7, 1863, for a unique innovation for cane mills. Straub's patent was for fenders, or curved arches, attached to the top plate and bottom plate, situated over and below the rollers, to guide the cane out of the discharge roller. By using the fenders rather than flanges on the rollers the mill would not become so easily jammed. The fenders acted much like a top and bottom turn plate guiding the bagasse out the discharge roller.

Sullivan and Hurdean, Zanesville, Ohio

The ironworks of Sullivan and Hurdean were located on South Third Street in Zanesville, Ohio, and produced a variety of cast-iron products, including both coal and wood cook stoves; parlor stoves; stoves for churches and schools; "Amalgam Bells;" hollowware; sad irons; fire fronts; and agricultural implements such as plows and cultivators. In the *Daily Zanesville Courier* they advertised that cane mills were kept on hand at all times and they were constantly manufacturing their popular models in four different sizes. Their mills were guaranteed inferior to none, and if any broke during normal usage they would be repaired free of charge. Sullivan and Hurdean manufactured sugar kettles and sold "Jacobs' Evaporators," an evaporator patented by C. Jacobs on August 6, 1861, and judged simplest and best in use at the 1862 Ohio Sorghum Convention held in Columbus, Ohio, in January 1862.

D.T. Sutherland Machine Works and Foundry, Bainbridge, Georgia

The D.T. Sutherland Machine Works and Foundry, Bainbridge, Georgia, did a general machine shop and foundry business in manufacture, repairs, and retail merchandise. Mr.

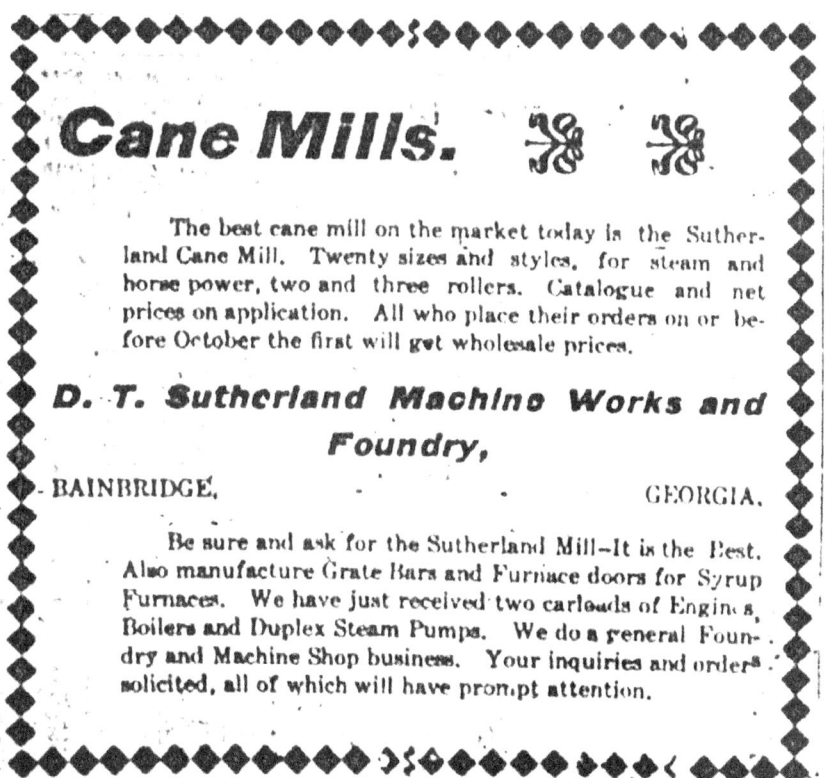

An ad for the Sutherland Machine Works of Bainbridge, Georgia (courtesy of Quitman Free Press, Quitman, Georgia.)

A Sutherland Machine Works cane mill in a scrap pile (photograph by John Dean, Hartford, Alabama).

Sutherland, a native of Ireland, emigrated to Scotland, then to the United States, settling in Bainbridge, Georgia. Products from his foundry were sold across a wide territory of the Deep South. In addition to cane mills, the company manufactured grate bars and furnace doors for syrup furnaces, and were dealers in steam engines, boilers, and Duplex Steam Pumps. While Mr. Sutherland was a very private person he left a lasting memorial in the beautiful wooden arches in the First Presbyterian Church of Bainbridge. The forms for the arches were made at the foundry and stand for the glory of God and a testament of excellent workmanship.

The cane mills they manufactured, which they claimed to be the "best mill on the market," as advertised in *The Quitman Free Press*, were manufactured in twenty sizes and styles, two and three rollers, adapted for steam or horsepower.

Julian M. Swoop Company, New Orleans, Louisiana

Julian M. Swoop was a native of New Orleans and a graduate of the Jesuit and Soule commercial colleges. He entered into business with his father, S. Swoop, who was part of the Shakespeare and Swoop Company, manufacturers of sugar mill equipment, an establishment which stood for nearly a century at 913 Girod Street, between Baronne and Dryades

Streets. At an earlier time the company was known as Shakespeare, Smith and Company. Apparently Julian's father gained controlling interest in the company, then passed it on to his son. In a 1905 listing Julian M. Swoop is listed as a manufacturer of sugar cane equipment. Swoop retired in 1924 and died at his home in Bay St. Louis, Mississippi, on July 22, 1930, and his obituary was carried in *The Times-Picayune* of New Orleans.

Syfan Machine Works and Foundry, Waycross, Georgia

C.T.W. Syfan was the owner and operator of the Syfan Machine Works and Foundry at the south end of Brunel Street in Waycross, Georgia. While the company did all types of iron and brass castings, they gave special attention to boiler work. They advertised that locomotive repairing and rebuilding was the specialty of this early 1900s foundry and machine shop. Though the early 1900s saw the rise of the gasoline engine as an alternative source of power, the steam engine made a great contribution to the world's agriculture and industry. In fact, few singular inventions have had greater impact than this one machine. The oldest steam engine of which we have record was built by a first century Greek named Hero, of Alexandria, but it was never developed beyond the "toy" stage. Giovanni Branca and the French physicist Denis Papin, along with the English engineers Thomas Savery, Thomas Newcomen and John Calley, all made significant contributions to the development of the

Syfan Machine Works & Foundry,

C. T. W. SYFAN Proprietor.

—MANUFACTURERS OF—

Iron and Brass Castings,

SPECIAL ATTENTON TO
BOILER WORK.

ALL KINDS MACHINERY
REPAIRED.

LOCOMOTIVE REPAIRING
AND REBUILDING A SPECIALTY.

Shops at the South end of Brunel Street,
WAYCROSS, GA.

Casting in Foundry every second day.

Though boilers were Syfan Machine Works' main business, the company also manufactured cane mills (courtesy James Britton and Okefenokee Regional Library, Waycross, Georgia).

steam engine. In 1765, the Scottish instrument maker James Watts conceived and built an engine with a separate water-cooled condenser chamber. He developed the crankshaft, double-acting pistons, governor, flywheel, and high-pressure steam engines, and is often referred to as the inventor of the steam engine as we know it today. By the 1830s there were several steam engines being developed for agricultural use. The "Forty-Niner," built by A.L. Archambult in Philadelphia in 1849, was one of the first steam engines produced in America. In 1855, Obed Hussey, who also developed a reaper, developed a self-propelled traction engine used primarily for plowing.

The first railroads were developed to haul coal from the mines and the cars were drawn along the rails by horses. In 1822, George Stephenson envisioned a steam engine pulling the cars along the rails. Then this self-made engineer, who didn't learn to read until he was seventeen, convinced a group of businessmen to try it on their new railroad from Stockton to Darlington, England. Three years later the railroad opened with a locomotive fully powered by steam—the first steam railway. By 1848, when Stephenson died, nearly 6,000 miles of railroad had been built in England and in America, and it was the railroad which tied together and helped develop this frontier nation. The Southern states advanced railroad transportation more quickly than did the Northern states. There were two periods of intense activity. One was from 1828 to 1839, which began with the construction of the Baltimore and Ohio Railroad. Charles Carroll, the lone surviving signer of the Declaration of Independence, turned the first shovel of soil to begin construction of this railroad on July 4, 1828. The B&O was the first significant railroad in the South and in the nation, and its little primitive locomotive, "Tom Thumb," has been immortalized. The other period of active railroad building was from 1850 to 1860, the decade prior to the Civil War.

Pictured is a roller made by the Syfan Machine Works of Waycross, Georgia.

The steam engine had numerous applications, from stationary power machines for threshers to steam traction machines for agriculture, to railway locomotives, to coaches, boats, and ships. Therefore, such companies as Syfan Machine Works and Foundry played an important role in the manufacture and repair of steam boilers that kept the wheels of industry and agriculture turning.

From an advertisement in the *Waycross Herald*, May 5, 1900, one could assume that much of Syfan's business involved repair and rebuilding of all types of machinery, especially locomotives and boilers. Syfan Machine Works and Foundry did iron castings and advertised "castings in foundry every second day." Among numerous items Syfan made were cane mills, our particular point of interest. Thus far this researcher hasn't found any metal frame or three roller vertical mills, though Syfan did produce rollers for wooden frame mills. So Syfan Machine Works and Foundry, Waycross, Georgia, joins the numerous American foundries in producing cane mills for the syrup and sugar industry of our nation.

Thomas, Mast and Company, Springfield, Ohio

What was to become the largest manufacturer of agricultural implements in the United States, Thomas, Mast and Company, was founded in Springfield, Ohio, in 1856 by John H. Thomas and Phineas P. Mast. The sprawling plant, which lay on Warder Street east of Limestone, along Buck Creek, began with a humble product line of cider mills and grain drills. Thomas retired from the business in 1871 and the firm was incorporated as P.P. Mast and Company, with C.O. Gardiner, A.W. Butt, C.R. Crain, and W.C. Downey, all of whom were connected with the firm, brought into partnership. Their "Buckeye" line of implements now included seed drills, fertilizers, sowers, plow sulkies, cider mills, harrows and sorghum mills.

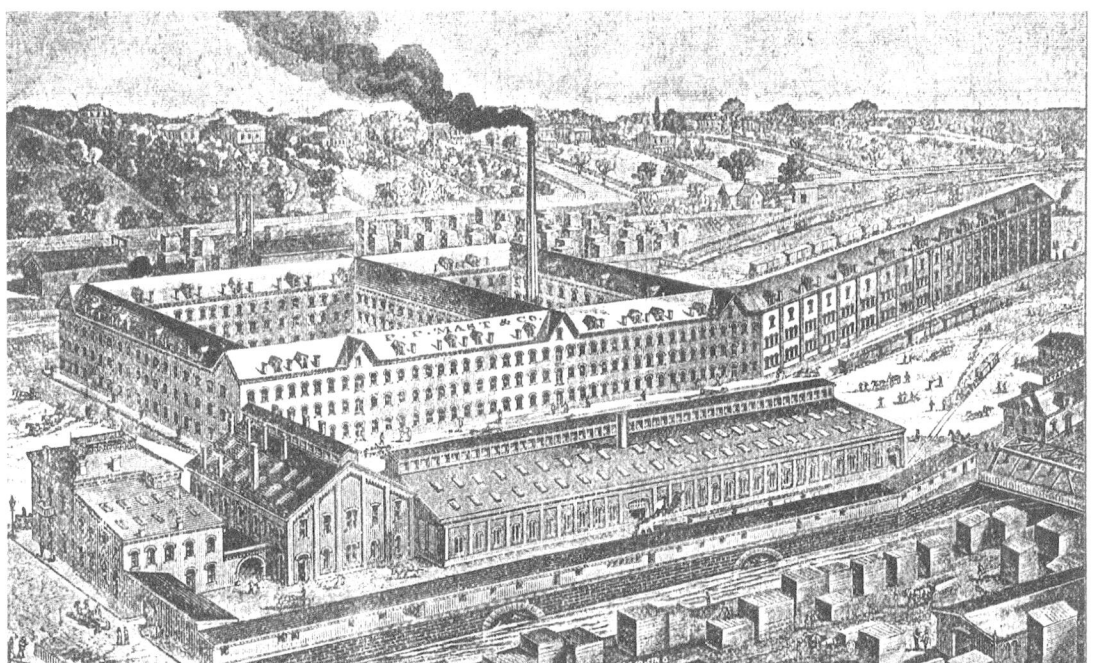

The Thomas, Mast and Company plant in Springfield, Ohio (courtesy Rockford Public Library, Rockford, Illinois).

In the mid 1880s the firm employed about 500 men, ran full steam the year around, and at peak seasons had to operate twenty-four hours a day. As the business grew the company had to continually add space and machinery to their facilities, as indicated in *History of Manufactories of Springfield, Ohio*, W.F. Austin, publisher. Branches were opened in St. Louis, Philadelphia, San Francisco, Kansas City, and St. Paul. Though the majority of their implements were sold in the United States, P.P. Mast and Company shipped their goods to Canada, Australia, Mexico, and South America. When Mr. Mast died in 1898 Charles R. Crain became president and served in that capacity until the firm was sold to the American Seeding Company in 1910. Thomas, Mast and Company manufactured two models of Buckeye sorghum mills, a horizontal roller No. 1 mill and a vertical roller No. 2 mill. The company advertised that these mills were constructed on the pattern of Southern sugar cane mills, but were manufactured expressly for the Northern Chinese cane. They claimed their mills were no longer an experiment but had been fully tested without a single report of a roller or shaft breaking though subjected to the power of four horses.

The Buckeye Sugar Mill No. 1 weighed 1,200 pounds and was built with three horizontal rollers which weighed 200 pounds each. The wrought iron shafts were 2½" in diameter and ran in "anti-friction" boxes. The mill was capable of grinding 100–125 gallons of juice per hour and was designed to be powered by horse, steam or waterpower, but not by a sweep. The Buckeye No. 1 cost $130 at the plant in 1860.

The Buckeye No. 1 was a horizontal roller mill (courtesy Rockford Public Library, Rockford, Illinois).

The Buckeye Sugar Mill No. 2 was a less expensive mill, with three vertical rollers powered by a sweep. The main roller was 15" in diameter and the two small rollers were 7½" in diameter with wrought iron shafts. This mill was capable of grinding 40–60 gallons of juice per hour, weighted 850 pounds, and cost $87.50 at the plant.

Thomasville Iron Works, Thomasville, Georgia

The Thomasville Iron Works, Thomasville, Georgia, was begun in 1871, and was the second oldest business in the city. C.B. Thompson and C.L. Thompson, both widely respected businessmen and citizens, served the company as president and vice president respectively. The ironworks carried on general machine shop work, had a foundry and blacksmith shop, and were agents for the Fairbanks-Morse gasoline engine, the Hoe saw, American steam pumps, the American Injector Co., the Ohio Injector Co., and the DeLoach Mill Manufacturing Company. The company was able to do light or heavy foundry, blacksmith, machine shop, and steelwork, and had extensive trade from Georgia, Florida and Alabama. They manufactured hydraulic wheel presses which they shipped as far north as Cincinnati and as far east as New York State. A large, well equipped machine shop faced S. Stevens Street, while the iron foundry with its cupola and core oven faced S. Lee Street near the heart of Thomasville. A separate pattern shop and pattern shed were also on the ironworks complex. The company manufactured large quantities of "White Way" lampposts, which were shipped

This Thomasville mill was produced by the Thomasville, Georgia, plant (photograph by Tommy Clayton, Hilliard, Florida).

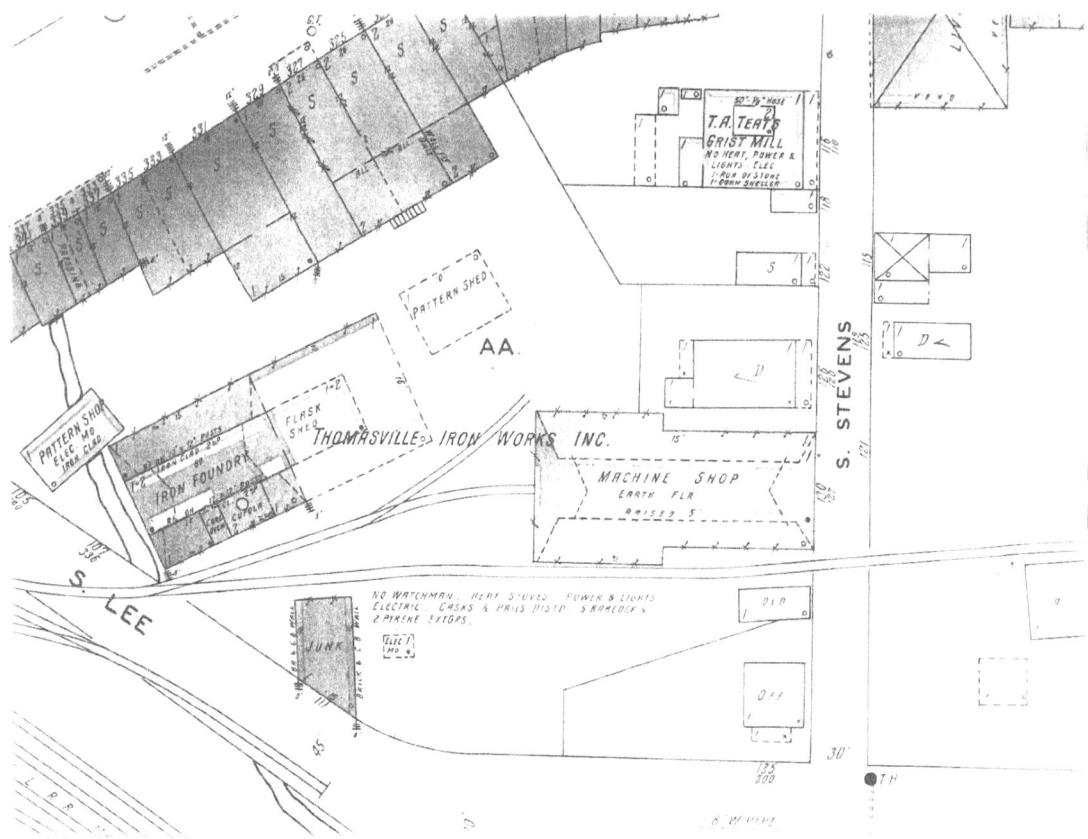

The industrial plat for the Thompson Foundry and Machine Co. (courtesy of Thomasville Genealogical, History and Fine Arts Library, Thomasville, Georgia).

to cities and towns all across Florida. In fact, the difficulties in collecting for these lampposts finally led to bankruptcy and the demise of the company, according to *Thomasville, Georgia Up-to-Date, 1926*.

The Thomasville Iron Works manufactured cane mills in two and three roller models. They offered the two roller mills in an "iron frame if preferred."

Thompson Foundry and Machine Company, Thomasville, Georgia

The Thompson family had been instrumental in the formation of the Thomasville Iron Works, which was also called "Thompson's Foundry" locally. At some point, apparently in the mid 1940s, the name became Thompson Foundry and Machine Company, with Cicero L. Thompson, serving as president, Cicero L. Thompson, Jr., vice president, and Mrs. B. Mabel Thompson secretary and treasurer. The company continued its ironworks industry with changes demanded by a changing market.

While some companies discontinued the manufacture of their cane mills, Thompson Foundry and Machine Co. continued their line into the 1940s. One of their large horizontal power mills is shown on the facing page. The Thompsons were civic minded persons and built an opera house in the city.

This huge mill was made by the Thompson Foundry and Machine Company.

Tredegar Iron Works, Richmond, Virginia

One of the largest and most extensive iron works in the South was the Tredegar Iron Works of Richmond, Virginia. The massive enterprise had its beginning in 1837 when its founder, Frank B. Deane, Jr., established an ironworks in the city. Deane named his ironworks Tredegar Iron Company as an honor to his engineer and superintendent, Rhys Daviers, who received his training at the Welsh ironworks of the same name. In 1838 Tredegar merged with an adjoining foundry, the Virginia Foundry Company, to establish the Tredegar Iron Works. The company produced railroad spikes, car wheels, rail-connecting plates and numerous other railroad related products. Joseph Reid Anderson, a West Point graduate, became the company's agent in 1841. Anderson, a trained engineer, was young and ambitious, and was willing to venture. He first leased the company, then purchased it in 1848 and began what was to become a three-generation Anderson name association which lasted for more than one hundred years.

Anderson stressed Southern manufacturing and promoted his company and encouraged others all over the South. His company built forty-one locomotives on his five acre site between 1850 and 1855, and most of those were for Southern rail systems. In the 1850s he built engines and boilers for two navy frigates. Business was expanding to the degree that he had to build a new locomotive shop in 1852. The Tredegar Iron Works actually existed as a series of separate companies and partnerships operating on the same physical site. In 1863, a massive fire reduced the facilities to a pile of ashes. All the machinery was ruined, workmen lost their tools, and sixteen new cannons finished for new gunboats were ruined. However, by July 1863, the foundry had been rebuilt and was at full blast.

The postwar recovery of the company was remarkable, as seen in Wright's work, *Richmond Since the War*. The ironworks reorganized in 1867 with a capital of one million dollars.

A bridge was built across the river with three-rail tracks to allow for both narrow and wide gauge locomotives, with connections running southward and also joining the northern system on the Richmond side of the river. During this time Tredegar had the capacity to work 2,500 hands and had an unlimited supply of water power, which resulted in a production capacity more than double that before the war. The company manufactured over 2,000 freight cars annually and its car-wheels were in wide demand. Tredegar received orders from all the principal railroads in America, from Canada, Cuba, Peru, Brazil, and other parts of South America.

The Tredegar Iron Works began making sugar mills in the 1840s, manufacturing and equipping numerous mills and engines in Louisiana. This thrust continued into the 1850s, when Anderson opened an agency in New Orleans to further expand his sugar and lumber mill business. Joseph R. Anderson loved Richmond, loved the Southland, and promoted it at every opportunity. While he did have periodic difficulties in race relations and labor disputes, he was a public minded individual who was elected to the Richmond city council in 1847 and to the state legislature in 1852. He won reelection in 1853.

John Turl's Sons, Inc., Newburgh, New York

John Turl's Sons, Inc., was founded in Newburgh in 1845 but it was not until 1902 that the company incorporated, with facilities at Washington and S. Water streets. In 1914 the company moved to larger facilities on River Road in New Windsor and employed about one hundred workers. The name was changed to Turl Iron and Car Company in 1925 and they continued to manufacture sugar cane mills and cars for industrial plants. Turl's Sons also maintained a New York City facility at 26 Courtland Street. The company name does not appear in the *Newburgh city directory* after 1954.

P.H. Turner and Company, Madison, Wisconsin

P.H. Turner bought Brown's Foundry in Madison, Wisconsin, which was subsequently sold to E.W. Skinner. According to the minutes of the 1866 Wisconsin Sorghum State Convention, a Mr. Turner (first name unknown) exhibited his Improved Buckeye Cane Mill. This could have been Mr. P.H. Turner, who operated a foundry, or perhaps Don Carlos Turner, who, on March 14, 1865, received Patent No. 46,835 for a cane crushing mill. The uniqueness of his mill lay in yokes suspended by stirrups from the axis of the upper roller, supporting the lower journals in such a way that when one lower roller expanded or opened to receive the cane, the other contracted or shut in a way so as to produce the greatest amount of pressure. Other than these meager facts no other references to Turner's work have been found by the author.

United States and Cuban Allied Works Engineering Corporation, South Bradford, Pennsylvania

The United States and Cuban Allied Works Engineering Corporation had its beginning in the Blaisdell Machinery Company, which was founded in South Bradford in 1903

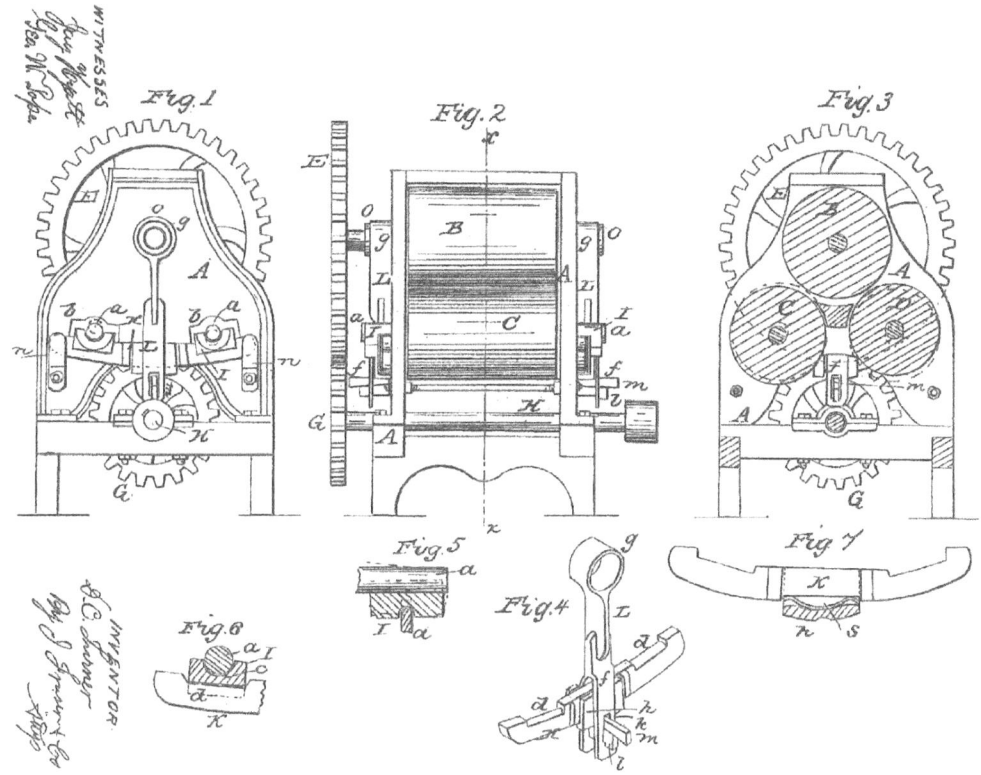

The uniqueness of Turner's patent lay in the stirrups supporting the lower rollers.

by Philo Blaisdell. This company became a noted manufacturer of steam, gas, and belt-driven compressors and vacuum pumps, and an interesting account is given in "Pictures from the Past," published in *Gas Engine* magazine. While its earlier machinery was used in oil fields and industrial applications, in 1918 the company was renamed the United States and Cuban Allied Works Engineering Corporation, with general offices in New York, and began production of the "Krajewski" sugar cane mills. (Please see the section on "Krajewski" for a more detailed account of this type mill.) In the early 1920s Hanley Ceramics bought the plant and manufactured brick making equipment. Later, Georgia-Pacific purchased the plant and began producing corrugated containers. A note of passing interest: Philo Blaisdell's son, George Blaisdell, was the inventor of the famous Zippo lighter.

Unknown Manufacturers

From time to time one comes across a mill which is simply different. There are contract mills made for local hardware stores or chains which are missing name plates, but these are usually recognizable by their design. The mills now referred to as unknown are mills whose designs are different and they bear no stampings, no nameplates and no parts numbers. Some earlier mills made by manufacturers in different cities are simply identical, except for different names stamped into the sides or tops of the mills. However, these unknown mills give us no clue to their identity. Yet, they are interesting and significant. If they could they would tell us their story. Someone who reads this and views these photographs perhaps can tell us the rest of their stories.

Above: An unknown mill under a shed near Bonifay, Florida. *Below:* This unknown mill near Ozark, Alabama, has no visible markings.

Above: This unknown mill near Dothan, Alabama, has no recognizable identification. *Below:* A wooden roller by an unknown maker (photograph by Tommy Clayton, Hilliard, Florida).

Above: An unidentifiable mill at a produce stand in Dothan, Alabama. *Below:* A "Tester" mill in Hilliard, Florida, by an unknown maker (photograph by Tommy Clayton, Hilliard Florida).

Above: An unidentifiable large two roller mill (photograph by Tommy Clayton, Hilliard, Florida). *Below left:* An unidentifiable mill beside the road (photograph by Bill Outlaw, Tallahassee, Florida). *Right:* Other than S.H. Co., St. Louis, nothing else is known of this mill (photograph by Butch Tindell, Elm Mott, Texas).

An unidentifiable mill originally from Kansas, (photograph by Rollin and Judy Nelson, Freeport, Illinois).

Utter Manufacturing Company, Rockford, Illinois

Isaac Utter was born January 17, 1809, in Eaton, New York, where he was raised and distinguished himself as a successful mechanic. Some of his fascinating story is related in *Portrait and Biographical Record of Winnebago and Boone Counties, Illinois*. After having built and operated a woolen mill in Warsaw, New York, he sold his business there and emigrated to Rockford, Illinois, in 1852, where he entered into a partnership with Orlando Clarke in a foundry and machine shop. Clarke had he established his business in Rockford in 1847, and now with his new partner established Clark and Utter, manufacturers of steam engines, machinery for flour mills and sawmills, and farm implements.

Upon Clarke's retirement in 1876, Utter bought his interests and the name was changed to Utter Manufacturing Company. Though he continued to manufacture farm implements, Mr. Utter was a supporter and encourager of the business community of Rockford and held numerous other business interests. He, Levi Rhodes, and his son, Charles M. Utter, built the Rockford Paper Company, of which he was a part for many years. A man of great determination and energy, Utter was a stockholder in the People's Bank and the Winnebago National Bank, and was a director and stockholder in the Second National Bank. He was also one of the original stockholders in a watch factory, a tack factory, and a silver-plate works. An industrious mechanical genius, Utter invented a number of implements relative to his factories, but never attempted to patent them. He, apparently, was a man of principle and integrity as well. Levi Rhodes, Utter's partner in the paper mill for almost a quarter

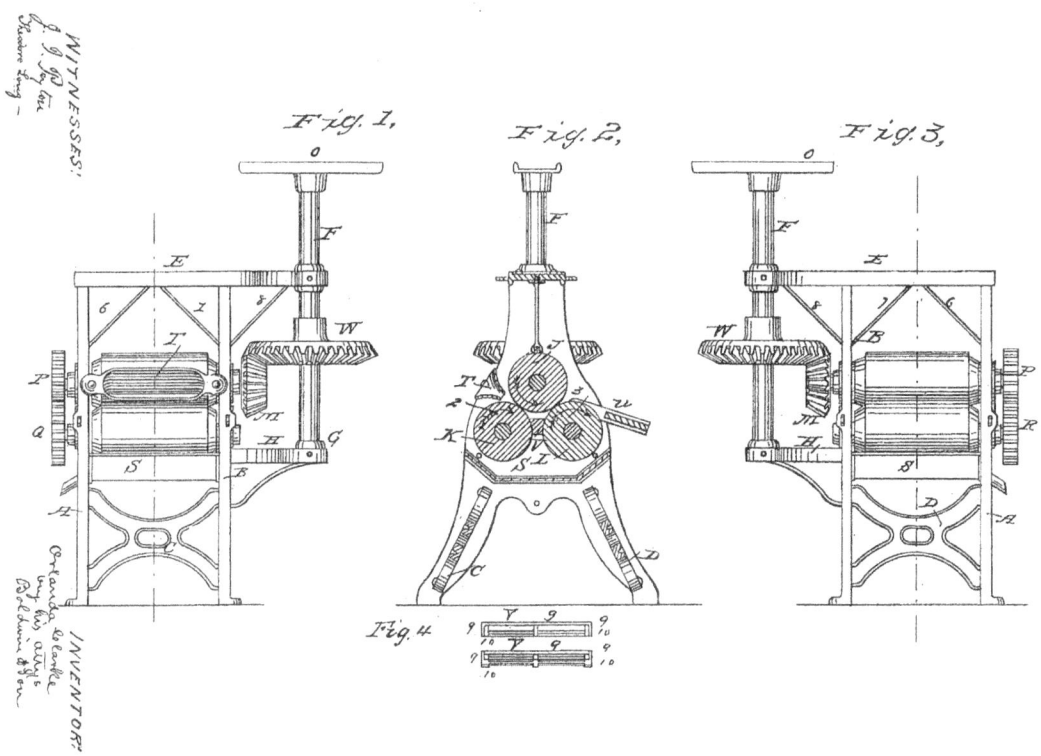

Utter's patent was designed to prevent the rollers from being clogged.

century, said of him, "He was a good man, upright and sincere. I could not ask [for] a better partner. For twenty-three years we were associated in the paper mill and in all that time there was never a word of difference or misunderstanding or any antagonism as to the plans and details of the business."

In 1876, the Utter Manufacturing Company advertised that they manufactured agricultural implements, including broadcast seeders; riding cultivators; flouring, grist, and sorgo machines; well drilling machinery; waterwheels; mill irons and general agricultural machinery. On January 29, 1867, a patent was granted to Rhodes, Orlando Clarke, assignor to himself and Isaac Utter, for a cane mill designed so as to prevent the rollers from clogging and juice from being wasted. The mill, secured by Patent No. 61,516, was a three horizontal roller animal powered mill. The top roller was stationary but the lower rollers were adjustable, and all were set in a metal frame. The Utter Manufacturing Company was the predecessor company of the Rockford Iron Works which occupied the foundry around 1900.

Valdosta Foundry and Machine Company, Valdosta, Georgia

Ed L. Thomas was an industrious businessman of Valdosta, Georgia, with interests in hardware, lumber, and ironworks. In January 1892, he was brought into the Thomas

Hardware Company, along with W.L. Thomas and W.C. Thomas as general partners. He was a partner in the Valdosta Lumber Company, but withdrew from the firm on July 26, 1897, presumably to concentrate on the foundry and machine shop business. By 1904 Mr. Thomas was proprietor of the Valdosta Foundry and Machine Company, operating out of the rear of a building at 619 West Savannah Avenue, Valdosta. The history of the company prior to 1904 is incomplete, but by 1908, Thomas had moved his business to 621 West Savannah Avenue , in its own building. Thomas was a devoted man, a man of integrity and faith, and was one of the founding members of the Tabernacle Baptist Church, later to be known as Lee Street Baptist Church. Some of the Thomas history may be read in "Way Back When" by Albert Pendleton.

In June 1911, Thomas began selling his equipment and inventory. On June 19, 1911, he sold a boiler, steam engine, gins, press, all shafting, pulleys, boxes, collars, couplings, and bolts to M.C. Cawthon, A.V. Knight and J.A. Studstill. He closed his foundry in Valdosta in 1913, and moved to Birmingham, Alabama, where he established the Thomas Foundries, later known as the Thomas Grate Bar Co. This business was to make Mr. Thomas a wealthy man.

A 1904 Valdosta Foundry and Machine Company advertisement in the *Quitman Free Press,* Quitman, Georgia, advertised engines, boilers, sawmills, columns, sills, lintels, ventilators, and all kinds of castings. "Our prices will sell you," was their motto. Advertisements in the local paper listed new and used equipment. Their cane mills can be seen with an "FM Co. Valdosta, GA" stamping.

Valdosta Manufacturing Company, Valdosta, Georgia

Another Valdosta, Georgia, foundry manufacturing cane mills was the Valdosta Machinery Company, with city directory listings at both 800 and 801 River Street. At some point, either before or after the life of the Valdosta Manufacturing Company, the property was

Valdosta Machinery Co. mills were similar to others made in south Georgia.

known as the Southern Foundry Company. About all the history located of this company is in the Valdosta city directory, 1913–1914, where the company is listed with J.F. Lewis, president; R.D. Stevens, secretary and treasurer; and D.A. Finley, general manager. By the summer of 1920 the property had changed owners. Cane mills manufactured by this Valdosta company are stamped VMC.

Washington Iron Works, Newburgh, New York

The Washington Iron Works, Newburgh, New York, really came into prominence in the mid to late 1850s when this recommendation concerning their steam engines appeared in the December 17, 1859, *Scientific American,* stating, "It is an excellent combination of known devices, for the production of a compact, efficient and cheap PORTABLE ENGINE." Founded under the auspices of Mailer, Rains and Company, the Washington Iron Works was located at the junction of Water and Washington streets in south Newburgh. The foundry occupied 235 feet on the Hudson River and along both sides of Water Street. The main building was located on the west side and the company rented buildings along the east side for various production purposes. It maintained a large dock into the river from the eastern portion of the complex, and the Erie Railroad passed directly by the ironworks. Therefore, the company could avail itself to either rail or water transportation for its raw materials and finished goods. The south portion of the main building contained the foundry. While it used both Scottish and American iron in its castings, the Washington Iron Works advertised its boilers as made with the "best American iron." As was characteristic for the day, castings were done in "green sand."

Adjacent to the foundry was the blacksmith shop where their wrought iron work was done. The expansive machine shop occupied the large part of two floors, and was capable of making anything from the largest steam engine to the smallest cider mill. One lathe in the machine shop was capable of turning a wheel fourteen feet in diameter. The wide range of products made and the excellency of workmanship brought numerous orders from the Southern states. The foundry prided itself in "filling all orders on short notice."

In 1866, the Washington Iron Works began making engines for the famous engineer and creative genius, William Wright. During the Civil War the ironworks employed a thousand men to help in the war cause. However, its prosperity did not continue, and in March 1870, the Washington Iron Works went bankrupt. J. Bigler and Company completed the contracts for the company. William Wright then rented the buildings and began production himself. Unfortunately, the buildings burned in the winter of 1870, destroying Alexander Cauldwell's Boiler Shop as well.

Rebuilding, Wright and his partners, J. Wilson Stratton and John A. McNulty, produced the Corliss engine with Wright's patented cutoff. This company employed around two hundred men for years, paying good wages in their time of prosperity. McNulty withdrew from the company and Stratton died, leaving Wright as the sole owner. Now this famous mechanic determined to fulfill a life-long dream—to build a model machine shop. Against the advice of friends and fellow business acquaintances, William Wright built his model machine shop when he was almost eighty years old. His dream was short lived. In the crash of 1893 Wright lost everything, including his house on Grand Avenue. He lived his final days in the New York City area and died at almost ninety without leaving a dollar.

During the height of its productivity, the Washington Iron Works made portable engines, from three to thirty-five horsepower, marine and stationary steam engines and boilers, propellers and propeller engines, gristmills, sawmills, bark mills, brick machinery, steam

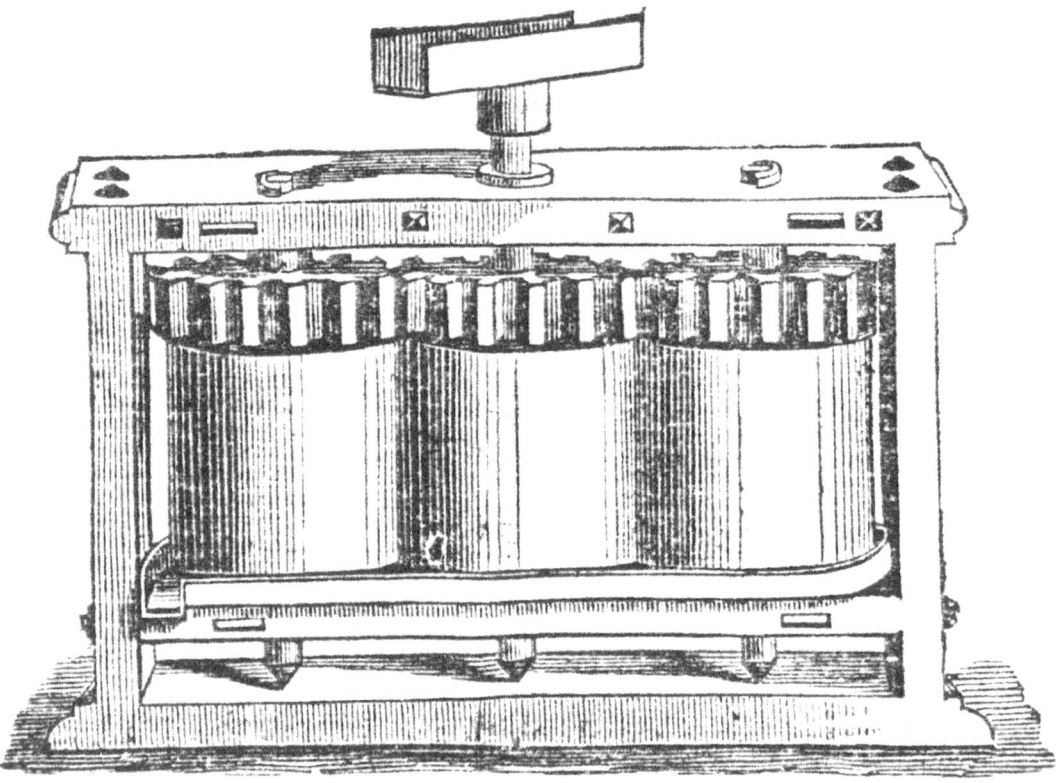

Washington Iron Works' mill had rollers in a straight line.

gauges, water indicators, fire regulators, wrought- and cast-iron pipe, shafting, hangers, and pulleys, iron and brass castings, wrought- and cast- iron railing for fences and verandas, cane mills and sugar pans. An early brochure from the company advertised vertical mills in two and three-roller styles in two sizes.

Vertical Roller Mills

This engraving represents a vertical three-roller mill, but two and three-roller mills with iron frames were also available. This model had a cast-iron pan to catch the juice so that it did not come in contact with the wood.

Chart for Washington Iron Work's Three-Roller Vertical Cane Mills

No. Of Rollers	Roller Size-D × L	Frame Type	Price
Vertical 2	15" × 12"	Wood	$90.00
Vertical 2	15" × 12"	Iron	$100.00
Vertical 3	15" × 16"	Wood	$125.00
Vertical 3	15" × 16"	Iron	$150.00

Horizontal Roller Cane Mills

The Washington Iron Works manufactured a series of three-roller horizontal cane mills as well. These came set in a heavy iron frame with journals turning in brass boxes. The rollers could be adjusted by set screws to give the pressure needed for various size cane.

Washington manufactured its horizontal mills in four sizes.

Chart for Washington Iron Work's Horizontal Cane Mills

Roller Size-D × L	Price
10" × 18"	$250.00
15" × 18"	$440.00
16" × 26½"	$700.00
8" × 20"	$840.00

These mills were configured for animal power. Most small units were kept on hand and large units were made to order in any size desired. In addition, the foundry produced sugar pans, ranging in size from thirty to one hundred fifty gallons, both deep and shallow patterns and ranging in price from $7 to $37.50. The Washington Iron Works, Newburgh, New York, joined numerous other foundries in its significant contribution to the early American sugar and syrup industry.

H. Wells and Brothers, Harpers Ferry, Virginia

While circular sawmills seem to have been H. Wells and Brothers' main products, they did manufacture sorghum mills. Hiram Wells received a United States patent for automatic sawmill blocks on June 9, 1857.

West Point Foundry and Iron Works, Cold Spring, New York

The West Point Foundry and Iron Works manufactured heavy castings and forgings of all kind from gun-iron of guaranteed strength of 30,000 pounds per square inch. Established

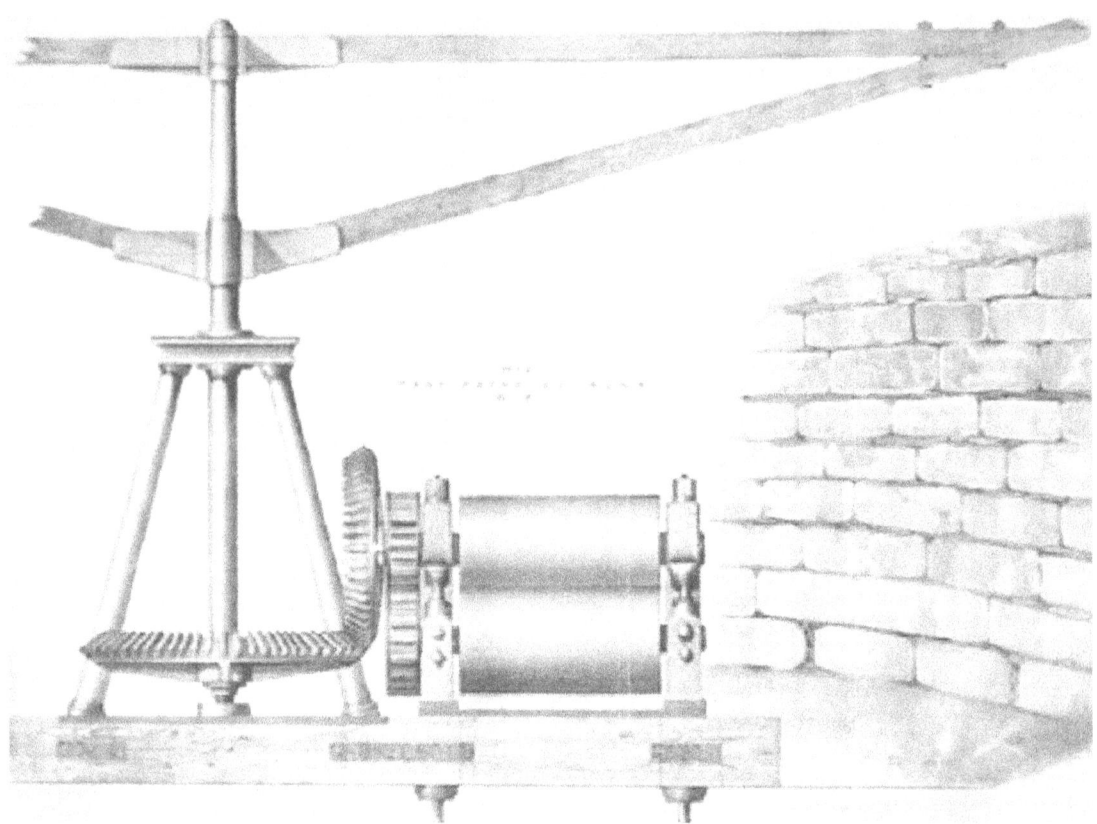

A West Point cane mill engraving found in its gallery (courtesy Putnam County Historical Society & Foundry School Museum, Cold Spring, New York).

as an association in 1817 by Gouverneur Kemble and others, the foundry was located at Cold Spring, New York, but named West Point after a larger town across the river. The foundry was originally designed for casting and boring cannon for the United States Army and Navy. In 1851 R.P. Parrott leased the shares of Kemble and the other stockholders. By 1869 the foundry was leased by Pauling, Kenble and Company, 30 Broad Street, New York City, and manufactured marine and stationary engines; Cornish and other pumping engines; flour mills; cattle mills; clarifiers and tanks; sawmills; engines for blast furnaces; presses for cotton, oil and paper; boilers; rifled cannon; wrought iron bridges; wrought iron freight cars; water and gas pipes; shot and shells; iron piers for bridges; waterwheels; cane mills and kettles. The foundry did steamboat repair at the foundry as well.

West Point Foundry and Iron Works became known for its "Rifled Cannon," which became the main armament of the army and navy during the Civil War. Known as "Parrott Guns," they were used successfully against Fort Macon and Fort Pulaski, at the shelling of Fort Sumter from Morris Island and upon the city of Charleston. Early on, when orders for military cannons could not sustain a constant workforce, the foundry turned to the manufacture of steam engines, boilers, and general heavy castings. The foundry produced the engines for the United States' naval steamers *Missouri* and *Merrimac*. The company also built the first locomotive manufactured in America for actual service on a railroad. This was the Best Friend of Charleston. Then they built the second locomotive used in rail service, the West Point, purchased by the South Carolina Canal and Railroad Company in 1831.

Above: This is a West Point beam steam engine engraving (courtesy Putnam County Historical Society & Foundry School Museum, Cold Spring, New York). *Below:* A West Point steam powered mill (courtesy American Society of Mechanical Engineers).

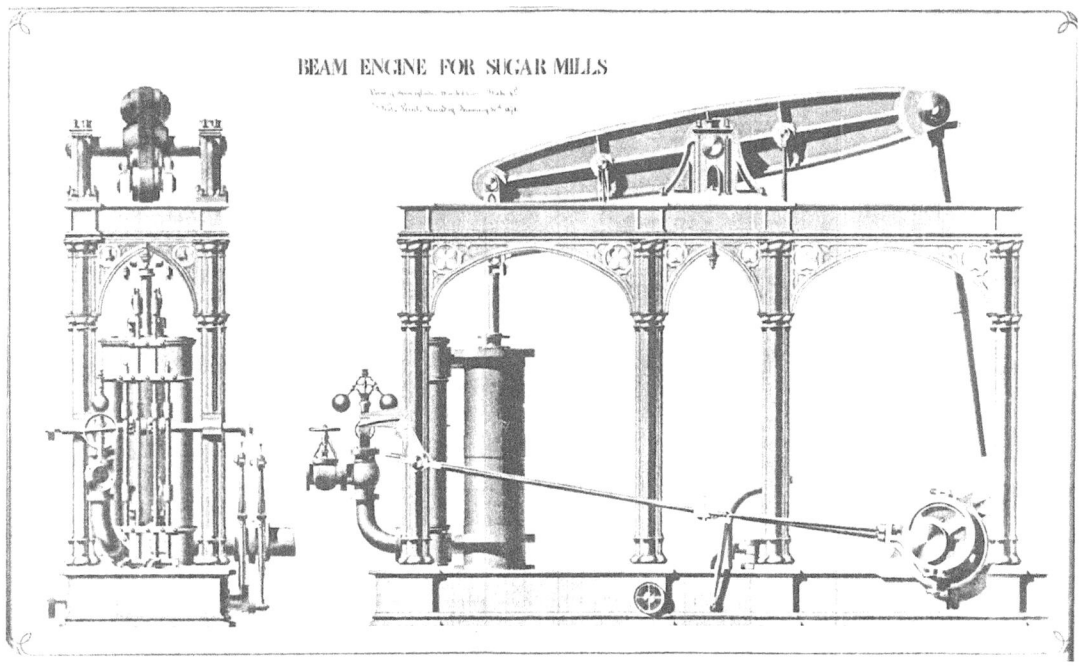

A view of a West Point mill and steam engine in Puerto Rico (courtesy American Society of Mechanical Engineers).

Through the years the company manufactured marine and stationary engines for a variety of applications. The West Point Foundry manufactured cane mills and kettles, and their mills have been found in sugar producing countries. A beautiful illustration of an animal powered mill is on display at their gallery in Cold Spring, New York. The American Society of Mechanical Engineers has been excavating a large steam powered mill at Hacienda La Esperanza, a National Historic Mechanical Engineers' Landmark at Manati, Puerto Rico. You can visit their web site at http://Files.ASME.org/ASMEORG/Communities/history/landmarks/5563.pdf. Excavations are also underway at the foundry's remains at Cold Spring. The Michigan Technological University Industrial Archaeology faculty has been leading work teams at the old site since 2001. You can visit their web site at www.westpointfoundry.org/researchnotes.html.

S.R. White and Brothers, Norfolk, Virginia

Seth March operated an agricultural warehouse in Norfolk as early as 1866. He died in 1870 at the young age of 58. Silas R. White is listed as the proprietor of S. March and Co., manufacturer of agricultural implements, iron and carriage materials, in a 1874–75 city directory. In the intervening years S. Rodney and Lewis B. White join Silas R. in the business, and by 1880 the company became S.R. White and Brothers. In 1888 steam engines were added to their product list.

According to the *Farm Implement News Buyer's Guide*, S.R. White and Brothers had a long list of agricultural implements, including D Arrow, Daisy, and I.A. Special cultivators; "I.A." Special and Little Joe fourteen-tooth harrows; Boy D Arrow, Carolina, D Arrow, Dixie Pattern, White's D Arrow, Farmer's Friend, White's Carolina, White's Chilled, White's Clipper, and White's Stonewall walking plows; Farmer's Friend walking plows for hillsides; Buckeye, Favorite, Valley Chief, White's Buckeye, White's Favorite one-hole hand corn shellers; Defender and White's Defender two-hole hand or power corn shellers; Eclipse one row cotton planters; Centennial, Eureka, Ives and Sinclair one row corn planters; peanut planters; rice and pea planters; Excelsior, Favorite, Valley Chief, White's Excelsior, and White's Favorite cider mills; wine presses; Defender cylinder feed cutters; Smith's Patent lever feed cutters; plow stocks; syrup evaporators and cane mills.

S.R. White died in 1896. Lewis B., Alpheus R., Arthur M., and William E. White, perhaps the brothers along with some of S.R.'s sons, continued the business. In 1911 the company became S.R. White's Sons. For the next forty years the company produced agricultural implements but finally closed its doors to business in 1950.

Whiting Iron Works, New Orleans, Louisiana

The Whiting Iron Works were manufacturers of sugar cane mills for the growing Louisiana sugar industry. No further details have been discovered by this author.

Whitney Iron Works, New Orleans, Louisiana

The Whitney Iron Works, 181 Tchoupitoulas Street in New Orleans, was founded May 18, 1883, by an incorporated company of capitalists that included George Pandely, Newell Tilton, C.M. Whitney, and George I. Whitney. They purchased Charles G. Johnson's New Orleans Foundry and Machine Works, a spacious facility covering virtually an entire block bounded by Tchoupitoulas, Constance, St. Joseph and Julia streets. The ironworks were conveniently arranged to include a machine shop, blacksmith shop, pattern shop, boiler shop, molding shop and a drafting room. Improvements were made and the new company set itself to produce sugar making machinery, plantation machinery and railroad work. The company became well known, employed only competent, skilled workers, and guaranteed its work as first class. One of the innovative products the company manufactured was a filtering press and washer to filter more juice from the cane. They claimed they could increase juice production by seven percent by using the washer and filter. Whitney also manufactured some of the largest cane mills ever ordered in that day, and claimed they gave better extraction than any in the country; they were featured in an article in the *Times Democrat* in New Orleans on March 5, 1893.

Other products manufactured by the one hundred fifty employees included steam boilers, steamboat machinery, steam fittings, gas fittings, boiler tubes, rubber belting, rubber hose, hose nozzles, hose couplings, valves, water gauges, pipe cutters, portable railroads, oil pumps, hoisting engines, cotton presses and sawmills.

Daniel Wilde Foundry, Washington, Iowa

Daniel Wilde, who operated a foundry in Washington, Iowa, brought the first portable steam engine into Washington County in December, 1876. He intended to use it for threshing, but it turned out to be quite a sight to behold. Scores of people turned out to see this

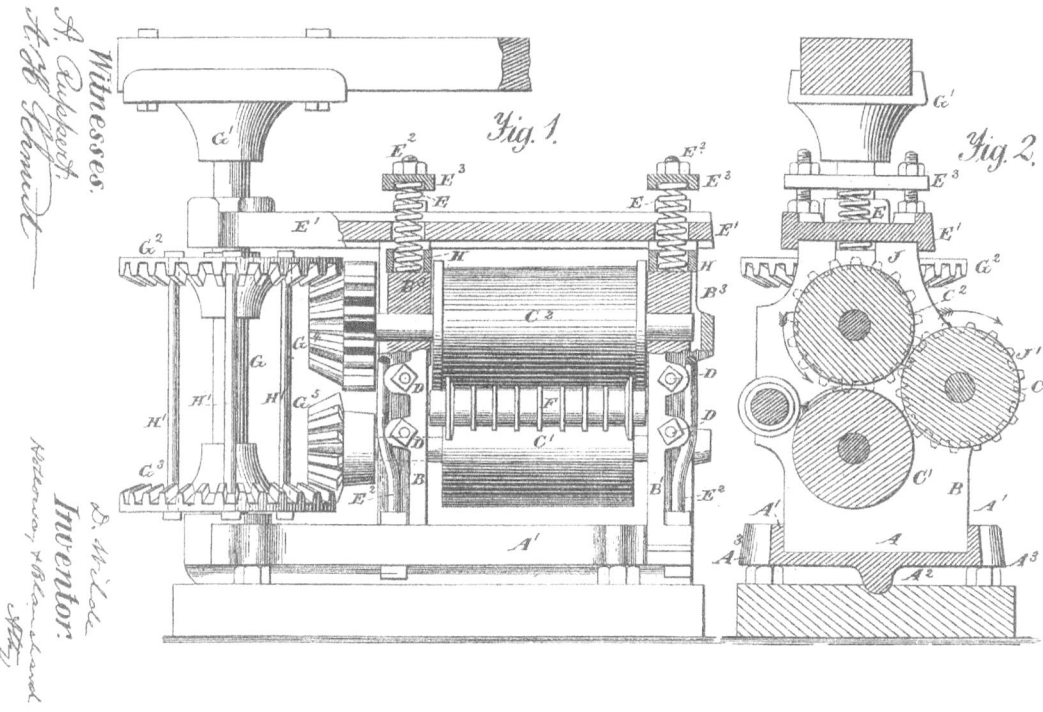

Above: Daniel Wilde's patent featured two horizontal crushing rollers, one set directly above the other. *Below:* The uniqueness of this mill is in the rollers running in corresponding channels.

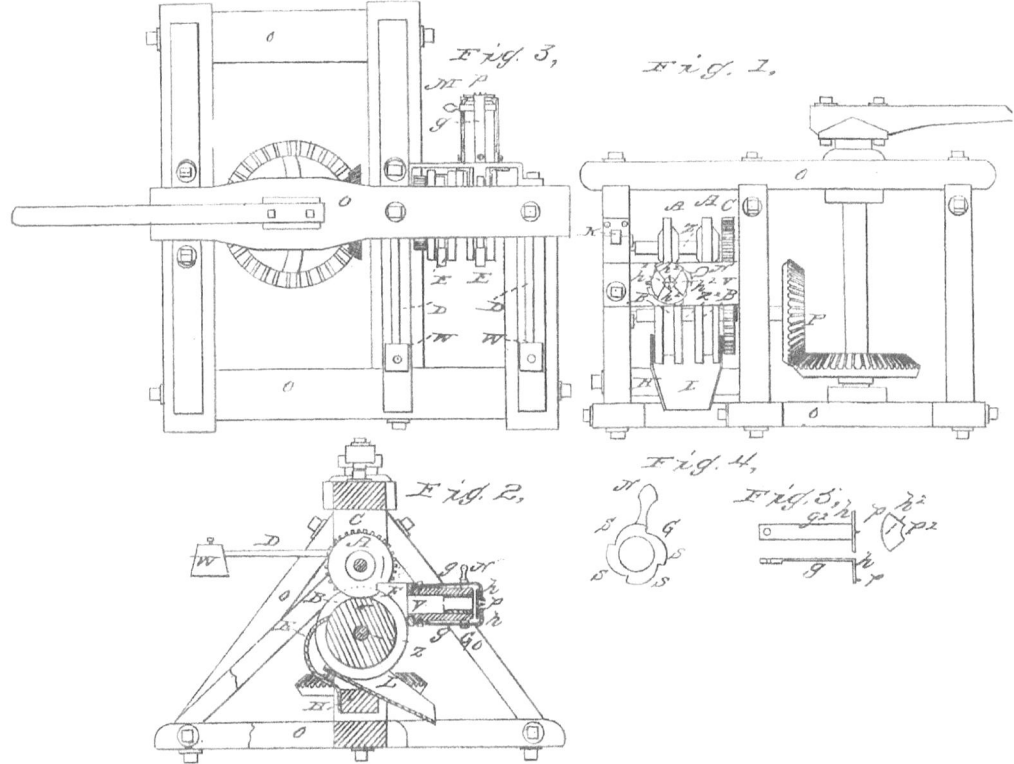

"street locomotive" lumber through town, steaming up and down hills with ease at approximately "3¼ to 4 miles per hour." This was a difficult period for our nation, and for Washington County it was no different. A county "poor house and farm" was voted in by the citizens, and, while this provided some relief for the wards of the county, there was a segment of society for whom extreme measures seemed to be required. In November 1877, Daniel Wilde and his foundry were hired to build some iron cells for several "incurable insane" residents. Wilde's heart was in the life of his town. After two fires within weeks of each other struck Washington, residents voted in some city councilmen who were ready for change. These councilmen appointed a special committee on April 2, 1883, including Wilde, to study the water supply and fire apparatus needs of the town. Within a few months they made their report and it was adopted by the city. A water reservoir was dug and firefighting equipment was purchased.

Daniel Wilde also applied himself to improving the cane mill. With the widespread propagation of Chinese cane, or sorghum, numerous sugar mills were established across America. On March 21, 1882, Wilde was awarded Patent No. 255,228 for a cane mill with certain improvements. His mill featured two horizontal crushing rollers, one set directly over the other and driven directly by a vertical turning shaft. The discharge roller was so designed that it would give upward movement to the bagasse, causing the juice to flow downward into a reservoir. A roller, or drum, was set between the crushing rollers and discharge roller to act as a turn plate. The vertical rise and fall of the upper crushing roller was regulated by sets of coil springs. A top beveled gear on the turn shaft powered the upper crushing roller and a beveled gear on the lower shaft powered the lower crushing roller. The upper crushing roller was cogged and powered the discharge roller.

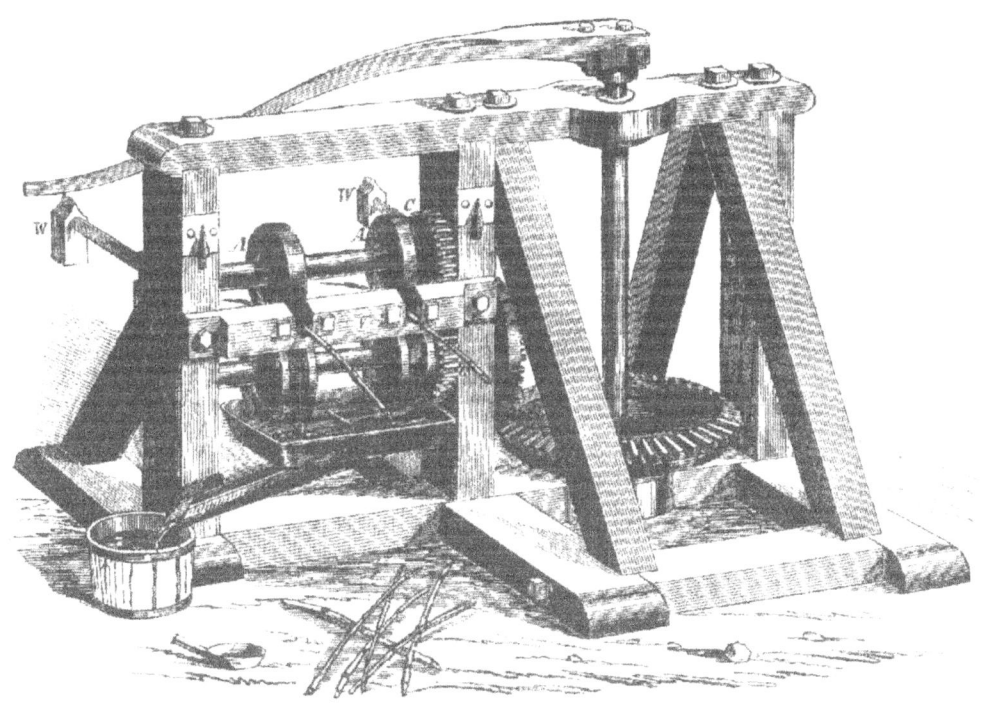

An engraving of Bassett's Challenger cane mill.

Winchester, DeWolf and Company, Whitewater, Wisconsin

Winchester, DeWolf and Company of Whitewater, Wisconsin, manufactured the Challenge Cane Crusher, based on the design of Daniel Bassett. Bassett received United States patent No. 24,922 on August 2, 1859, at the onset of the American sorghum industry. The uniqueness of the Bassett mill consisted of two tongued rollers mounted on a horizontal shaft set to run in corresponding circular channels on the rollers below. Equal-sized cog wheels were placed on each shaft, when meshing with each other insured simultaneous motion in opposite directions. The shaft of the upper rollers was set in boxes at either end, which allowed some vertical movement. Tension, or pressure, was applied by means of levers upon which weights were placed. Since the cane was confined to a small space and the pressure was localized, great velocity could be attained with safety. This unique mill was featured in *Scientific American* on September 24, 1859.

Winship and Brothers, Atlanta, Georgia

When Joseph Winship moved his family to Atlanta few could have imagined the impact the Winships would have on the religious, educational, economic, and industrial life of the growing community. This impact is told in such volumes as *Atlanta and Its Builders*, by Thomas H. Martin, and *The History of Georgia*, by Clark Howell. Joseph came from an old line of New England Puritan stock, and his wife, Emily, was the daughter of a distinguished Virginia family. Born in New Salem, Massachusetts, on August 29, 1800, Joseph received his early education and became an apprentice in the boot and shoe trade. Moving South with his employer, he located in Monticello, Georgia, where he worked for two years. Trying to further his career, Joseph went into merchandising, opened a business in Jones County, and later moved to Clinton, Georgia. With his brother, Isaac, he opened a boot and shoe business in Forsyth, Georgia, and established a factory and a tannery. He later sold his interest in the business to his brother and returned to merchandising in Clinton. In 1845 he gave up this business and opened a cotton gin factory in Morgan County, Georgia. The next big transition in Joseph's career came in 1851 when he turned the cotton gin business over to his two sons-in-law and moved to Atlanta where he began manufacturing freight cars. This business, Winship Machine Works, so prospered that he saw the need to open an iron foundry in order to manufacture the needed castings and supplies rather than depend upon outside sources. His sons, Robert and George, operated the foundry. A fire destroyed the freight car factory in 1856 and the Winships, concentrating on the iron foundry business, decided not to rebuild. At this point Joseph brought his sons into partnership and the business became Joseph Winship and Sons. Upon Joseph's retirement in 1873 the business became Winship and Brother. The older son, Robert, was born in Forsyth, Georgia, on September 27, 1834. He received his education in the schools of Jones and Morgan counties, moved to Atlanta with his family, and became a partner with his father in business. During his active career, Robert conducted his business with such industry, integrity, and energy that he won the high esteem of the people of Atlanta. Because of failing health he retired from active involvement in the business in 1884. He died on September 9, 1899.

George, the younger son, was born in Clinton, Georgia, on December 20, 1835. He received his education at the academy in Clinton, and, like Robert, moved to Atlanta with his family. As a seventeen-year-old youth he entered the ironworks business of his father and became skilled in the machinists' trade. George also had great financial

Above: Winship's nameplate on one of their mills. *Below:* This Winship cane mill is similar to others of the area in that era.

ability and abundant energy. He was a director of two building and loan associations, a director of the Atlanta Home Insurance Company, a director of the Trust Company of Georgia, a director of the Merchants Bank of Atlanta, a director of the Atlanta Ice and Coal Company, and president of the Atlanta Banking and Savings Company. He also served as water commissioner of the City of Atlanta, and served in the Confederate army as a member of Cobb's Legion.

George was known for his "lofty Christian life." Bishop W.A. Candler, for whom the Candler School of Theology in Atlanta is named, wrote of George, "His moral characteristics are industry, punctuality, charity, modesty and serene faith." The deep religious piety of his parents took root in George's life and bore beautiful fruit. He was a trustee of Emory College for many years, and a trustee of the Georgia State School of Technology.

During the Civil War the company produced guns and supplies for the Southern troops, but those were hard times. The 1864 march of General Sherman through Atlanta left the company in ruins. The Winships had to resort to selling a prime piece of real estate to help finance rebuilding their company as a result of the war. However, the company did rebuild and was soon prosperous as Winship Brothers. In 1884 the company was incorporated as Winship Machine Company, with George serving as president and Robert as vice president. At that time they manufactured cotton gins, direct steam and screw cotton presses, engines, boilers, shafting, pulleys, gearing, sawmills, cane mills, fertilizer machinery, iron and brass

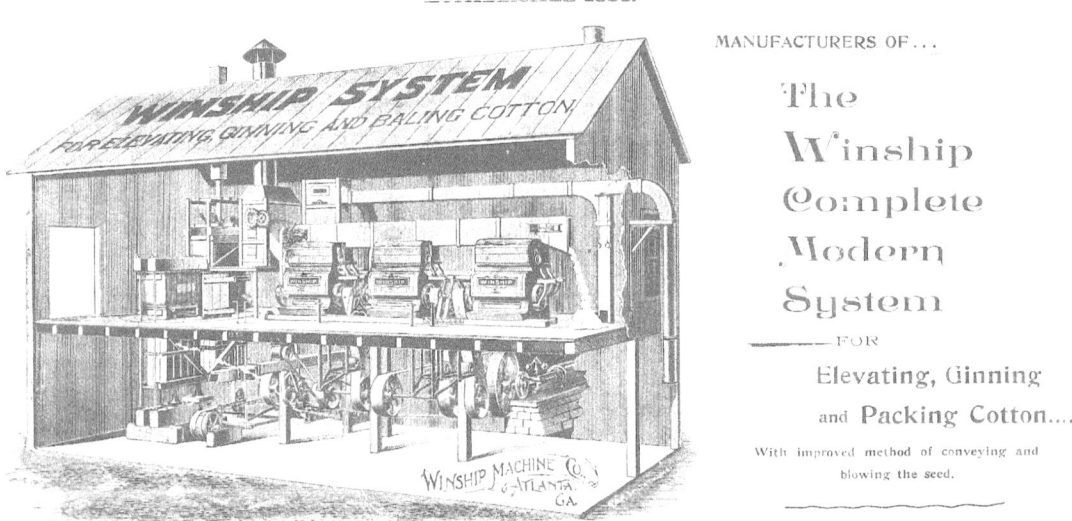

Though Winship made cane mills, cotton gins became the main product (from *A Commercial History of the State of Georgia*, edited by T. Edgar Harvey, published by The Georgia Division of the Travelers' Protective Association of America, 1897, page 59, image provided by the Special Collections Department of the Atlanta-Fulton Public Library).

castings. When Robert retired, his son, Charles Robert, succeeded him as vice president. By 1902 winship had discontinued most of its product line and was concentrating exclusively on the manufacture of cotton gins, becoming one of the largest iron plants in the Southern states. Charles succeeded his uncle, George, as president and served in that capacity until 1899, at which time the company merged with the Continental Gin Company. Two-roller vertical cane mills similar to the Morven and Quitman mill may be found across southern Georgia.

Wood and Mann Steam Engine Company, Utica, New York

The Wood and Mann Steam Engine Company of Utica, New York, with a branch at 96 Maiden Lane, New York City, claimed to have the oldest, largest and most complete works in the United States devoted exclusively to the manufacture of portable engines and sawmills. They manufactured the inclining celebrated Corliss patent variable cutoff steam engines from 4 to 500 horsepower. Wood and Mann also manufactured slide valve stationary engines, portable engines, circular Mulay and gang sawmills, wheat and corn mills, circular saws, pulleys and shafting, and sugar cane mills. From a series of advertisements in *Scientific American* it seems the company added cane mills to their product line in 1869.

O.E. Woodbury, Madison, Wisconsin

At the 1866 Wisconsin Sorghum State Convention, O.E. Woodbury exhibited his Adjustable Sugar Mill. No information has been found as to the foundry of which Woodbury was a part, but he received Patent No. 50, 978 on November 14, 1865, for his mill. A feature of his mill was the unique way a lower roller and upper roller were hinged to swing open. This novel approach would allow for easy lubrication, cleaning or scraping the main roller, and allow some yielding to the pressures of a heavy load.

Woodruff and Beach Iron Works, Hartford, Connecticut

The Woodruff and Beach Iron Works was in business in Hartford, Connecticut, as early as August 1855, manufacturing high and low pressure steam engines to order. Their

From 4 to 500 Horse-Power.
INCLUDING
The celebrated Corliss Cut-off Engines, Slide Valve Stationary Engines, Portable Engines, etc. Also, Circular, Mulay, and Gang Saw Mills, Sugar-Cane Mills, Shafting, Pulleys, Castings, etc.; Lath, Wheat, and Corn Mills, Circular Saws, Belting, etc.
SEND FOR DESCRIPTIVE CIRCULAR AND PRICE-LIST.
WOOD & MANN STEAM ENGINE COMPANY,
UTICA, NEW-YORK.
Warerooms, 42 Cortlandt Street, New-York. Aug. ly.

A Wood and Mann advertisment of its products, including cane mills.

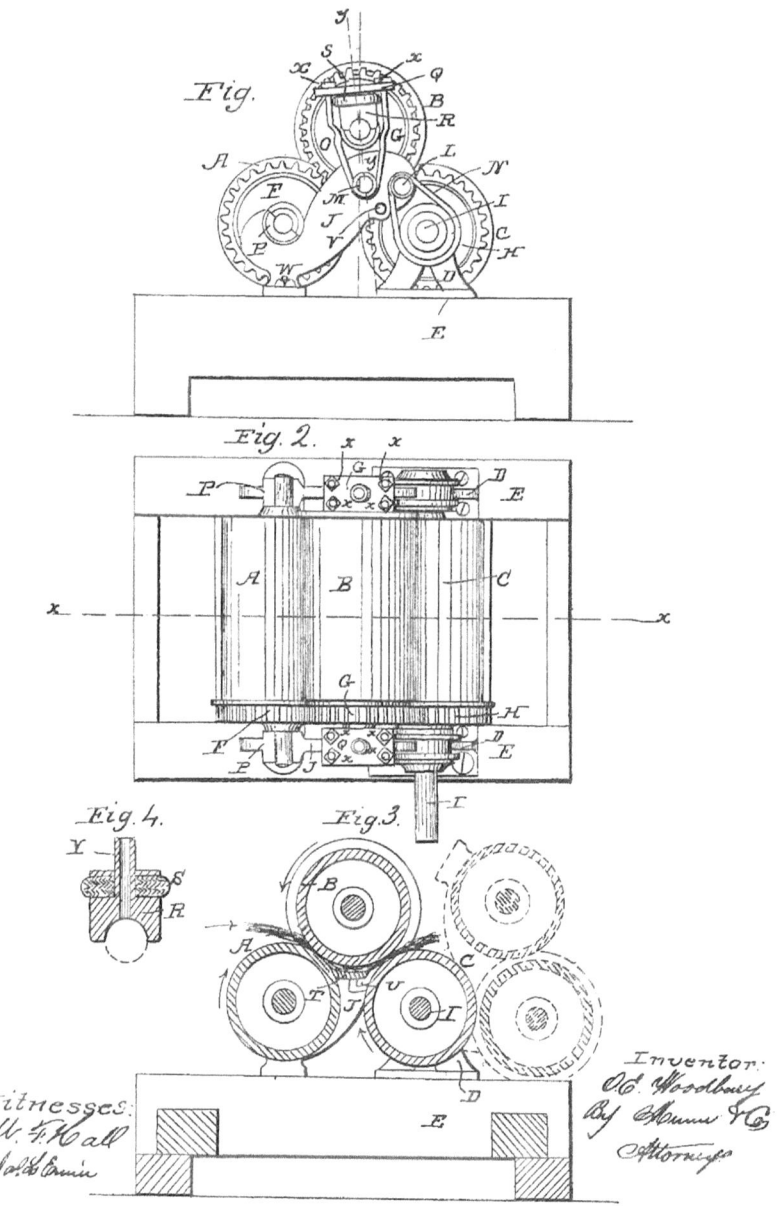

The upper and lower rollers were hinged to swing open on this mill.

product list at that time also included powder mills, paper mills, flouring mills, and sugar mills. They also did iron, brass, and composition castings to order. In 1863 their extensive complex was further enlarged to accommodate castings for some large governmental contracts. They built the engines and boilers for the celebrated *Kearsarge*, the gunboat *Nipsic*, and the *Piquot*. Two immense cranes capable of lifting and moving 40 to 50 tons were installed, and later another steam crane with a 75 ton capacity was erected. A cylinder for one of the frigate's engines required 13 tons of metal, which was melted and cast in April 1864. Each of the ships' engines weighed about 500 tons and required about two years to complete.

In 1874, the foundry and extensive collection of patterns of Woodruff and Beach were leased to the Hartford Foundry and Machine Company, which continued business as Woodruff Iron Works. The Woodruff and Beach Iron Works and the firm of Woodruff and Beach were dissolved.

Woodruff Iron Works, Hartford, Connecticut

The Woodruff Iron Works, 223 State Street, Hartford, Connecticut, consisted of a foundry and machine shop and held one of the largest stocks of patterns in New England. They manufactured steam engines of all sizes; boilers; pumping engines and pumps; feed pumps and safety valves; powder, paper, and flour mill machinery; cider mills; clothiers' screws; builders' screw jacks; hydraulic presses; Waters' patent heaters; water gates; fire hydrants; shafting; couplings; pulleys; and fly-wheels of all sizes. Woodruff manufactured sugar mills as well. In 1874, the foundry and machine shop of Woodruff and Beach Iron Works were leased to the Hartford Foundry and Machine Company, along with their large assortment of patterns, and the business continued as the Woodruff Iron Works according to *The Manufacturer and Builder*, March 1874. The Woodruff and Beach Iron Works and the firm of Woodruff and Beach were dissolved.

While the company made a variety of machinery, including cane mills, building steam engines and boilers was a special branch of their business. One engine of special interest was a cotton-press engine on order from Wilmington, North Carolina. The cylinder of this engine was 51 inches in diameter, it had a seven-foot stroke, weighed seven tons, and generated 1,000 horsepower. Not all of their engines were of this size, however, and they built a variety of sizes for governmental navy contracts and civilian use as well.

Woodruff Machinery Manufacturing Company, Winder, Georgia

George W. Woodruff, cofounder and president of the Woodruff Machinery Manufacturing Company, Winder, Georgia, was a man of varied interests, unique business acumen, and great initiative. He graduated from the Perry-Rainey Institute, Auburn, Georgia, in 1897 and taught school for a brief time at the Bold Springs School in Walton County. Business, apparently, was more

A vertical roller mill made by Woodruff Machinery of Winder, Georgia.

A horizontal roller mill made by Woodruff Machinery of Winder, Georgia.

to his liking. He moved to Winder in 1898 and founded the Woodruff Hardware Company in 1910. After his brothers, Robert L. and Albert J., joined the firm the hardware business was expanded to become the Woodruff Machinery Manufacturing Company. Their farm machinery line included hay presses, sawmills, cane mills and other related agricultural implements which were shipped all across the United States and into Canada. A branch office and showroom was opened in Atlanta on Forsyth Street. The Woodruff Hardware Company was one of the first local dealers in farm tractors and automobiles. An interesting account of this era is found in *Beadland to Barrow*, by C. Fred Ingram.

After the Woodruff brothers dissolved their partnership, George W. opened a harness-making business. Not one to sit idle, George became a partner in the Winder Manufacturing Company, and founded and became president of Carwood Manufacturing Company, where he served until his death in 1943. Always interested in agriculture, Woodruff owned farms in Barrow, Walton, and Gwinnett counties. He also loved his county, his state, and its people. Consequently, he spent the last years of his life as a member of the Georgia legislature. The Woodruff Machinery Manufacturing Company manufactured both vertical roller and horizontal roller cane mills, though no record of specific sizes has been found. George W. Woodruff sold his heavy machinery and foundry business to Ludger Lanthier in 1927 and it became the Lanthier Machine Works.

Bibliography

Adey, P. *Sugar from Cane*. New York: Longman, 1974.

Albert, Bill. *World Sugar History Newsletter* 14 (December 1989). University of East Anglia: Norwich, UK.

Appleton (Wisconsin) Motor. February 15, 1866.

Arkansas Experiment Station. "Sorghum and Sugar Cane Culture." Bulletin no. 22 (December 1892). Fayetteville: Arkansas Industrial University.

Armes, Ethel. *The Story of Coal and Iron in Alabama*. Birmingham, AL: Book-Keepers, 1972.

Arnold, James R., and Robert Wiener. *The Timechart of the Civil War*. St. Paul, MN: MBI, 2001.

Augusta (Georgia) Chronicle, July 29, 1885.

Austin, W.F. *History of the Manufacturers of Springfield, Ohio*. W.F. Austin, 1884.

Ballou, William Hosea. "Sugar-Cane and Sugar-Making." *Cosmopolitan*, February 1890.

Barnes, A.C. *The Sugar Cane*. New York and Toronto: John Wiley & Sons, 1974.

Baumheckel, Ralph, and Kent Borghoff. *International Harvester Farm Equipment*. St. Joseph, MI: American Society of Agricultural Engineers, 1997.

Bennett, James R. *Tannerhill and the Growth of the Alabama Iron Industry*. McCalla, AL: Alabama Historic Ironworks Commission, 1999.

Bessemer, Henry. *Sir Henry Bessemer, F.R.S.: An Autobiography*. London: Institute of Metals, Offices of Engineering, 1905, rpt. 1989.

Binford, J.H. *History of Greene and Sullivan Counties, State of Indiana*. Chicago: Goodspeed Bros., 1884.

Blumenthal, Maurice. *Half-Century's Progress of the City of Brooklyn*. New York: International Publishing Co., 1886.

Bowker, R.R. "A Lump of Sugar." *Harper's New Monthly Magazine*, June through November 1886.

Brandes, E.W., and G.B. Sartoris. "Sugarcane: Its Origin and Improvement." In *Yearbook of Agriculture, 1936*, by Henry A. Wallace (secretary of agriculture). Washington, DC: United States Department of Agriculture, 1936.

Brant and Fuller. *History of Vanderburgh County, Indiana*. 1889. Rpt. New York: Thomas and Hudson, 1994.

Broadhead, D.M., and N. Zummo. *Sugarcane Culture and Syrup Production*. Washington, DC: United States Department of Agriculture, Agriculture Research Service, ARS-61, 1988.

Brooks County Genealogical Society. *Brooks County Georgia: Echoes of Its People*. Vol. 2. Madison, FL: Jimbob, 2000.

Bryan, A. Hugh. "Sorghum-Sirup Manufacture." Farmers' Bulletin no. 477, United States Department of Agriculture. Washington, DC: February 9, 1912, rev. February 1918.

"Catalogue of Cane Mills, Etc., Etc., Etc." List of products manufactured by the Clark Sorgo Machine Co., Cincinnati, OH. 1864.

Church, Charles A. *Past and Present of the City of Rockford, Illinois, and Winnebago County Illinois*. Chicago: S.L. Clarke Publishing Co., 1905.

Cincinnati Times Star. The City of Cincinnati and Its Resources. Cincinnati: The Cincinnati Times Star Co., 1891.

Cist, Charles. *Sketches and Statistics of Cincinnati in 1859*.

Cleveland Press, Cleveland, Ohio. February 27, 1930.

Collier's Encyclopedia. Editorial director, Lauren S. Bahr. New York: Collier's, 1971. Vol. 7 of 24.

Conner, T.D. *Ironwork of Savannah*. Savannah, GA: T.D. Conner and Writeplace, 2004.

Craven, Wesley Frank. *The Southern Colonies in the Seventeenth Century, 1607–1689*. Baton Rouge: Louisiana State University Press, 1949.

Dacus, J.A., and James W. Buel. *A Tour of St. Louis, or the Inside Life of a Great City*. St. Louis: Western Publishing Company, Jones and Griffin, 1878.

Dahlberg, J.A. "Classification and Characterization of Sorghum." In *Sorghum: Origin, History, Technology, and Production*, C.W. Smith and R.A. Frederiksen, eds. New York: John Wiley and Sons, 2000.

Daily Zanesville Courier. Zanesville, Ohio, March 27, 1863.

Dale, J.K., and C.S. Hudson. "Sugar-Cane Juice Clarification for Sirup Manufacture." Bulletin no. 921. United States Department of Agriculture, Bureau of Chemistry. Washington, DC: Government Printing Office, November 9, 1920.

Daniel, Larry J., and Riley W. Gunter. *Confederate Cannon Foundries*. Pioneer Press, June 1977.

Daniels, John, and Christian Daniels. "The Origin of the Sugarcane Roller Mill." *Technology and Culture* 29, no. 3 (July, 1988): 493–535.

Davis, Robert S., Jr. *Cotton, Fire and Dreams: The Robert Findlay Iron Works and Heavy Industry in Macon, Georgia, 1839–1912*. Macon, GA: Mercer University Press, 1998.

Deerr, Noel. *Cane Sugar*. Manchester, England: Norman Rodger, 1911.

_____. *The History of Sugar*. Two vols. London: Chapman and Hall, 1950.

_____. *Sugar and the Sugar Cane*. Manchester, England: Norman Rodger, 1905.

Delorit, Richard J., Louis J. Greub, and Henry L. Ahlgren. *Crop Production*. 5th ed. Englewood Cliffs, NJ: Prentice-Hall, 1984.

Devor, John, and Post Express Printing Company. *Rochester and Post Express: A History of the City of Rochester*. Rochester, NY: Post Express Print Company, 1895.

Dew, Charles B. *Bond of Iron*. New York: W.W. Norton, 1994.

Dodge, Bertha S. *Plants That Changed the World*. Boston: Little, Brown and Co., 1959.

Doyle, Joseph B. *20th Century History of Steubenville and Jefferson County, Ohio*. Chicago: Richmond-Arnold Publishing Co., 1910.

Dunlap, Thomas, comp. and ed. *Wiley's American Iron Trade Manual*. New York: John Wiley and Son, 1874.

Durham, Walter T. *Nashville, the Occupied City: The First Seventeen Months—February 16, 1862, to June 30, 1863*. Nashville: Tennessee Historical Society, 1985.

_____. *Reluctant Partners: Nashville and the Union, July 1, 1863, to June 30, 1865*. Nashville: Tennessee Historical Society, 1987.

Dyess, Ernest L. "Resurrection of the Syrup Mill." In *Divine Appointments*. Camden, AL: Pebble Hill, 1998.

Eaton, Clement. *A History of the Old South*. New York: Macmillan, 1949.

Edlin, Herbert. *Atlas of Plant Life*. New York: John Day, 1973.

Ellis, Franklin, and Samuel Evans. *History of Lancaster County*. Philadelphia, PA: Everts and Peck, 1883.

Encyclopedia Americana. International ed. Danbury, CT: Grolier, 1994. Vol. 25 of 30, pp. 850–856.

Evansville Courier. Evansville, Indiana, February 9, 1941.

Farm Implement News. *Buyer's Guide: A Classified Directory*. Vol. 13. Chicago: Farm Implement News Company, Publishers, 1903.

Farm Implement News. *Buyer's Guide: A Classified Directory*. Vol. 32. Chicago: Farm Implement News Company, Publishers, 1923.

Farm Machinery, for Dealers Only. Vol. 15, no. 7—Old Series. St. Louis and Kansas City. July 1887.

Ferris, E.B. "Sugar Cane for Syrup Making." Bulletin no. 129. Mississippi Agricultural Experiment Station. Agricultural College, December 1909.

Flynt, Wayne. *Mine, Mill & Microchip*. Northridge, CA: Windsor, 1987.

Fulton, Charles J. *History of Jefferson County, Iowa*. 2 vols. Chicago: S.J. Clarke, 1912–1914.

Galloway, J.H. *The Sugar Cane Industry*. Cambridge: Cambridge University Press, 1989.

General Business Review of Highland County, Ohio. Newark, OH: Historical Publishing Company, 1892.

Golden, John P., II. "The First Hundred Years: 1882–1982." In *The History of Goldens' Foundry and Machine Company*. Columbus, GA, 1989.

Green, Allen Ayrualt. *The Making of a Steam Engine*. Chicago: Allen A. Green, 1904.

Greeno, Follett Lamberto, ed. *Obed Hussey, Who of All Inventors Made Bread Cheap*. Follett Lamberto Greeno, 1912.

Hair, James T. *Iowa State Gazetteer*. Chicago: Bailey and Hair, 1865.

Hancock, Ralph, ed. *How It Works: The Illustrated Encyclopedia of Science and Technology*. New York: Marshall Cavendish, 1977. Vol. 17 of 20, pp. 2290, 2291.

Hardy, John. *Selma: Her Institutions, and Her Men*. 1879. Rpt. Spartanburg, SC: Reprint Company, 1978.

Harlan, J.R., and J.M.J. DeWet. "A Simplified Classification of Cultivated Sorghum." *Crop Science* 12 (1972): 172–176.

Harrington, H.H. "The Manufacture of Cane Syrup." Bulletin no. 68. College Station: Texas Agricultural Experiment Station, July 1903.

Hedges, Isaac A. *Sugar Canes and Their Products, Culture and Manufacture*. St. Louis, MO: Isaac A. Hedges, 1879.

Hedges, Free & Co. *Experiments with Sorghum Sugar Cane; Including a Treatise on Sugar Mak-

ing; also, a Descriptive Catalogue of Sugar Making Apparatus, Farm Implements, Etc. Cincinnati: Hedges, Free & Co., 1859.

Hennig, Helen Kohn, and Columbia (SC) Sesqui-Centennial Commission. *Columbia: Capital City of South Carolina.* Columbia: Columbia Sesqui-Centennial Commission, 1936.

History of Wilmington. New York: Press of Moss Engraving Company, 1894.

Hitchcock, A.S. *Manual of the Grasses of the United States.* Vols. 1 and 2. New York: Dover, 1935.

Hogan, William R. *The Texas Republic: A Social and Economic History.* Norman: University of Oklahoma Press, 1946.

Humbert, Roger P. *The Growing of Sugar Cane.* Amsterdam, London, New York: Elsevier, 1963.

Huntsville (Alabama) Post, December 27, 1900.

Huntsville (Alabama) Weekly Mercury, January 31, 1900.

Hurst, R.H., and W. Scott. "Memoirs of the Imperial College of Tropical Agriculture." *Sugar Technology Series.* No. 1, *Cane Syrup.* St. Augustine, Trinidad: July 1929.

Hurst, William C. *Making Syrup for Profit.* Athens: University of Georgia College of Agriculture Cooperative Extension Service, June 1982.

Huxley, Anthony, botanical ed. *The Encyclopedia of the Plant Kingdom.* New York: Chartwell, 1977.

Indiana Magazine of History 4, no. 3. "Austin Seward" (September 1908): 103–116.

Industries of New Orleans. New Orleans: J.M. Elstner, 1885.

Ingram, C. Fred, ed. *Beadland to Barrow: A History of Barrow County, Georgia, from the Earliest Days to the Present.* Compiled by the Barrow County Historical Society. Atlanta: Cherokee, 1983.

Irvine, J.E. *Theoretical and Applied Genetics, An International Journal of Plant Breeding Research.* H.C. Becker, editor-in-chief. Heidelberg, Germany: Springer-Verlag (February 1999): 186–194.

Jackson, Walter M. *The Story of Selma.* Birmingham: Birmingham Printing, 1954.

James, Peter, and Nick Thorpe. *Ancient Inventions.* New York: Ballantine, 1994.

Janesville Gazette. Janesville, Wisconsin, October 3, 1865; March 16, 1912.

Janesville Historic Commission. *City on the Rock River: Chapters in Janesville's History.* Janesville, WI: Janesville Historic Commission, 1998.

Janesville Recorder. Janesville, Wisconsin, February 27, 1907.

Johnson, Paul C. *Farm Inventions in the Making of America.* Des Moines, IA: Wallace Homestead, 1976.

Jones, C.E. *Madison, Dane County and Surrounding Towns.* Madison, WI: William J. Park Company, 1877.

Jones, Charles C., Jr., and Salem Dutcher. *Memorial History of Augusta, Georgia.* From its settlement in 1735 to the close of the eighteenth century, by Charles C. Jones, Jr.; from the close of the eighteenth century to the present time, by Salem Dutcher. Spartanburg, SC: Reprint Company, 1980.

Kargau, E.D. *Mercantile, Industrial and Professional Saint Louis.* St. Louis: Nixon-Johes Printing Co., 1902.

Kimball, Gregg D. *American City, Southern Place.* Athens: University of Georgia Press, 2000.

Kimber, C.T. "Origins of Domesticated Sorghum and Its Early Diffusion to India and China." In *Sorghum: Origin, History, Technology, and Production,* C.S. Smith and R.A. Frederiksen, eds. New York: John Wiley and Sons, 2000.

King, Edward. *The Great South.* Baton Rouge: Louisiana State University Press, 1972.

King, Norman, R.W. Mungomery, and C.G. Hughes. *Manual of Cane-Growing.* Australian Agricultural and Livestock Series. Sydney: Angus and Robertson, first published 1953, rev. and enlarged 1965.

Land, J.E. *Industries of Indiana.* Indianapolis: J.E. Land.

Land, John E. *Macon: Her Trade, Commerce and Industries, 1892–3.* J.E. Land, 1893.

Land, Jno. E. *Pen Illustrations of New Orleans, 1881–82.* New Orleans: Published by the author, 1882.

Leighton, Desmond. *Sugar.* New York: Priory Press, Hove Crane, Russak, 1977.

Lewis, W. David. *Sloss Furnaces and the Rise of the Birmingham District.* Tuscaloosa: University of Alabama Press, 1994.

Litvin, Martin, and George Churchill. *Voices of the Prairie Land.* 2 vols. Galesburg, IL: Mother Bickerdyke Historical Collection, 1972.

Louisville Post. The City of Louisville and Its Resources. Louisville, KY: The Louisville Post Company, 1892.

Mack, Norman, ed. *Back to Basics.* New York: Reader's Digest, 1981.

Mansfield (Ohio) News, October 13, 1929.

Manufacturer and Builder 3, no. 12 (December 1871): b010, Wood and Mann advertisement.

Manufacturer and Builder 7, no. 12 (December 1875): 290, Newburgh Steam Engine advertisement.

Marsh, Barbara. *A Corporate Tragedy: The Agony of International Harvester.* Garden City, NY: Doubleday, 1985.

Martin, John. "Sorghum Improvement." In *Yearbook of Agriculture, 1936,* by Henry A. Wallace (secretary of agriculture). Washington, DC: United States Department of Agriculture, 1936.

Mask, Paul L., and William C. Morris. *Sweet Sorghum Culture and Syrup Production.* Alabama Cooperative Extension Service. Auburn: Auburn University, 1991.

Maxwell, Francis. *Modern Milling of Sugar Cane*. London: Norman Rodger, 1932.

Mazumdar, Sucheta. *Sugar and Society in China*. Cambridge and London: Harvard University Asia Center, 1998.

Meginness, John F. *Biographical Annals of Lancaster County*. Chicago, IL: J.H. Beers, 1903.

Mintz, Sidney W. *Sweetness and Power*. New York: An Elisabeth Sifton Book, Viking, 1985.

Mollenhoff, David V. *Madison: A History of the Formative Years*. 2nd ed. Madison: University of Wisconsin Press, 2003.

Montgomery, Morton L. *History of Reading*. Reading, PA: Times Book Print, 1898.

Moore, Alma Chestnut. *The Grasses, Earth's Green Wealth*. New York: Macmillan, 1960.

Murty, B.R., and J.N. Govil. "Descriptions of 70 Groups in Genus Sorghum Based on a Modified Snowden's Classification." *Indian Journal of Genetics* 27 (1967): 75–91.

Needham, Joseph. *Science and Civilisation in China*. Vol. 6, *Biology and Biological Technology*, part 3, "Agro-Industries: Sugarcane Technology," by Christian Daniels. New York: Cambridge University Press, 1996.

(New Orleans) Times-Democrat, March 5, 1893.

(New Orleans) Times-Picayune, Wednesday, July 23, 1930.

Newton County Historical Society. *Neosho: A City of Springs*. Rev. ed. Newton County (MO) Historical Society, 1992.

One Hundred Fiftieth Anniversary. New Orleans: Stratton Baldwin, 1972.

Osbourn, Mona, comp. *History of Neosho and Newton County Missouri*. 1942.

Owen, C.E. *Owen's Gazetteer and Directory of Jackson County, Iowa*. Davenport, IA: Owen Publishing Company, 1878.

Owen, Thomas McAdory. *History of Alabama and Directory of Alabama Biography*. Vol. 4 of 4. Spartanburg, SC: Reprint Company, 1978.

Parker, John P. *His Promised Land: The Autobiography of John P. Parker, Former Slave and Conductor on the Underground Railroad*, Stuart Seely Sprague, ed. New York: W.W. Norton, 1996.

Phillips, Ulrich Bonnell. *Life and Labor in the Old South*. Boston: Little, Brown, 1949.

Pillsbury, Richard, and John Florin. *Atlas of American Agriculture*. New York: Simon & Schuster Macmillan, 1996.

Putnam, Sallie B. *Richmond during the War: Four Years of Personal Observation*. New York: G.W. Carleton, 1867.

Qingshan, L., and J.A. Dahlberg. "Chinese Sorghum Genetic Resources." *Economic Botany* 55 (2001): 401–425.

Quitman Free Press, Quitman, Georgia.

Randolph, J.W. *Experiments with Sorghum Sugar Cane and Treatise on the Manufacture of Syrup And Sugar*. Revised from the ed. published by Hedges Free & Co., Cincinnati. Richmond, VA. 1864.

Rasmussen, Wayne D., ed. *Readings in the History of American Agriculture*. Urbana: University of Illinois Press, 1960.

Republican Register. Galesburg, IL, August 23, 1893, and October 7, 1899.

Richardson, Jesse M., *Alabama Encyclopedia*. Vol. 1. Northport, AL: American Southern, 1965.

Rose, R.E. "Sugar Production in Florida." From *Florida Quarterly Bulletin*. Tallahassee: October 1, 1910.

St. Louis Star. The City of St. Louis and Its Resources. St. Louis, MO: St. Louis-Sayings, 1893, pp. 132–133.

St. Louis Up to Date: The Great Industrial Hive of the Mississippi Valley, St. Louis, Mo. Consolated Illustrating Co., 1895.

Savannah Morning News. "Men Who Lead in Trade." Saturday, September 5, 1896, p. 7.

_____. Sunday, October 4, 1903; Monday, October 5, 1903; Tuesday, October 6, 1903.

Schroeder, Joseph J., Jr., ed. *Sears, Roebuck and Co. Fall 1897 Consumers Guide*. Northfield, IL: DBI.

_____. *Sears, Roebuck and Co. Fall 1900 Consumers Guide Catalogue No. 110*. Northfield IL: DBI, 1970.

Scientific American (New Series) 1, no. 4 (July 23, 1859): 49 (Report of Hedges' cane mill).

_____. (New Series) 1, no. 8 (August 20, 1859): 120 (report of Cook's air car).

_____. (New Series) 1, no. 12 (September 17, 1859): 192 (report of E.J. Horn's cane mill).

_____. (New Series) 1, no. 13 (September 24, 1859: 208 (report of Bassett's cane mill).

_____. (New Series) 10, no. 24 (June 11, 1864): 376 (report of S.L. Denney's sorghum mill).

_____. (New Series) 11, no. 15 (October 8, 1864): 225 (report of Skinner's cane mill).

Scott, Jane. *Botany in the Field*. Englewood Cliffs, NJ: Prentice-Hall, 1984.

Shirley, Michael. *From Congregation Town to Industrial City: Culture and Social Change in a Southern Community*. New York and London: New York University Press, 1997.

Sloane, Eric. *The Seasons of America Past*. New York: Funk & Wagnalls, 1958.

Smith, C.W., and R.A. Frederiksen, eds. *Sorghum: Origin, History, Technology and Production*. New York: John Wiley and Sons, 2000.

Smith, Dudley. *Cane Sugar World*. New York: Palmer, 1978.

Society for Industrial Archeology. *Guidebook to Tours and Sites in Savannah, Georgia*. Twenty-eighth Annual Meeting, Savannah, Georgia, June 3–6, 1999.

Spencer, A.P. "Sugar-cane and Syrup Making." Bulletin no. 118. Gainesville: University of Florida Agricultural Experiment Station, 1913.

Stevenson, G.C. *Genetics and Breeding of Sugar Cane*. London: Longmans, Green, 1965.

Stewart, F.L. *Sorghum and Its Products*. Philadelphia, PA: J.B. Lippincott & Co., 1867.

Stubbs, William C. *Sugar Cane*. Vol. 1. State Bureau of Agriculture and Immigration. Baton Rouge: Louisiana State University Press. June 30, 1897.

Thomasville, Georgia, Up-To-Date: Describing its resources, enterprises and opportunities and the men behind them. 1926.

Tompkins, Peter, and Christopher Bird. *The Secret Life of Plants*. New York: Harper and Row, 1973.

Vaughan, J.G., and C.A. Geissler. *The New Oxford Book of Food Plants*. Oxford: Oxford University Press, 1997.

Viola, Herman J., and Carolyn Margolis, eds. *Seeds of Change*. Washington and London: Smithsonian Institution, 1991.

Wall, Joseph S., and William M. Ross, eds. *Sorghum Production and Utilization*. Westport, CT: Avi, 1970.

Wallace, Henry A. (secretary of agriculture). *Yearbook of Agriculture, 1936*. Washington, DC: United States Department of Agriculture, 1936.

Welty, Susan Fulton. *A Fair Field*. Detroit: Harlo, 1968.

Wendel, C.H. *Encyclopedia of American Farm Implements & Antiques*. Iola, WI: Krause, 1997.

_____. *150 Years of International Harvester*. Osceloa, WI: Motorbooks International, 1993.

Western Historical Company. *The History of Jackson County, Iowa*. Chicago: Western Historical Company, 1879.

_____. *The History of Rock County, Wisconsin*. Chicago: Western Historical Company, 1879.

Wheeler, Richard. *Sword Over Richmond*. New York: Harper and Row, 1986.

Wiley, W.H. "Manufacture of Table Sirups from Sugar Cane." Bulletin no. 70. United States Department of Agriculture, Bureau of Chemistry. Washington, DC: Government Printing Office, 1902.

Wilford, John Noble. *The Mysterious History of Columbus*. New York: Alfred A. Knopf/ Random House, 1991.

Williams, Eric. *From Columbus to Castro: The History of the Caribbean, 1492–1969*. New York: Harper and Row, 1970.

Worsley, Etta Blanchard. *Columbus on the Chattahoochee*. Columbus, GA: Columbus Office Supply, 1951.

Yoder, P.A. "Growing Sugar Cane for Sirup." Farmers' Bulletin no. 1034. United States Department of Agriculture. Washington, DC: United States Printing Press, March 1919, rev. July 1925.

Zim, Herbert S. *Plants: A Guide to Plant Hobbies*. New York: Harcourt, Brace, 1947.

Index

Acme cane mill, Sears 259
Adams, John M. 198
Addison, New York 186
Adjustable Sugar Mill, Bevitt 64
Adjustable Sugar Mill, Woodbury 329
Africa 17, 27
Agricultural Implement Manufactory 53
Aikin, William 234
Alexander, J. E. 54
Alexander, John, and Company 88
Alexander and Son cane mill 55
Alexander and Son Plow Works 54
Alexandria 17
Allen, Gerald B. 156
Amazon cane mill, Deere 129
Amazon cane mill for Steam Power, Deere 129
Amazon cane mill for water power, Deere 131
Amazon cane mill with high ratio gearing, Deere 130, 131
Amber cane mill, Brennan 86
America cane mill, Bell 63
American Mammoth cane mill, Squier 295
American Seeding Company 86
Americas 18, 20
Anderson, Joseph Reid 307
Angola 18
Ansonia, Connecticut 150
Arab Conquests 17
Argentina 19
Assyria 27
Athens, Georgia 56
Athens Foundry and Machine Works 56
Atlanta, Georgia 326
Atlantic Islands 18

Atlas cane mill, Bell 63
Augusta, Georgia 198
Aurora Horizontal cane mill, Blymyer 78
Australia 17
Avery, B. F. and Sons 57
Azores 18

Baldwin, A., and Company Ltd. 58
Baldwin, Albert 58
Baltimore, Maryland 213
Bangladesh (Pakistan) 17
Barbados 19
Barbados Experiment Stations 24
Barber, Dr. C. A. 12
Bassett's Mill 326
Belknap, W. B. 58
Belknap Hardware Company 58
Bell, C. S., and Company 60
Bell, Charles Singleton 60
Belleville, Illinois 141
Bellevue, Iowa 63
Bellevue Foundry and Machine Shop 63
Belt, Raymond 197
Belt's Cane Mill 198
Bessemer, Henry 44
Bevitt, George W. 64
Bevitt's Mill 64
Bihar Orisa 17
Blandy, F. J. L. 64
Blandy, Henry 64
Blandy's Improved Sugar Mill, Blandy's 65
Blandys' Steam Engine Works 64
Bloomington, Indiana 262
Blue Grass (New) cane mill, Belknap 60
Blue Ribbon cane mill, Deere 127
Blymyer, Day and Co. 82

Blymyer Iron Works Company 65
Botanic Station, Barbados 23
Bouganville 16
Bounty cane mill, Bell 63
Brandes, Dr. E. W. 12
Brazil 19
Brennan, Thomas 82
Brennan and Company 82
Brooklyn, New York 87, 114, 209, 240
Brown, William Riley 107, 279
Buckeye Sugar Mills, Thomas, Mast and Company 303
Buenos Aires 19
Buerkens, Barney 86
Buerkens Manufacturing Company 86
Buffalo, New York 284
Burdon, William 87
Burdon, Hubbard and Company 87
Burlington, Iowa 88
Burlington Foundry and machine Works 88
Burma 17

Cairo 17
Canal Point, Florida 25
Canary Islands 18
Canton, Illinois 228
Cape Verde Islands 18
Carolina 20
Carr's Mill 51
Carroll, Robert 190
Cathay 17
Central City Iron Works 88
Challenge cane mill, Winchester DeWolf and Company 326
Champion cane mill, Bell 63
Champion cane mill, Haven 179, 180

Champion cane mill, Sears 260
Charleston, South Carolina 239
Chase, O. L., Mercantile Co. 88
Chattanooga, Tennessee 89
Chattanooga Plow cane mills: No. 7 91; Nos. 11–14 90; No. 16 91; Nos. 22–25 91; No. 34 93; No. 44 92, 94; No. 45 93; No. 45-A 93; No. 46 96; No. 60 97; No. 70 94; No. 71 93; No. 72 93; No. 92 95; No. 109 96; Nos. 111–114 93; Nos. 122–124 91; No. 144 92; No. 145 93; No. 145-A 93; No. 171 93; Nos. 222–224 91
Chattanooga Plow Company 89
Chicago, Illinois 199, 212, 258
China 17
Christiana, Pennsylvania 99
Christiana Machine Company 99
Cincinnati, Ohio 65, 101, 125, 178, 218, 298
Clark, W. H. 101
Clark cane mills: Back Geared Horizontal 103; New Style 102, 103; Old Style 101, 102, 103; Sweep Below 103; Victor 101, 102, 103
Clark Sorgho Machine Company 101, 104
Clarksville, Virginia 57
Classification by outward Appearance 20, 21
Cleveland, Ohio 135, 178, 192
Climax Adjustable Sugar Mill, Skinner 265
Climax cane mill, Bell 62
Climax cane mills, Nos. 0–4, Parlin and Orendorff 229
Clinton Foundry 105
Close, Hiram, Perry and Cushman 105
Coe, R. 88
Coimbatore, India 17, 24
Cold Spring, New York 319
Coldwell-Wilcox Company 105
Coleman, H. Dudley 105, 106, 107
Coleman, H. Dudley, Machinery Company 105, 106
Collinge, John's design 43
Colon Horizontal Mill, Blymyer 79
Columbia, South Carolina 56
Columbus, Christopher 18
Columbus, Georgia 149, 210, 342
Columbus Iron Works cane mills: Nos. 12, 14, 16, 18 two roller mills 110, 111; Nos. 0–3 three roller mills 112; Nos. 18 and 20 horizontal roller mills 113

Columbus Iron Works 107–111, 113, 114, 160, 162
Congaree Iron Works 114
Continental cane mill, Nos. 1–4, Parlin and Orendorff 229
Continental Works 107, 108, 111, 160, 161, 269
Cook, D. M. 115, 116
Cook, Captain James 13
Cook Cane Mills 116
Cook Islands 20
Cook's Mill 116
Cora cane mill, Fulton 156, 157
Cornell, J. B. and J. M., Company 123
Cortes 19
Crete 18
Crockett, E. 124
Crockett's Iron Works 124
Crusaders 20
Cuba 19
Cyprus 18

Dahlberg, Dr. Jeff 27
Dake, Frederick E. 187
Dake's Mill 188
Daniels, Christian 13, 41
Daniels, John 42
D'Antignac, William H. 198
Day, J. H., and Company 125
Dead Sea 17
Deane, Frank B. 307
Deely, Robert 125
Deely, Robert and Company 125
Deere, John 125
Deere, John and Company 125, 126, 127, 201
Deerr, Noel 6, 40
Delta cane mill, Bell 63
DeMarce, Anthony 132
DeMarce, Anthony Machine Shop 132
DeMarce cane mill 132
Demerara 20
Demorest, Georgia 133, 134
Demorest Foundry and Machine Works 133, 134
Demorest Mill 133, 134
Denmead, A. W. 213
Denney, S. L. 100
Dennis, W. T. 47
Dennis' Mill 47
Denny's Mill 100
deWet 27
Diamond cane mill, Squier 289
Diamond Heavy Duty cane mill, Squier 290
Dickinson, C. H. 46
Dickinson's Mill 45
Diebert, Bancroft and Ross 134
Diebert, John 134
Domestic cane mill, Bell 63
Double barrel cannon 56
Doubleuse (trash-returner) 43

Drummond, William 234
Duryea, Hendrick V. 47
Dyas, Robert 220
Dyer, Edward F. 135
Dyer Company 135
Dyer's Mill 135, 136

Easter Island 20
Eastwood Brothers and Carson 136, 137, 138
Eclipse cane mill, Bell 63
Eclipse cane mill, Parlin and Orendorff 229
Economist cane mill, Bell 63
Economist cane mill, Haven 179, 180
Economist cane mill, Oyler 222
Eddy, Thompson and Company 139
Edgar, William 209
Edge Runner 37
Edge Runner Mill 37
Egypt 27
Emerson, Ralph 139
Emerson Manufacturing Company 139, 140, 141
Emerson's Mill 139
Ethiopia 18
Etienne de Boré 20
Eureka cane mill, Blymyer 80
Evansville, Indiana 186, 253, 258
Excelsior cane mills: Favorite, Numbers 9–13 149; Nos. 30 and 31 147; No. 39 (Pony) 145, 146, 147; Nos. 40, 41 145; Nos. 42, 43 144; Nos. 42A and 43A 145; Nos. 44 and 45 142, 144; No. 50 141, 142, 143; St. Louis Vertical Mill 147, 148, 149
Excelsior Foundry Company 141
Experimental Stations, Origins of 22

Fairfield, Iowa 132
Farmer's Choice cane mill, Bell 63
Farrel, F. 150
Farrel cane mill 150
Farrel Foundry and Machine Company 150
Favorite cane mill, Excelsior 149
Feed guide 47
Ferdinand, King 18
Field, J. A. 151, 152
Field, J. A., and Company 151, 152
Fiji 20
Findlay, Robert 153
Findlay, Robert Iron Works 153
Florida cane mill, Squier 292
F.M. Co. cane mill, Valdosta Foundry and Machine Company 316
Forest King cane mill, Mansur 209

Foster, John Reinhold 13
Franklin Iron Works 154
Frost, J. P. 154, 155
Frost cane mill 154, 155
Frost Manufacturing Company 154, 155
Fulton Iron and Manufacturing 156
Fulton's Sugar House Mill 157

Galesburg, Illinois 154
Galloway, J. H. 40
Galveston, Texas 105
Garland cane mill, Blymyer 79
Gates, Philetus W. 157
Gates, P.W., and Company 157, 158, 159
Gates cane mill 157, 158, 159
Gem cane mill, Blymyer 75
Gem cane mill, Squier 292
Genoa 18
Giant cane mill, Eastwood 136
Giant cane mill, Mount Airy 217
Gleason, Solomon Wilson 159, 160
Gleason, S.W., and Company 159, 160
Globe cane mill, Bell 63
Globe Special cane mill, Bell 63
Gold Medal cane mill, Bell 63
Gold Medal cane mill, Oyler 224
Golden, George Jasper 162
Golden, John Poitevent (Porter) 160
Golden, Theodore (Theo) Earnest 160
Goldens' cane mills: Nos. 1–4, standard three vertical rollers 163, 164, 165; Nos. 1X–4X 166; Nos. 2XX–4XX 166; Nos. 8 and 9 horizontal mills for horse power 167, 168; Nos. 12, 14 and 16 two vertical roller mills 170; Nos. 12X, 14X and 16X 171; Nos. 18XX and 20XX 171; Nos. 27, 36, 45, 54 and 63 horizontal power mills 167, 168
Goldens' Foundry and Machine Company 160, 161
Golding, William 221
Gomera 18
Great South-Western cane mill, Manny 206
Great Western cane mill, Blymyer 70
Great Western Horizontal Mill, Blymyer 71
Great Western Premium cane mill, Pearson and Aikin 234, 235
Gregory, Edward G. 88
Grimm Manufacturing Company 175

Grundmann, Theodore 47
Grundmann's Mill 47

Harlan 27
Harpers Ferry 319
Harris, Daniel 250
Harris, James 175, 176
Harris Manufacturing Company 175, 176
Harris' Mill 175, 176, 177
Hartford, Connecticut 177, 329, 331
Hartford Foundry and Machine Company 177
Hartford Sorghum Machine Company 177
Hasskarl, Justus Karl 13
Haven, James L. 178
Haven, James L. Company 178
Hawaiian Islands 16
Hedges, Free and Company 181
Hedges, Free cane mills: Double geared vertical mill 183; Horizontal back geared mill 184, 185; Horizontal mill with vertical shaft 184; Improved Sugar Mill 182; Single geared vertical mill 183
Hendrie, Charles 88
Henerey, W. S. 185
Henerey, W. S., and Company 185
Henry the Navigator 18
Hero cane mill, Nos. 50–55, Rumsey 248
Hewes and Phillips 185
Hildago cane mill, Mansur 209
Hillsboro, Ohio 60
Hispaniola 18
Hitch, J.W. 214
Holtz, F., Company 186
Holtz, Ferdinand 186
Hopkins, Lambert 198
Horn, E. J. 186
Horn's Improved Cane Crusher 186
Hudson, Ohio 175
Hudson City, New York 186
Hudson Machine and Iron Foundry 186, 187
Hunt, Thomas E. 187
Hunt, Thomas 47
Hunt, Dake and Company 187
Hunt's Mill 47, 187
Huntsville, Alabama 187
Huntsville Foundry and Machine Works 187–189

Ile de Bourbon (Réunion) 18
Imperial cane mill, Nos. 1–4, Parlin and Orendorff 229
Improved Gold Basis cane mill, Manny 204
Improved Kentucky cane mill, Blymyer 75

Improved Kentucky cane mill, Nos. 0–4, Parlin and Orendorff 229
Indented rollers 43
India 16
Indianapolis, Indiana 187
Indonesia 16
Indus Valley 29
International Harvester Company 89, 199
International Harvester Company cane mills: Nos. 111–114 fluted rollers 201; Nos. 44A, 144A, 45A and 145A 201; No. 171 201; Nos. 192 and 192A 201
Invincible cane mill, Sears 261
Iran (Persia) 17
Iron headstock 43
Iron sleeves 43
Irvine, Dr. J. E. 14
Isabella, Queen 18
Isosceles triangle design 43

Jamaica 19
Janesville, Wisconsin 175
Java 16
Java Experiment Stations 23
Jefferson Foundry 190
Jericho 17
Jesuits 19
Jeswiet, Dr. 12
Jones, John 241
Jordan River 17
Jumbo 88 cane mill, Bell 63

Kansas City, Missouri 88
Kashgar 17
Kehoe, William 191
Kehoe Iron Works 190–192
Kehoe Rollers cane mill 192
Keim, Benneville 243
Keim, George M. 243
Kentucky cane mill, Brennan 85
Kentucky Giant Mill B 77
Kentucky Horizontal Mill A, Blymyer 76
Kenwood cane mill, Sears 261
Kenya 18
Kilby Manufacturing Company 192
King of the South cane mill, Baldwin 58
Kingsland and Douglas cane mill 193
Kingsland and Douglas Manufacturing Co. 192
Krajewske-Peasant Company 194, 195
Krajewski Crusher cane mill, United States and Cuban Allied Works 194
Kratz, C. Foundry 194
Kratz, Christian 194

la Couture, Jacques Francois Dutrone 43
Laub, G. H. 46
Laub's Mill 73
Lebanon 17
Leeds, Jedechal 196
Leeds' Foundry and Machine Shop 196
Leeward Islands 19
Lester, John H. 196
Linnaeus, Carl 12
Little Giant cane mill, Sears 260
Logan, Ohio 197
Logan Foundry and Machine Shop 197
Lombard Iron Works 198
Lone Star cane mill, Bell 63
Louisiana 20
Louisiana cane mill, Squier 295
Louisiana No. 2 cane mill, Squier 295
Louisville, Kentucky 57, 82, 234

Macon, Georgia 124, 153, 253
Madagascar 18
Madeira 18
Madison, Wisconsin 64, 264, 308, 329
Magee, Alexander 203
Magee, Alex. and Company 203
Magnolia cane mill, Deere 128, 129
Malta 18
Manny, Abraham J. 204
Manny and Company 204
Mansfield, Ohio 65, 115
Mansur, Alvah 208
Mansur and Tebbetts Implement Company 208
Marquesas 20
Mast, Phineas P. 303, 304
Mauritius 18
Mazumdar, Sucheta 40
McCormick, Cyrus 199
McCormick-Deering 199
McDonough, John J. 203, 251
McDonough and Ballantyne 203
McMinnville, Tennessee 136
Mediterranean Sea 17
Mexico 19
Miller and Marsden 209
Minneapolis-Moline Company 57
Mintz, Sidney W. 40
Mobile, Alabama 209
Mobile Pulley and Machine Company 209
Mohawk cane mill, Nos. A–C, Rumsey 248
Moline, Illinois 125
Monahan, James 239
Monahan and Parry 211
Monarch cane mill, Bell 63
Monitor cane mill, Bell 63
Montgomery, Alabama 211

Montgomery Iron Works cane mill 212, 213
Montgomery Manufacturing Company and Iron Works 211
Montgomery, William, and Company 211
Monument Iron Works 213
Morgan Iron Works 214
Morris, Henry G. 214
Morris, Stephen P. 229
Mortar and Pestle Mill 36
Mortar and Pestle 35
Morven, Georgia 214
Morven Foundry and Machine Works 214
Morven Mill 215
Mount Airy, North Carolina 216
Mount Airy Iron Works 216
Mount Airy Mill 217
Mozambique 18
Mulligan, Thomas 250
Munn, Abraham G. 82

Nashville, Tennessee 280
Navidad 19
Needham, Joseph 41
Nelson, N. O. 217
Nelson, N. O., Manufacturing Company 217
Neosho Manufacturing Company 217
Neosho, Missouri 54, 217
New Amber cane mill, Mansur 209
New Blue Grass cane mill, Belknap 60
New Canton Vertical Mills, No. 0–4, Parlin and Orendorff 229
New Clipper cane mill, Nos. A–C, Parlin and Orendorff 229
New Decatur, Alabama 220
New Guinea 11
New Improved Cook Mill, Cook 117
New Live Oak cane mill, Blymyer 76
New Orleans, Louisiana 58, 105, 107, 134, 135, 196, 221, 230
New South cane mill, Bell 63
New Superior Horizontal Mill, Cook 135
New York, New York 105, 123, 125, 194, 196, 211, 214
Newark, New Jersey 185
Newburgh, New York 105, 218, 308, 317
Newburgh Steam Engine Works 218
Niles, James 218
Niles, Jonathan 218
Niles cane mill, Blymyer 72
Niles Works 218

Norfolk, Virginia 322
Norris Works 220
Norristown, Pennsylvania 220
North Alabama Engineering Company 220
Northwestern Sorgho Company 221
Northwestern Sorgho Co. cane mill 221
Novelty Iron Works 221

Ohio Horizontal Mill, Blymyer 78
Opal Mill for hand power, Blymyer 74
Orgall, Andrew 43
Oyler, George K. 222
Oyler, George K., Manufacturing Company 222
Oyler cane mills Economist Mill 222; Gold Medal Mill 224; Pioneer Mill 222; Plantation Mill 225; Plantation Mill with Sweep Below 226; Western Mill 224

Pakistan (Bangladesh) 17
Palestine 17
Paragon cane mill, Bell 63
Paraguay 19
Parker, John P. 237
Parlin and Orendorff Company 89, 228
Pascal Iron Works 229
Payne and Joubert 230
Peacock, George 230
Peacock Mill 231, 232
Peacock's Foundry 230
Pearl cane mill, Squier 290
Pearson, Aikin and Company 234–236
Pearson, Elisha A. 234
Pearson cane mill, Aikin and Company 235, 236
Pella, Iowa 86
Pemberton, Dr. C. E. 12
Perfection Cane Mills, Spotless 282, 283
Perfection Horizontal Mills, Spotless 282, 283
Persia (Iran) 17
Peru 19
Peruvian Three Roller Mill 40
Philadelphia, Pennsylvania 151, 214, 229
Philippines 16
Phillips, Arthur M. 190
Phoenix Foundry and Manufacturing Company 237–239
Phoenix Foundry cane mills, Ripley, Ohio: Phoenix Horizontal Mills 239; Phoenix Vertical Mills 239
Phoenix Iron Works 239
Pioneer cane mill, Bell 63

Pioneer cane mill, Haven 179
Pioneer cane mill, Manny 206
Pioneer cane mill, Oyler 222
Pioneer cane mill, Squier 288
Pioneer Iron Works 240
Pizarro 19
Plantation cane mill, Oyler 225
Plantation cane mill with sweep below, Oyler 226
Poderoso cane mill, Bell 63
Poe, James M. 198
Pole Mill 37
Polo, Marco 17
Porto Santo 18
Portuguese 11
Powell, Eugene 46
Press, static 38
Proefstation Oost Java, Paso-eroean, Java 5, 23
Progresso cane mill, Bell 63
Puerto Rico 19
Pusey, Joshua L. 214
Pusey and Jones Company 214

Quitman, Georgia 242, 267
Quitman Machine Works 242
Quitman Mill 242

Reading, Pennsylvania 243
Reading Iron Company 243
Réunion (Ile de Bourbon) 18
Rhodes 18
Rhodesia 18
Rhumphius 13
Richmond Foundry 243
Richmond, Virginia 53, 243, 281, 307
Rio Grande cane mill, Mansur 209
Ripley, Ohio 234
Rival two roller mill, Rumsey 248
Rockford, Illinois 139, 244, 309
Rockford Iron Works 244
Roebuck, Alvah Curtis 259
Rogers, Eddy P. 141
Rogers, George B. 141
Rost and Heiny 244
Rourke, John 244
Rourke, John, Iron and Brass Works 244
Rourke cane mill 245
Rowland, T. F. 114
Roxiburgh 13
Ruby cane mill, Squier 291
Rumsey, L. M. 247
Rumsey, L. M., Manufacturing Company 247
Rumsey cane mill, Nos. 1–4, Rumsey 248

St. Louis, Missouri 116, 151, 156, 203, 204, 208, 217, 222, 247
St. Louis cane mill, Excelsior 147
St. Louis cane mill, Magee 204

Salem Iron Works 248
Samoa 20
Sanders, Newell 89
Santo Domingo 19
São Tomé 18
Savannah, Georgia 159, 190, 203, 211, 239, 244, 249, 250, 251, 253
Savannah Iron and Brass Foundry and Machine Works 249
Savannah Iron Works 250
Savannah Locomotive cane mill 251
Savannah Locomotive Works and Supply Company 251
Savannah Machine Works 253
Saville cane mill 297
Saville cane mill, Stauffer and Eshleman 297
Scantling, Thomas 253
Scantling, Thomas, and Sons 253
Schofield, John Shepley 253
Schofield, J. S., and Son 253
Schofield cane mill 256
Schultz, Thuman and Company 258
Schwartz, Stuart B. 41
Sears, Richard Warren 258
Sears cane mills: Acme 259; Champion 260; Defiance 260; Invincible 261; Little Giant 260
Sears, Roebuck and Company 258
Selma, Alabama 88, 230
Seward, Austin 262–264
Seward, Austin, and Son 262–264
Seward's Mill 262, 267, 264
Seyfert, Simon 243
Seymour, W. S. 47
Seymour's Mill 47
Shakespeare, Joseph A. 264
Shakespeare Iron Works 264
Shensi 17
Sicily 18
Sitwell, George 43
Skinner, E. W. 264, 308
Skinner, E. W., and Company 264–267
Skinner's Mill 264
Smeaton's triangle design 43
Snowden 27
Society Islands 13
Sorghum: basic races 27–28; original imported varieties 31, 32; origins 27; uses 29
Sorghum bicolor 27–29
Sorghum family 26–27; *Andropogoneae* 11, 27; *Gramineae* 11, 27; *Panicoideae* 27; *Poaceae* 27
Sorghum groupings 29
Sorghum varieties: Atlas 31;

Black Amber 28; Brandes 32; Chinese Amber 28; Chinese Sugarcane 28; Collier 32; Colman 31; Dakota Amber 30; Dale 31; Early Amber 32; Folger 31; Georgia Blue Ribbon 32; Goose-neck Sorghum 31; Hodo 32; Honey 31; Honey Drip 31; Iceberg 32; Kansas Orange 30; M 8 I-E 32; McLean 32; Minnesota Amber 30–31; Orange Sorghum 31; Planter 32; Red Amber 31; Red-Top Sorghum 31; Sart 32; Sourless Sorgo 30; Sugar Drip 31–32; Sumac 31; Texas Seeded Ribbon 31; Theis 32; Topper 76-6 32; Tracy 32; Waconia Amber 30; White African 32; Wiley 32; Williams 32
Sorghum, forage 29
Sorghum, grain 29; Bicolor 29; Caudatum 29; Durra 29; Guinea 31; Kafir 29
Sorghum, specialty 29; Broom-corn 29; Sweet Sorghum 30
South Africa 18
South Bradford, Pennsylvania 308
South Pacific Islands 12
Southeast Asia 16
Southern Machinery Company 268–267
Southern Machinery Mill 267, 268
Southern Plow cane mills: Improved Columbus Belt Powered Mills 279; Improved Columbus Three Roller Mill, Nos. 11–15 271, 272, 273, 276, 277, 278; Southern Plow Horizontal Mill No. 5 276; Southern Plow Horizontal Mills, Nos. 18 and 20 276; Standard Vertical Mills, Nos. 0–3 271; Two Roller Mills, Nos. 12–18 273, 274, 275
Southern Plow Company 269
Southern Queen cane mill, Cook 117
Southern Sorgho Machine Company 280
Southwestern Agricultural Works 74
Spain 18
Spaugh, W. T. 249
Speciale, Pietrio 40
Speedwell, New Jersey 280–281
Speedwell Iron Works 280–281
Spotless Company 281–283
Spotless Jumbo cane mill 282, 283
Spraugh, J. E. 216
Springfield, Missouri 139

Springfield, Ohio 303
Squier, George L. 284, 285, 288
Squier, George L., Manufacturing Company 284–288
Squier's Mills cane mills: American Mammoth 295, 296; Diamond 289, 290; Diamond Heavy Duty 290; Florida 292, 294, 295; Gem 292; Louisiana 294, 295; Louisiana with cane carrier 295; Pearl 290; Pioneer 288, 289; Ruby 291, 292, 293; Texas 291, 292, 293
Star cane mill, Bell 63
Star cane mill, Field 151
Star cane mill, Mansur 209
Star cane mill, Nelson and Company 217
Star cane mill, Rumsey 248
Static Press cane mill 38
Stauffer, Eshleman and Company 266, 297, 298
Steubenville, Ohio 190
Straub, Isaac 298, 299
Straub, Isaac, and Company 298, 299
Straub's Mill 298, 299
Sudan 18
Sugar: first 17
Sugar cane family: *Andropagonae* 11; *Glumiflorae* 11; *Gramineae* 11; *Saccharum* 11
Sugar cane origins 11
Sugar cane species: *S. Barberi Jeswiet* 11; *S. Officinarum L* 12; *S. Robustum Brandes and Jeswiet* 12; *S. Sinense Roxb.* 13; *S. Spontaneum* 13; *Saccharum edule* 13
Sugar cane varieties: ; Ainakea 20; Aleijada 19; B.109 19; B.147 19; B.208 19; B.306 19; B.H.10/12 24, 26; B.O.3 17; B.O.17 17; B.O.50 17; Bandjarmasin hitam 23; Batramic 21; Batavian Striped 21; Bois Rouge 19; Badilla 16; Bamboo Canes 16; Black cane 19; Black Cheribon 25, 26; Black Java 21; Black Manila 24; Black Tanna 19; Blue Ribbon 25; Bois Rouge 19, 21; Brekeret 21; Bronzeada 19; Brouicius 247 24; Burbon 12, 21, 24; Burke 21; Caledonia 12; Caledonian Queen 21; Canne Morte 24; Cavengerie 16; Cayana-10 25, 26; Cayanna Antiga 19; Cayanninha 19; Cheribon 12, 23, 24; Chinea 13; chu-che 17; Chunnee 24, 26; Cirzenta 19; Co.205 17; Co.213 17; Co.221 17, 24; Co.281 17; Co.285 17; Co.290 17, 24, 25; Co.291 24; Co.310 17; Co.413 17; Co.L.54 17; C.P.28/11 25; C.P.28/19 25; C.P.29-116 26; C.P.36-111 26; C.P.52-48 26; C.P.67-500 26; C.P.807 25; Creole 17, 26; Crystallina 19, 25; Culleroah 17; D.74 20, 24; D.95 25; Dama 21; Drard 21; E.K.2 23; E.K.28 23; Elephant 21; F.31-407 26; Ferrea 19; GA.64-188 26; Ganna 17; Georgia Green 15; Georgia Yellow Gal 15, 25; Geru 16; Gogari 16; Goru bunu bunana 16; Goru seela scelana 16; Governor Lees 21; Grande Savanne 21; Green Ribbon 21, 25; Hawaiian 25; Hillii 21; Home Green 25; Home Purple 20, 25; Home Ribbon 20; Home Striped 25; Horne 21; Imperial 19; *Irimolu S. Fragile* 16; Iscamgine 16; Japanese Cayana 25; Java 21; Kaludai Boothan 24; Kansar 26; Kara – karawa 21; Kassoer 23, 26; Kavangire 26; Keening 21; Keni Keni 21; Khera 26; Ko Kea 20; Kulloa 16; Kullore 16; Lahaina 20, 21, 23; Lakona 21; Large Green 21; L.C.P.85-384 25; Loethers 23, 24; Louisiana Purple 25; Louisiana Striped 26; Louzier 19; lu-che 17; Malabar 20; Mamuri 21; Mani 21; Manteiga 19; Meera 21, 24; Mungo 26; Muntok 24; N.G.64 16; Nanal 17; Nara Tara 21; N:Co.310 17; Oliana 20; Otaheite 18–21, 26; Othageute 12; Palania 20; Papaa 20; Paunda 17; *Piaverae S.obscurum* 16; Pindar 17; Po-a-ole 21; P.O.J.33 24; P.O.J.36 24; P.O.J.100 23, 24; P.O.J.139 24; P.O.J.161 24; P.O.J.181 24; P.O.J.213 24; P.O.J.228 24; P.O.J.2364 23; P.O.J.2878 23; POP.63-1 26; POP.63-12 26; Port Mackay Cavangere 24; Preanger 26; Purple Bamboo 24; Purple Mauritius 21; Purple Striped 25; Purple Transparent 21; Purple Transparent Cheribon 19; Q.75 18; Q.83 17; Queensland Creole 21; Ragnar 18; Rappoe 21, 24; Red Ribbon 21, 24; Red Fiji 23; Red Manila 24; Restali 17; Rose Bamboo 20, 24; Rox Louizer 19; *Rurutu S. Rubicundum* 16; Russel 21; Salangora 19; Samsara 17; Samuri 21; S.C.12/4 24, 26; Selangore 21; Simpson cane 21, 25; Singapore 21; Striped Bamboo 24; Striped Cheribon 19; Striped Tip 20; Tamarind 19; Tekeha 26; Transparent 12; Tanna 12; To avae 16; To oura 16; *To uti S. Atrorubens* 16, 24; Uba 13, 26; Ukh 17; Vagabonde 21; Vaihi 16, 20; Vico 21; Violet Ribbon 21; Vitu-Haula 21; Vulu Vulu 21; White Manila 24; White Tanna 19; White Transparent 19, 24, 26; Yellow Caledonia 20; Yellow Bamboo 20; Yellow Tip 20; Yontanzan 26; Zwart Cheribon 26
Sugar Experimental Station, Louisiana 25
Sullivan, Indiana 244
Sullivan and Hurdean 299
Superior Heavy Horizontal Mill, Cook 122
Superior Horizontal Mill for animal power, Cook 118
Superior Horizontal No. 39 Mill, Cook 118
Superior Horizontal No. 50 Mill, Cook 122
Superior Horizontal Power Mill, Cook 119
Superior Horizontal Power Mill with double back gear, Cook 120, 121
Sutherland, D. T. 299
Sutherland, D. T., and Machine Works and Foundry 299
Sutherland cane mill 299
Swaziland 18
Swoop, Julian M. 300, 301
Swoop, Julian M., Company 300, 301
Syfan, C. T. W. 301–303
Syfan Machine Works and Foundry 301–303
Syfan Rollers cane mill 301, 302, 303
Syria 17
Szechwan 17

Tanzania 18
Texas cane mill, Squier 291, 292, 293
Thailand 17
Thomas, Ed 315, 316
Thomas, John H. 303–305
Thomas, Mast and Company 303–305
Thomasville, Georgia 305, 306
Thomasville Iron Works 305
Thompson, C. B. 305
Thompson Foundry and Machine Co. cane mill 306
Thompson Foundry and Machine Company 306
Tiger cane mill, Rumsey 248

Tilt Hammer Mill 38
Tonga 20
Tonking (Vietnam) 17
Topaz cane mill, Blymyer 74
Trahern, D. E. 244
Tredegar Iron Works 307–308
Trojan cane mill, Bell 63
Tropic cane mill, Bell 63
Turl's/John Turl's Sons 308
Turner, P. H. 308
Turner, P. H., and Company 308
Turner's Mill 308, 309
Turpin, William 198

Underwood, F. C. 268, 269
United States and Cuban Allied Works 308, 309
United States Department of Agriculture 30
Unknown Mills 309–314
Utica, New York 329
Utter, Isaac 314, 315
Utter Manufacturing Company 314
Utter Manufacturing Company Mill 314, 315

Vail, Alfred 280–281
Vail, Judge Stephen 280–281
Valdosta, Georgia 315–316
Valdosta Foundry and Machine Company 315
Valdosta Manufacturing Company 316
Velasque 19
Victor cane mill, Blymyer 67
Victor cane mill, Nos. 0, 1 Jr., 1, 2, 3, 4, 6, Rumsey 248
Victor Horizontal Mill, Blymyer 72
Victor cane mill with sweep below, Blymyer 70
Vietman (Tonking) 17
Virgin Islands 19
Virginia 20
VMC cane mill, Valdosta Manufacturing Company 316
von Lippman, Edmund 40

Wallace Line 16
Washington, Iowa 323
Washington Iron Works 317–319
Washington Iron Works cane mills: Horizontal Mills 318, 319; Vertical Mills 318
Waycross, Georgia 301
Wells, Hiram 319
Wells, H., and Brothers 319
West Point Mills 319, 320, 321, 322
West Point Steam Powered Mill 321
Western cane mill, Bell 63
Western cane mill, Oyler 224
West Point Foundry and Iron Works 319–322
White, Silas R. 322–323
White, S. R., and Brothers 322–323
Whitewater, Wisconsin 326
Whiting, Augustus 296–297
Whiting Iron Works 322
Whitney Iron Works 323
Whittaker, James 243
Wilde, Daniel 323–325
Wilde, Daniel, Foundry 323–325
Wilde's Mill 323, 324, 325
Wilmington, Delaware 241
Wilson, William 63
Winchester cane mill, DeWolf's Mill 326
Winchester, DeWolf and Company 326
Wind powered mill 42
Winder, Georgia 331
Winship, Joseph 326–329
Winship and Brother 326–329
Winship Mill 326, 327, 328, 329
Winston-Salem, North Carolina 248
Winter, Joseph Samuel Prince 211
Wood and Mann Steam Engine Company 329
Woodbury, O. W. 329
Woodbury Mill 329
Woodruff, George W. 331, 332
Woodruff and Beach Iron Works 329–331
Woodruff Horizontal Mill 332
Woodruff Iron Works 331
Woodruff Machinery Manufacturing Company 331, 332
Woodruff Vertical Mill 331
Wray, Leonard 28
Wright, William 317

Yemen 17

Zanesville, Ohio 64, 299
Zanzibar 12

www.ingramcontent.com/pod-product-compliance
Lightning Source LLC
Chambersburg PA
CBHW081537300426
44116CB00015B/2661